UNKNOWN GODS

UNKNOWN GODS

THE ONGOING STORY OF RELIGION IN CANADA

REGINALD W. BIBBY

First published in 1993 by
Stoddart Publishing Co. Limited
34 Lesmill Road
Toronto, Canada
M3B 2T6
(416) 445-3333

Canadian Cataloguing in Publication Data

Bibby, Reginald W. (Reginald Wayne), 1943–
Unknown gods : the ongoing story of religion in Canada

ISBN 0-7737-5606-X

1. Canada — Religion — 20th century.   I. Title.

BL2530.C2B52 1993   306.6′0971   C93-094471-2

Book design: Brant Cowie/ArtPlus
Typesetting: Tony Gordon Ltd.
Printed and bound in Canada

Stoddart Publishing gratefully acknowledges the support of the Canada Council, the Ontario Ministry of Culture, Tourism, and Recreation, Ontario Arts Council, and Ontario Publishing Centre in the development of writing and publishing in Canada.

*To those who value faith
and believe in its potential
to enrich lives*

CONTENTS

PREFACE

I n 1987 when *Fragmented Gods* was published, I wasn't sure what to expect. Since the early 1970s, I had been carrying out research on religion in Canada, and presenting and publishing the findings primarily within the academic community. The book represented an attempt to pull together the diverse material, and broaden the audience to people across the country with an interest in religion. Frankly, I had a fair amount of apprehension about how the book would be received.

The response has been overwhelming. It has been good to see the book used extensively in universities and colleges. But what has been especially gratifying has been the widespread receptivity to the research by Canadians from all parts of the country and by a seemingly endless array of groups who have welcomed me into their presence over the past several years. The response has provided further proof that people who value faith are well aware that organized religion is experiencing tough times. But the willingness of such folk to read, reflect, and act also suggests that large numbers are determined to do everything they can to turn things around.

Things obviously haven't been standing still. And since the 1980s, things haven't been getting any better for the churches. Consequently, if anything, the need to understand the cultural environment in which ministry is being attempted has become more important rather than less. New information and new ideas need to be shared, making it possible for innovative strategies to be put into place. *Unknown Gods* provides me with the opportunity to continue the conversation we started in 1987.

My participation this time is characterized by less restraint and more passion. The times call for honesty and directness; churches are dying at a time when the culture needs what they historically have had to offer. It's my hope that my research and ideas will help to clarify perception, stimulate thought, and contribute to the response I believe is so urgently needed.

As usual, it seems like years have been squeezed into months in completing this project. For the most part it has been enjoyable, yet I confess I'm beginning to wonder if such efforts can ever be completed without the pain of excessive stress and a lack of moments to "ski and be." I'm about to embark on a short trip to Wales, which I hope will bring back some semblance of normalcy.

Life for me is immensely enjoyable, in large part because I am able to spend so much of my time thinking and writing, teaching and learning, and focusing on topics I find both interesting and worthwhile. Over time, a fairly extensive number of players have been helping to make it all possible. Organizationally, the University of Lethbridge continues to provide me with the resources and the tranquillity to do my work. Those are not small gifts. The Lilly Endowment's religious division, headed by Craig Dykstra, and the body it supports, the Louisville Institute for the Study of Protestantism and American Culture, under the leadership of James Lewis, have been extraordinarily generous in providing full funding for the two most recent surveys, PROJECT CAN90 and PROJECT TEEN CANADA 92. Their warm support and consistent encouragement have greatly enriched the quality of my day-to-day work.

In addition, the research and personal support of some extremely talented, stimulating, and upbeat individuals have been adding much to the ongoing effort. They include my son and senior research associate, Reggie, Jr.; Michèle Therrien, Jim, Tony, and Craig, my daily computer allies; Les Visser, who has looked after the bills and reports; Suzanne Lehouillier, who has headed up data entry, and her father, Jules, who, along with Michèle and Dianne, have been looking after French translations. There have been a large number of people in the trenches, including Dave, Russ, Tine, Mark, Nicky, Joe, Rob, and the sometimes forgotten Ken McKay. I thank them all. Don Posterski, of course, has worked with me on the PROJECT TEEN CANADA youth surveys. His contribution is very deeply appreciated.

As the final hours of manuscript preparation tick down, I again am conscious of the superb job that Maryan Gibson has done in working as copy editor. I thought I was a pretty good writer until we met; this is our third effort together. Don Bastian, the managing editor at Stoddart, has been there through all five of my books to date. I continue to greatly value his expertise and friendship.

And, as always, I thank my family. My mother, at 75, continues to cheer me with an energy I envy; Dad, who is two years her senior, also provides me with solid support. They are cherished. Thanks also to some people who have been there over the long haul — Grant, Gwen, Ted, Stan, Marilyn, Hal, Brian, and Jo. Together, these people and organizations continue to make it enjoyable to explore what is happening to the gods in our time.

REGINALD W. BIBBY
Lethbridge, Alberta
July 1993

Paul stood in front of the Areopagus and said:

> *Athenians, I see how extremely religious you are in every way. For as I went through the city and looked carefully at the objects of your worship, I found among them an altar with the inscription, "To an unknown god." What therefore you worship as unknown, this I proclaim to you.*

> *When they heard . . . some scoffed; but others said, "We will hear you again about this."*

> *— Acts 17.22ff*

INTRODUCTION

On April 4, 1993, the Canadian religious community and Canadian media were buzzing over the religious event of the year — maybe the decade, probably more. U.S. President Bill Clinton, a Southern Baptist, had attended the morning service of Vancouver's First Baptist Church. In a front-page story the next day, the *Vancouver Sun* wrote that the church was full for the early Sunday morning service for the first time that anyone could remember. "After all," the paper added, "it's not every day that one gets to worship with, or just plain worship, the most powerful leader in the world."

Later that same Sunday, another event, which received far less publicity, took place in the Cactus Club finger-food restaurant about four blocks away on Robson Street. Four people — two young men in their mid-20s, a fairly defunct Roman Catholic woman in her mid-30s, and a former Baptist minister — sat for several hours exchanging stories and ideas. Three of the four are not religious in the conventional sense of the word, while the fourth — the former minister — is regarded with caution by many of the religious types who know him. Their focus was life's mysteries — strange coincidences that cry out for explanations, such as thinking about someone and then seeing them, or having a dream that literally comes true.

One of the young men spoke in detail about two perplexing experiences in Europe — being in a shed and feeling the need to flee, only to find out later that three suicides had taken place there; on another occasion, sleeping in a house that reputedly was "haunted," and hearing "someone" open his bedroom door, walk across the floor, touch his arm, and then leave the room — an invisible someone he could hear and feel, yet not see.

The young woman was intrigued but, reflecting her degree in

psychology, insisted on not abandoning rational procedures in evaluating such things. Yet she spoke of her own inability to find meaning in her work and much of her life, pointing out that things conventional were not for her.

The other young man for the most part was content to listen with fascination to what the others had to say. He noted in the course of the evening that he himself is sensitive to the spiritual side of life, reading and reflecting on what "it's all about." But for the most part, he said, his questions still haven't been answered.

As for the former minister, well, he was once more rather taken by the enthusiasm for such matters, and still again found himself asking, "Where on earth are the churches?" I should know. The recalcitrant clergyman, you see, was me.

The three people I was with are all in the market for religion. They are intrigued with mystery; they are searching for meaning. And all have a sense of religious memory — links to previous Roman Catholic and Protestant religious traditions. What they also have in common is that they don't associate their intrigue and quest with the kinds of things that organized religion has to offer. With or without President Clinton in the pews, they had given no thought to attending First Baptist earlier in the day. Or any other church for that matter.

Something's seriously wrong. Canadians are asking religious questions at a time when the nation's churches have never been emptier. Over the course of history the churches have had significant things to say about those mystery and meaning issues that are so important to large numbers of people. Why is it, then, that people don't make the connection? Why are the gods and what they have to say about mystery and meaning not better known? And why is it that the churches are landing-places for geographically mobile members, including Baptist presidents, while the masses have their meetings about mystery and meaning in Cactus Clubs?

This is what this book is all about.

The Data Base

In probing the Canadian religious scene, I am making extensive use of the ongoing surveys I have been carrying out as part of the Project Canada Research program at the University of Lethbridge. To date, four national adult surveys have been completed — in 1975, 1980,

1985, and 1990. In addition, I have conducted three complementary national youth versions with the help of Don Posterski — in 1984, 1988, and 1992. My game plan is to run the surveys through the year 2000, at which point I intend to turn my attention to making improved sense of it all from venues limited only by my imagination and resources.

The surveys provide comprehensive trend data on Canadian adults and teens. Their highly representative samples make it possible to generalize to their respective populations with considerable accuracy, easily matching the claims of typical national polls. To the extent that bigger is better, the four adult surveys have embraced a total of some 6,000 adults, the youth counterparts about 10,000 teenagers. What is particularly important, however, is the design; carried out over the time, the surveys make it possible to (1) chart change among adults and teens and (2) enrich the trend analysis by comparing older and younger Canadians. Further, each new adult survey includes some people from the previous one, meaning that we have individuals on file who have participated since 1975, some since 1980, others since 1985, providing invaluable and rare panel data.

I have no illusions, however, that my data sets are enough. Consequently, the analyses and thought in this book draw heavily from Statistics Canada materials, notably the most recent, 1991, census and earlier versions, along with the 1991 General Social Survey, consisting of some 14,000 cases. Readers should note that my projections about religious involvement in the future that appear in chapter four are based, not on my own surveys, but on the GSS with its much larger sample size. In addition, with the help of Ann Oram of York and Wendy Watkins of Carleton, along with the generosity of Gallup Canada, I have experienced the delight of being able to retrieve, analyse, and report on some wonderful old surveys going back as far as 1945.

"Hard data" still aren't enough. Consequently I have invited a large number of people to bring their ideas to this examination of religion in Canada, by drawing very heavily on a wide range of written materials. They include journal articles and books, newspaper columns and accounts, and recent articles drawn from some twenty of the religious groups' magazines and newspapers. This extended conversation subsequently includes research colleagues, academics, journalists, religious leaders, church members, and many other interested observers. You may well be among them.

Three quick points. A project like this is exhausting but never exhaustive. Particularly when I attempt to get inside the worlds of religious groups, I find that qualitative description is disappointingly incomplete. I again have tried to provide helpful aerial snapshots and accurate broad outlines. Readers and practitioners will need to fill in the details and amplify, clarify, and correct the claims I am making. I hope you will share such information with me.

Second, my interest has been in religion in Canada generally. The book obviously gives much attention to the Christian tradition because of its numerical dominancy; however, my interest is much greater. As with *Fragmented Gods,* I ask those involved in faiths other than Christianity to permit me to use the term "church" as a shorthand term for "religious group," and for people who come from such backgrounds as Baptist, Pentecostal, Alliance, Nazarene, Evangelical Free, Mennonite, and Reformed to allow me to group them as "conservative Protestants," sharing in a believers' church tradition.

Third, although I always seem to make this plea, it seldom is taken seriously. It needs to be, so let me try again. Books have a tendency to be applauded and rejected, not on the basis of their ideas, but on the basis of ideology and methodology. To not be seen as coming from the appropriate ideological or theological direction, or to be viewed as "quantitative" rather than "qualitative," frequently terminates the discussion before it has a chance to begin. First and foremost, I invite you to take on my ideas.

As with its 1987 predecessor, I expect that this book will be greeted with a variety of emotional reactions. But once more, my greatest hope is that it will help to clarify what is currently taking place, make people think, and lead to an enrichment of faith and life. May it also contribute to the unknown becoming known.

PART I
WHAT'S HAPPENING
IN THE CHURCHES

The decline in service attendance and group membership that began in Canada around 1950 for Protestants and 1965 for Roman Catholics is continuing in the 1990s. Exceptions to the pattern are minor — few groups are being spared. What's more, the situation is not being turned around by baby boomers, new Canadians, or efforts to reach the unchurched. Beyond numerical involvement, relatively few Canadians give evidence of being profoundly influenced by any organized faith. But it's not just that growing numbers of people are ignoring religious groups and their messages. The proportion who express confidence in religious leaders has dropped markedly in the past decade. Of considerable importance, what to date has been a serious numerical decline problem will expand into nothing less than a full-scale crisis for most religious groups within the next 25 years. The United and Anglican Churches will be among those that may well be almost decimated.

1

THE CONTINUING EXODUS

The post-World War II dropoff in both religious group membership and weekly attendance, which I documented in *Fragmented Gods* in 1987, has not come to an end.

To refresh memories, the attendance decline among Protestant groups can be traced back to the late 1940s. A similar slide also began to characterize Roman Catholics by the mid-1960s — coinciding not only with the conclusion of Vatican II (1962–65) but also with the accelerated modernization of Quebec. "Other faith" groups, such as Jews and Buddhists, seemed to experience similar drops in regular service attendance. Virtually no Protestant denominations, not even the previously high-flying Pentecostals — are deviating from the downward pattern. Obviously one can cite local and perhaps even regional exceptions. But nationally the pattern is clear: things are not improving in the 1990s.

EMPTIER PEWS

People recall happier days. Former publisher John Irwin remembers Sundays in Toronto when he was growing up in the 1940s. "At Bloor and Yonge, you could walk down the middle of the street with your eyes shut and not get run over," he says. "Everyone was in church."[1] Mark Twain allegedly once commented on a visit to Montreal that "One cannot stand on a street in Montreal and throw a brick without breaking a church window."[2] These days, with weekly attendance coming in at only about 15% in Montreal, chances are pretty good that no one would be hit by the brick.

Irwin and Twain were solidly in touch with reality. The first national poll on religious service attendance I have been able to uncover was carried out by the Gallup organization in 1945. It found that approximately 65% of the population 21 and over had attended a religious service in the three weeks following Easter Sunday. A similar poll taken around the same time in the U.S., covering a four-week period, found that a lower proportion of Americans — 58% — had attended a service. Allowing for the fact that some of the 65% of Canadians had not attended in all three weeks, a reasonable adjustment might peg the weekly attenders at about 60%.

The 1945 survey also found some interesting patterns by age, gender, and region. Some 69% of those under the age of 30 had attended during the three-week period, slightly *above* the 64% level for both people 30 to 49 and those over 50. The figure for women was 73%, for men 61%. Regionally, Gallup reported that Quebec led the country, at about 90%. While specifics were not given, the company did say in its May 12, 1945, release that "the whole of Eastern Canada has a better record than the West. In some Western provinces, the poll found more people who had not attended than had." Gallup suggested a very practical reason for the difference: people in the West might have had to travel greater distances in order to attend a service.[3]

By the 1950s, the six in ten who claimed to be worshipping in the nation's churches, synagogues, and temples had slipped to five in ten; by the 1970s, to three in ten. It now stands at just over two in ten. The attendance decline has been pervasive:

- As recently as the mid-1960s, close to 80% of **Roman Catholics** were in church at least once a week. Today, just over 30% of RC's are attending that often.
- In the case of **Protestants,** in the late 1940s, around 50% maintained that they were weekly church-goers, with the figure still close to 40% at the end of the 1950s. Now, barely over 20% report that kind of involvement.
- **Other religions** are faring little better. The collective attendance level for Canadians who identify themselves as Jewish, Hindu, Buddhist, Sikh, and so on, came in at about 35% in the mid-1950s. It dipped to just under 15% in the 1970s, and — even with greater numbers since that time as a result of immigration — has not risen noticeably.

A major study of Catholicism commissioned by the Assembly of Quebec Bishops has documented the numerical problems of Roman

Catholics in Quebec specifically. Released in late 1992 and entitled *Risquer l'avenir* (Risking the Future), the study's findings included the following:[4]

1. Local communities have seen a serious decrease in the number of people attending Sunday Mass. The decline evident 20 years ago has only continued, including not only a minority of the general population but a minority of the baptized.
2. The average age of Christian community members is higher than that of the general population, often 50-55 years. The report says, "This raises a certain amount of concern." As one respondent put it, "If you look at the congregation on Sundays, the average age . . . It's no laughing matter. Something will have to be done, and soon."
3. The number of priests declined steadily between 1970 and 1990, resulting in one priest frequently providing the pastoral care for three or four parishes; it has, however, made way for the involvement of the laity in pastoral tasks.
4. Between 1970 and 1990, gross revenues have not diminished in most communities. However, they have become insufficient to provide for the maintenance of buildings and services and for the hiring of pastoral staff.

The number of practising Catholics in a Montreal parish such as Saint-Yves has dropped from about 25% in 1970 to 7% today. "We hardly ever see young couples or adolescents," explains the parish secretary, Monique Fortin. "As for the younger ones, the picture is even bleaker." The situation in Saint-Yves is not an exception to the provincial rule. The study found that even in some rural parishes, the rate of practising Catholics is less than 10%.[5]

Among the Protestant denominations, regular weekly attendance is particularly light for Canada's two largest mainline bodies, the United and Anglican churches, describing only about 15% of the people who identify with those two groups.

Attendance is highest for conservative Protestant groups, at almost 50%. Yet even the conservative Protestants are showing signs of plateauing. The 1985 PROJECT CANADA survey found that close to two in three of these evangelicals claimed to be attending almost every week. Available data suggest that a change has been taking place in the past few years, whereby increasing numbers of conservatives show signs of following the pattern of other Canadians in treating weekly attendance as optional.

TABLE 1.1. **WEEKLY SERVICE ATTENDERS IN CANADA: 1957–1990***			
In %'s			
	1957	1975	1990
NATIONALLY	53	31	23
ROMAN CATHOLIC	83	45	33
Outside Quebec	75	49	43
Quebec	88	41	29
PROTESTANT	38	26	22
Anglican	24	24	15
United Church	40	28	15
Lutheran	38	19	10
Presbyterian	38	11	13
Conservative	51	40	48
OTHER FAITHS	35	13	12

*1957: % indicated attend services on a typical Sunday; 1975 & 1990: % said attend services "Almost every week" or more. "Other" refers to faiths other than Christian. In this and subsequent tables, unless indicated otherwise, the 1975 and 1990 samples for Lutheran, Presbyterian, and other faiths have been combined with 1980 and 1985 respectively because of insufficient numbers in a single year.

SOURCES: 1957: March Gallup poll; 1975 & 1990: PROJECT CANADA Survey Series.

Among the Pentecostal Assemblies of Canada, for example, between 1980 and 1986, membership jumped from 136,000 to 185,000 — an increase of 49,000. Yet, rather than accelerating in recent years, by 1992 membership reached 222,000 — an increase of 37,000.[6] Don't get me wrong — these aren't bad figures, given the present "religious economy." But they do suggest that, even among the groups that allegedly are experiencing growth, net additions are relatively modest.

If you think this national attendance news is grim, keep in mind that, if anything, the figures might be slightly inflated. Some people still seem to think they should exaggerate their attendance to the pollster — particularly when their group expects them to be in church. Researcher Arnell Motz has done some checking. He called churches in Vancouver and obtained their actual attendance counts for a given Sunday. He found that, although 18% of Vancouverites said that they had been in church, in reality only about 7% seem to have shown up.[7] The moral of the story? What people are saying is not always what they are doing.

DECLINING ROLLS

Membership in a local church or parish is at best a crude indicator of involvement in the 1990s. There are many Protestant groups, including a good number of the Pentecostal and nondenominational persuasion, that simply do not stress formal church membership. It's a reflection of the individualistic times: such groups encourage people to attend, but they don't ask them to sign on the proverbial dotted line.

In contrast to this vague Protestant tie between identification and membership, to identify oneself as a Roman Catholic means, theologically, that one *is* a member of the Roman Catholic Church. Regular attendance, however, seems to be the behavioural prerequisite of people actually seeing themselves as members of a local parish. So it is that, as of the early 1990s, 28% of the country's Roman Catholics say they are members of a parish — about the same proportion who indicate they are weekly attenders (33%).

The same argument for the tendency to *identify with a tradition* versus *attend and take out membership* seems to have even more support among people who identify with other world faiths. The extent to which Jews, for example, attend services is generally recognized to be secondary to their tendency to be involved in a local synagogue. One Toronto woman points out that her children believe in God and know they're Jewish, but the family attends synagogue only twice a year on high holidays — not every Saturday the way she did when she was a child. "People consider it an imposition on their time," she comments, adding, "I hate to say that, but it's probably what it is."[8]

Yet, even in the case of "other faith" groups, membership levels have been decreasing. Over the past 20 years, attendance has remained at around 15%, but membership has slipped from about 50% to 30%. Despite the assumed lifeblood of immigration, these findings suggest that people in "other faith" groups are experiencing the secularization that is part of their broader acculturation experience.

Keeping in mind these problems in interpreting the meaning of membership in a local congregation, it is perhaps still of value to note that membership in Protestant denominations, where formal ties continue to be widely encouraged, is also down dramatically in the last half of this century.

- Some 80% of Protestants were members of local churches in the mid-1950s; the figure now stands at just under 40%. There are very few denominational exceptions.
- The mainline United Church, Anglican, and Lutheran groups have experienced major membership declines, from more than 80% to 30%. The Presbyterian drop has been from about 65% to 30%.
- Conservative Protestants have also shared in the membership decline. Over the past 35 years, formal membership in Baptist and other evangelical groups has slipped from around 85% to 55%.

Perhaps most disturbing for the conservative Protestant denominations is the finding that, as with attendance, membership knew a lofty height as recently as 1985, when 70% of affiliates claimed ties with a local congregation. If the drop involved only membership, it perhaps could be written off as reflecting a growing disinclination for evangelicals to join churches. Unfortunately, the 1985–90 membership slide from 75% to 55% has been matched by an attendance slide from some 65% to 50%.

TABLE 1.2. **CONGREGATIONAL MEMBERSHIP IN CANADA: 1957–1990**		
In %'s		
1957	1975	1990
NATIONALLY 82	48	29
ROMAN CATHOLIC 96	56	28
Outside Quebec 91	67	38
Quebec 99	**	18
PROTESTANT 80	51	37
Anglican 74	50	30
United Church 84	52	35
Lutheran 86	62	32
Presbyterian 64	54	30
Conservative 86	51	55
OTHER RELIGIONS 37	49	32

**Membership for Francophones unknown.

SOURCES: 1957: March Gallup poll; 1975 & 1990: PROJECT CANADA Survey Series.

MINIMAL EXCEPTIONS

In the past, religious leaders have found some consolation and hope in the fact that the research findings on decline did not indict everyone. Some have been rightfully able to claim that membership and attendance problems "might be affecting other groups — but not us." Apart from denominational differences, it's also been possible in Canada's past to suggest that there have been variations in group involvement in such characteristics as region and community size, as well as gender, education, and age.

- In less industrialized areas of the country, such as Quebec, the Atlantic provinces, and later the Prairies, people have tended to be more involved in the churches than their counterparts in Ontario and British Columbia.
- Similarly, secularization has been more pronounced in urban areas than in rural parts of Canada, as well as more common among men, people with higher levels of education, and younger Canadians.

Such impressions have had some support, but perhaps not as much as folk wisdom had taken for granted. An analysis of the results of a Gallup poll in the mid-1950s shows that, at that time:

- Quebec easily led the country in attendance and membership, but people in the Prairies and in Ontario were more likely than those in the Atlantic area to claim that they were church members. Then, as now, people living in B.C. were the least inclined to be involved in religious groups.
- Outside Quebec — where little variation by any variable existed — attendance and membership were somewhat higher in smaller communities than the larger cities, among women rather than men, and slightly more common among people over the age of 30 than those younger.
- Education, however, was not having a diminishing effect on involvement. The 5% or so of Canadians who had gone to university were just about as likely as others to be church members, and somewhat more likely to attend every week.

What's particularly startling, however, is the discovery that none of these factors makes much difference anymore. A comparison of the levels of church attendance and membership in the mid-1950s with those of the 1990s reveals that participation has dropped significantly for Canadians in almost all of these variable instances (see TABLE 1.3). The four-decade comparison clearly shows that increasingly low levels of attendance and membership now characterize a majority of Canadians:

- in *all* parts of the country;
- in small communities, as well as the large cities;
- who are either women or men;
- of all educational levels;
- who are older, as well as younger.

TABLE 1.3. **WEEKLY ATTENDANCE AND MEMBERSHIP BY SELECT CHARACTERISTICS: 1957–1990**

In %'s

	Attendance		Membership	
	1957	1990	1957	1990
NATIONALLY	53	23	82	29
REGION				
QUEBEC	83	23	97	16
OUTSIDE QUEBEC	43	24	77	34
Atlantic	50	41	54	49
Ontario	44	21	77	31
Prairies	48	22	82	36
B.C.	25	22	54	27
COMMUNITY SIZE*				
more than 100,000	40	19	68	27
10,000–99,000	49	28	80	31
less than 10,000	44	30	81	33
GENDER*				
Female	47	25	82	32
Male	40	22	71	27
EDUCATION*				
Degree or More	49	27	72	41
Some Post-Secondary	—	18	—	25
High School or Less	43	25	77	24
AGE*				
18–29	36	14	68	17
30–49	44	30	79	26
50 & over	46	43	78	40

*Quebec excluded for 1957 due to lack of variability.

SOURCES: 1957: March Gallup poll; 1990: PROJECT CANADA Survey Series.

Such national survey information confirms what our grandparents and parents have witnessed firsthand: there has been a sharp decline in attendance and membership in Canada over the last half of this century. What has to be disturbing for religious leaders about the drop is the extent to which it has been experienced right across the country and across all social categories. Pockets of resistance are few.

Still, that's not to say people who value faith have abandoned hope that better days are just ahead, even in the tough religious times of the 1990s.

2

SOME UNFOUNDED HOPES — AND FEARS

I n the midst of the numerical woes of Canada's religious groups, there have been a number of developments in recent years that have contributed to hope. They are centred around three interesting possibilities: (1) young parent baby boomers are returning to the churches; (2) new immigrants are becoming involved in religious groups; and (3) the "unchurched" are being recruited in growing numbers.

Ironically, however, all three of these areas have also been associated with considerable anxiety. Some people are troubled about the possibilities that younger Canadians are increasingly turning their backs on religion; that Canada is becoming a multi-faith mosaic; and that the unchurched are not being reached in appreciable numbers. Those three concerns have been joined by a fourth — that, in the midst of all the problems the country's religious groups are experiencing, new competition, primarily in the form of New Age religion, is only making a bad situation worse.

Such people will be relieved to learn that much of the anxiety is unwarranted. Unfortunately, so are the hopes.

BABY BOOMERS

The news came as a shock, but a welcome one at that. Just when Canadians and Americans who value organized religion thought that most young adults had given up on the churches, the news came from south of the border that a miracle was in the making. Baby boomers — people born between approximately 1945 and 1965 in the two decades following the Second World War — were said to be coming back. As downcast clergy looked whimsically out their church windows, they allegedly were taking in a startling new sight — young couples coming up the sidewalks with their children, en route to the churches![1]

In its cover story of December 17, 1990, *Newsweek* drew on the research of American sociologists Wade Clark Roof, David Roozen, and Jackson Carroll in proclaiming that "the boomers are back!" Their research, said *Newsweek,* revealed that, although two-thirds of baby boomers have dropped out of organized religion, "more than one-third of the dropouts have returned" in recent years. According to the story, above all, "the return to religion is fueled by the boomers' experiences of becoming parents — and the realization that children need a place where they can learn solid values and make friends with peers who share them." This return of the boomers has subsequently become something of an American folk-wisdom fact.

The news of their return has not gone unnoticed in Canada. *Maclean's,* inspired by the *Newsweek* piece, ran an article six months later entitled "Saving the Boomers"[2] In lieu of available data supporting the case for the return of the boomers, the writer — relying on quote and anecdote — focused on the attempts churches are making "to lure members of the baby boom generation back into their pews."

Still, primarily because of the influence of the American media, the rumour has spread that large numbers of baby boomers are making their way back to Canadian churches. In September 1991, the newspaper *ChristianWeek* ran a front-page story entitled "Are Canadians Really Going Back to Church?" Writer Doug Koop noted:

> *The sense that more Canadians are choosing to go to church is gaining legitimacy in the public mindset. . . . On an anecdotal level, stories of neighbours eager to ask questions about God abound. Reports of churches that are growing and of burgeoning spiritual interest are common.*[3]

But, asked Koop, "Are Canadians really going back to church?" Here's what we know so far.

The American Situation

In an examination of baby boomers born between 1945 and 1954, David Roozen and his associates[4] found evidence supporting a return to the churches.[5] Weekly church attendance for these older baby boomers had increased between the early 1970s and early 1980s from 33% to 42%. The size of the increase was found to be fairly similar for all denominations. A major accompanying factor was family cycle: during the ten-year period, the percentage of older boomers who married and had school-age children increased from 9% to 40%. While the attendance level of the younger half of baby boomers, born between 1955 and 1965, did not match that of the older boomers, their involvement level was still slightly higher than that of the older half when the latter was the same age in the early 1970s. According to the Roozen research, attendance was on the upswing for boomers.

Analyses through the late 1980s in the U.S. have found similar patterns. By the end of the 1980s, the attendance level of the younger baby boomers had caught up to that of the older boomers. In addition, these new studies found modest increases in a variety of beliefs and practices, along with a greater tendency for young Americans to say that religion has importance in their lives. The case seems tight: American baby boomers are making a religious comeback.

Two Important Questions

The U.S. findings, however, leave two major questions unanswered. First, to what extent does the comeback trend differ from that of previous post-adolescent generations? Second, is the magnitude of the return sufficient to warrant the generalization that the boomers are coming back?

Regarding the first question, in at least the detectable past, *some* people from all emerging generations have gone back to church when they hit their late 20s and 30s. Postadolescence is the primary period of renewed religious involvement. Those who see the return of baby boomers as a novel phenomenon might do well to heed the admonition of Ecclesiastes that "there is nothing new under the sun."

For example, my 1985 study of close to 1,800 active and inactive Anglicans in Toronto, the country's largest diocese, found that almost 60% of both the self-proclaimed "actives" and "inactives" were highly involved during their preteen years. From age 13 to 24, the involvement levels for current actives dipped to 33%, for inactives to 17%. However, to the extent that young Anglicans returned to church, the trend began when they were around age 25 and virtually ended by 40. That pattern characterized both postwar and prewar generations.[6]

In short, both earlier generations and postwar baby boomers exhibited the same tendency to drop out in adolescence and then return during their years of marriage and rearing children.

As for the second important question concerning the magnitude of the return of young adults, it's significant that the Anglican study in Toronto found that, with each new generation, some people returned. But a larger number did not. Such findings are consistent with those of Wade Clark Roof and his colleagues in the U.S. Focusing on the 96% of baby boomers who say they were raised in a religious tradition, Roof found that, as of about 1990:

- 42% had remained involved continuously ("Loyalists");
- 22% had dropped out and returned ("Returnees");
- the remaining 36% were still uninvolved ("Dropouts").

Roof and Loeb's[7] findings brought a light rain to the homecoming parade of baby boomers, cautioning that "returnees" in reality constitute a smaller proportion of Americans than "dropouts."

The Canadian Situation

Fortunately we don't have to rely on conjecture. Information is available in the form of national surveys that allow us to take a firsthand look. An examination of the data shows that the attendance level for people born in the first decade after the Second World War — so-called older boomers — increased modestly from 12% in 1975 to 17% by 1985. At that point, these older boomers were between the ages of 30 and 39. Similar to the Toronto Anglican situation, attendance seems to have levelled off by the time the boomers hit 40; as of 1990 it had risen only slightly higher, to 19% (see TABLE 2.1).

In the case of younger baby boomers, who were born between 1956 and 1965 and therefore were younger than 35 as of 1990, there was no sign as yet of the return found in the U.S. research. This appears to be primarily because, to the extent Canadian boomers are returning, the largest number who do so reappear by about age 35. As of 1990, these younger boomers were exhibiting attendance levels very similar to those of the older boomers when the latter were the same age in the 1970s and 1980s. There may well be a slight attendance increase for these younger baby boomers in the next ten years, as they hit their mid-30s and beyond. But the present patterns suggest that, as with the older boomers, the attendance increase will be only minor. Some Canadian boomers are coming back; most are not.

TABLE 2.1. **ATTENDANCE PATTERNS OF THE POSTWAR GENERATION IN CANADA: 1975–1990**

% Attending Weekly

SURVEY YEAR	Older Boomers 1946–55	Younger Boomers 1956–65	Total Boomers 1946–65
1975	12 (20–29)	** (10–19)	14 (10–29)
1980	13 (25–34)	26 (15–24)	15 (15–34)
1985	17 (30–39)	15 (20–29)	16 (20–39)
1990	19 (35–44)	13 (25–34)	15 (25–44)

**Insufficient numbers to compute table percentages. Bracketed figures refer to age that survey year.

SOURCE: PROJECT CANADA Survey Series.

More significant than these slight increases in the attendance levels of young Canadians is the finding that the pools of young Canadians who are coming back are ever smaller. Yes, it's true that between 1975 and 1990 baby boomer attendance increased — from about 12% to about 20%. But their near-final attendance level pales when compared to the attendance levels of prewar generations. The 20% figure for boomers at age 40 is more than ten percentage points below that of 40-year-olds just 15 years ago. It also is only about half the involvement level of Canadians 55 and over today (see TABLE 2.2). The impressionistic observation of Robert Bast of the Reformed Church in America is accurate: baby boomers are only half as likely to be in church as their parents were.[8]

The message? Some boomers *are* coming back. But they are not coming back in sufficient numbers to replace the more active members of prewar generations, who soon will be gone. The net result is a steady downturn in church attendance nationally — from 31% in 1975 to a current level of some 23%. The national decline in service attendance will continue in at least the foreseeable future.

Such a predictable return of the latest new cohort of young adults consequently hardly signals a massive resurgence of interest in religion; that in turn calls for academics to conjure up profound social and cultural causal explanations.

From the standpoint of Canadian church leaders who are dusting off the pews and expecting standing-room-only crowds, the picture is not pretty. Some of the baby boomers — perhaps one in five — will become regular attenders. But the vast majority will not.

TABLE 2.2. **ATTENDANCE IN CANADA BY AGE COHORTS: 1975–1990**				
% Attending Weekly *(Baby Boomers Boxed)*				
AGE COHORT	1975	1980	1985	1990
20–24	12	26	15	14
25–29	12	10	15	6
30–34	24	15	15	15
35–39	31	25	21	18
40–44	33	29	28	20
45–49	36	22	33	31
50–54	37	32	27	25
55-plus	44	44	43	38
NATIONALLY	32	28	25	23
SOURCE: PROJECT CANADA Survey Series.				

Here again some religious groups claim to be the exceptions to the research finding rule. "That might be happening out there," comes the protest, "but fortunately my church is different." The objection may sometimes be valid.

In the case of the return of baby boomers, however, leaders need to be cautious in claiming an exemption from what we have just observed. An examination of what boomers themselves have to say about their attendance patterns, according to their religious groups for 1990, suggests that *no* Canadian group is gaining more boomers than they are losing. One partial exception is conservative Protestants, where younger boomers are reporting attendance increases; older boomers, on the other hand, are not (see TABLE 2.3).

It may well be that evangelical Protestant denominations are doing a better job than other groups when it comes to providing programs that appeal to young parents. The problem they appear to share with their religious group colleagues, however, is how to keep such people highly involved as their children move into their teens and beyond.

TABLE 2.3. **SELF-REPORTED ATTENDANCE PATTERNS OVER THE PAST FIVE YEARS: 1990**			
In %'s			
People Born Before 1946 (45 & over)	Older Boomers 1946–55 (35–44)	Younger Boomers 1956–65 (25–34)	Total Boomers 1946–65 (25–44)
RC: QUEBEC			
Increase 13	12	8	10
Decrease 29	21	38	30
No Change 58	67	54	60
RC: OUTSIDE QUEBEC			
Increase 11	14	14	14
Decrease 15	12	24	19
No Change 74	74	62	67
ANGLICAN			
Increase 5	16	10	12
Decrease 11	15	15	15
No Change 84	69	75	73
UNITED CHURCH			
Increase 5	8	7	7
Decrease 20	14	35	23
No Change 75	78	58	70
CONSERVATIVE			
Increase 6	15	22	19
Decrease 21	22	5	12
No Change 73	63	73	69
SOURCE: PROJECT CANADA Survey Series.			

Overall, the pattern is clear: Canadians born in either the prewar or postwar periods are both more likely to say they have been attending services less frequently in recent years.

- The situation is particularly bleak in the case of **Roman Catholics in Quebec** and the **United Church**, where baby boomers who report they are attending less often are outnumbering those who report attending more often by three to one.
- Postwar **Roman Catholics elsewhere** and **Anglican** baby boomers are not returning in large numbers. But at least the proportions

who indicate they are attending less are — by age 35 — being matched by those who say they are attending more.

- In the case of **conservative churches**, boomers younger than 35 tend to claim a pattern of increasing involvement. As just noted, however, the problem here is that, to date at least, evangelicals show just as strong a tendency as many of the people in the mainline groups to become less involved as they get older. Secularization, in the form of social mobility, may function to pull conservatives into a more normative attendance line.

The Boomer Bust

Contrary to rumour, the postwar generation is not in the process of making a mass return to Canadian churches. No one should be particularly surprised. The national attendance decline has rather obvious implications for intergenerational participation. Not only are parents not attending services as frequently as their parents and grandparents, they also are not as likely to expose their children to church life. In a 1957 Gallup poll almost three in four Canadians said they had gone to Sunday school when they were children; 60% said they had attended regularly.[9] As of the early 1990s, that figure has dropped to one in four. Consequently, the question of whether or not Canadians are *returning* to church is increasingly irrelevant; an ever-growing majority have *never* been actively involved. It's not a matter of returning; it's a matter of becoming involved for the first time.

And therein lies the challenge facing those who value faith. It would be nice if leaders could simply wait for baby boomers to come knocking. Unfortunately most won't. But that's not to say that boomers and other Canadians are closed to what religion has to offer.

	N	Attend Weekly	Hi Enjoyment Rel Group	Religion Very NB	Confi-dence in Leaders	Future: Gain Influence
Boomers	231	19	9	23	33	19
Their Teens	3990	18	6	24	39	16

TABLE 2.4. **OLDER BABY BOOMERS* AND THEIR TEENAGE OFFSPRING**

In %'s

*Older boomers: born between 1946 and 1955; teens were born between 1973 and 1977, when boomers ranged in age from 18 to 31.

SOURCES: PROJECT CAN90 and PROJECT TEEN CANADA 92.

NEW CANADIANS

To Canadians who have grown up with cultural diversity, it's easy to assume that immigration is something common to virtually all nations. In fact, such is far from the case. Even though Canada has a relatively small population compared to other countries, for some time now, Canada has been second only to the United States in the number of immigrants it has been receiving.

Things are not about to change. Demographers tell us that if our population is to remain at its current level — let alone grow — our immigration figures will have to rise even higher. The reason is simple: our number of births are not offsetting our number of deaths. In lieu of adequate natural increase, we need more "human imports" if we are to continue to have what experts regard as an adequate national population.

It's not uncommon for people to express concern about rising levels of immigration, especially in tough economic times. Ironically, the fact of the matter is that the actual number of people coming to Canada from other countries has not increased markedly in recent years. If anything, the figures were down in the 1980s from the levels, for example, of the 1950s and 1960s.

What has changed are the dominant countries from which new arrivals are coming. Over time, the major countries of origin have moved from Britain and France through Western, Eastern, and Southern Europe, to Third World countries, notably Asia and Central America. The implications of both the past and present immigration patterns for religion have been dramatic.

Dealing with Diversity

Historically, immigrants brought the religions of their homelands to Canada. Seen through the eyes of the host aboriginal peoples, Christianity was a foreign religion, first imported by newcomers from Britain and France. With the arrival of other Europeans and their diverse expressions of the faith, something of a "Christian mosaic" began to emerge.

This post-sixteenth-century religious monopoly continued largely uncontested through the 1950s. As late as 1971 — the year the federal government officially declared Canada a multicultural country — some 90% of the populace indicated that their ancestral roots were European. Not coincidentally, in the same year, virtually the same percentage also identified themselves as Protestants or Roman

Catholics. The runner-up to the Christian religion was not another world religion, but rather the "nothing" category.

Globalization and population movements have raised new questions about the extent to which societies will variously experience cultural conflict, pluralism, and assimilation. Canada's fairly unique response to our own growing cultural diversity consequently provides a valuable case study regarding the cultural and religious possibilities of diversity.

Since the 1950s, Canada has been among the few nations in the world practising explicit pluralism. In October 1971, the federal government announced that the official policy giving guidance to our cultural diversity would be multiculturalism. Canada was to be no melting pot. Instead, Canadians of diverse backgrounds would be encouraged to cultivate their national heritages, be guaranteed the opportunity to participate fully in Canadian life, and share their cultures with each other. The collective result, declared the prime minister of the day, Pierre Trudeau, would be "a richer life for us all."

As a result of the official enshrining of multiculturalism, Canadians have become highly sensitive to the official rights and privileges of all peoples and all cultures, including all religions. Any sense that the historically dominant Christian religion is being given a privileged position in such areas of public life as schools and even the military is met with considerable resistance.

Canada, so the thinking goes, is a country of many mosaics. Beyond the cultural mosaic, we have a moral mosaic, a family structure mosaic, a lifestyle mosaic, a political mosaic, a sexual orientation mosaic, and of course a religion mosaic. Alvan Gamble, a Baptist, sums up the common perception: "Demographic trends show that the Christian population is diminishing as immigrants arrive from non-Christian cultures.[10] The landscape allegedly is shifting. For example, in early 1993 Dr. Suwanda Suganisiri, the former president of the Buddhist Council of Canada, was claiming Buddhists now number around 300,000. Carleton anthropology professor Brian Givens was saying that Buddhism was Canada's second fastest-growing religion, behind only evangelical Protestantism.[11]

The Apparent Reality

Given that religious diversity appears to be increasing in Canada, the responses of religious groups have been fairly predictable, lying along a continuum between polar extremes.

There are some who attempt to *embrace diversity*. Groups like the United Church of Canada applaud the presence of many faith communities. For example, in 1991 the denomination's Alberta Conference "celebrated" religious diversity at its annual meeting, using the theme "Faith — A Multi-Coloured Garden."

A second fairly common response is to *accept diversity*. This position recognizes that the age of Christian dominance in Canada is over, and is resigned to the reality that the clock will never be turned back. It's therefore important to accept the new situation with dignity, if not delight. Author and church leader Don Posterski, for example, in recent years has been urging evangelicals to accept that "We are no longer in a majority, and we need to learn how to live with it."

A third response has been to *use diversity*. Many evangelical groups, taking an exclusive approach to the Christian faith, see the influx of immigrants from Third World countries as representing a great opportunity for evangelism. The mood is consequently fairly upbeat. Evangelicals like Enoch Wan treat immigrants as a "new mission field" and attempt to equip churches to "reach them."[12]

A fourth response, possibly most prevalent among older Canadians in a variety of religious groups, including mainline varieties, is to *reject diversity*. The breaking up of "Christian Canada" is seen by such people as unfortunate. They are not particularly inclined to proselytize the newcomers; they just wish things could stay the way they were.

In actual fact, all four responses may be largely out of touch with the Canadian reality.

A Melting Pot in a Mosaic

An examination of religious identification in Canada since the first census in 1871 through 1991 reveals that, for all the immigration that has taken place, the proportion of Canadians lining up with religions other than Christianity has changed very little. The only new development that stands out statistically has been the post-1960s tendency of an increasing percentage of people to indicate they have *no* religious preference.

There are three obvious factors that have contributed to such religious stability. First, as noted, the vast majority of immigrants to Canada prior to the 1980s came from European countries where

Christianity has been dominant. Their children tended to retain their parents' Protestant and Catholic ties, resulting in an overwhelming Christian monopoly in this century.

TABLE 2.5. **RELIGIOUS GROUP IDENTIFICATION IN CANADA: 1871–1991** *In %'s*					
	RC	Protestant	Other	None	Totals
1871	43	56	1	<1	100
1901	42	56	2	<1	100
1941	42	52	6	<1	100
1971	44	46	5	5	100
1991	47	37	4	12	100

SOURCE: Derived from Statistics Canada census data.

TABLE 2.6. **ANCESTRY OF THE CANADIAN POPULATION: 1871–1991** *In %'s*						
	British	French	Other European	Asian	Aboriginal	Other	Totals
1871	60	31	7	<1	1	1	100
1901	57	31	9	<1	1	1	100
1931	52	28	18	<1	1	1	100
1961	44	30	23	1	1	1	100
1981*	40	27	19	3	3	8	100
1991*	40	23	25	4	2	6	100

*Includes multiple origins. Appeared for first time in 1981.

SOURCE: Derived from Statistics Canada census data.

Second, despite the rise since the 1980s in the number of people coming from Asia and other Third World countries, what is often not recognized is the fact that large numbers of these people *also* have been arriving as adherents to the Christian faith, rather than other world religions. As Roger Nostbakken, the president of the Lutheran Theological Seminary in Saskatoon, has pointed out,[13] a global village of 1,000 people in the 1990s would actually consist of:

- 329 Christians;
- 174 Muslims;

- 131 Hindus;
- 61 Buddhists;
- 52 animists;
- 3 Jews;
- 34 members of other religions;
- 216 people without any religion.

Since Christianity is the most numerically dominant religion in the world, we hardly should act shocked that people who come to Canada are not adding all that much to the literal religion mosaic. Frequently what they are really bringing are cultural variations on the Christian religion. It's true of many individual immigrants; it is also true of many so-called "ethnic churches."

- As of 1992, there were more than 60 Chinese-speaking Christian congregations in Vancouver alone.[14]
- In Edmonton, where there are some 10,000 people from the Philippines, an Alliance Filipino congregation is booming and has just purchased an available United Church building; it's only one of about eight such groups across Canada.[15]
- In Toronto, the relatively small Canadian Baptist Federation could recently claim no less than five relatively new ethnic congregations in the city — Assyrian, Japanese, Chinese, Middle Eastern and Taiwanese.[16] Multicultural ministry expert Roland Kawano of the United Church says that altogether, as of the early 1990s, Toronto had 60 Korean congregations for a community of more than 30,000 people, and 60 Chinese congregations serving a much larger population of close to 300,000.[17]
- In Calgary, there were at least nine Christian Korean congregations alone — reflecting the fact that 25% of South Koreans today are Christians.[18]

The vast majority of these ethnic church members usually have arrived in Canada as Christians. The Korean Christian Church in London, Ontario, provides a fairly typical illustration of the nature of ethnic churches. A Presbyterian congregation, it was founded in the 1960s by five Korean families who moved from Toronto. A product of an extensive Presbyterian presence in Korea — which in turn has its origins in missionary efforts dating back a century — the church is composed of a core of immigrants, supplemented by second-generation families. Its most recent senior minister was part of the ministerial staff at the 30,000-member Young Nak congregation in Seoul; the assistant minister also was from Korea, where his parents were active Presbyterians. The church has two Sunday services, one in Korean and the other in English, that tend to appeal to older and younger members respectively. Korean professors and students at the University of Western Ontario are among those involved in the church.[19]

As of 1991, about one in three Asians born outside Canada were identifying with Protestantism or Roman Catholicism — virtually the same proportion as those who were claiming ties with other world religions. Most of the remaining third indicated that they did not identify with any religion. Immigrants from Latin American countries — including South America, Central America, and the Caribbean — tended to arrive in Canada as Roman Catholics. Newcomers from Africa — who constituted 5% of immigrants between 1980 and 1990 — were the only continental departure from the tendency to identify with Christianity. Some 60% of African emigrants identified with religions other than Christianity; still, more than one in three said that they were either Roman Catholics or Protestants (see TABLE 2.7).

A third reason for the ongoing dominance of Christianity is religious assimilation. For all the talk about having a multicultural society, a good case can be made for the reality of two dominant cultures: one in English-speaking Canada that is influenced dramatically by the United States, the other in Quebec with its French and Québécois roots.

To live in Canada is to be predictably influenced by the dominant host cultures. Relatedly, immigrants and their children frequently intermarry. The net result is that acculturation and assimilation contribute to a tendency for many to abandon the religion of their parents and grandparents, and identify with Protestantism and Roman Catholicism.

And so it is that, as of 1991:

• Close to five in ten people born in Canada who trace their national backgrounds to Third World countries say they are Protestants or Roman Catholics;

- an extremely high four in ten indicate they have no religious preference;
- just one in ten identify with other world faiths.

	Other Faiths	Xn	Rom Cath	UC	Ang	Pres	Luth	Bap	Other Evans	None	Totals
TABLE 2.7. RELIGIOUS IDENTIFICATION OF CANADIANS OF NON-EUROPEAN ANCESTRY: 1991 _In %'s_											
Born in Canada	10	48	20	12	2	<1	1	5	8	42	100
Born Outside of Canada	32	46	29	1	2	<1	<1	4	10	22	100
Asia	36	37	26	1	1	<1	<1	2	6	27	100
Africa	60	35	21	10	3	1	<1	<1	<1	5	100
Latin America	7	79	41	<1	6	1	<1	9	21	14	100

SOURCE: Derived from the 1991 General Social Survey, Statistics Canada.

Further, the 1992 PROJECT TEEN CANADA national survey of the country's 15- to 19-year-olds found that the parents of visible-minority youth who were born outside Canada were slightly more inclined to identify with religions other than Christianity (45% versus 28%). However, indicative of gradual acculturation, among visible-minority adults who have been born in Canada, Christianity is the preferred identification (44% versus 39%).

The 1992 youth survey uncovered another noteworthy finding concerning religious assimilation. Only 1% of teenagers whose parents were either Roman Catholic or Protestant were personally identifying with other world religions (see TABLE 2.8). But by the time young people whose parents adhered to other world faiths had hit their late teens, 12% had come to identify with the Christian religion. These included 14% of young people born in Canada, and 9% of those born outside Canada.

These findings suggest that, despite the official proclamation that Canada is a multicultural and multireligious country, considerable religious assimilation is taking place, with the movement being almost totally in the direction of the Christian faith. Put bluntly, when it comes to religion in Canada, the mosaic is largely a myth. It therefore is not surprising that the _Maclean's_ 1993 survey "portrays

Canada as an overwhelmingly Christian nation, not only in name, but in belief."[20]

TABLE 2.8. **INTERGENERATIONAL RELIGIOUS IDENTIFICATION**				
In %'s				
		Teens' Religion		
Parents' Religion	Christian	Other	None	Totals
Christian	89	1	10	100
Other Faiths	12	74	14	100
Teens Born in Canada	14	70	16	100
Teens Born Outside				
Canada	9	81	10	100
None	20	1	79	100
SOURCE: PROJECT TEEN CANADA 92.				

However, the jubilation in the Christian camp should probably be short-lived. When the nation's dominant religious style is short on commitment and long on consumption, religious assimilation is not necessarily the win it's cracked up to be.

The Price of Religious Assimilation

Many Asians who arrive as Christians appear, if anything, to be somewhat more religiously committed — or at least more religiously conservative — than their Canadian counterparts. *United Church Observer* writer Catherine Rodd, points out, for example, "At an age when most Caucasians wouldn't be caught dead admitting they go to church, the teens in ethnic congregations are eager and enthusiastic." She tells of one Vancouver teen from the Philippines who "was shocked when the youth group she joined cancelled their Bible study to squeeze in a rehearsal for their Christmas play." The young woman commented, "That would never have happened at home."[21] Stuart Lightbody of the Christian and Missionary Alliance has suggested that the spiritual vitality of the ethnic churches is contagious, and may serve to revitalize faith in this country.[22]

However, the mini-institutions — families, churches, temples, media — of those immigrants who hold on to religions including Christianity cannot be expected, in the long run, to stem the tide of North America's mighty socializing and secularizing influences. Further, given that acculturation and assimilation are realities in Canada, there is no reason to believe that immigrants, in the course of becoming more and more like the rest of us, will exhibit higher levels of religious commitment.

And they don't. As new Canadians and their children are exposed to North American and French Canadian lifestyles, they tend to do two things: identify with the dominant Christian religion and follow the lead of other Canadians in becoming highly selective consumers in their "use" of religion.

- In the case of Asian immigrants, for example, the younger they are when they arrive in Canada, the more likely they are to identify with the Christian faith in their later adult life. However, participation is another story. Some 25% of those who immigrated to Canada when they were younger than 13 have proceeded to become weekly attenders, far below the 80% level for those Christian Asians who came to Canada when they were 30 or older (see TABLE 2.9).
- Latin American immigrants differ in being much more inclined to identify with Christianity, regardless of when they arrived in Canada. But, similar to Christian Asians, the inclination to attend services on a weekly basis is inversely related to the age one sets foot in Canada. Almost the same proportion of those who were younger than 13 when they arrived — 23% — have gone on to become weekly churchgoers in adult life, far below the 60% level for those who were older than 30 when they came to this country.

The Reverend Danny Huang of Willowdale's Taiwanese United Church says that even within youth groups, there are noticeable differences between the teens born in Canada and those born elsewhere.[23] An evangelical college student from Malaysia told me that cultural assimilation in the sexual realm, for example, doesn't even necessarily take very long:

> *When Asians come to Canada, their morals go down — they become more relaxed and open. Like, they start to sleep around. Back home in the Asian countries, sleeping around is stigmatized. People have exclusive partners. They might have sex with different people, but not as openly as the Canadians. But over here, they change.*

Such findings suggest that the social and cultural factors that erode the desire for people born in Canada to participate in organized religion have a similar impact on new arrivals, especially those who are young. In time, most are no more likely than other Canadians to be either highly involved or religiously committed.

People coming to Canada can greatly enrich our collective life. Moreover, they, like the rest of us, are receptive to many of the things that religion historically has had to offer. However, like the baby boomers, they don't represent some kind of miracle cure for the problems of the churches. Rather, they represent part of the great opportunity that is facing religion in our time.

TABLE 2.9. IDENTIFICATION AND CHRISTIAN ATTENDANCE BY AGE WHEN EMIGRATED: 1991

In %'s

	Asian Immigrants					Latin American Immigrants				
		Religious ID			Ctn		Religious ID			Ctn
	Cty	Other	None	Total	Wkly	Cty	Other	None	Total	Wkly
Age When Came										
under 13	43	25	32	100	25	64	11	25	100	23
13–18	38	22	40	100	54	86	7	7	100	30
19–29	36	39	25	100	64	81	6	13	100	45
30+	33	42	24	100	79	78	9	13	100	60
TOTALS	36	37	27	100	78	8	14	44	100	44

SOURCE: Derived from the 1991 General Social Survey, Statistics Canada.

EVANGELISM AND ITS EUPHEMISMS

If groups can't grow the easy way, by adding child and geographically mobile members, there's one last possibility: the recruitment of outsiders. Usually the term used is "evangelism"; in other instances, "faith sharing." Regardless of the word, the concept is one of reaching out beyond one's boundaries.

Experiencing the growing numerical crisis firsthand, religious groups have not stood still.

- Conservative Protestant denominations such as Baptists, Pentecostals, and the Christian and Missionary Alliance have viewed the current situation as representing an unprecedented opportunity for outreach and have accelerated their evangelistic efforts.
- The national umbrella organization for many such groups, the Evangelical Fellowship of Canada, has spearheaded an effort

known as Vision 2000, which is attempting to facilitate evangelism through training, research, and the overall co-operative effort of more than 40 denominations and para-church organizations.[24]

- Anglicans worldwide have declared the 1990s to be the decade of evangelism. In British Columbia, saying they are "disturbed by the secularization" of the province and "challenged by the influx of immigrants,"[25] Anglicans have embarked on an evangelistic effort using high-profile promotion to supplement and support personal witness.

- Lutherans have given the green light to a major campaign for attracting new members throughout the next decade, adopting a mission plan that calls for growth of 1% annually. The plan includes forming outreach ministries, starting new congregations, and enlarging existing ones.[26]

- Pope John Paul, in a 1991 encyclical that represented the Vatican's first major statement on missionary work in a quarter-century, announced an aggressive campaign to spread Roman Catholicism. Pointing to new fronts including Eastern Europe and Asia, the Pope warned against "the belief that one religion is as good as another."[27]

- And then there's the case of Presbyterians — yes, seemingly reserved and solid middle-class Presbyterians. In at least the recent past in North America, Presbyterianism has not been synonymous with "witnessing" and "proselytizing." Yet, in the face of declining numbers and an aging membership, denominational leadership summoned clergy and lay leaders to a national conference on "mission and evangelism" on the outskirts of Toronto in the fall of 1988. I was there as a guest resource speaker and couldn't resist suggesting to them — playfully and warmly, I hope — that, in the face of their numerical problems, their rediscovery of evangelism amounted to their "converting a demographic necessity into a theological virtue."

There's no doubt about it: Canada's religious groups, perceiving the religious market to be opening up as increasing numbers of people cease to be involved in the churches, are attempting to solve their numerical problems by upgrading their recruitment efforts. In what sounds like a cyclical argument, having not been able to keep their people, they are increasing their efforts to recruit them — and presumably keep them. Logically and practically, it is not an easy task. It also is not one with which they are having much success.

The General Picture

For starters, from the standpoint of participation in religious groups, it's very apparent that the people who are *currently* involved usually are the same people who were involved when they were younger.

- Some 80% of Canadians who at present are attending services on close to a weekly basis were doing the same thing when they were growing up.
- Close to another 10% were going to churches a few times a month to monthly.
- Only about 2% of today's weekly attenders were going to services seldom or never as youngsters.

What's more, the situation has changed little since 1975 (see TABLE 2.10). Then, as now, more than 80% of the weekly churchgoers had been attending services that often as young people. Then, as now, only 2% of the weeklys had been yearlys or nevers as children. These findings, incidentally, are consistent with those of Don Posterski and Irwin Barker; in their 1992 survey of close to 800 of Canada's most active church members, they found that a mere 7% had been raised in unchurched homes.[28]

TABLE 2.10. **CHILDHOOD INVOLVEMENT OF CURRENT WEEKLY ATTENDERS: 1975 & 1990**		
In %'s		
	1975 (339)	1990 (267)
Nearly every week or more	83	81
Two-three times a month	5	5
About once a month	2	3
Several times a year/yearly	8	9
Less than once a year	1	1
Never	1	1
TOTALS	100	100
SOURCE: PROJECT CANADA Survey Series.		

A peek at these previously inactive Canadians reveals that only about 10% have in fact "graduated" to a near-weekly attendance level. The same can be said for just over 10% of those who previously attended a handful of times a year. While it's fair to say some inroads are being made to the unchurched market, the gains to date are modest.

Moreover, a comparison with the situation in 1975 shows that, despite the accelerated attempts in recent years to reach outsiders, there has actually been a *lower* rate of success (see TABLE 2.11). Reflecting church recruitment efforts prior to the mid-1970s, as of 1975 about 15% of the yearlys and nevers had moved up into the weekly-plus category over their lifetimes, as had over 25% of those who had previously been in the "several times a year" category. Both levels are well above those for 1990.

The churches are relearning what the committed have known well for some time: "sinners" are hard to reach.

There's more, however, to the story of the childhood attendance patterns in the pre-1950s versus now. It's not just that groups have been having difficulty attracting the previously inactive. They've also been finding it very hard to *keep* the people they have. At a time when only about 10% to 20% of those marginally involved as children have become regular attenders, around 70% of those who were that highly involved in their early years have passed the incoming new recruits on their way out the church doors. That's up slightly from 65% in 1975.

TABLE 2.11. **CURRENT INVOLVEMENT BY CHILDHOOD ATTENDANCE: 1975 & 1990**

In %'s

Level in Childhood	N	Weekly Plus	1–3 Month	Sev Times a Year	Once Year	Never/ Rarely	Totals
1990							
Weekly+	738	29	11	19	15	26	100
One-three month	153	14	13	14	21	38	100
Several times year	110	13	8	25	16	38	100
Yearly or less	148	10	5	7	16	62	100
1975							
Weekly+	803	35	9	21	14	21	100
One-three month	84	18	18	26	14	24	100
Several times year	46	26	9	26	10	29	100
Yearly or less	158	15	2	15	15	53	100

SOURCE: PROJECT CANADA Survey Series.

Attrition is a major problem for Canada's religious groups. Limited recruitment is being offset by limited retention. The age-old dilemma referred to earlier is blatant in these numbers: how do groups recruit *outsiders* when what they are doing appears inadequate to retain the majority of *insiders*?

Pseudo-Evangelism: Switching

In lieu of reaching out to large numbers of religiously inactive Canadians, religious groups frequently seem to confuse the recruitment of people from other churches with the reaching of outsiders. For the most part, I think it is an honest mistake.

As we have just seen, the vast majority of people who are the most active in the country's religious organizations today are the people who were very active when they were younger. But that is not to say they have necessarily remained involved with the same groups over their entire lifetimes.

In fact, a number of observers, taking their cues from the American rather than Canadian scene, have been arguing lately that denomination no longer matters much in this country. Lutheran official Jim Chell told a 1993 conference on shared ministry that they are "pioneers in a postdenominational age."[29] Christian Reformed leader John Van Til was quoted as saying, "People don't join a church because of denominational loyalties; they join because of someone else who goes there, or because that's where they experience acceptance." His colleague Arie Van Eek agreed, claiming that "denominational loyalty is eroding."[30] Don Posterski and his co-author Irwin Barker have recently informed us that "denominational walls are tumbling down."[31] Looking at the American scene, church planting expert Lyle Schaller says that adults born in the 1950s and 1960s don't carry the institutional loyalty of older generations. "Parents and grandparents stayed with their denomination, but people from age 40 down to 25 don't have that denominational loyalty," says Schaller. "They shop around."[32]

But are the walls actually tumbling down?

An examination of the current affiliation of respondents by their parents' affiliation suggests that a measure of movement between Canada's dominant religious groups certainly has been taking place.

- About 5% of adults from **Roman Catholic** homes have moved into mainline Protestant — United Church, Anglican, Presbyterian, utheran — churches. Only a small percentage have switched to the conservative Protestants or to other world religions. Given that Roman Catholics make up approximately 45% of the Canadian population, such seemingly trivial percentages nonetheless translate into some solid numbers — about 340,000 moving to the mainliners, and about 65,000 to both it the conservative Protestants and other faiths.

- The **mainline Protestant** churches likewise have seen about 10% of their affiliates defect to other groups, divided almost evenly between the Roman Catholics and Conservatives. Because the mainline churches make up about 35% of the nation's population, these percentages represent about 265,000 people in each instance. Another 50,000 have shifted to other religions.

- The **conservative Protestants**, constituting only about 7% of the Canadian population, are — along with the 5% of people identifying with other faith groups — the most vulnerable of religious groupings to defection. The reason is simple: population size. The likelihood that a person who is raised a Baptist (3%) or Pentecostal (1.5%) will marry outside the conservative fold is obviously much greater than it is for the average Roman Catholic (45%) or mainline Protestant (35%). And so it is that some 20% of conservatives shift to other groups, with most of these people — about 170,000 — moving over to the mainliners.

- Facing the same retention problems, groups such as **Jews, Hindus,** and **Muslims** (each less than 1%) have seen about 20% of their adherents — some 150,000 people — move over to the Christian groups, almost totally to Roman Catholicism and mainline Protestantism.

What also is readily apparent from an examination of intergenerational movement is that, in all group instances, the most popular destination for those who defect is the no-religion category. These people tend to be younger single Canadians, who nevertheless frequently tell us in our surveys that they expect to turn to religious groups in the future for pivotal rites of passage — ceremonies such as weddings, baptisms, and funerals.

This "none" category thus appears to continue to be a highly transitory zone, a sort of resting place, that many will abandon with the onset of marriage and children. Consistent with such an argument, apart from temporary "nones," it's interesting to note that 40%

of Canadians who came out of homes where their parents claimed no religion are now lining up with the country's religious groups. Almost all of them opt for Christianity (see TABLE 2.12).

TABLE 2.12. **RESPONDENTS' AFFILIATION BY PARENTS' AFFILIATION**							
In %'s and 1000s*							
			Respondents' Affiliation				
Parents' Affiliation	N	RC	Mainline Prot	Cons Prot	Other	None	Totals
Roman Catholic	475	87% 5,873	5 338	1 67	1 67	6 405	100 6,750
Mainline Protestant	349	5% 263	85 4,462	4 210	1 52	5 263	100 5,250
Conservative Protestant	68	<1% 2	16 168	64 671	2 21	18 188	100 1,050
Other Faiths	34	11% 82	7 52	<1 1	75 562	7 53	100 750
None	74	12% 72	18 108	9 54	1 6	60 360	100 600

*For illustrative purposes, based on a national population figure in the post-1950s, less young children, of about 15 million.
Percentages of the population: RC's 45, Mainline Protestants 35, Conservative Protestants 7, Other 5, None 8.
Parents' affiliation is based on father's religious preference; the correlation between father and mother's preference is very high, 0.77.

SOURCE: PROJECT CAN90.

Switching, as such, doesn't necessarily translate into people becoming more involved in their new groups. The key factor appears to be the attendance norm of one's new setting. Individuals who switch to the mainline Protestants pretty much imitate the prevalent attendance level. The same is true for those who shift to the conservative Protestants, the Roman Catholics, and other faiths (see TABLE 2.13).

Not only is switching relatively uncommon, then, but it doesn't necessarily result in heightened participation — except, perhaps, in the evangelical Protestant case, where currently one in two people who have "switched in" are attending weekly. But even here, one needs to be cautious. An examination of new conservative recruits from other groups reveals that half of them were weekly attenders when they were growing up, with almost all who attended often accompanied by their mothers and half of them with fathers.[33]

In sum, intergenerational switching does not automatically result in higher involvement. When it does, there is good reason to believe that many switchers are simply continuing their patterns of high participation elsewhere. Switching may look like evangelism and sound like evangelism. But for all the motion and commotion, it usually is not evangelism.

TABLE 2.13. **INVOLVEMENT LEVEL OF PEOPLE "SWITCHING IN"**

In %'s

		N	Weekly	Monthly	Several Times a Year	Yearly or Less	Totals
Mainliner	All	401	14	10	17	59	100
	Switchers	50	8	8	11	73	100
Conservative	All	92	49	9	11	31	100
	Switchers	28	49	4	20	17	100
Roman Catholic	All	498	32	11	23	34	100
	Switchers	29	33	5	13	49	100
Other Faiths	All	44	18	13	26	43	100
	Switchers	9	16	19	<1	65	100

Note: No. of "switchers in" is obviously small, especially in the "other faith" instance. They nonetheless are included for heuristic value.

SOURCE: PROJECT CAN90.

Involvement Without Identification

One final qualifier needs to be added about switching. As people look at individuals in their churches from different backgrounds, they are inclined to assume that, because they are now attending and perhaps have become members, they have switched; they have cut their ties with the religious groups of their childhood.

This might be largely an illusion. Religious identification is a psychological and emotional variable. People can attend a United Church for practical reasons — its location, marriage, enjoyment of the minister, and so on. That's not to say, however, that they cease to regard themselves as Anglican, Lutheran, Roman Catholic, or whatever. One Anglican priest in the Hamilton area, for example, told me of a member who left for a nearby Presbyterian church and its choir, complaining that he "couldn't stand the way that Anglicans sing." On a visit to the area hospital sometime later, the minister noted that the former member's name happened to be on the hospital list — complete with his "Anglican" affiliation!

Similarly, in surveying the conservative Protestant scene, it doesn't take a sophisticated analyst to recognize that a given Christian and Missionary Alliance Church includes those who continue to see themselves as Baptists and Mennonites, to merely start the list of people in the evangelical family.

The 1990 national survey reveals that this pattern of "involvement without identification" ranges from about one in three people who attend conservative Protestant churches to one in four for those attending mainline congregations to perhaps one in 50 for those worshipping in Roman Catholic churches (see TABLE 2.14).

TABLE 2.14. **GROUP WITH WHICH ONE IS INVOLVED BY GROUP WITH WHICH ONE IDENTIFIES (In %'s)**

People Attending Monthly or More

Group with Which Involved	N	Group With Which Identify					
		Main	Conserv	RC	Other	None	Total
Roman Catholic	212	1	1	98	<1	<1	100
Mainline	69	73/95*	3	1	<1	1	100
Conservative	42	3	67/84*	8	3	2	100

*The first figure refers to involvement and identification with the *same* denomination (e.g., Anglican–Anglican, Baptist–Baptist); the second figure includes those who are involved with a *different* denomination in that grouping from the group with which they identify (e.g., Anglican–United, Baptist–Alliance).

SOURCE: PROJECT CAN90.

Quite clearly, noteworthy numbers of Protestants are happy to participate in the life of given congregations and parishes, but may well not be identifying psychologically and emotionally with the denominations of which these groups are a part. They also appear to show a much greater willingness in the 1990s than in the past to "network" — to work together and share faith together. In the words of Glen Scorgie, the dean of the North American Baptist College, "a growing number of Canadian Christians no longer hesitate to clamber over established boundaries to link up with kindred spirits."[34] Across Canada, ecumenical initiatives are common. In Prince Edward Island, 15 denominations are participating in transdenominational events through a co-operative effort known as "Island Vision."[35] In the city of Calgary, the co-operation level between churches is uncommonly high, extending to a covenant — produced by Pastor Jim Wallace and the city's evangelical Ministerial Association — that discourages transfer growth involving disgruntled members, as well as the criticism of other churches; it has been signed by some 35 conservative and mainline ministers.[36]

Co-operation, however, does not mean that denomination no longer matters. If it didn't matter, people would readily discard their previous denominational identities when they became involved with a new group. The fact that they don't adds further support to the argument that it is not only extremely difficult for religious groups to recruit seemingly inactive Canadians, it's also not easy to randomly recruit geographically mobile churchgoers.

Despite their claims that "denominational walls are tumbling," Posterski and Barker's 1992 findings for active Protestant church members support rather than refute the stability of identification argument. True, they found that 55% of their active member sample said they had "switched denominations" during their lifetimes. However, much of that switching was within the evangelical and mainline families — of the Mennonite-to-Baptist and Anglican-to-United varieties. Some 71% of the laity in mainline groups were in fact raised in mainline denominations; similarly, 63% of the members active in conservative churches were brought up in evangelical denominations.[37] What's more, when asked how important they would rank denomination in deciding to switch to another church, 59% of their mainliners, 66% of Pentecostals, and 46% of their other conservative Protestants said "high." Overall just 18% gave denomination a "low" ranking.[38]

When data on intergenerational loyalty among Roman Catholics are factored in to their Protestant findings, one can see that the walls may have some chips missing. But they're not exactly crumbling.

Canadians — to a much lesser extent, it seems, than Americans — are hanging on to the religious identification of their parents and grandparents. In a Canada where we officially value the preservation of cultural histories and are suspect of those who want us to give them up, perhaps the finding is not all that surprising. As University of

Washington sociologist Rod Stark commented to me recently, "It's not at all clear that the Canadian religion economy has been deregulated."

**FIGURE 2.1. THE CALGARY COVENANT:
A COVENANT OF THE CHURCHES OF CALGARY**

Unity is at the very heart of God (John 15:22). In Calgary, there is but one true church and Jesus is its head (Ephesians 4.4-6). When Christians love each other and walk together in unity, the world is convinced of the truth of the gospel and reality of God (John 15:23).

One of the aspects of church life that erodes the unity of the Church of Calgary is the constant "circulation of the saints" between churches. This often breeds a spirit of competition, suspicion, and criticism.

In order to promote the unity of the Body of Christ in Calgary, to build up the Kingdom of God in this city and not my own personal church kingdom, and in order to declare to the people of this city the unity of the pastors and leaders of the churches of this city, I agree to the following:

1. I will never seek to draw people away from another congregation. I will not engage in criticizing another church or state or imply that my church is superior.
2. I will pray regularly for the other assemblies within our city and earnestly endeavour to keep the unity of the Spirit in the bond of peace.
3. I will rejoice when God blesses my fellow pastors and sister congregations.
4. When I know that a person from another church is attending my church, I will make a personal call to the pastor of that church and see if he is aware of what is happening. If there are problems or conflicts that have not been satisfactorily dealt with, I will seek to meet with the pastor and the people involved to address these matters.
5. Within my own denomination or fellowship, I will follow carefully the official procedure laid down for the transfer of members. I will never recommend transfer or receive transferees without dealing first with any unresolved problems related to the people transferring.

Signed: _____

Church: _____

The Conservative Protestant Case

But surely, one might think, there are some groups such as Pentecostals and grassroots charismatic congregations,[39] including those that are part of John Wimber's Vineyard movement,[40] that are having considerable success in reaching the unchurched. The possibility has been an intriguing one to observers in the United States, Canada, and elsewhere. In 1972 an American mainline churchman, Dean Kelley, released a book entitled *Why Conservative Churches Are Growing;* it explored the apparent success of evangelical Protestant denominations at a time when groups such as the Methodists, Presbyterians, Episcopalians, and Lutherans were declining. In the ensuing twenty years, the book has sparked vigorous debate as to the nature and sources of the two apparently divergent patterns. A general assumption seems to be that the decline in the market shares of the mainliners has resulted in an opening up of the religious market for conservative Protestants. According to the argument, because the evangelical groups address the demand for meaning through stressing supernatural and spiritual issues, they have been experiencing significant market gains.

Further, although it is difficult to demonstrate empirically, it appears that many conservative Protestant denominations are characterized by a certain vitality and drive that frequently makes them qualitatively different from many mainline groups. Such a qualitative difference, seen by observers like Kelley as tied to demands and commitment, may have important implications for apparent quantitative differences between conservative and mainline groups.

Since the early 1970s I have collaborated with University of Calgary sociologist Merlin Brinkerhoff in exploring the nature of conservative church growth. The study initially involved 20 randomly selected evangelical congregations in Calgary. Historically a hotbed of evangelical activity, this city of 700,000 recently has been described by church-growth expert Peter Wagner as one of four cities in North America — and the only one in Canada — where Christian revival is likely to happen during the 1990s.[41]

In early 1971 Brinkerhoff and I met with church personnel and went over the membership additions for the period 1966–70. New members were classified as coming into the churches through one of three pathways: (1) *reaffiliation,* where they were regarded by the church as Christians upon their arrival (for example, through transfers); (2) *birth,* meaning that the new member had at least one evangelical parent or guardian prior to age ten; and (3) *proselytism,* where they did not fit into either of the first two categories and in effect had come in from outside the evangelical community.

We found that 72% of the new additions had come through reaffiliation, while 19% were in reality children of evangelicals. Only about 10% had come from outside the evangelical sector, with the key recruitment links being relational in the form of friendship and marriage.

In 1982, aware of the ongoing claims that conservative Protestants were continuing to know numerical gains in contrast to mainline Protestants and Catholics, we returned to the same churches and catalogued their new additions for 1976–80. There had been four congregational casualties, dropping the original 20 congregations to 16. We found little departure from the pathway proportions that we had observed a decade earlier.

Still, through the early 1990s, as we have seen, Canadian national data point to higher participation levels for conservative Protestants than for mainliners, while census data indicate that the evangelicals are at least holding their own, at a time when mainliners and Catholics are shrinking. Consequently there seemed to be merit in returning still again to Calgary and exploring whether things have been changing.

In early 1992 we did so, and found the 16 churches from ten years earlier still intact. Once more replicating our earlier procedures, we examined the additions to the 16 groups for the period 1986–90. Further, aware that a number of new and seemingly burgeoning evangelical congregations had been appearing in Calgary in recent years, we supplemented the original 16 churches with four grassroot groups that had appeared since 1980 — three of which were charismatic. This subsample made it possible to explore the possibility that the growth patterns of these new congregations might differ from our somewhat more "routinized" evangelical churches.

We found that the original 16 had continued to experience a slight increase in the proportion of outsiders they had recruited during 1986–90, while their additions through birth were somewhat down from previous years. The mainstay pipeline source of reaffiliation was virtually the same, at around 70%. The modest changes in the birth-proselytism mix may in large part have reflected the fact that, as these congregations aged over the post-1960s, the pool of children available as new members in many instances had diminished. As a result, the recruitment of outsiders became increasingly necessary to organizational viability. Here, as perhaps is often the case, evangelism took place not so much because it *should* but because it *had* to. To repeat the aforementioned comment yours truly offered the Presbyterians, what was theologically virtuous was in reality driven by what was demographically necessary.

As for the four grassroot evangelical groups, their pathway proportions closely resembled the 16 original congregations. An examination of a sample of people actively involved in these four fledgling churches — using church telephone directories in lieu of formal membership lists — revealed almost identical proportions of religious backgrounds to the people who joined the original groups.

TABLE 2.15. **SOURCES OF NEW MEMBERS: ORIGINAL AND GRASSROOT CHURCHES**				
	% 's			
Period	Reaffiliation	Birth	Proselytism	Totals
ORIGINAL				
1966–70	72	19	9	100
1976–80	70	17	13	100
1986–90	72	13	15	100
GRASSROOT				
1986–90	71	15	14	100
SOURCE: Derived from Bibby and Brinkerhoff, 1992:3–4				

What the research concerning new members has made very clear is that, since at least the 1960s, conservative Protestant groups in this particular Canadian city have had limited success in recruiting people from outside the evangelical community. Beyond percentages, the actual number of outsiders recruited *per church per year* was only *1.3* between 1966 and 1970, *2.6* for 1976–80, and *2.9* between 1986 and 1990! This rather dismal picture persisted over time, despite the fact that almost all these congregations were engaged in an array of evangelistic efforts. Nor were the churches particularly small: two, for example, had some 1,000 members each.

A FOOTNOTE: NUMBERS AREN'T EVERYTHING

To return to the phrase that Benton Johnson, the editor of *The Journal for the Scientific Study of Religion*, coined back in 1973 in the course of revising our paper on that first Calgary study, the project seems to provide substantial support for the argument that evangelical church growth involves not so much the penetration of secular society, as the "circulation of the saints."

That phrase and the idea behind it has gained wide acceptance in the past two decades. American sociologists Wade Clark Roof and William McKinney[42] have co-opted it in a matter-of-fact fashion to describe the movement of church members in the U.S. And Canadian author Ron Graham, in his best-selling journalistic account of religion in Canada, *God's Dominion*,[43] used the phrase as the title for his chapter on conservative Protestants.

However, having had twenty years both to fill out our findings and reflect more fully on them, Brinkerhoff and I have become increasingly uncomfortable with such widespread acceptance of the "circulation of the saints" thesis. We're surprised, in fact, that for two decades our academic colleagues have failed to give the thesis the criticism it so richly deserves. While it has much merit, we believe it also suffers from three major flaws:

1. Low Proportions Versus Normative Proportions

Since 1973, we have assumed that the 70–20–10 distribution for reaffiliation-birth-proselytism means that evangelicals are not adding many outsiders. In the Calgary case, as we have just pointed out, the argument is sound: 2.3 outsiders per church per year over fifteen years is not very many — regardless of how one plays with the figures.

Yet obviously, if the total population of new members is sufficiently large, the 70–20–10 distribution may be just fine, perhaps quite normal. A healthy congregation, after all, will add new members through all three pathways. There would be something wrong with a church located in a normal North American setting if people on the move geographically ignored it or if no members' children ever joined. The important issue, then, is not that the proselyte proportion has to exceed the levels of the reaffiliation and birth pathways. Rather, the overall pool of new additions needs to be of sufficient size to ensure that the 10% of outsiders translates into numbers that reflect the church's attempts to reach out to people beyond the boundaries of the evangelical community. In short, 70–20–10 does not necessarily mean that the saints are merely circulating.

2. Immediate Patterns Versus Life-long Patterns

The focus of our Calgary research has been the immediate religious group history of new members. We have asked only about the most recent previous church tie and not about a person's religion of birth.

Consequently, our finding that only 10% of new members have come from outside the evangelical community cannot be interpreted to mean that, over lifetimes, only 10% of new members have made such a transition, which would leave people with the impression that conservative Protestants recruit very few people from the mainline and Roman Catholic camps. Quite clearly, many people who come from other evangelical churches originally appeared as outsiders. However, they are passed on to the next evangelical church as re-cycled "sinners" who, in our research, have been counted as "saints." This is an important point that American researchers Robin Perrin and Armand Mauss have recently underlined in the light of research on Vineyard congregations in Washington and Oregon.[44]

The fact of the matter is that the PROJECT CANADA national surveys have documented the difference for some time. When we asked Canadians in 1990, for example, about their life-long affiliational patterns, we found that a total of somewhere around 30% of current evangelicals had come from other groups, while another 10% claimed they had no religious background (see TABLE 2.16).

Putting that 30% national figure together with our Calgary findings, the picture that emerges is one where new members in any evangelical church setting include perhaps 10% who have come *directly* from outside the evangelical community, and another 20% who have come *indirectly*, via other conservative churches. Perhaps another 10% have actually had little or no ties with a religious tradition — although, I suspect, this figure is inflated.[45] The remaining 60% are life-long "circulating saints." Such findings do not dispel the circulation thesis. But they do suggest the need for caution in concluding that conservatives are having almost no success in reaching people beyond the borders of their groups.

3. Growth Versus Vitality

On the surface, Canadian evangelicals appear to be readily winning the switching competition. After all, some 20% of all conservative Protestants come from the United, Anglican, Lutheran, and Presby-terian churches; another 8% have Roman Catholic roots. By way of comparison, a mere 3% of mainliner Protestants and less than 1% of

Roman Catholics have evangelical Protestant origins. It looks like a trouncing. The other religions of Canada, by the way, do not appear to be either a significant source of recruits or destination for defectors.

The apparent margin of victory for the evangelicals in the switching competition is, in reality, very small. The reason lies in the vast differences in the sizes of the religious groups involved. As noted earlier, conservatives make up only about 7% of the Canadian population, compared with around 35% for mainliners and almost 45% for Catholics. Although 30% of those who join the evangelical ranks come from outside the evangelical community, that percentage translates into only about 425,000 people. On the other hand, even though the conservatives who defect to the mainline and Catholic camps make up only 4% of the total of those groups, that seemingly harmless loss represents almost 400,000 people.

If we move beyond religious switchers and focus on who is bringing in the largest number of previous "nones," then perhaps we have the biggest surprise of all: the mainline Protestants' 4% total translates into 280,000 people — *twice the number of conservatives*, at 140,000. Even the Roman Catholics are adding more nones (180,000) than the evangelical groups.

TABLE 2.16. **CURRENT AFFILIATION BY ORIGINAL AFFILIATION: In %'s and 1000s***						
Select Canadian Groups: 1990						
			Parents' Affiliation			
Own Affiliation	Cons Prot	Mainline Prot	Roman Catholic	Other	None	Totals
Conservative Protestant	61 834	21 286	8 112	<1 28	10 140	100 1,400
Mainline Protestant	3 210	86 6,020	6 420	1 70	4 280	100 7,000
Rom. Cath.	<1 180	4 360	93 8,190	1 90	2 180	100 9,000
Other	4 40	5 50	16 160	74 740	1 10	100 1,000
None	17 272	12 192	27 432	2 32	42 672	100 1,600

*Based on a national population figure in 1990, less young children, of about 20 million. Percentages for the groups: RC's 45, Mainline Protestants 35, Conservative Protestants 7, Other 5, None 8.

SOURCE: PROJECT CAN90.

Still, we need to be careful. Proportionately the conservative Protestants are bringing in more outsiders than anyone else. Further, because of their relatively small size, the evangelical groups have to work extremely hard just to stay where they are and not be absorbed by the mainline Protestants and Catholic majority. According to the first Canadian census of 1871, conservatives made up 8% of the population. Currently they continue to stand at about the same level.[46]

Consequently their failure to experience extremely large net gains should not obscure an intriguing finding: 8% of the religious population has been going head-to-head with approximately 80% of the mainline Protestant and Catholic population and coming out the winner by a slight margin! Given the pressures of intermarriage, acculturation, and the considerably inferior organizational resources, for such a little religious company to fare so well is nothing less than a remarkable accomplishment. The net gains point to considerable vitality among conservative Protestant denominations.

What's more, rather than diminishing, that vitality shows signs of contributing to ongoing strength, relative to the mainliners. As we will see shortly, national analyses of weekly attendance by age show that evangelicals are succeeding in holding their own across their age groups — in sharp contrast to the other Protestants and Roman Catholics.

Nevertheless, the bad news is that neither the evangelicals nor the mainliners are having particular success in reactivating the growing pool of Canadians who are not involved in the churches. Evangelism and its euphemisms are not resuscitating Canada's ailing religious groups. Beyond the negative implications for the organizations themselves, perhaps there is a much more tragic human result: that large numbers of Canadians who might benefit from and, indeed, may *need* the message and ministries of the churches are being left largely untouched.

THE NEW COMPETITORS

It's one thing for a relationship not to work out; it's another to watch the other person become involved with someone else. Canada's established religious groups have been more than a little concerned that they are losing people to some new religious movements. As I reported in *Fragmented Gods,* as of the mid-1980s the new groups on the block were not having an awful lot of success. Still, that was then.

According to some observers of the contemporary religi[   ]
the anxiety on the part of people associated with Canada's h[   ]
dominant groups is well warranted. They argue that, somewhat ironically, the decline of existing forms of religion will automatically
trigger the appearance of new ones. The demand for religion is
constant; what is changing are the groups that are supplying it.

What the Theorists Say

SECULARIZATION
TION; NB

Such an argument goes back at least as far as French sociologist Emile
Durkheim (1858–1917). While he is typically associated with the
secularization thesis, there is an important wrinkle to his thinking that
is often not given the emphasis it warrants. While recognizing that
traditional religion in Europe was in a serious state of decline in the
late nineteenth century, Durkheim maintained that religion was
anything but dead. Unlike such thinkers as Auguste Comte and
Sigmund Freud, he didn't see the advance of science as eliminating
religion. On the contrary, he pointed out that the two types of
thinking had co-existed since the birth of science and would continue
to do so. Scientific thought, said Durkheim, is simply a more perfect
form of religious thought and progressively replaces it. However,
religion will always have an important speculative function because
science "is fragmentary and incomplete; it advances but slowly and is
never finished; but life cannot wait." Religious explanations may be
forced to retreat in the face of the steady advance of science, but
religion never surrenders.[48]

Moreover, according to Durkheim, because religion has its very
source in social life and carries out an array of important collective
and individual functions, it will survive. "The old gods are growing
old or are already dead, and others are not yet born," he wrote.
However, while he noted that "there are no gospels which are immor-
tal," he added, "but neither is there any reason for believing that
humanity is incapable of inventing new ones."

In a stimulating contemporary update, American sociologists Rodney Stark and William Bainbridge have maintained that religion is
guaranteed an indispensable role when it comes to the meaning of
life and death. Only references to supernaturally grounded ideas,
they say, can provide plausible answers to these so-called ultimate
questions. As a carrier of explanations based on supernatural assumptions, religion plays a unique and irreplaceable role in human
affairs.[49]

Viewing religious activity as dynamic and ever changing, Stark and Bainbridge make extensive use of a market analogy. Secularization, they say, is a process found in all "religious economies." Some religions and some groups are always losing ground. But because the market for religion remains, the activity only increases and the competition intensifies as old groups and new groups struggle to gain, retain, and enlarge market shares.

Such activity sees breakaway sects attempt to rejuvenate fading traditions, while new groups — what Stark and Bainbridge call cults — attempt to bring consumers something new. Revival and innovation are consequently central features of the religion marketplace. Precisely in the geographical areas where conventional religion is weakest, cults will be strongest — vying for the chance to seize the market.

Secularization, in the minds of Stark and Bainbridge, is therefore a process that stimulates religion, rather than extinguishes it. The never-ending human quest for meaning ensures religion's viability.

According to such thinking, leaders of traditional religious expressions in Canada have much to worry about. In addition to being concerned about decreasing interest in what they have to offer, they have to face the very real possibility that people are turning elsewhere.

One of the most publicized options has been the so-called New Age movement. There has been concern that significant numbers of young people are not just staying away from the churches, but are being lured away by the cults — including Satanism and witchcraft.

The New Age Movement

Since the early 1980s and the publication of Marilyn Ferguson's *The Aquarian Conspiracy,* New Age thought has received considerable exposure. Early thinkers, according to Professor James Beverley, included the founder of theosophy, Madame H.P. Blavatsky, along with the famous medium Edgar Cayce. Prominent current leaders, he says, include Ferguson, David Spangler, Fritjof Capra, Carlos Castaneda, and, of course, Shirley MacLaine.[50] Some observers have tended to associate the movement with what they regard as the idiosyncracies of MacLaine,[51] and, as one Toronto writer has put it, "with beliefs and practices often thought of as being, well, flaky. Meditation. Astrology. Tarot cards. Reincarnation. Out-of-body experiences. Dream analysis."[52] In the late 1980s, *Globe and Mail* columnist Bronwyn Drainie wrote that it's "rather like spiritual Silly Putty."[53]

However, it now is very clear that New Age has become a significant religious-spiritual movement, acknowledged by such well-known futurists as John Naisbitt[54] and Alvin Toffler.[55] Whether people support it or denounce it, says one Toronto journalist, the New Age movement "has become too widespread to write off as the self-indulgent ramblings of a fringe group."[56]

New Age thought has focused heavily on such themes as the tapping of one's potential, personal spirituality, the spirit world, and a major shift in consciousness with the arrival of the twenty-first century. Naisbitt, for example, notes that the movement has its roots in the human potential movement and the complex awareness of "the oneness of creation, the limitless potential of humanity, and the possibility of transforming the self and today's world into a better one."[57]

The movement has nonetheless tended to be ideationally eclectic and organizationally diffuse. Canadian New Age expert Linda Christensen says the range of beliefs is so great that it makes it very difficult to define New Age thought. In fact, she says, "there is such diversity that if one approaches the New Age as a highly systematized belief structure one would inevitably discover it to be full of contradictions." Christensen argues that the chief interest for many of the people involved is not so much beliefs as it is transformation, largely understood in terms of healing and wholeness with self, others, nature, and the world at large.[58]

As for organization, Christensen points out that the movement is essentially a grassroots "decentralized mega-network."[59] Naisbitt writes that there are no membership lists, and it is difficult to pin down the actual number of people involved — although he cites one estimate that the figure in the U.S. is perhaps 5% to 10% of the population.[60]

What is far easier to document is the interest in New Age materials. Books, magazines, music, and what seems like an unending number of activities, courses, and services, have become extremely popular.

- The size of the New Age sections in bookstores, for example, are the envy of any number of disciplines, including religious studies — and, yes, certainly sociology.
- New Age bookstores and magazines are popping up in major cities across Canada. Publications like Toronto's *Dimensions,* Vancouver's

Common Ground, and Montreal's *Guide des Resources* inform readers of varied activities and programs taking place. As of mid-1993, *Common Ground* had a print run of 100,000 and claimed a readership of 300,000.[61]

- Places like B.C.'s Vision Mountain Leadership Training Centre in Nelson offer an array of courses, with the 1993 selections including topics like "Consensus Decision Making," "Body Mind Harmonizing," "Experiencing the Clown," and "Transformational Therapy."[62]

- According to *Guide des Resources,* which has a circulation of close to 100,000, in Montreal alone, there are some 10,000 people making their living from New Age–related businesses.[63]

The assumption is that New Age thought is being adopted by significant numbers of North Americans and others as an alternative to traditional religion. This is the major reason many U.S. evangelicals have resisted it so aggressively[64] and such organizations as the Christian Research Institute in Calgary watch it so closely. CRI spokesman Dan Hardock has commented that while the movement can offer something real for people to hang on to, it can be dangerous because of its close association with the occult. Says Hardock, "Some of these things are sort of like dealing in spiritual dynamite."[65] A few PROJECT CAN90 respondents also expressed apprehension. One evangelical mother of five from PEI said, "It's totally dangerous and a manipulation of Satan." A Full Gospel mine worker from Manitoba commented, "New Age is a religion that sets God and self as equals." And a 45-year-old suburban Toronto Anglican woman described New Age as "dangerous stuff."

Journalists and other observers, including the people on the street, have joined religious leaders in sensing that New Age may be filling religious gaps. One Toronto New Age bookstore manager, Gerry Warner, told an interviewer that the movement is filling a gap left by mainstream religions. "People are finding that typical and traditional techniques aren't working," he said. "People in the movement are a lot of recovering Catholics and such — people who haven't been happy with the religion or the faith they were born into."[66]

Warner's impressions warrant a closer look. The 1990 national survey probed the extent to which Canadians are (a) familiar with New Age thought, (b) personally interested in such thinking, and (c) participating in any New Age activities, groups, or networks. The survey has found that

- about 30% of Canadians say they are familiar with New Age ideas;
- some 11% of people across the nation indicate they are either "somewhat interested" (8%) or "highly interested" (3%) in New Age thought;
- 3% report that they are involved in New Age activities, 2% in actual groups, and 2% in networks;
- variations among the most highly interested by their religious identification, age, gender, and region of residence are very slight.

Although the percentages for interest and participation are small, this is not to say that the numbers are insignificant: 3% of 20 million adults translates into some 600,000 Canadians, 11% into just over two million.

These findings, however, do not address the obvious question: to what extent are Canadians adopting New Age thought as their new religion versus adding some of its attractive features to their conventional religious expressions? Just because someone pays attention to her horoscope does not mean she has abandoned Catholicism, any more than giving credibility to psychic powers means that someone has deserted the United Church.

An examination of the role New Age thinking plays in Canadian lives reveals the following:

- the vast majority of people most interested in New Age thought — 81% — continue to identify with Roman Catholicism (53%) or Protestantism (28%);
- only 14% say they have no religious preference;
- just 5% actually identify with some other kind of religion, with New Age presumably what most of these have in mind;
- a full 75% of this core of people who are the most enthusiastic about New Age thinking indicate they have *no intention* of abandoning their traditional groups.

Subtracting the Roman Catholics and Protestants, this means that *less than 1%* of Canadians currently are *exclusively involved* in New Age religion. Consistent with these findings, the latest Canadian census (1991) has found that only 1,200 people explicitly say that their religion is "New Age." Some 40% are in B.C., about 30% live in Ontario, and 20% in Alberta. Just *15* "covert" New Agers are from Quebec, for example.[67] For the vast majority of the approximately 10% who do have some interest in the movement, New Age thought seems to function as a supplement rather than a substitute for traditional faiths.

Consequently, rather than seriously altering the religious status quo in Canada, New Age religion seems to follow the pattern of most new entries into the Canadian religion market, offering consumers optional items that can be added to more conventional religious beliefs and practices. The interest in the New Age movement provides, it appears, further evidence that Canadians in the 1990s continue to be very much into "religion à la carte."

A Note on the Self-Development Craze

A movement that sometimes overlaps with New Age is the self-help movement. Having its most recent roots in the human potential movement of the 1960s, it has mushroomed into a multimillion-dollar industry. Modern-day experts such as Anthony Robbins and such self-help programs as Context Training, Personal Best, and Omega are telling North Americans how they can tap their potential in unprecedented ways. The array of messages are widely available through lectures, seminars, workshops, books, and audio and video tapes — frequently hyped through a growing number of television "infomercials."

The 1990 PROJECT CANADA survey found that no less than one in five Canadians indicated they had taken a personal development course in the previous year! They included one in three people under the age of 35, one in five between the ages of 35 and 54. Enrolment was almost equal for women and men.

Is the self-help movement proving to be an alternative to involvement in organized religion for many Canadians? Knowing that a person has taken one course in the past year hardly provides us with an adequate measure of their interest. But for what it's worth, unlike the New Age movement, self-development does appear to have particular appeal to a large number of young people and, perhaps significantly, to almost one in three Canadians who claim no religious affiliation.

Clearly the self-help movement is a development worth watching.

TABLE 2.17. **INTEREST IN THE NEW AGE MOVEMENT AND THE SELF-HELP MOVEMENT**

In %'s

		The New Age Movement			The Self-Help Movement
			Participate in:		Taken Self-Dev. Course in
	Highly Interested	Activities	Groups	Networks	Past Year
Nationally	3	3	2	2	21
Roman Catholic	4	3	2	3	25
Quebec	2	4	4	5	25
Outside Quebec	6	2	<1	1	26
Protestant	2	2	1	<1	13
Anglican	2	1	<1	<1	12
United Church	2	2	2	1	12
Conservative Prot	2	<1	<1	<1	11
Other	6	5	6	4	27
None	4	3	2	1	29
18–34	3	2	1	1	33
35–54	3	3	2	2	18
55+	4	3	3	2	6
Female	4	4	2	2	22
Male	2	2	1	2	19

SOURCE: PROJECT CAN90.

Cults

The comprehensive PROJECT TEEN CANADA project I have carried out with colleague Don Posterski has vividly documented the apathetic relationship our nation's young people have with organized religion. As we reported in our book, *Teen Trends,* the attendance level of today's young people is the lowest of any teen cohort in more than half a century. Further, about half of those who are involved in religious groups do not appear to be associating a lot of joy with the experience. Overall, teenagers are placing limited value on established forms of religion and, if anything, see religion's significance in Canadian life as diminishing in at least the immediate future. It doesn't add up to an encouraging picture for religious leaders.

There has been much speculation about what young people *are* embracing. Excessive indulgence in a number of so-called pleasurable pursuits, notably drugs and sex, has, in previous decades, been feared by adults generally and nervous parents specifically.

There also has been concern that the nation's young people will fall prey to mysterious and aggressive new religious and quasireligious movements. In the 1970s and early 1980s, new entries, including the Moonies, Hare Krishna, and the Children of God, were seen as seducing daughters and sons and employing sinister brainwashing techniques. The assumption was that no one in their right mind would willingly join such groups. Evening newscasts told the story of young people being kidnapped on street corners and being lured away from airports. In retrospect, we overreacted. Relatively few young people were ever inclined to turn to any of the new movements.

These days, the possibilities continue to chill spines. It's one thing for parents to find that their teenagers are sleeping in on Sunday mornings — or are not in their bedrooms at all. It's quite another to learn that some teens in the community are participating in black magic, making suicide pacts, and — worst of all — encouraging our own kids to join in.

Considerable publicity has been generated in Canada about the extent to which teenagers are engaging in two kinds of "religious" behaviour that most people find more than a little disturbing — Satanic cults and witchcraft. The first is generally regarded to be destructive, incorporating rites involving violence and even death. Witchcraft, actually, the ancient European religion of Wicca, is often confused with Satanism. In fact, Wicca followers don't practise so-called black magic. Although it has a strong supernatural and magical flavour, it nonetheless, according to United Church Interfaith Dialogue Officer Paul Newman, "is an authentic, respectable religion that works for the health and well-being of its followers." On that basis, Newman was willing to write a letter in 1992 supporting a Calgary Wiccan practitioner seeking visitation rights to his young child.[68]

In 1990 the Canadian media gave extensive play to the growth of Satanism among young people, stimulated in large part by the claim that three teenage suicides in Lethbridge, Alberta, were linked to a Satanic-inspired death pact. Despite all the publicity, the RCMP maintained that no such link was found. Throughout the year, prominent newspapers such as the *Globe and Mail* ran articles on the spread of Satanism in Canada. *Globe* writer Timothy Appleby told the country that "an estimated 2,000 individuals have stepped forward claiming to have been abused in satanic cults." In his opening story, he began by describing this revelation of two young women in a Winnipeg counsellor's office:

Two young women speak of seeing babies torn apart and eaten. They speak of drinking blood. They speak of children being raped, lowered into graves and urinated on. "Many times I saw people killed, many times," said a woman who calls herself Selina. "My best friend was burned alive at a ceremony. We were about ten. We weren't allowed to cry." She says she has personally killed lots of people. "I was made to, with a dagger."[69]

Experts such as sociologist Stephen Kent at the University of Alberta are well aware that some young people are indeed involved in Satanic activities. He personally has interviewed more than a dozen who claim to have survived Satanic experiences. "What's remarkable is that we're getting similar accounts of what seem to be separate groups," says Kent. "The points of commonality include rituals in secluded areas, usually with people in robes of different colors, with chanting and, occasionally, human sacrifices which usually involve children."[70]

As for witchcraft, it also is evident from the testimonies of experts and current and former members that witchcraft, or Wicca, groups do exist, and include young people. It's estimated that 6,000 Canadians embrace the religion.[71] In the Calgary court case just referred to the judge listened while the defendant described his religion as one that is "nature based" and sees God as having "many faces." The judge, Karen Jordan, decided to grant the man visitation rights to his son, observing, "Is this [Wicca] so different from the beliefs of the millions of adherents to the Hindu faith?"[72]

It's difficult to get an accurate reading on just how many Canadians — young or old — are participating in either Satanism or Wicca. Statistics Canada doesn't exactly get a firm count in the course of carrying out the census, and other surveys aren't much help either. In light of the stigma associated with both kinds of activity, the people involved — especially in the case of Satanism — are not particularly anxious to tell outsiders about their participation. Even in the Wicca instance, admission can carry a high cost. The footnote to the Calgary judge's benevolent view of the defendant's religion is that she did, nevertheless, admit that the man's religion does conjure up images of "scorpions, cauldrons and magic wands."[73] As for dialogue officer Paul Newman, who wrote the letter in the man's defence, he found himself facing criticism from his denomination.[74] So much for the survey possibility.

Another method of probing the level of involvement, however, is to ask a large sample of people about the extent to which they are aware of other people participating in such activities or groups. The method is hardly perfect. But the expectations that individuals will volunteer such nonpersonal information that will reflect their actual contact with people who are involved would seem to be reasonable.

The 1992 PROJECT TEEN CANADA survey used such a procedure. We asked 15- to 19-year-olds how common Satanic or witchcraft group involvement and practices are "among teens you know." In both instances slightly fewer than one in ten said participation is "fairly common." About three in ten indicated it is "fairly uncommon," while around six in ten reported it is "nonexistent." Differences by region, community size, gender, and race were very minor.

For one in ten teens to say participation among people they know is "fairly common" does not mean that one in ten teens are participating. In some situations, especially smaller schools and communities, the involvement of a few people in an entire school or town could result in a "fairly common" response. Such activities make for hot copy; the word quickly gets around, with the data subject to the same hyperbole and distortion of anything that hits the gossip line.

TABLE 2.18. **INVOLVEMENT IN SATANISM AND WITCHCRAFT**

"There has been some talk about young people having an interest in Satanism and witchcraft. Among teens you know, how common is:"

In %'s

	NAT	BC	PR	ON	QUE	ATL
Involvement in Satanic Groups or Practices						
Fairly Common	8	8	10	8	7	10
Fairly Uncommon	32	33	35	36	22	39
Is Nonexistent	60	59	55	56	71	51
Involvement in Witchcraft Groups or Practices						
Fairly Common	7	8	8	7	7	7
Fairly Uncommon	28	26	33	30	21	32
Is Nonexistent	65	66	59	63	72	61

SOURCE: PROJECT TEEN CANADA 92.

As Don Posterski and I indicated in our book *Teen Trends,* we do not mean to minimize the impact of these activities on some teenagers and their parents.[75] But the fact remains, as with new religious movements generally, a relatively small proportion of Canadian teenagers participate in Satanism and witchcraft.

Not Yet Replaced

While Durkheim, along with Stark and Bainbridge, saw new gods coming into being to replace the old, in actual fact the old religions that have dominated the stages of the Western world for centuries — namely, Protestant and Roman Catholic variations of Christianity — remain the dominant religions in Europe and the Americas, including Canada.

There are a number of reasons why new religious movements have had such difficulty in making significant inroads:

- Established groups — similar to established companies — already have an emotional and psychological lock on most of the customers. Many people don't feel comfortable switching to a group that is new to the point of being labelled a sect, let alone a cult.
- There also is social pressure. To switch to a new religious organization is a form of religious deviance. It carries with it the risk of being stigmatized by family and friends.
- Then, too, the established groups don't give up market shares without a fight. New religious movements in the 1970s, for example, were commonly met with vigorous opposition in the form of the anti-cult movement. The New Age movement, as mentioned, has been similarly attacked by some of the existing groups, notably the fundamentalists, and particularly in the United States.

Beyond becoming overtly hostile, religious groups can neutralize the lure of new competitors by co-opting some of their more attractive and innocuous features. As I pointed out in *Fragmented Gods,* Canadian groups over time, consciously and perhaps often unconsciously, have responded to varied consumer demand by engaging in "menu diversification." The groups that historically have held a monopoly on the country's religion market — notably the Roman Catholics, United Church, and Anglicans — have increasingly diversified and enlarged their religious menus. Today's Roman Catholic, Anglican, or United Church member therefore has the option of being detached or involved, agnostic or evangelical, unemotional or charismatic. As a result, there's little need to switch.

* * *

In short, the hopes and fears surrounding baby boomers, new Canadians, outsiders, and new religious movements are largely out of touch with reality. The facts are:

- The boomers aren't coming back.
- Immigrants fairly quickly imitate the low participation tendencies of other Canadians.
- The unchurched are scarcely being touched.
- The new religions typically fare worse than the old ones.

But don't unfasten your seat belt quite yet. The problems of organized religion do not stop there.

3

SOME MAJOR SETBACKS

In a major reshuffling of power in the course of the century, social and cultural changes in Canada and elsewhere have altered the role religion plays in the lives of societies and individuals. At the societal level, industrialization and postindustrialization have led to a redefinition of religion's rightful place, and in the process has stripped religion of much of its previous authority over life. At the individual level, religion has also been highly marginalized, so that it has a limited influence in the day-to-day living of most people.

It's as if a top executive in a major corporation has been relieved of most of his duties. To the extent that religion aspires to speak to all of life, the redefinition of its rightful place in both the societal and personal instances has represented a significant demotion. And, like the executive, religion has had to endure a range of consequences — social, psychological, emotional, and financial.

As if things were not bad enough, the demoted executive's image has also been tarnished by charges of sexual impropriety.

THE LOSS OF AUTHORITY

A 25-year-old Catholic newspaper reporter summed up the current situation succinctly when she told us in the PROJECT CAN90 survey, "I don't see religion as having much power at all in the nation's affairs." A retired chemist similarly commented, "The major issues of the day seem to me to have little to do with religion and morality; economic and political factors are far more important."

There was a time not all that long ago when religion had significant authority in Canada. The Roman Catholic Church, which historically has been the church of close to one in two Canadians, had considerable clout when it spoke on matters of faith and life, especially in pre-1960 Quebec. To varying degrees, Protestant groups such as Anglicans and the United Church, along with evangelical groups, could likewise speak to their people and have a chance of being taken seriously by a good number.

It's hard to make a case for the authority of religious groups today. Sure, the churches still speak out. Declarations from the Canadian Council of Catholic Bishops, the Canadian Council of Churches, the Evangelical Fellowship of Canada, and so on are common. Many ministers still attempt to advise and admonish their congregations.

What is not at all clear, however, is whether all these words carry much weight. These are the 1990s, not the 1950s. For most parishioners, the national body or pastor or priest or rabbi merely offer another opinion — another viewpoint in a world of points and counterpoints. In the end, the authority to decide which position to take, says our culture, lies with the individual. Anything else is viewed as inappropriate — intimidation, bullying, dogmatism, brainwashing, a violation of our basic rights and freedoms. Such is the nature of individualism in our day.

If religious leaders suspect it, politicians know it. That's why they typically do not take the proclamations of religious groups too seriously. They know the former clout is no longer there.

Social scientists, for some time now, have been offering an explanation for what has been happening to religion in Europe and elsewhere. Their thinking is helpful, as well, in understanding religious developments in Canada.

Secularization in Theory

Many of the early analysts of religion held the view that religion is inherently false and that consequently, in due time, it would be discarded by "thinking" people. Such a positivistic view assumed that as societies became more advanced, greater illumination and economic well-being would relegate religion to history.

The founding father of sociology, Auguste Comte,[1] for example, maintained that civilization has been passing through three stages of thought — the theological, the metaphysical, and the positive; religion, belonging to the earliest stage of development, was gradually abandoned. Similarly, anthropologist James Frazer[2] saw human intellectual development evolving from magic through religion to science. Sigmund Freud[3] predicted that religion would gradually be replaced with science, which, in his view, was a far more responsible and superior means of dealing with reality. Karl Marx[4] likewise saw religion as a drug-like panacea that would no longer be needed once the problem of oppressive social conditions was resolved.

The secularization viewpoint, however, has not been limited to those who have regarded religion's demise as inevitable because it is either primitive or untrue. A large number of observers have seen religion's influence as decreasing because of the nature of advanced societies. Durkheim[5] and economist Adam Smith[6] were among the earliest proponents of such a position. Since the 1960s, perhaps the most prominent and unequivocal spokesman for the secularization thesis has been Oxford University's Bryan Wilson,[7] followed closely by transplanted European Peter Berger, now of Boston College,[8] and German sociologist Thomas Luckmann.[9] Secularization is seen by such thinkers as having institutional, organizational, and personal components.[10]

On the *institutional* front, say these thinkers, increasing specialization in advanced societies leads to a reduction in the authority religion wields over the various areas of life. For example, unlike the situation in less complex settings, religion no longer has control over an advanced society's political and educational spheres.

Such specialization, or "social differentiation," can be seen in the loss of influence of the church in European countries since at least the Reformation. Closer to home, secularization at the institutional level has been experienced by the Roman Catholic Church in Quebec since approximately 1960.[11] In their 1992 report, the Quebec bishop's research committee wrote:

> Quebec has become a modern society, with all the advantages and limitations of this type of society. The Church no longer plays the important role it used to play. The various social institutions have gradually conquered their autonomy with respect to the Church. . . . [Men and women] refer less and less to religious interpretations in determining the meaning of their lives.[12]

Even today, comparisons between the roles of churches in Canada's rural communities versus urban areas illustrate the same reality. In smaller places, it's still common for churches to carry out a number of social and community functions, complete with the potluck supper. In the big cities, however, churches frequently do little more than perform rites of passage and provide a place of worship.

In the *organizational* area, the argument goes, religious groups, over time, move in the direction of conforming to what is happening in the so-called secular world. Sociologist Max Weber,[13] for example, in discussing the movement from sect to church, has spoken of the tendency of religious groups to experience what he calls "routinization." Worship becomes more formal and less spontaneous; beliefs become more structured; the religious community itself becomes more organized.

Observers such as American social historian H. Richard Niebuhr,[14] drawing on the thinking of Weber and Ernst Troeltsch,[15] have argued convincingly that the history of Christianity has been characterized by a church-sect cycle. Groups of people, concerned about the loss of original ideals, have broken away to form sects, only to evolve into formal denominations themselves, which in turn have given way to further idealistic sects. In the 1960s, a number of works appeared that were particularly vocal about the way in which religious groups were selling out to culture. Among the best known were Pierre Berton's *The Comfortable Pew*[16] and Peter Berger's *The Noise of Solemn Assemblies*.[17] The issue of religion's sellout to culture has been virtually dropped in the 1990s, largely because the reality has by now been pretty much taken for granted.

At the *personal* level, there has been a widespread "secularization of consciousness" — a change in the way people interpret their worlds. Most people no longer feel any need to explain what is happening in their lives in terms of the gods. What happens is viewed primarily as the result of strictly human factors, such as environmental influences or personal characteristics. Once venerated other-worldly ideas are forced to compete with this-worldly claims on this-worldly terms.[18]

Life's questions and previous mysteries are dealt with pretty much by resorting to the physical and social sciences, the humanities, and medicine. The ultimate questions concerning the meaning of life and death are seen as interesting, but beyond resolution; one's attention is best given to more practical and pressing matters. Religion neither tends to interpret life nor inform behaviour.

In a capsule:

- Secularization is seen as a process in which religion has decreasing importance for societies, individuals, and even the religious groups themselves.
- The territory over which religion has authority diminishes, socially and personally.
- Its supporting groups are co-opted by society.

Religion's role is specialized, its influence marginalized, its organizations routinized.

A number of proponents of the secularization thesis still allow that the process is hardly without occasional disruptions. Princeton sociologist Robert Wuthnow,[19] for example, has pointed out that variations can readily be observed even among certain age cohorts, such as American youth in the 1970s who embraced spiritual ideas in surprising numbers. He writes that "discontinuities in the secularization process need to be acknowledged as the rule, not the exception, in religious change."

Secularization advocates also are quick to differentiate between church religion and religion more generally. Luckmann,[20] for example, has little doubt that religion survives beyond its traditional expressions in forms he calls "invisible religions." Berger, as well, sees an ongoing vigorous interest in the supernatural, summarized in the title of his book, *Rumor of Angels*.[21]

But as they look at Christianity and its churches, the proponents of the theory of secularization see the long-term process as moving in one direction — toward a decrease in the importance and authority of the church.

Secularization in Practice

Anyone scanning how life is lived in Canada in the 1990s will have difficulty disagreeing with most of what has just been said. At the organizational level, the churches have indeed been relegated to a relatively narrow religious role in Canadian life.

Churches are not expected to address all of life. On the contrary, in a day when specialization is the name of the cultural game, organizations are not wise to become too diversified. To do so is to run the risk of easily being outspecialized by niche-oriented competitors. The old cliché — jack of all trades, master of none — has become a guideline for organizational oblivion.

Despite this age of specialization, many religious groups still attempt to say much about everything — the economy, politics, immigration policy, the environment, global concern, and so on. The problem is that they have difficulty being taken seriously, let alone experiencing success. Further, their ability and credibility are not being enhanced by their shrinking numerical and financial resources. The result, in the words of United Church minister Neil Young, is that "our briefs on issues and our petitions for action get tossed on the pile with everyone else's."[22]

Even the media — those meaning-makers whose opportunity to shape minds is unmatched by any information source in history — have not been able to resist poking fun at religious groups, which, in the media's mind, try to say too much. About three years ago, Toronto political cartoonist, Andy Donato, sketched an elderly God-like man reading a newspaper with the headline, "Catholic Bishops Speak Out on Free Trade." Behind him, with his hand on the older man's shoulder, was a younger Christ-like figure saying, "Father, forgive them, for they know not what they do."

It's not just that people in the media, along with politicians and economists, fail to show deference to religious groups; they typically live out life without much reference to religion. *Maclean's* writer Mary Nemeth recently made the observation that in "an overwhelmingly Christian populace, there is a near-total absence of religious discourse in Canadian politics, the media and advertising."[23]

Perhaps even more troubling, however, is that Canadians are also less than unanimous in telling the churches to come alive and jump into all of life. A full 40% of the Canadian populace maintain that "ministers should stick to religion and not concern themselves with social, economic, and political issues." Those who hold such a view are far from fringe fundamentalists. They also aren't just the nominally involved. On the contrary, they consist of:

- a majority of Roman Catholics in Quebec, including the regular attenders — as well as a third of the RC's in the rest of the country, regulars and otherwise.
- about three in ten people who have United Church and Anglican ties, with two of these three being those who attend twice a month or more.

- some 35% of conservative Protestants — although this does not represent a *decrease* from the 45% who favoured staying out of societal matters in 1975.
- approximately three in ten Canadians who adhere to other faiths.

Still further, nationally, opposition to involvement in life beyond the religious sphere has, if anything, been slightly increasing rather than decreasing, from 37% in 1975 to 39% in 1990. The reason for the slight rise lies primarily with Roman Catholics in general and Quebec Catholics in particular. Noting the pattern, the 1992 bishops' report on religion in Quebec included this quote from one Catholic concerning the church's intervention on the economy: "I feel that this is too political an issue for the Church to be concerned. . . . It smells too much of politics."[24]

Somewhat ironically, Catholics in general are becoming less accepting of religion's involvement in social and political matters, at a time when conservative Protestants are becoming more accepting. Hans Daigeler, who worked with the Canadian Conference of Catholic Bishops before entering politics in Ontario, says, "There seems to be a tacit understanding that religion is a private matter — they don't want you to come out and be a Holy Roller."[25]

Catholics consequently may not have been as upset as some Protestants were when Toronto Archbishop Aloysius Ambrozic fired Carl Matthews, publisher and editor of the archdiocese of Toronto's official paper, the *Catholic Register,* in the fall of 1992. Matthews had written an editorial urging readers to vote yes in the October referendum on the Charlottetown accord.[26] True, the independent *Catholic New Times* in a February editorial asked, "Since when is it wrong for a Catholic editor — even an official one — to take a stand on a national issue?"[27] Yet, survey findings (see TABLE 3.1) suggest there's a good chance that many Roman Catholics agreed with the archbishop's belief that Matthews had overstepped his journalistic boundaries. It's interesting to note that an editorial in the national *Anglican Journal* the same month also called for a yes; it was presumably deemed acceptable![28]

All this doesn't exactly add up to an enthusiastic mandate for religious leaders to become social activists. Be careful, though, with your interpretation. I'm not saying for a moment that clergy and other leaders shouldn't charge forth, if they feel so inclined. What I *am* saying is that, when they lead such charges and look back over

 oulders, they often will find themselves with a less than
_ming supporting force.

TABLE 3.1. **RELIGIOUS INVOLVEMENT IN LIFE**

"Ministers should stick to religion and not concern themselves with social, economic, and political issues."

% Agreeing

	Nat	RCOQ	RCQ	Ang	UC	Cons	Other	None
All Affiliates								
1990	39	35	55	29	30	35	32	46
1975	37	30	48	33	31	45	39	49
Regular Attenders*								
1990	33	31	55	32	18	21	**	**
1975	31	27	44	27	23	24	**	**

*Attend services twice a month or more.
**Too few cases to compute stable percentages.

SOURCES: PROJECT CAN75 and PROJECT CAN90.

Secularization and Pluralism

It's not even particularly clear that when religious groups stick to religion, they have a lot of freedom to be very assertive, Charter of Rights ideals notwithstanding. I've been among those arguing for some time now that we have made the mistake of thinking that a pluralistic society such as ours is only possible when we essentially declare that everything's relative. We have thought that if we are to be a country of many cultures, many lifestyles, many religions, many everythings, we cannot pronounce judgments on the merits of our various possibilities.

Academics have, in fact, played the role of high priests who have legitimized the "everything's relative" idea. They have reminded us that everything is personally and socially constructed, reflecting the ideas and characteristics of individuals and societies. Consequently nothing is really better or best. To think in those terms is to be "ethnocentric."

The result of laying out such pluralistic guidelines is that the already reduced territory over which religion is allowed to have authority is, in effect, reduced even further. The demoted executive not only has a smaller area; he also has a smaller say over his smaller area.

In playing by the pluralistic rules and being solid multi-everything citizens, religious groups find themselves severely restricted. To begin with, they are called upon to recognize that ours is now a multi-faith country. The principles of tolerance and acceptance are the norm. It's not only that conflict is frowned upon; there also is little appreciation for competition. Aggressive and imaginative efforts to recruit other groups' members, for example, are not the Canadian way.

The pluralistic rules go further. In addition to the coexistence norm, another important guideline exists: there is no place for truth claims. If a variety of lifestyles, moralities, and religions are all to have a place under one societal roof, each must be seen as valid options for the populace. Truth has to be seen in terms of personal preference. A society that is multicultural in the broadest sense of the term cannot permit proponents of one cultural style or sexual orientation, abortion view or world view, to impose their positions on others. The diplomatic way to resolve the problem of diverse outlooks is to decree that they all are relative.

Religious groups in Canada must operate within such a relativistic environment. Service the customers. Offer viewpoints. Make pronouncements that endorse such broad societal ideals as equality and justice. But don't get too specific. And don't get too general. Know your place. Stick to religion. Above all, don't use the T-word.

Tragically, religious groups cannot even turn to their affiliates and members for support in rising above such pluralistic handicaps. The problem here is that academics have done their work well: relativism has caught on well in Canada. No, it's not that people can clearly articulate the concept. But the educational sector has been joined by the other key idea-instilling institutions, such as the media and government, in convincing Canadians that there are few things in our culture that are superior to others.

I'm not exaggerating. My 1990 national survey of adults found that some 65% endorse the idea that "everything's relative." In addition, no less than 50% maintain that "what is right or wrong is a matter of personal opinion." Such relativistic thinking is even more prevalent among our young people; as of 1992 the same statement about "right and wrong" being "a matter of personal opinion" was endorsed by almost 65% of Canada's teenagers. Significantly, Canadian adults and youth who are active in religious groups are just about as likely as those not involved to subscribe to a relativistic view of life.

TABLE 3.2. **RELATIVISM AND RELIGION**

% Agreeing

	Nat	RCOQ	RCQ	Ang	UC	Cons	Other	None
"Everything's relative"								
Adults: 1990								
All	65	62	76	64	60	51	75	75
Churchgoers*	58	62	67	45	38	51	**	**
"What's right or wrong is a matter of personal opinion"								
Adults: 1990								
All	50	50	61	51	40	34	75	75
Churchgoers	41	47	53	45	44	17	**	**
Teens: 1992								
All	64	63	59	73	67	52	70	68
Churchgoers*	57	57	58	70	64	45	69	**

*Attend services twice a month or more.
**Too few cases to compute stable percentages.

SOURCES: PROJECT CAN90 and PROJECT TEEN CANADA 92.

In days of yore, prophets could emerge from the wilderness and proclaim to the citizenry, "Thus saith the Lord." In the last days of the twentieth century, such prophets are scarce. In a multicultural Canada, they would be ridiculed, perhaps arrested, maybe hospitalized. Stripped of the ability to speak with acknowledged authority, religious leaders become little more than additional voices in the galaxy of interest groups. They have no special credentials, receive no preferential treatment. In fact, given the problems lately that leaders have been associated with in matters of sexuality and finances, they are well aware they have to choose their issues and words very carefully.

The pluralistic rules have done much to immobilize religion in Canada, making it difficult for groups to expand, as well as exert a strong influence by speaking out loudly and with certainty. When religion has to be worried about expanding its membership base, and be concerned about the dangers of being prophetic, it loses its body and its voice. There's not much more to lose — except its credibility.

THE LOSS OF CONFIDENCE

Nothing seems to upset people more than improprieties involving sex and money. Since approximately 1985, Canadian churches have indirectly and directly been associated with too much activity in both areas.

Confidence Breakers

The problems are well-known. In the late 1980s, a series of scandals focusing on sex and money brought down a number of high-profile American televangelists. Among the best known were Jim Bakker and Jimmy Swaggart. In Canada, Queensway Cathedral's Ralph Rutledge — whose thriving Toronto ministry was highlighted in *Fragmented Gods* — was quietly moved from the leadership of his congregation to a counselling program. Tight-lipped church leaders simply acknowledged that indiscretionary behaviour had taken place.[29]

Far more damning for religion's image have been the disclosures of sexual misconduct involving Roman Catholic priests. If their behaviour had involved adult women, single or even married, we would have had a serious *scandal* on our hands. But the news that the people involved were males, and that the males were young boys, escalated the scandal into an *atrocity*. The facts spoke for themselves: trusted Roman Catholic priests were violating their oaths of celibacy by engaging in sex. Worse than that, they also were flagrantly repudiating explicit Roman Catholic teachings by engaging in homosexual acts. Still worse, these guardians of children, working in orphanages, group homes, and residential settings, were exploiting them for their own sexual gratification. The nation was outraged.

The allegations spread like an epidemic:

- More than a dozen Roman Catholic priests were charged and convicted of sexual misconduct involving boys at the Mount Cashel orphanage in Newfoundland.
- In Ontario the apparent physical and sexual abuse of boys at training schools operated by the Christian Brothers in the towns of Alfred and Uxbridge near Toronto was so extensive that a compensation package of $23 million — up substantially from a $16 million tentative settlement just six months earlier — was negotiated between the church, the Christian Schools of Ottawa, and the Ontario government in June of 1993. As many as 650 alleged victims are eligible to apply for compensation, which will include counselling, vocational skills upgrading, and payment for pain and suffering.[30]

- In Kingston a choirmaster sexually abused more than a dozen choirboys over a 15-year period; he subsequently was sent to prison. In 1993 criminal charges of sexual abuse were also laid against a former chorister.[31]
- In Manitoba aboriginal leader Phil Fontaine acknowledged that he himself had been sexually abused in an Indian residential school. He maintained that such behaviour had been widespread prior to the school's being phased out in the 1960s. In February 1991 an aboriginal woman appearing on CTV's "The Shirley Show" told a nationwide audience how she had suffered physical and sexual abuse at a Presbyterian-run school in Birtle, Manitoba — a claim church officials subsequently found verified by former residents both there and at a school in Kenora.[32]
- In Saskatchewan, highly respected group home operator Father Lucien Lareé was charged with sexual misconduct involving both males and females. He was later cleared in a controversial trial and decision, and has moved to the U.S. His Bosch homes for children were closed.
- In British Columbia the bishop of Prince George resigned in July 1991 after being charged with raping and assaulting native women in a diocesan residential school in the 1960s. The charges were later stayed at his Vancouver trial in December 1992 because of procedural infractions by lawyers for the crown.[33]
- In May 1993 ABC's "Primetime Live" carried a ten-minute feature informing all of North America of the physical and sexual abuses carried out in Quebec's Roman Catholic orphanages in the pre-1960s. As many as 15,000 orphans, the program claimed, had been abused — some even murdered. According to the story, these "Orphans of Duplessis" — named after the repressive premier who ruled Quebec from the late 1930s through the 1950s — had filed a $1.2 billion lawsuit; an apology from the church was also being sought.[34]

Public interest in understanding what has been happening in the realm of sexual abuse is bound to increase with the news, in June of 1993, that the controversial mini-series, *The Boys of St. Vincent,* the fictional story of sexual abuse in a Catholic orphanage in the 1970s, won the grand prize at the Banff International Television Festival — Canada's first solo victory in the festival's 14-year history. It also won the best mini-series award. The film has been described by Catholic

Children's Aid Society supervisor Paul McAuliffe as "a sensitive and insightful treatment of a story where no one lives happily ever after."[35] Although the series was shown nationally on CBC in December 1992, it did not air in Ontario or Quebec, because a judge ruled it might prejudice the trials of four Christian Brothers facing criminal charges in Ontario.[36] In full distribution, including video cassette, it will only heighten awareness of such problems. Says Sister Brenda Peddigrew, who grew up on Mount Cashel Road less than a hundred yards from the orphanage, "We have to watch it so it won't happen again."[37]

Beyond scandal and abuse, there has been, of course, a third major area of controversy involving sex. Prophecy has its price. In 1987 the United Church of Canada released a highly controversial report on sexual orientation. The report recommended that homosexuals be seen as full-fledged members of the church and, as such, be eligible for ordination as ministers. Needless to say, the recommendation was picked up enthusiastically by the country's media, who essentially interpreted the proposal as meaning that homosexuals were going to be ordained as United Church clergy. What had been intended as recognition of full membership in the church took on the appearance of being an aggressive new movement on the part of the denomination's leadership to put gays and lesbians into United Church pulpits from coast to coast!

Nonetheless, despite calls for careful study of the proposals, emotion seems to have played a major role in how people responded. Between at least 1984 and 1990, the issue dominated United Church life. Following the adoption of the "full membership status" concept in 1988 by the church's general council meeting in Victoria, about 25,000 members and some ten congregations left the denomination.[38]

The position of the church was hailed by many leaders within the denomination as groundbreaking and progressive, painful yet necessary. For other leaders, it was yet another sign that the United Church was defying the authority of the scriptures, selling out to culture in an attempt to stay in step with the times.

If the rank-and-file member was a shade confused, there is good reason to believe that the word that described nominal adherents was probably "dismay." Given that the vast majority of these marginal types joined other Canadians in disapproving of homosexuality and feeling somewhat uncomfortable around gays and lesbians, more than a few appear to have been muttering, "What on earth is going on in my church?"

On the heels of their problems, religious groups have attempted to regroup:

- Anglican bishop Peter Mason, with primate Michael Peers present, apologized to victims of sexual abuses and their families in early 1993 at St. George's Cathedral in Kingston, speaking first to 100 people outside the church, and later to 600 inside at an evening service. Many of the 100 were former members who had picketed the cathedral for more than a year.[39]
- The Baptist Union of Western Canada, in addressing pastoral sexual misconduct, has prepared a "Moral Failure Document" and a supplementary protocol statement that articulates 15 principles. Included is the following: "It is always a professional misconduct for an accredited minister within the BUWC to enter into sexual relations with a child, a congregant, a person he or she is counselling, a fellow employee or a volunteer worker."[40]
- In 1992 the United Church adopted a new policy on sexual abuse aimed at eradicating any such behaviour on the part of its members, ministers and otherwise. "Sexualization of a relationship between a minister and someone under his/her pastoral care," for example, is regarded as "an unethical boundary violation."[41]
- In addition to negotiating compensation packages, the Roman Catholic Church — through the Catholic bishops — has produced a report, *From Pain to Hope,* and study kit, *Breach of Trust/Breach of Faith,* dealing with the pastoral care and rehabilitation of victims, as well as guidelines aimed at preventing further incidents.[42] A two-year project has been launched to co-ordinate the church's response to allegations of abuse in Indian residential schools. Included are proposed "healing workshops" involving both natives and nonnatives.[43]
- Religious leaders like Archbishop Peers have proposed that groups have a clear posture toward sexual abuse, including acknowledging and being responsive to the claims of victims, establishing policies for behaviour involving church personnel, and engaging in education and prevention.[44]

In the midst of allegations, charges, convictions, apologies, and compensation, there is, of course, a real danger that clarity, truth, and justice are sometimes lost.[45] Mass indictment and mass apologies undoubtedly result in many innocent individuals being sacrificed. Not every person who worked in a home or a residential school is guilty. In February 1993, for example, a former Christian Brother was acquitted of beating and raping students; the key witness was accused by the judge of perjury, saying he may have adopted another boy's true story for financial gain.[46] Journalists are among those who make statements to the effect that a major reason for the aboriginals' "social upheaval" is "the residential school and the type of slavery mentality it created."[47] Yet, the historical fact of the matter, says researcher Thomas Lascelles, is that only about one in six native students even went to residential schools. The rest either attended reserve schools or those in neighbouring white communities.[48]

These days, such facts matter little. The seriousness of the documented offences have been sufficient to warrant widespread criticism and cynicism. It might not be totally just. But substantial damage has been done.

A Confidence Reading

All three areas of controversy appear to have contributed in a major way to a critically important trend: there has been a dramatic drop in public confidence in religious leaders in the past decade.

- In 1980 approximately 60% of Canadians said that they had "a great deal" or "quite a bit" of confidence in religious leaders, virtually unchanged from the early 1970s.
- By 1985 the confidence level had dropped to about 50%.
- As of 1990 the level of confidence had plummeted to 37%.

In the very short 1985–90 period, the confidence drop was:

- close to 25 percentage points among people identifying with the United Church;
- around 20 points for Anglicans and conservative Protestants;
- about 15 percentage points for Roman Catholics.

The widespread nature of the confidence decline is also apparent in the findings for Canada's teenagers. In 1984 some 62% of the country's 15- to 19-year-olds said that they had a high level of confidence in religious leaders. By 1992 that figure had fallen to 39%.[49]

TABLE 3.3. **CONFIDENCE IN RELIGIOUS LEADERS BY RELIGIOUS GROUP: 1985–90**

% Indicating "A Great Deal" or "Quite A Bit"

	1985	1990
NATIONALLY	51	37
ROMAN CATHOLICS	62	47
PROTESTANTS	52	32
Anglican	46	24
United Church	50	27
Conservatives	68	50
OTHER	30	41
NONE	10	15

SOURCE: PROJECT CANADA Survey Series.

What is particularly dramatic and telling is the decline in confidence by region. Undoubtedly reflecting the controversies mentioned, the 1985 to 1990 drops in confidence have been 40% to 30% in B.C., 51% to 33% in the Prairies, 46% to 31% in Ontario, 54% to 48% in Quebec, and — by far the greatest slide in confidence — from 74% to 40% in the Atlantic provinces.

TABLE 3.4. **TEEN AND ADULT CONFIDENCE IN INSTITUTIONS**

"How much confidence do you have in the people in charge of . . ."

% Indicating "A Great Deal" or "Quite a Bit"

	The Police	The Schools	Radio	TV	Court System	Relig Orgs	Your Prov Govt	The Fed Govt
ADULTS								
1990	70	55	52	55	43	37	30	13
1985	74	56	—	43	48	51	30	29
TEENS								
1992	69	67	65	61	59	39	32	27
1984	77	69	—	—	67	62	41	40

SOURCES: PROJECT CANADA and PROJECT TEEN CANADA Survey Series.

And no, it's not just a case that Canadians are feeling disillusioned with all their major institutions, including religion. Both the adult and youth surveys show that no other Canadian institution — with the exception of the much maligned federal government — has experienced a loss of public confidence in recent years that begins to match that experienced by religion.

Down but Not Out

The obvious question that arises from all this is: "To what extent are people staying away as a result of their waning confidence?" The short answer appears to be: "Not much." Most people who previously attended church don't appear to be either staying home or heading elsewhere. They may be upset with their leaders to varying degrees, perhaps disillusioned and demoralized. But surprisingly, to date at least, they are showing no signs of making a massive move toward the church exits. While attendance levels are down slightly since the mid-1980s, they in no way match the magnitude of the confidence-decline levels.

To be sure, there are regional exceptions. Archie Patrick, a community planner and educational consultant who works for ten chiefs and about 15 reservations in the Prince George, B.C., area, maintains that the history of sexual abuse at the Catholic residential school there has had serious effects. A graduate himself of two residential schools, Patrick notes that 100% of the native people were baptized into the Catholic Church 20 years ago. He estimates that "less than 5% of our people go to church now. "The faith," he says, "has been falling apart here."[50]

There also are organizational exceptions. Susan Mader Brown of King's College in London, Ontario, says that the "drastic reduction in seminary applications" experienced by Roman Catholics in the early 1990s, for example, was at least in part the result of "the negative perception of priests provoked by the scandals."[51]

Overall, however, the survey findings suggest that, despite all that has happened, for most people religion — even in its organized expression — is far more than the actual personalities involved. In a June 1993 address to a Retail Council of Canada convention, pollster Allan Gregg of Decima Research told his audience that retailers are getting hit by the same kind of anger Canadians have been directing at politicians. Consumers, he said, have lost their faith in once-trusted stores and brand names, just as they've lost their faith in political leaders.[52]

Surprisingly, when it comes to religion, Canadians are showing a remarkable "brand" allegiance. The thinking of the affiliated masses seems to be along the lines of, "The leaders might be messing up, but my faith and my church are still important to me." Of course developments have been upsetting. Who's surprised to learn that 37% of Roman Catholics reported in the 1993 *Maclean's* poll that "their faith was shaken by revelations of sexual abuse in the church"?[53] What is perhaps surprising is that while many have been shaken up, most are hanging in.

TABLE 3.5. **CONFIDENCE AND SERVICE ATTENDANCE: 1985–90***				
	1985		1990	
	Confidence	Attendance	Confidence	Attendance
NATIONALLY	51	26	37	23
British Columbia	40	19	30	22
Prairies	51	23	33	22
Ontario	46	23	32	21
Quebec	54	27	48	23
Atlantic Canada	74	42	40	41

*Confidence: "A Great Deal" or "Quite A Bit";
Attendance: Almost every week or more.

SOURCES: PROJECT CAN85 and PROJECT CAN90.

I'm not talking here about only the most devout active members. It's also interesting to observe that the decline in confidence has not been matched by a reduced tendency of the nominally involved to look to the churches for weddings, christenings, funerals, and the like. An analysis of the desire for such rites of passage in the future, according to levels of confidence people have in religious leadership, reveals virtually *no difference* between those who have high levels of confidence in leaders and those who do not. Both categories of Canadians are equally likely to say they will turn to religious groups when the time comes for such ceremonies and sacraments to be carried out!

The loss in confidence and the rise in stigma have certainly not made things easier for the country's religious groups. Still, the findings point to a rather remarkable amount of resilience and patience in large numbers of Canadians. In a literal sense, all has not been lost.

TABLE 3.6. **CONFIDENCE IN LEADERS AND DESIRE
FOR RITES OF PASSAGE**

*% Anticipating Turning to Religious Groups for Ceremonies
Relating to Birth, Marriage, and Death*

	Birth	Marriage	Death
High Confidence	26	28	60
Low Confidence	26	29	60

SOURCE: PROJECT CAN90.

THE LOSS OF INFLUENCE

It's a shade difficult to exert a lot of influence when your responsibilities have been dramatically diminished and your credibility severely questioned. Such is the situation with religion in the Canadian '90s.

Sure, there are some who will protest that the legacy of religion — notably the Christian tradition — can be seen in current culture. They will point out that our values, our social programs, our laws, the fact that we are allegedly known as a gentle nation, all have their roots in our Judaeo-Christian past.

But to ask for that acknowledgment of religion's historical influence on our culture is almost like an author asking for a footnote in someone's new book. Much more significant, it seems to me, are the findings that, today, religion's direct impact on the lives of Canadians is neither very unique nor very comprehensive.

The Legacy Argument

The secularization thesis — whereby religion is seen as losing authority and thereby its influence — has certainly not gone uncontested. Some observers maintain that religion's importance has tended to remain fairly constant over time. Two of the most prominent people who have held this viewpoint are sociologist Talcott Parsons and sociologist-priest-novelist Andrew Greeley.

In a very influential essay written three decades ago, Parsons[54] maintained that it's a mistake to equate either the decline of the church's authority over life or the growing individualistic approach to religion with religion's losing influence. He noted that Christianity continues to have an important place in the present Western world, notably in the United States. While the spheres over which religion has had direct control and authority have decreased, so-called secular conduct, says Parsons, knows the ongoing influence of religion. The reason? Religious values, such as tolerance and decency, have been institutionalized. "I suggest that in a whole variety of respects modern society is more in accord with Christian values than its forebears have been," he wrote, being careful to add that the difference is relative and that "the millennium definitely has not arrived."

As for highly personal expressions of religion, Parsons argued that such a pattern is consistent with both "the individualistic principle inherent in Christianity" and the emphasis on differentiation in modern societies. The result is that religion has become a highly "privatized" personal matter, differing from earlier expressions in that it's less overt and less tied to formal group involvement.

For Parsons, rather than being in a state of decline, Christianity has been both institutionalized *and* privatized. Similar to the traditional family, religion "has lost many previous functions and has become increasingly a sphere of private sentiments." But, he insists, "it is as important as ever to the maintenance of the main patterns of the society, though operating with a minimum of direct outside control."

One might conclude from reading Parsons that all is well on the religious front. Individuals still take religion seriously, but are keeping their commitment to themselves. Religious groups have not lost influence; they have already helped to shape their culture's values and, if anything, are in a better position than ever before to concentrate on religion.

Andrew Greeley[55] goes even further than Parsons, asserting for some time now that secularization is a myth. Greeley acknowledges that religion today certainly faces secular pressures and is not important to everyone. However, he maintains that such realities are not unique to our time. He specifically challenges six claims that are common to the secularization position, arguing that

1. Faith is not being seriously eroded by science and higher education.
2. Religion is no less significant in daily life than in the alleged great ages of faith.
3. Participation levels are not down compared to earlier.
4. Religion does continue to have a widespread impact on life, but in less obvious ways.

5. Private commitment does have consequences for the public sphere.
6. The sacred remains are highly visible in everyday life.

According to Greeley, religion continues to flourish. Rumours of its decline and death have been grossly exaggerated.

There clearly is a measure of merit in such legacy arguments. It's true that identification with religious traditions remains high and that allegiance to specific religious groups is fairly stable over time. Parson's observation that the importance of the family will ensure that the overwhelming majority will accept the religious affiliation of their parents — "unless the whole society is drastically disorganized" — has proved sound.

However, it's difficult to find support for the assertions of Parsons and Greeley that individuals are privately as devout as their predecessors. Extensive research in North America and Europe has consistently found that levels of commitment by any number of measures have been dropping during this century.[56] Further, rarely have researchers been able to identify a clear-cut link between commitment and attitudinal and behavioural consequences for the vast majority of people who exhibit either private or public commitment.

To put it bluntly, if people are just as religious as they were in the past, they neither know it nor show it. Canada is no exception.

Reasonable Expectations

Ideas these days obviously have a number of core sources. The key "mind-makers" have been clearly identified. Individually they consist, in sociological jargon, of our "significant others" — parents, friends, partners, teachers, and so on. Social scientists describe these key sources in collective form as "reference groups" and appropriately define them as "people whose ideas are decisive for us." The key institutions? The family, the media, education, government, and, yes, for some, religion.

Suppose you had to predict an individual's attitudes on a given subject — Asian immigration, for example. You were allowed to obtain information on just *one* aspect of the individual and could pick from a list of his or her occupation, gender, income, education, hours of TV viewing, gender, and religion. Big dollars are riding on the outcome. Which variable would you choose? Most of us would probably opt for information about *education*. After all, what can TV viewing or religion tell you about whether or not someone is or isn't enthused about Asians coming to Canada?

Now try the exercise with a person's attitudes on other subjects — use of leisure time; favourite magazines, sports, and movies; the quality of clothes and furnishings; what part of town the person lives in; political views and party preference; bilingualism and multiculturalism; beliefs about God and life-after-death; views on premarital sex, homosexuality, and abortion.

Chances are, if you are in step with most Canadians, you won't place your money on religion until you come to the last two categories. The fact that you don't suggests that, apart from idealism, you yourself see religion as something that influences supernatural beliefs and perhaps sexuality. Apart from that, compared with other factors, it just doesn't carry all that much weight.

TABLE 3.7. **PERCEIVED IMPORTANCE OF SELECT FACTORS**

"How important do you think the following are in predicting how a person thinks and acts?"

% Indicating "Very Important"

	Nationally	18–34	35–54	55+
Their educational level	46	42	44	56
Their occupation	30	32	23	37
Their age	28	27	24	32
Their income	22	21	17	30
Their religion	18	17	16	23
Size of community	14	14	10	19
Their nationality	13	12	12	14
Their astrological sign	2	1	3	4

SOURCE: PROJECT CAN80.

Take young people, for example. In *Teen Trends,* we argued that they probably have never been better informed, at least on a "headline knowledge" level. However, we also maintained that they have never been more "American." Their heroes in virtually every area of life are "made in America." They range from Michael Jordan in sports, to Stephen King and V.C. Andrews in literature, and Dan Rather and Connie Chung in news. The only notable regional exception is Quebec, where heroes tend to be French Canadians, with the Americans in hot pursuit.[57]

There's little mystery behind the major source of such mind-shaping. It's not the school system and it certainly isn't religion. It's the American media, led by television and, more specifically, by cable television. We've always been influenced by American culture. The difference is that the advent of cable has meant that our exposure to life, American-style, has grown exponentially. That is what's significant about the "hero" findings. We are looking at how the world is being put together by the first Canadian generation that has literally grown up with cable television. And what we are seeing is that, to an unprecedented extent, U.S. television is constructing reality for all Canadians.

If Canadian educators are having trouble keeping up with television when it comes to both the amount of information they can disseminate and their ability to influence people, it should shock no one that religious groups are finding the going more than a little rough in our new information society. Think of the obvious hurdles:

- Religious groups are just one information source among many.
- The amount of access to people is very limited, maybe two hours a week tops with their most active members, much less with nominal adherents.
- Like many educators, religious groups frequently use technology inferior to the high-tech, high-sound, high-graphic, high-energy world of television. As I keep asking university colleagues, "Why are we still using blackboards and chalk?"

Religious groups do, however, attempt to clear such hurdles:

- They lay claim to authority in many spheres of life. The Roman Catholic Church, for example, may just be one voice among many, but it maintains that its voice is nevertheless the one that counts the most. Evangelical groups also frequently make the same claim.
- They recognize that their access to people is limited. Still, they are trying to increase that access both through encouraging higher levels of participation in church events and through the use of their own media forms — including magazines, newsletters, books, audio tapes, and videos. Attempts continue to be made to gain regional and national television exposure, particularly through the Vision TV cable outlet.

- Of considerable importance, Roman Catholics have been success-fully expanding their school systems across the country during the past few decades and have been emulated by an increasing number of conservative Protestant groups, Jews, and others.
- Within resource limits, religious groups are increasingly co-opting technology — computers, VCRs, video recorders, and state-of-the-art sound systems. In more and more congregations, the basement blackboard — thank heavens — is in danger of extinction.

So here's what the present situation seems to add up to. Religion attempts to speak to all of life, but it tends to be relegated to a specialized sphere. When religion does speak up, it finds itself competing with many alternative voices, including those from economic, political, and academic directions, which are inclined to see religion as overstepping its boundaries.

The reigning champions of information these days, however, are actually the media — who can easily outperform the economist, politician, professor, and priest when it comes to getting ideas out, being persuasive, and shaping minds. Politicians, crafty as they are, learned a long time ago that if they wanted to influence society, they had to make use of the media. Religious groups have gradually caught on to the idea, but this side of a scandal or a controversy typically have not been hot copy for the media and typically have lacked the resources to go it alone. To their credit, religious groups have been several steps ahead of academics, who have not made good use of television largely because many, if not most, refuse to acknowledge its power to influence and educate, and unapologetically still choose chalk.

We would therefore expect that

- religion would influence individual Canadians to the extent that they accept the authority of religion;
- the committed would differ little from others in areas that receive broad cultural endorsement — such as interpersonal values like honesty and compassion;
- they would, however, differ from other Canadians in areas where their religious groups have taken positions that conflict with the culture — such as Roman Catholics and evangelicals being opposed to premarital sex and abortion, or the United Church endorsing the possibility of ordaining homosexuals.

The Current Situation

To start with, the 1990 PROJECT CANADA survey has found that 26% of Canadians say religion is "very important" to them. Another 30% indicate it is "somewhat important." The remaining 44% say religion is either "not very important" (24%) or "not important at all" (20%). The "very important" levels range from:

- 56% among conservative Protestants;
- 37% for people identifying with faiths other than Christianity;
- 33% for Roman Catholics outside Quebec, 28% in Quebec;
- 20% each for people identifying with the United and Anglican churches;
- 2% for those who say they have no religious preference.

In probing religion's influence, I want to explore the differences between those who see religion as highly important to them and those who do not. I have two reasons in mind, one organizational, the other psychological.

First, there is a very high correlation between a person's maintaining that religion is important and that person's service attendance. Some 78% of those who regard religion as "very important" are weekly or monthly attenders. Conversely, only about 1% of Canadians who say that religion has no importance to them attend monthly or more.[58] To focus on those who see religion as significant is to get a good measure of the possible impact of organized religion on these people.

TABLE 3.8. **SERVICE ATTENDANCE BY IMPORTANCE PLACED ON RELIGION**

In %'s

Importance placed on Religion	N	Weekly	Attendance Monthly	Yearly	Never	Totals
Very Important	313	63	15	19	3	100
Somewhat Important	357	22	15	54	9	100
Not Very Important	292	3	5	68	24	100
Not Important At All	241	<1	1	54	45	100

SOURCE: PROJECT CAN90.

Second, social psychologists tell us that self-image is a key determinant of attitudes, feelings, and behaviour. Self, they say, is a product of a variety of roles we play — such as our occupation, being a parent, and, for some, being religiously devout. To the extent that people define themselves as religious, they would be expected to endorse many of the ideas held by the groups in which they are involved.

I want to use teenagers as something of a comparison group, allowing us, for example, (a) to see if differences persist when age is held constant, and (b) to explore possible variations across generations. The measure I want to use to tap religion's importance to young people — in lieu of having exactly the same item in the youth survey as the adult counterpart — is self-professed commitment. Some 24% of teenagers indicated in the 1992 survey that they are "committed" either to Christianity or to another religion; 76% indicated they are not. Once again, there is a high correlation between professed commitment and service attendance,[59] meaning that we can get a glimpse of the possible impact organized religion has on the country's young people.

VALUES

When asked what they want out of life, almost everyone places high value on good relationships — family life, friendships, and being loved. Adults to whom religion is very important are somewhat more inclined than other Canadians to place a high value on relationships, while devout teens slightly exceed other young people in the importance they place on family life.

Next to relationships, freedom — with all that the term connotes, from being free to be able to think and act to being free of pressures and strain — is also valued supremely. Freedom is equally valued by the committed and others, whether they are adults or teenagers.

Beyond relationships and freedom, Canadians openly acknowledge the importance of success and comfortable living. Such goals differ little by the significance of religion in one's life, although religiously committed adults are somewhat more likely than others to put a high value on success.

When we move from what people want out of life to *individual* characteristics such as cleanliness, hard work, intelligence, creativity, and imagination, differences between the religiously committed and others are few; they are limited to being clean and working hard, and disappear among younger people. A negative interpretation is that religious groups are not instilling in the committed a unique appreciation for creative reflection and uninhibited imagination.

TABLE 3.9. **SELECT TERMINAL VALUES BY IMPORTANCE OF RELIGION**			
% Viewing as "Very Important"			
Adults		Teenagers	
HI	LO	HI	LO
Family life	94	79	71	57
Being loved	88	78	83	79
Friendship	87	74	84	85
Freedom	86	84	86	86
Success	71	61	77	76
A comfortable life	62	64	68	70

SOURCES: PROJECT CAN90 and PROJECT TEEN CANADA 92.

However, when we turn to *interpersonal* characteristics, some striking differences by the importance of religion in one's life become readily apparent. Virtually all the traits examined — from honesty to politeness to generosity — are more highly valued among larger proportions of the committed than others.

TABLE 3.10. **SELECT INSTRUMENTAL VALUES BY IMPORTANCE OF RELIGION**			
% Viewing as "Very Important"			
	Adults		Teenagers	
	HI	LO	HI	LO
INDIVIDUAL				
Cleanliness	81	64	73	72
Hard work	70	54	57	47
Intelligence	61	57	57	56
Creativity	40	37	45	45
Imagination	39	42	—	—
INTERPERSONAL				
Honesty	97	86	76	68
Concern for others	81	57	69	69
Politeness	79	56	59	52
Forgiveness	78	47	71	55
Generosity	68	45	52	37

SOURCES: PROJECT CAN90 and PROJECT TEEN CANADA 92.

Further to the concern expressed in *Teen Trends,* it's perhaps significant that teenage endorsement levels of these interpersonal traits tend to fall below the levels of adults — including committed teens relative to committed adults. Indicative, as well, of the "institutionalization of caring" is the finding that young people who are not especially religiously committed are just as likely as the devout to say that "concern for others" is very important to them. Compassion, officially, is in. Yet, in the next breath, teens are less inclined to endorse the very kind of values that translate such alleged social concern into practice — integrity, courtesy, a willingness to forgive, and giving beyond what's required.

In the midst of the noise caused by the heavy traffic of the information society, religion's voice shows signs of being heard with some clarity in the interpersonal realm.

SEXUALITY

The sexual realm is a zone in which religion continues to have much to say. The Roman Catholic Church's views on sex outside of marriage, homosexuality, and abortion are well-known. Evangelical Protestant churches also have tended to hold fairly conservative views about sex. They have been disproportionately prolife and have advocated premarital sexual abstinence;[60] a few have links with such programs as Teen Aid and Challenge 93.[61] Fairly conservative sexual views have also been held by a number of other world faiths, notably Islam, Hinduism, and — to a lesser extent — Judaism. Somewhat more liberal views have been espoused by the mainline groups, with the United Church being particularly vocal in recent years about the need to respect homosexuality as a legitimate sexual preference — not forgetting, of course, that there have been some loud dissenting voices within these groups.

Given such different group emphases, it's important not only to look at general differences *between* people who are religiously committed and other Canadians, but also to explore variations *among* the committed.

What we find again is support for the argument that the high valuing of religion is associated with "differences." In the sexual realm, the committed in every group are more apt to disapprove of:

- premarital sex and homosexual relations;
- homosexuals being entitled to the same rights as other people;
- homosexuals being eligible for ordination as ministers;
- the availability of legal abortion either on demand or when the health of the woman involved is endangered.

Religion appears to have an influence on the sexual attitudes of many of the committed. Their views consistently differ from those for whom religion is not particularly important. These differences, however, are relative. When we stand back and take a look at what the committed are thinking, versus what their churches are saying, we get a far less clear-cut picture:

- More than half of the highly committed approve of premarital sex, including over 60% of Roman Catholics and 20% of evangelical Protestants.
- Close to one in five approve of homosexual relations, with the same proportion maintaining that homosexuals should be eligible for ordination; the evangelicals are the only group to express almost unanimous disapproval.
- Almost nine in ten of the highly committed agree that a woman should be entitled to a legal abortion if her health is seriously endangered, including some 85% of devout Roman Catholics; it's abortion on demand that most of the committed (85%) oppose.

TABLE 3.11. **SEXUAL AND ABORTION ATTITUDES BY IMPORTANCE OF RELIGION**														
% Approving														
	NAT		RCOQ		RCQ		ANG		UC		Cons		Other		None
	Hi	Lo	Hi	Lo	Hi	Lo	Hi	Lo	Hi	Lo	Hi	Lo	Hi	Lo	
Sexual Attitudes															
Premarital sex	51	90	59	89	67	91	59	92	44	34	22	83	28	55	99
Homosexual relations	17	40	21	38	26	39	15	39	12	35	3	16	48	49	65
Homosexuals															
Same rights as others	70	84	78	84	73	88	63	87	85	85	47	69	70	87	90
Eligible ordination	19	41	21	38	15	29	33	38	23	40	6	15	34	67	67
Abortion Available															
Mother's health	86	98	80	95	93	98	83	99	99	96	76	97	95	99	99
On demand	15	46	5	34	10	36	25	50	30	52	6	23	32	63	65

SOURCE: PROJECT CAN90.

These findings show that religion is making a difference in the lives of *some* of the committed, so that — collectively — those who see religion as important tend to have more conservative views on sexuality and abortion than other Canadians. However, at the same time, large numbers of people who place a high value on religion break with the party line, particularly in approving of sex outside marriage, as well as abortion under certain circumstances.

Here, as with interpersonal values, religion shows signs of being taken seriously by some of the committed. On the other hand, its voice is also being ignored by many of its most faithful followers.

QUALITY OF LIFE

Basing my observations on the 1985 PROJECT CANADA national survey, I noted in *Fragmented Gods* that the committed tended to differ very little from other Canadians in their self-reported levels of happiness and satisfaction. Such a situation did not mean that religion was not an important source of well-being for some people. It did mean, however, that large numbers of Canadians were experiencing similar amounts of happiness and satisfaction through pathways other than religion.

As of the 1990s, people who say that religion is very important to them are slightly more likely than others — including the religious "nones" — to indicate that they are "very happy," that they receive a high level of enjoyment from family life, and that they are "pretty well" satisfied with their incomes. The exception to the national rule are those people who are committed to faiths other than Christianity; they do not tend to differ significantly from less committed adherents.

TABLE 3.12. **QUALITY OF LIFE BY IMPORTANCE OF RELIGION**														
In %'s														
	Nat		RCOQ		RCQ		Ang		UC		Cons		Other		None
	Hi	Lo	Hi	Lo	Hi	Lo	Hi	Lo	Hi	Lo	Hi	Lo	Hi	Lo	
General Happiness "Very Happy"	94	86	95	88	96	93	90	86	88	79	95	72	88	90	83
Enjoyment from Family High	65	57	63	58	64	58	61	58	64	63	75	19	41	63	49
Financial Satisfaction "Pretty Well"	27	22	25	20	31	27	33	23	40	25	18	16	15	28	22
SOURCE: PROJECT CAN90.														

But speaking of significance, as in 1985, the differences between Canadians who highly value faith and those who do not are very small. Religion may contribute to some people feeling happier and more satisfied, and even result in marginally more of the committed feeling more upbeat and content than others. It's clear, however, that the trails to the top of the well-being mountain are many. Religion provides just one such pathway.[62]

The Roman Catholic School Case

In view of the difficulty religion has in having its voice heard in the information era, the increase in the number of private and public religious schools in recent years is obviously a significant development.

While a large number of religious groups have been involved, the group that has received both the highest profile and the largest amount of public funding has been the Roman Catholics.

In a presentation to the National Catholic Education Association Conference in Toronto in 1990, Brian McGowan asserted that the justification for publicly funded Catholic education lies in an "alternative vision" to the contemporary North American lifestyle.[63] According to Catholic thinking, the school, church, and family ideally work together to create that alternative vision in young people. What is not especially apparent, however, is how successful the three complementary sources are collectively in producing youth who are different from any other young people.

The 1992 PROJECT TEEN CANADA national survey allows us to address this important question of religious impact particularly well in the Roman Catholic case because of the size of the sample — 1,245.[64] In short, large numbers of Catholics who were enrolled in Roman Catholic schools can be compared with (a) Protestants and other non-Catholics in the public schools and (b) Roman Catholic students who were attending the non-Catholic schools.

Here, then, we have a snapshot of the net influence of home, church, and school on young Roman Catholics. More important, we can assess whether or not that net influence is producing different kinds of youth from those found outside the Catholic educational system.

The examination provides mixed news for RC educators. To start with, 48% of students in the Catholic system say they are getting fairly high levels of enjoyment from school, slightly above the 41% figure for students in the public system.

But the impact findings are not quite as positive. With respect to *religion*, Roman Catholic students in Catholic schools outside Quebec are somewhat more likely than other students to attend services, hold core beliefs, and — along with Catholics in the non-Catholic systems — describe themselves as religiously committed.

In sharp contrast, students in the Roman Catholic schools within Quebec report the lowest attendance and personal commitment levels in the country — mirroring adults in the province. There's an interesting paradox here: those levels largely reflect what is happening in the lives of their parents. Yet as Toronto religious studies professor, Peter Beyer, points out, those same parents believe that their children ought to learn about the Roman Catholic faith in school. One poll in the 1980s, says Beyer, found that 40% of Québécois preferred "a Catholic school where the religious dimension covers all aspects of school life."[65]

Somewhat surprisingly, Roman Catholic teens, regardless of their school system, are less inclined than non-Catholic young people to indicate they receive a high level of enjoyment from their religious group, as well as place a high value on participation.

TABLE 3.13. **INVOLVEMENT, BELIEFS, AND COMMITMENT RELIGION AND SYSTEM***				
In %'s				
Non RC Public (1672)	RC Public (515)	RC RCOQ (330)	RC RCQ (400)	National (3990)
INVOLVEMENT				
Weekly Attendance 26	24	33	12	24
Enj't Rel. Grp: High 18	11	15	11	16
Invm't: Hi Valued 21	5	8	4	13
BELIEFS				
Existence of God 88	94	95	91	91
Divinity of Jesus 63	67	77	61	65
Life after Death 64	68	80	64	67
SELF-IMAGE				
Com. Christian 29	39	37	23	29
Com. Another Faith 6	<1	1	<1	3

*The system categories are non-Roman Catholics in public (non-Catholic) schools; Roman Catholics in public (non-Catholic) schools; Roman Catholics in Catholic schools outside Quebec; and Catholics in Catholic schools in Quebec.

SOURCE: PROJECT TEEN CANADA 92.

As for *interpersonal values*, traits such as honesty and generosity tend to be endorsed by similar proportions of students, regardless of which school system they're in. Roman Catholic schools, churches, and families may be having something of a positive influence; the findings suggest, however, that the influence is not unique to Catholic institutions.

TABLE 3.14. VALUES BY RELIGIOUS ID & SYSTEM				
% Indicating "Very Important"				
	Non RC Public (1672)	RC Public (515)	RC RCOQ (330)	RC RCQ (400)	National (3990)
Honesty	73	68	68	75	71
Concern for others	71	68	67	41	64
Forgiveness	67	65	68	51	63
Politeness	57	55	59	56	57
Generosity	46	38	45	40	43
SOURCE: PROJECT TEEN CANADA 92.				

What has to be disconcerting for adult Roman Catholics, however, is their collective inability to seriously influence their young people's *sexual attitudes and practices*, such as:

- Teenage Catholics show no less of a tendency than other teenagers to approve of premarital sex when love is involved. If anything, they are slightly more likely than other teens to be sexually involved!
- Young Roman Catholics outside Quebec are somewhat less likely than other teens to approve of homosexual relations. In Quebec, however, the opposite is true: almost one in two Catholics attending RC schools in that province say that they approve of homosexual relations. Interestingly, Roman Catholic youth, regardless of where they are attending school, are slightly more inclined than other teenagers to maintain that "homosexuals are entitled to the same rights as other Canadians."
- Roman Catholic youth outside Quebec are slightly more likely than others to be opposed to the availability of legal abortions; their Quebec counterparts, however, think pretty much the way non-Catholics do.
- The attitudes of young Catholics toward unmarried people either

living together or having children are fairly similar to those of non-Catholics, and in the Quebec instance, more permissive.

But let's not get lost in comparative analyses. Against the ideals put forth by the Roman Catholic Church, where sexual relations are to be engaged in only by married heterosexuals, and where there is to be no direct attack on the fetus:

- Some 85% of young Roman Catholics approve of premarital sex when love is involved.
- More than one-half are currently sexually involved.
- Around 30% approve of homosexual relations.
- About 85% feel that a legal abortion should be possible when rape is involved, some 30% for any reason.

TABLE 3.15. **SEXUAL AND FAMILY ATTITUDES BY RELIGIOUS ID AND SYSTEM**				
% Approving				
	Non RC Public (1672)	RC Public (515)	RC RCOQ (330)	RC RCQ (400)	National (3990)
Premarital sex: if love	78	92	79	93	84
Premarital sex: if like	49	58	41	89	57
Sexually involved personally	47	57	51	54	52
Homosexual relat'ns	31	32	22	48	33
Homosexual rights	67	75	72	81	72
Abt'n: rape involved	86	87	76	91	85
Abt'n: for any reason	40	35	24	38	36
Unmarried, living together	80	93	81	93	85
Unmarried, having children	60	70	53	85	66

SOURCE: PROJECT TEEN CANADA 92.

These findings on sexuality, when combined with those pertaining to values and involvement, tell the story of the significant difficulties that the country's largest religious group is having in its efforts to influence its adherents.

Other groups are likewise trying to have an impact on their young people through stressing the interdependent roles of family, church, and school. The Roman Catholic example, however, suggests that when religious groups have to go head-to-head with the myriad socializing influences found in Canadian culture more generally, it is extremely tough to come out the winner.

* * *

There's no doubt that religious groups in the 1990s are still trying to have an impact on the lives of Canadians. But for all the efforts, in the minds of those who are nominally involved, religion's voice is just one among many — even in the areas of values and sexuality.

More disturbing is the finding that even among those Canadians who regard faith as very important, the influence of religion is not readily apparent. As the *Risking the Future* report has observed in the Quebec Catholic instance, what is disturbing is not just the drop in the number of practising Catholics; it's also the impoverished faith of the participants.[66]

Further, our examination of students in the Roman Catholic system suggests that, even when religious groups attempt to increase their influence by operating their own schools, they are experiencing very modest amounts of success.

An important qualifier is in order here. In contrast to the claims of Parsons and Greeley — that the legacy of religion's past influence is evident in the population's widespread adoption of such Judaeo-Christian values as honesty and compassion — the Canadian facts suggest that those kind of civility traits are on the wane. In the area of interpersonal relations, those who value faith tend to differ from their more secular counterparts. The problem is that even among the committed, relational values are not unanimously endorsed. Today's individualism has seemingly neutralized many basic interpersonal values that presumably were more widely endorsed earlier in this century.

A number of observers are also saying that religion actually needs to reacquire some of the turf it previously yielded, such as certain social services and even education, now that governments are having problems delivering what is required in those areas. For example, *Presbyterian Record* editor John Congram recently wrote: "The Church should seize the opportunity to reclaim some of the territories previously ceded to the state in the belief the state could do a better job." He adds: "Today, in many cases, the state has run out of money if not generosity."[67]

It is highly questionable, though, to what extent religious groups have either the will or the ability to marshal the required resources, especially in light of their own numerical and financial problems.

Having some kind of unique or special influence is not easy in the information age. Yet, the mandate of people who value faith calls them to keep on trying. The alternative is to yield totally to culture. The gods would not be pleased.

4

THE IMMINENT CRISIS

I n the face of the evidence indicating that things are looking extremely bleak on the religious front, there are always some who attempt to find hope in the observation that "things go in cycles." More than a few individuals in more than a few audiences have reminded me over the years, "Yes, religion may be down now. But it's only a matter of time until things rebound." These optimists might be surprised and relieved to find that a good many social scientists agree with them.

Such prominent sociologists as Pitirim Sorokin, Kingsley Davis, and Daniel Bell have maintained that societies oscillate between an emphasis on "rationality" and "irrationality," between a moving away from religion and a moving toward it.

Sorokin's[1] well-known thesis, for example, is that history consists of a pendulum-like fluctuation between "ideational" and "sensate" cultures. The ideational period is characterized by ideals and spiritual concerns, while the sensate period is a time when a society emphasizes material values. Davis[2] has maintained that there is "a limit to which a society can be guided by sheer rationality." Secularization, he wrote, will therefore "likely be terminated by religious revivals of one sort or another," complete with new sects. But religion is unlikely to be replaced by secular substitutes.

In like manner, Bell,[3] a social forecaster from Harvard, sees people in postindustrial societies as experiencing the limits of modernism and alternatives to religion. He writes that "a long era is coming to a close. The theme of Modernism was the world beyond. . . . We are now groping for a new vocabulary whose keyword seems to be limits." Bell maintains that new religions will arise in response to the core questions of existence — death, tragedy, obligation, and love.

This oscillation argument has become increasingly popular in recent years. Social analyst Jeremy Rifkin,[4] for example, has claimed that it accounts for the emergence of the charismatic movement and for the accelerated success of evangelical Christianity. Intentionally or not, the American research that we have examined on baby boomers has fed the idea that the pendulum is swinging once again in a proreligious direction. Also contributing to such an expectation has been the proclamation of prominent futurists John Naisbitt and Patricia Aburdene in their best-selling book, *Megatrends 2000,* that the world is on the verge of a massive return to spirituality.

In fairness to these observers, it must be said that they are not necessarily or even particularly thinking in terms of a return to organized religion, especially to those groups the religious establishment has comprised. Many of the pendulum proponents are thinking of spirituality much more generally. Nevertheless, their prophecies are frequently co-opted by those hoping for the rejuvenation of existing religious groups.

THE AGING CHURCH

An examination of people's current involvement by age, however, reveals little support for such optimism. On the contrary, the findings only underline something of the incredible proportions of organized religion's coming crisis. What is readily apparent is that religious involvement belongs to earlier periods in Canadian life. Times have been changing, our culture has been evolving. The impact on religion has been profound.

Where the Action Is

The data on involvement and commitment tell a straightforward story. The most devout people in the country are Canadians 55 and older. They attend more, give more, profess more, and endorse more.

- Better than 40% are both local church members and weekly attenders, compared to around 25% of people in their late-30s to mid-50s and less than 20% of Canadians under the age of 35.
- The major financial contributors to the churches are people 55 and older. In 1990, for example, they gave more than all other younger Canadians combined.

- Almost five in ten of those who are 55-plus say religion is very important to them, versus just over two in ten of Canadians 35 to 54, and less than two in ten under 35.
- Older Canadians also are far more likely than younger ones to express high levels of confidence in religious leaders.

Further, these patterns of higher involvement and commitment among older Canadians are consistent across *every* religious group in the country. In every instance, the core members are drawn disproportionately from older people.

It doesn't take a brilliant demographer to deduce the obvious. Morbid though the prediction might be, futurist John Kettle is telling us we are on the verge of an era when funeral home franchises will constitute a major growth industry as the boomers' parents — and in turn the boomers — leave the scene over the next several decades. "We're talking about a multi-million-dollar industry," says Kettle.[5] What will be good for that industry will *not* be good for the religion industry. The disappearance of people 55-plus over the next three decades will have nothing less than dramatic consequences for organized religion in Canada.

TABLE 4.1. **INVOLVEMENT AND IMPORTANCE BY AGE FOR SELECT RELIGIOUS GROUPS**

		Nat	RC	Prot	Ang	UC	Cons
		%'s					
MEMBERS	18–34	18	18	27	20	18	49
	35–54	31	32	32	31	21	50
	55+	42	38	49	39	58	70
WEEKLY ATTENDERS*	18–34	14	15	22	7	8	54
	35–54	23	30	23	13	12	56
	55+	37	51	31	21	25	62
RELIGION IMPORTANT	18–34	16	18	20	12	8	44
	35–54	23	28	22	13	9	55
	55+	45	57	40	32	40	61
CONFIDENCE IN LEADERS	18–34	28	38	24	14	16	45
	35–54	35	44	29	29	23	47
	55+	47	62	39	38	47	

SOURCES: PROJECT CAN90; *1991 General Social Survey, Statistics Canada.

THE EMERGING GENERATION

A perusal of the publications of Canada's religious groups in the past year or so suggest they are trying to keep up a brave front when it comes to the interest levels of their young people. To the extent that the groups value clear perception, I am not sure why.

- The Evangelical Lutheran Church in Canada's Labyrinth gathering in Kingston in the summer of 1992 drew some 900 young people "from Victoria to Halifax."[6]
- In August 1993 thousands of Canadian Roman Catholic young people were among the half-million youth who converged on Denver for a five-day, World Youth Day conference, a biannual event attended by the Pope.[7]
- The *United Church Observer* ran a front-cover story in January 1993 featuring the picture of three teens and the heading, "In Church and Happy: Five Successful Youth Groups." The story noted that youth involvement has dropped from more than 20,000 to about 14,000 in the past 15 years. "But individually, it's a different story," readers were told, and were turned in the direction of five groups "that hum along very nicely, sustained by a unique combination of energy, commitment, direction and faith."[8]

More in touch with the mainline reality, it seems to me, are the thoughts of Carolyn Pogue. Writing for the *United Church Observer* in 1993, Pogue had this to say: "It's no secret that the United Church is aging. It's no secret that basements, gymnasiums and sanctuaries are not crowded with youth or young adults."[9] Similar sentiments have been expressed in the Quebec bishops' 1991 research report on religion in that province: "There are very few teenagers and young adults at gatherings and in committees. Their absence was beginning to show 20 years ago; now it is a general fact." The report cites one woman who says, "My children almost automatically quit going to church when they reach 14 years of age; they turn away from the church and live in a way that is completely different from what I have wished for them."[10]

Despite what seems like an obvious strategy move, few of the country's religious groups, especially the mainliners, act as if they've caught on. Not many appear to have followed the 1989 lead of a denomination like the Canadian Baptist Federation, which has been working hard just to hold its own, in stating that it will "encourage local church youth ministry as a vital priority for the 90s."[11]

In addition to youth programs, conservative Protestant groups seem to be among the few who also recognize the importance of having "feeder" youth educational programs that enable religious organizations to literally grow their own. Pentecostal minister Robert Jones writes, "The best model to ensure that the church is a tomorrow place comes from a yesterday institution — Sunday school."[12] Highly respected Baptist minister and former lawyer Don Burke comments, "Sunday School, which for 200 years has been the major recruitment, teaching, and evangelistic arm of church life, is almost gone in Canada." He notes, however, that "Baptists are one of the few major denominations that still offer Sunday school to all ages."[13]

The overall lack of involvement of children and teenagers in church programs over the past decade or so is beginning to show — dramatically. We now have some solid readings on the religious inclinations of Canada's youth. The 1984 and 1992 PROJECT TEEN CANADA national surveys asked teenagers about their attendance levels and the importance of religion in their lives.

The findings have been consistent: organized religion does not fare well. Just 18% are weekly attenders today, down from 23% in the early 1980s. Some 24% describe themselves as religiously committed, down markedly from 39% only a decade ago. Nationally, the one bright spot seems to lie in the finding that eight in ten young people continue to identify with religious traditions. They say they are Roman Catholics, United, Anglican, Presbyterian, Baptist, or Jewish.

There are, however, some striking differences by denomination that may well have profound implications for the immediate future:

- teenagers who identify with conservative Protestants are the most involved and most committed of any category in the country;
- larger numbers of Roman Catholic teens see themselves as committed than attend services on a weekly basis;
- involvement and salience levels are lowest for young people affiliated with the mainline Protestant groups, notably the United, Anglican, and Lutheran churches.

		Nat	RCOQ	RCQ	Ang	UC	Cons	Luth	Pres	Other	None

TABLE 4.2. INVOLVEMENT AND IMPORTANCE OF TEENS BY SELECT RELIGIOUS GROUPS: 1984 AND 1992

%'s

		Nat	RCOQ	RCQ	Ang	UC	Cons	Luth	Pres	Other	None
Weekly	1984	23	38	17	13	17	43	25	18	12	3
Attenders	1992	18	28	11	14	13	60	16	31	19	2
Religion	1984	39	60	48	23	25	47	32	21	47	2
Important*	1992	24	33	20	21	24	59	31	45	32	1
Confidence	1984	62	78	67	60	62	78	71	58	40	21
in Leaders	1992	39	47	40	48	46	67	47	44	49	10

*View selves as "committed" to Christianity or another faith.

SOURCES: PROJECT TEEN CANADA 84 and PROJECT TEEN CANADA 92.

As we discussed in the context of baby boomers, these patterns for Canadian teenagers are, of course, no accident. Growing numbers of young Canadian parents are not involved or committed. As a result, only about one in four are exposing their children to religious groups. Fewer adults than in the past have a faith to pass on. As the cycle repeats itself between new generations, involvement and commitment will further dissipate. What we have is an ever downward spiral:

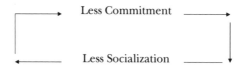

And so it is that in 1975, 74% of adult Canadians could report they had attended religious services when they were growing up. Yet, by 1990, the proportion making that claim had slipped to 64%. Further, in 1975, 35% of Canadians with school-age children said they were exposing them to religious instruction, such as Sunday school. By 1990, the figure had slid to 28%.

The surveys of teenagers reveal that, as an aggregate, 15- to 19-year-olds largely mirror the religious styles of their parents. As they reach adulthood, they do what their parents do — they keep their religious affiliations, but take their religion in very small pieces, that is, selected beliefs, practices, and professionally rendered services. Young people are following in parental footsteps in having religions that are characterized by consumption rather than commitment.

TABLE 4.3. EXPOSURE TO RELIGIOUS INSTRUCTION BY PARENTS OF SCHOOL-AGE CHILDREN: 1975–90		1975	1990
_In %'s_			
NATIONALLY	Regular	35	28
	Often	9	7
	Sometimes	31	27
	Never	25	38
ROMAN CATHOLIC*	ALL	43	36
	Outside Quebec	49	38
	Quebec	38	35
PROTESTANT*	ALL	30	23
	Anglican	24	12
	United Church	35	21
	Conservatives	48	52
OTHER		31	17

*Figures for religious groups: "regular."

SOURCE: PROJECT CANADA Survey Series.

In terms of religion, the newest generations of Canadians appear to differ little from Canadian adults. Both their religious identifications and religious styles seem to be largely inherited, with minimal disruption or innovation. Significantly, some 90% of teens with Protestant parents claim to be Protestants. The same is true for 90% of Catholics from Catholic homes. These are almost identical to the intergenerational retention figures for adults — 91% in the case of Protestants, 86% in the case of Catholics.

THE NUMBERS CRUNCH

The numerical implications for religious groups seem to be obvious. Still, there are those who refuse to give up. As Scott Peck points out, it's common for organizations to spend an enormous amount of effort trying to deny and ignore the fact that they are facing a crisis. When they finally do wake up to the fact, it may be too late.[14]

Problem? What Problem?

If there are some observers who want to argue that things go in cycles and that all will eventually be well, there are others who insist on downplaying the numbers. At their worst, some people in this camp simplistically dismiss people who are concerned about numbers as bean counters, and presumably embrace the idea that quality is more important than quantity. I would remind them that the quality-versus-quantity cliché may not have as much truth to it as one of its amendments: The mark of quality is not necessarily the absence of quantity.

Duke University theologian and pastor William Willimon recently told the *United Church Observer* about a church he once served that gave him what he refers to as a "really dumb argument." It goes, he says, "We're really faithful because we've lost so many members. We're paring down now to the really committed. Mainly they'd pared themselves down to people who were too trifling and lazy to move anywhere else and shouldn't have flattered themselves so." He adds, "Big numbers are not a guarantee of faithfulness but neither are small."[15]

In the Christian tradition, for example, the early church — while epitomizing integrity — was a church that grew in a rather hostile cultural environment. Maybe things aren't supposed to work that way in our day. But people need to be careful before they presumptuously make a virtue of the fact that their message is appealing to very few Canadians. If they are mistaken, all they are doing is dignifying disaster.

A related line of thought sees the remaining core of committed Christians as "significant minorities." The deadwood that was part of the church in the late 1950s and 1960s is now gone, and what is left are faithful remnants.[16] This thinking, as well, can be presumptuous. The remaining Christians might indeed be significant minorities. They also might simply represent all that is left; there might not be anything particularly significant about the remnants at all. In fact, our findings so far seriously question the assumption that they are particularly special or different.

Other observers accept the fact that numbers are important. But they question the alarm that people like myself express about the current situation. Andrew Greeley, for example, acknowledges that numbers are significant. However, he maintains that, in the U.S. at least, there is no "new" numbers problem. Things are really no worse now than they were in the past.[17] Recently, Greeley's somewhat maligned argument has received highly reputable support from Rodney Stark and Roger Finke. In their book, *The Churching of America, 1776–1990,* they argue that religious participation in America has, if anything, increased over time. In 1776, they say, fewer than 20% of Americans were active in the churches, compared to more than 60% today.[18]

The problem with all this is that it doesn't apply particularly well outside the United States. The information we have on religious participation in Europe, for example, points to clear decreases in service attendance over time, corresponding to periods of industrialization and postindustrialization. Some examples:

- in England, weekly church attendance is around 3% to 5%; in the past 20 years, the churches in Britain have lost more than 2 million members, 5,000 clergy, and have closed 2,000 church buildings;[19] a city such as Liverpool has experienced an attendance drop from 70% in 1831 through 30% in 1891 to a current level of less than 10%;[20]
- regular service attendance levels in such places as France, Belgium, Holland, Italy, Greece, and the Scandinavian countries are estimated to be no higher than 5% to 10%, and only slightly higher in Australia and New Zealand.[21] It's generally conceded that such extremely low levels represent a drop from both the immediate and distant past.

Apart from the situation elsewhere, including the U.S., let no one be mistaken: the numbers problem in Canada *is* real. And it will get worse before it gets better.

Religion in the Year 2015

Given that (a) most people who will return to churches after an adolescent hiatus have done so by their mid-30s and (b) the involvement levels of teenagers in Canada are even lower than adults, a reasonable projection of what the numerical situation will look like in the foreseeable future can be made by examining the present 18- to 34-year-old cohort. Let's simulate the future, and have them age about 25 years. By then they will have replaced many older Canadians and, in turn, will have been replaced by today's teens and preteens. It's true that some people who are older will probably be more committed. But our youth data suggest that some adults who are younger will be less committed.

		Nat	RC	Prot	Ang	UC	Cons	Other
TABLE 4.4. MEMBERSHIP AND ATTENDANCE PROJECTIONS FOR SELECT RELIGIOUS GROUPS (In %'s and 1000s) *2015 Based on Membership and Attendance Levels of Current 18- to 34-year-olds*								
MEMBERS								
1990	% of pop. 20 million	29	12	16.5	3.6	5.5	4.6	1.5
	number	5,800	2,400	3,300	720	1,100	920	300
2015	% of pop. 25 million	18	8	10	2.0	1.3	4.2	.5
	number	4,500	2,000	2,500	500	325	1,050	125
WEEKLY ATTENDERS								
1990	% of pop. 20 million	23	13.5	8.5	1.1	1.9	4.7	1
	number	4,600	2,700	1,700	220	380	940	200
2015	% of pop. 25 million	14	7	6	.4	.8	4.5	.7
	number	3,500	1,750	1,500	100	200	1,125	175

SOURCES: Membership, PROJECT CAN90; adult population, *Canadian Almanac; attendance, 1991 General Social Survey, Statistics Canada. Some numbers do not equal totals, due to rounding.*

In short, we can get a fairly reliable preview of how things will look in the future by using today's 18- to 34-year-olds as an index of where Canadian adults as a whole will be about 25 years down the road, in 2015:

- The inclination to be members of congregations will drop from today's 30% levels to around 15%. By then the proportion of Canadians who are weekly attenders will have tumbled from the current 23% level to about 15% as well.
- Such losses will not be minor for the country's religious groups. The percentage drops in membership and attendance will translate into significant numerical losses. As today's 18- to 34-year-olds age through the population, by the year 2015, religious groups may well have only about 4.5 million members — compared to a current 5.8 million. Weekly attenders will number about 3.5 million — versus 4.6 million today (see TABLE 4.4).
- Although the Roman Catholic Church will remain Canada's largest religious body, it will experience severe membership and attendance losses — particularly in Quebec. Relative to the population,

conservative Protestants will manage to hold their own, but will not significantly increase their market share.

- What looms as a particularly dramatic alteration of the religious landscape of Canada is the impact of aging on the previously dominant mainline Protestant denominations. By around 2015, conservative Protestants will have more congregational members than any mainline group. Perhaps of much greater significance, beyond membership, on any given Sunday there will be three conservatives in the pews for every mainline Protestant!

THE COMING RESOURCE CRASH

The resource implications, in terms of the loss of people, finances, and power with which to engage in ministry, are nothing less than staggering. Life for organized religion in Canada's twenty-first century looks extremely grim.

The Diminished Work Force

Churches are unique in that they rely heavily on volunteers to carry out their work. A conservative estimate puts the ratio of paid staff to volunteers at the local congregational level at about one to 100.

Currently a disproportionate number of the people carrying out the work of the country's religious groups are in the over-55 category. What's disconcerting is that there is little sign, except for possibly the conservative Protestants, their places are going to be filled by younger adults in the numbers that will be required in the next three decades.

Presumably the people who constitute the human-resource pool from which religious groups draw are those who attend on or close to a regular weekly basis. Using this measure, we can proceed to produce a snapshot of the churches' human-resource picture 25 years from now, and compare it with the resource situation today.

What we find is that collectively the primary pool of people from which the country's religious groups will be able to draw will shrink about one million in the next two to three decades — from about 4.5 million to 3.5 million.

- The Roman Catholic Church is on the verge of experiencing a dramatic drop in its human resources in Quebec — from about 1.2 people at present to half that number in about 25 years.
- The United Church and Anglican resource pools will be cut in half, from almost 2 million to fewer than 1 million in the United case,

and from more than 1 million to about 400,000 in the Anglican case.

- Lutherans and Presbyterians, currently with human-resource pools of fewer than 100,000, will see those numbers drop further, although the Presbyterian decline will be modest.
- Only Baptists and other conservative Protestant groups will have more people to work with than they do at present; but even so, the gains will be modest.

The nation's religious groups will find themselves facing the predicament of trying to respond to a growing Canadian population with volunteer work forces that for the most part will be decreasing in size. It's not an enviable situation.

TABLE 4.5. **HUMAN-RESOURCE POOLS OF GROUPS:
1991 AND 2015 (In %'s and 1000s)**

*2015 Based on Attendance Levels
of Current 18- to 34-year-olds*

	Nat	RCOQ	RCQ	Ang	Luth	Pres	UC	Baps	CPs	Other
1991										
% of pop (20M)	23	7.3	6.2	1.1	.4	.4	1.9	1.0	3.7	1.0
number	4.6M	1,460	1,240	220	80	80	380	200	740	200
2015										
% of pop (25M)	14	4.8	2.2	.4	.2	.3	.8	.9	3.6	.7
number	3.5M	1,200	550	100	50	75	200	225	900	175

SOURCE: 1991 General Social Survey, Statistics Canada.

Capital Chaos

The lack of people of course, has negative implications for more than the staffing of congregations. Lower numbers also mean lower revenues. It's particularly important to understand that the departure from the scene of Canadians older than 55 doesn't only mean that religious groups will be suffering a *quantitative* loss, which is bad enough. They will experience a severe *qualitative* loss as well. Older Canadians in the churches are not only the most committed and most active, they also tend to contribute the most financially, and without their contributions, churches are bound to suffer in quality.

A 1987 national survey of 1,000 Canadians carried out by Decima Research for the Canadian Centre for Philanthropy has provided us with some of the best information to date on financial contributions to religious groups.[22] Among the survey findings:[23]

- The proportion of Canadians who provided financial support to religious organizations increased from a low of about 35% for those younger than 35, through 55% for those 35 to 54 years old, to around 60%, for people older than 55.
- Canadians younger than 35 not only were the least likely to contribute, they also gave the least annually, on average, about $80 — half as much as the $160 median for 35- to 54-year-olds, and even further below the $170 that people 55 and older gave to the churches.
- People who attended services at least once a week gave an average of $460 a year; the average for everyone else, including those who were showing up one to three times a month, was around $100.
- The vast majority of religious contributions was directed specifically at the churches themselves. Only small percentages of Canadians indicated that they had donated money to radio or television programs (3%), missions (3%), or religious schools (2%). No other organization was cited by as much as 2% of the population.

The implications of these findings are obvious: The disappearance of older Canadians from the Canadian religious-group scene will be associated with a severe loss in revenue for the churches. There is little indication they are about to be replaced by a generation who even begins to match their religious commitment, involvement, and financial contributions.

To be sure, many of the country's religious groups consequently have come to realize the importance of tapping into the devotion and generosity of these aging Canadians before they leave the scene. "Planned giving" programs have been put into place, whereby members are encouraged to invest in annuity programs, to remember churches in their wills, leave behind an insurance policy, or to request that commemorative gifts be directed to their churches.

Crass though all this might sound to some, especially those already wary of religious groups' appeals for money, it has become an extremely common practice in Canada. Rather than engaging in something uniquely capricious, religious groups find themselves in stiff competition with a wide range of aggressive and well-trained rivals, such as charities, hospitals, universities, and political parties.

And not all Canadians are troubled by planned-giving proposals. In its national philanthropy survey, Decima found that, although only 6% of the population have made out wills that leave gifts to charity, an additional 27% said they would be willing to consider such bequests — meaning that the bequests segment stood at 33%. Decima concluded, "The data indicate that the area of wills is potentially a very fruitful one for charitable and non-profit organizations to explore . . . without any change in current attitudes."[24]

Still, it does not seem likely that such sources of revenue, important and sizable as they may be, can on their own prop up the churches in the long haul. Religious groups appear to face two practical problems: giving among younger members is not particularly high, and those who give the most are passing from the scene.

TABLE 4.6. **MEMBER PER CAPITA GIVING BY GROUP: 1990**	
MAINLINERS	$
Presbyterian	451
Anglican	385
Lutheran: ELIC	364
United Church	301
CONSERVATIVES	
Christian & Missionary Alliance	2393
Free Methodist*	1740
Associated Gospel	1478
Foursquare Gospel	1470
Baptist: Union of Western Canada	1427
Brethren in Christ	1332
Mennonite Brethren	1286
Reformed Church in Canada	1280
Baptist: Ontario and Quebec	1183
Baptist: North American	1165
Adventist	1152
Mennonite Church: Canada	1152
Evangelical Free*	1134
Church of the Nazarene	935
Disciples of Christ	804
Mennonite Conference*	752
Baptist: Atlantic	456

SOURCE: 1992 Yearbook of American and Canadian Churches. *1991 YAC.

The only bright spot appears to be the conservative Protestants. As with attendance, their per capita giving tends to be the highest in Canada. While other groups are losing ground, they seem to be holding their own. But as mentioned earlier, it is hardly a cause for jubilation.

Signs of the Times

As we scan the activities of the country's major religious groups, two dominant characteristics can be observed. The first is widespread financial concern. The second is organizational restructuring. For example:

- The United Church has seen its Mission and Service Fund — the source of its national programs — level off in recent years, with revenues for 1992 some $2 million below its targeted goal. Ministers and national church staff had their pay frozen for 1994.[25] Calls for major restructuring are being heard.[26] According to veteran *Observer* writer Bob Bettson, the two questions dominating the 1993 winter meetings of national divisions were: "What should the United Church look like in the 90s?" And, "How can the church pay for what it wants to do?"[27]

- The Anglican Church of Canada's national executive decided that its 1994 spending would be 2% below that of 1993, and that spending in 1995 would be 10% below the 1993 level. The cuts were aimed at reducing an accumulated deficit that now is about $1 million. At the national synod meeting in 1992, an Annual Appeal was approved to allow the church to continue current programs while avoiding debt.[28] The executive council is engaged in a "strategic planning process"; among the preliminary findings from the so-called learning stage is that people want a more "participatory" church, including better communications between the national structures, dioceses, and parishes.[29] Structural alterations would seem to be in the making.

- Faced with insufficient resources to engage in ministry, the Presbyterians have launched a Live the Vision campaign, aimed at raising a minimum of $10 million for Canadian and overseas projects.[30] In January 1992, the denomination completed a major restructuring of the national office, at a cost of close to $900,000.[31]

- The country's largest Lutheran body, the Evangelical Lutheran Church in Canada, has been unable to increase its annual budget of $3 million since its formation in 1985, making new program development extremely difficult. Dissension has resulted in funds not being passed on to synods and the national church. The church's 1991 convention adopted a Mission Plan for Becoming a Growing Church, a 10-year emphasis that to date has received mixed reviews and mixed support.[32] Restructuring is also being called for by a Steering Committee for Renewal and, according to former bishop Donald Sjoberg, is inevitable.[33]

- The Canadian Baptist Federation — comprised of Atlantic, Ontario-Quebec, and Western Canadian conferences — made a number of budget cuts in April 1993 in the face of an accumulated deficit of $60,000. The CBF attributed its dollar problems to decreases in regional and individual donor funding.[34] The Atlantic and Ontario-Quebec conventions were struggling. The Baptist Union of Western Canada has launched a Share the Light ministry fund aimed at raising funds for the development of new churches and the renewal of existing ones. Organizational renewal also is being called for; the BUWC, for example, established a Task Force on Organizational Renewal in June 1992.[35]

As we have already seen, Roman Catholics — particularly in Quebec — are also expressing concern. The 1990 Quebec bishops' report on the state of the church in Quebec was explicit in acknowledging the seriousness of the situation: "Many community members have become more conscious than 10 or 15 years ago of the urgency to do something drastic. They now realize clearly that by continuing on their current course, communities are simply heading for gradual extinction. Therefore, they are prepared to try something new and to take risks." The report has called for more emphasis on adult education, lay involvement, and even reconceptualizing what it means to be a Catholic.[36]

There also is concern among all Roman Catholics about priests being both older and fewer in number. If current trends continue, within just 10 years 85% of priests in Canada will be older than 50.[37] Seminary grads are not appearing in sufficient numbers to replace them. Montreal's Le Grand Seminaire, for example, had more than 300 seminarians enrolled in 1965; currently it has less than 100.[38]

As we move into the twenty-first century, we can expect to find groups struggling to adjust to the reality of diminishing resources. Similar to companies that are facing hard times, they will be downscaling and doing whatever is necessary to remain organizationally viable. Closures and mergers, shared facilities and shared ministries,[39] hiring freezes and layoffs, program reviews and revisions, will all be plentiful.

The situation for religious groups is tough. But what's really hard to take is that the churches are floundering at a time when they should be flourishing. As I will show shortly, culturally, market conditions seem to be excellent for religion. What's bewildering is why the country's religious groups are failing in such prosperous times.

POSTSCRIPT: IS IT THIS BAD EVERYWHERE?

The problems facing organized religion in Canada are hardly unique to this country. In virtually all highly advanced European societies, the norm is that only small cores of less than 10% of the population are involved in the churches; religious organizations play a very specialized role, functioning primarily to service the demand for rites of passage. The grand cathedrals built in the Middle Ages, says one commentator, David Marshall, "are grotesquely in excess of demand, functioning primarily as "tourist traps absorbing millions annually for maintenance."[40] London *Times* writer, Clifford Longley, sums up the situation in England this way: "The English have withdrawn their consent to the establishment of the Church of England . . . not by crowding into the cold streets to shout but by not crowding into its cold churches to sing and pray."[41]

Until recently Canada's relatively high level of church participation has been novel among highly advanced societies — easily the envy of religious leaders in places such as Britain, France, Germany, the Netherlands, and Scandinavia. Obviously that envy is diminishing.

· There is one country, however, where organized religion has not suffered from a great recession: The United States. Since the time polling began in the 1930s, fluctuations in attendance and membership have been very small. As of the early 1990s, the U.S. has what many regard to be a world-leading weekly church attendance level of 40%, which has changed little in 60 years. Likewise, congregational membership has remained steady for at least the same period. It currently stands at 69%; in the 1930s, the figure was 73%.

The important research of Finke and Stark, backing things up to the founding of the country in 1776, only makes the argument all the more conclusive. They have found that "the master trend of American religious history is a long, slow, and consistent increase in religious participation from 1776 to 1926 — with the rate inching up slightly after 1926 and then hovering near 60%.[42]

There's little doubt about it: over the course of American history, U.S. religious groups have succeeded in retaining their relatively high proportions of members and weekly attenders. Everyone is not a church member; but the majority are, and they back it up with impressive attendance patterns.

TABLE 4.7. **U.S. MEMBERSHIP AND ATTENDANCE: 1930s–1990s**		
	Congregational Membership	Weekly Attendance
1990s	69	40
1980s	68	41
1970s	70	40
1960s	73	43
1950s	73	46
1940s	74	37
1930s	73	35
SOURCE: *PRCC Emerging Trends*, 12:6, June 1990; 12:7, September 1990.		

Invariably analysts attempt to account for such high levels of participation by pointing to culture. Observers spanning from Alexis de Toqueville, through Will Herberg and Robert Bellah, to Robert Wuthnow and Wade Clark Roof have drawn attention to the close historical and ongoing link between religious involvement and what it means to be an American. Prominent Hartford Seminary sociologist, William McKinney, for example, recently quipped, "We're in some ways an incurably religious culture."[43]

Beyond general cultural determinants, however, there may be a very good and tangible reason for the higher levels of participation in the U.S. In their concluding remarks, Finke and Stark make the point that religious groups as such have been the key variable in determining the shape of American religion over time. Looking back over the 200-year period, they write: "We recognized that sudden shifts do occur in our religious economy, but these involved the rising and falling fortunes of religious firms, not the rise and fall of religion per se." Those who win, they suggest, are not that hard to identify:

Humans want their religion to be sufficiently potent, vivid, and compelling, so that it can offer them rewards of great magnitude. People seek a religion that is capable of miracles and that imparts order and sanity to the human condition. The religious organizations that maximize these aspects of religion, however, also demand the highest price in terms of what the individual must do to qualify for these rewards. . . . Thus, other things being equal, people will always be in favor of a modest reduction in their costs. . . . They usually succeed . . . because each reduction seems so small and engenders widespread approval. No doubt most Methodists were glad to be permitted to go to the circus, just as most Catholics probably welcomed the chance to skip mass from time to time.

. . . There comes a point, however, when a religious body has become so worldly that its rewards are few and lacking in plausibility. When hell is gone, can heaven's departure be far behind? Here people begin to switch away. Some are recruited by very high tension movements. Others move into the newest and least secularized mainline firms. Still others abandon all religion. These principles . . . reveal the primary feature of our religious history: the mainline bodies are always headed for the sideline.[44]

Consistent with H. Richard Niehbur's argument, the sect-to-church cycle has characterized American history. The market for religion in the U.S. has not changed over time. What *has* changed are the groups that service the market.

Key to the Niebuhr and Finke-Stark thesis, however, is this: religious groups have emerged that service the spiritual needs of Americans. While it can be assumed that those human needs are universally present, it cannot be assumed that the religious groups are.

Collectively, American religious groups — in the past and certainly in the 1990s — appear to be functioning as superior religious companies to their counterparts in places like Europe and — yes — Canada. If the Americans are world leaders in economics and education and entertainment and sports, they must be doing something right. We can hardly attribute their success in those areas to such a bland, all-encompassing factor as "culture." Organizational knowhow, investment, initiative, and imagination presumably have had something to do with how they have been and are currently performing.

The religious outcome, I suggest, is no less surprising. Led by the conservative Protestants, whose membership cards are held by about 30% of Americans — compared, incidentally, to only about 7% of Canadians — religious groups in the U.S. are functioning more effectively as organizations. Unlike many groups in Canada and Europe, American evangelicals, in particular, have the resources, the vitality, and a "product" that is in touch with ongoing spiritual and supernatural concerns. They are doing a superior job of meeting the ongoing market demand for such emphases. That's the main reason they have more names on their membership lists and more people in their pews.

Consistent with Finke and Stark's argument, the key to greater American involvement in religion may be not so much a reflection of *culture* as it is a reflection of *companies* — not the result of some kind of mysterious cultural determination, but rather the product of better religious organizations. Sound a shade preposterous? Highly respected economist Laurence Iannaconne has taken a look at religion in a variety of cultural settings and found that among Protestants, "church attendance and religious belief are greater in countries with numerous competing churches than in countries dominated by a single church."[45]

If these things are so, then Clifford Longley's recent suggestion in the London *Times* may be more profound than even he imagined: the best hope, he says, for what he calls the "spiritual corpse of the Church of England" is "that the Evangelicals will take it over before it is too late, and extract something from the wreckage."[46] What is needed, he senses, is new and greatly improved ownership and management.

And if Longley is right, if much of the problem is not culture but company, then religious groups in Canada would be wise to take notice. They'd be particularly wise to put an end to blaming the culture for their problems — which brings us to the second major feature of Canada's ongoing religious story.

PART II
WHAT'S HAPPENING IN
THE CULTURE

*I*f that were all that there is to the Canadian religion story, those who value faith and are in touch with reality would be in a state of despair. There's little doubt that organized religion is in very serious shape, its golden years apparently relegated to history.

But as we look out on the cultural landscape and watch the dust settle on the grey ruins of much of organized religion, we see an interesting spectacle. In the midst of the debris and desolation, a large number of green patches of spirituality can be detected. The temples may be disintegrating, but the grass is far from dead.

To look beyond organized religion to Canadian culture is to observe at least three important indicators of latent spirituality — the ongoing fascination with mystery, the search for meaning, and religious memory.

5

INTRIGUE WITH MYSTERY

W̶e need explanations. Most of us are not content simply to observe. We also want to understand. And so it is that in the not-so-rational Canadian '90s there is widespread fascination with experiences that do not have readily apparent explanations. There also is much bewilderment about the reality of death, and what, if anything, lies beyond it.

THE UNEXPLAINED

One of the two young men in the Cactus Club setting I mentioned in the Introduction talked of an experience he'd had in Sweden about two years earlier. He went to a shed to get wood for the kitchen stove. As he piled the wood into his arms, he became overwhelmed with a feeling of being almost "absorbed" by the setting. The feeling became so strong he found himself dropping the wood and running out of the shed. Later, he learned that some time before three people had committed suicide in that shed.

The Normality of the Paranormal

Put two or more people together, open up the subject of strange experiences and coincidences, and I guarantee that the stories will start coming. . . .

- A friend told me of having a dream while holidaying in Europe that her brother back in Alberta had lost his arm in an accident. Troubled, she called home the next day to find that, yes, he had been in an accident; the good news was that the arm had not been lost, just broken.

- A few years ago, two professors planned to meet for a couple of days at one of the professors' homes, in Idaho. The other was driving down from Canada; it was his first visit. About five hours before they were due to meet, the Canadian came to a small Idaho city of some 20,000 people and, after driving around for a few minutes, decided to call his family. His host was presumably at home, about 40 miles away. The visitor made a totally arbitrary choice to turn into a grocery store parking lot, having spotted a phone that was at the moment being used. As the person hung up, he opened his car door, and was about to head for the phone. Out of what seemed like nowhere appeared a stranger, who also wanted to use the phone. Who was the stranger? By coincidence, the very professor the Canadian had come to Idaho to meet.

- A former student of mine lost her husband in a plane crash. Her sister-in-law had a rather vivid and remarkable dream in which he appeared, discussing the pros and cons of heaven and telling her to tell his wife not to worry about him, that all was well. In the dream, his sister had the presence of mind to remind him that his wife probably wouldn't believe all this, and to give her some means of convincing her. He thought for a moment, then wrote down a strange word that made no sense to his sister. In relating the dream to his wife over the phone the next day, she repeated the peculiar word. There was a moment of silence on the line; the word, it turned out, was one the couple had learned and used playfully with each other during a stay in Australia. There had been no reason to share it with anyone — including his sister — once they were back home in Canada.

- Prior to a recent trip to Portland, I gave some thought to calling a friend whom I had met in England a dozen years earlier but not had contact with since. After trying and failing to locate the address from a letter I had received in 1981, I set the thought aside. The night before I was to leave, upon returning home and entering my office area, I discovered that my cat had somehow knocked a single brown envelope of old and new items off a pile of materials on my desk. One item that was protruding prominently out the end of that envelope was the mislaid letter from my Portland friend.

- And did I ever tell you about the time . . .

Canadians appear to have significant numbers of these kinds of somewhat puzzling "paranormal" experiences. Approximately one in two claim they themselves have experienced precognition — the anticipation of an event before it has happened. About the same proportion say they have experienced mental telepathy — an awareness of another's thoughts. Those levels, by the way, are almost identical to what Canadians reported in a Gallup survey in 1979.[1] As for God, close to one in two think they have experienced God's presence.

What's peculiar has been the extent to which these commonplace experiences have been slow to receive official recognition. Surveys and late-night conversations reveal that they are part of the biographies of an overwhelming majority of people; they are the norm rather than the exception. Yet, paranormal events have been largely ignored until very recently by closed-minded academics, who, frankly, have done us all a severe disservice by not at least taking the sheer volume of the claims more seriously. As Gary Wills puts it, "The learned have their superstitions, prominent among them a belief that superstition is evaporating."[2]

There's good reason to believe that much of the fascination with science-fiction novels and films, along with reports about unexplained experiences, is not just the result of wanting to be entertained with things that are literally out of this world. The success of such long-running series as "The Twilight Zone" may also be tied to the fact that some of the stories resonate with the personal experiences of large numbers of viewers. However, historically, religion has been critical of such happenings, while science has relegated them to the entertainment sphere. Consequently people who have found themselves in "strange coincidences" and having "supernatural experiences," haven't talked a lot. Who needs the stigma? Instead, they typically have dismissed their experiences as chance events, or — when the events have been particularly vivid — as something they should best keep to themselves. Unfortunately they haven't realized that most of the people they work with, sit beside, and pass in shopping malls have had similar experiences.

Little wonder that many people across Canada have been turning to less conventional sources than academics and clergy in the course of trying to make sense of the things that have been happening to them.

TABLE 5.1. **PARANORMAL AND SUPERNATURAL EXPERIENCES**

In %'s

	No	Yes, Def- initely	Yes, I Think So	No, I Don't Think So	No, Def- initely Not	Totals
Precognition	1196	21	26	28	25	100
Mental Telepathy	1279	20	32	48	—	100
God	1209	21	23	31	25	100

SOURCES: Telepathy, PROJECT CAN80; Precognition and God, PROJECT CAN90. The 1980 telepathy item options were "Yes, I'm sure I have," "Yes I think I have," and "No."

The Need for Explanations

Rationalists are inclined to want to dismiss alleged paranormal experiences as being the result of fear, gullibility, or the failure of education.[3] Such positivistic explanations, in my mind, are incredibly naive. To borrow some lines from Peter Berger, "the denial of metaphysics" may well "be identified with the triumph of triviality," a "shrinkage in the scope of human experience" that "constitutes a profound impoverishment."[4]

Once in a while, something dramatic happens that stretches our explanatory abilities — or results in a quick derogatory categorization. For example, this story hit newspapers across North America on April 16, 1992:

> LAKE RIDGE, VA. (UPI) — A church where statues have reportedly shed tears and a priest has exhibited mysterious wounds like those suffered by Jesus Christ will restrict Holy Week services to members.
>
> St. Elizabeth Ann Seton Church drew hordes of people following the news accounts of the "crying" statues and the mysterious ailments of associate pastor Rev. James Bruse.
>
> The church was forced to turn away worshippers.
>
> The crush of visitors has eased in recent weeks, but the 1,800-family parish decided to limit access to Mass beginning today to ensure that parishioners may attend Easter services.
>
> Tickets have been issued to registered members.
>
> "We had to do that because attendance was getting out of hand," said spokeswoman Marie Pelletier.
>
> "Parishioners haven't been able to get into the church," she said.

Assuming we give a story such as this some credibility, we are alternately fascinated and perplexed trying to account for it — especially if we have seen it with our own eyes.

Fortunately, most of what happens to us and around us can be accounted for fairly easily. Cause and effect are reasonably straight-forward:

- The room becomes dark because someone turned off a light.
- A door shuts because someone closed it.
- We think about someone, and phone them.
- A friend meets us in a restaurant because we arranged to get together.
- We don't see her again because she has died.

What makes life a bit more problematic is when cause and effect are not at all clear — which is sometimes the case:

- The room becomes dark, but no one has dimmed the lights.
- A door shuts, but no one has touched it.
- We think about someone, and they phone us.
- The long-forgotten friend is met coincidentally in a restaurant, the cause for pause being that we had a dream about her the night before.
- We think we have seen her again, even though she is dead.

Accustomed as we are to rational, or naturalistic, cause-and-effect relationships, we don't necessarily opt for alternative explanations of the supernatural variety. There may be no inclination to turn to what the psychic researchers or clergy, for example, have to say. We may well dismiss strange events as random or unexplainable.

Still, in the case of many Canadians, these kinds of experiences arouse immense curiosity. We want to know *why* they have happened. Science might be the first place we look for our explanations. But if science can say little or nothing, we may be willing to consider other kinds of explanations. As a group of psychologists have recently put it, for some people, "concepts such as 'God's plan,' 'original sin,' and 'the work of the devil' might answer questions that otherwise would be unanswerable, and explain behaviour that otherwise would be incomprehensible."[5] For other people, less conventional explanations pertaining to concepts like "tracking," "visualization," and "spirit guides" might be helpful.

The range of possibilities is probably endless. We find ourselves in a shopping mall of explanatory choices, where sales reps try to convince us their explanations are the right ones, where priests and gurus compete with psychics and healers. It's a buyers' market. Not everyone gets rich.

On September 1, 1992, for example, southern Albertans — increasingly socialized to appreciate concepts like aboriginal self-government and native spirituality — weren't sure how to respond when Wallace Mountain Horse, the spiritual leader of the Blood Tribe, announced that the reason a freak snowstorm hit the region in August and destroyed crops was the widespread religious disbelief in the area. Mountain Horse said the public, including members of his own tribe, ignored his invitation to help him in his efforts to call upon the god Thunder to stop the storm in its early stages. The snowstorm hit as a warning, he said, because "there's something lacking in the line of religion." Mountain Horse pointed out that his own crops were left untouched.[6] To the best of my knowledge, the spiritual leader's plea for repentance was largely ignored. People almost dare the gods to repeat the summer snowstorm. Then again, Noah had the last laugh. . . .

The tendency to look beyond science for answers isn't new. As I pointed out in *Fragmented Gods,* since the birth of modern science, people have readily supplemented scientific explanations with supernatural or nonnaturalistic ones. In fact, it might be more historically accurate to say they supplemented supernatural explanations with scientific ones. Sometimes it's because scientific explanations are not yet available, in which case, says an observer like Durkheim, we are impatient and "rush ahead to complete it prematurely."[7]

On occasion, however, we turn to nonscientific explanations because of a more serious limitation: the issue cannot be addressed by science, for it lies outside science's realm.

Death is such an issue.

THE UNKNOWN

There perhaps is nothing that remains a greater human mystery than death. We know we are going to die, and there is nothing we can do to prevent it. The only question is when — and whether it marks the termination of our existence.

Concern About Dying

Some Canadians are more anxious than others about dying. Approximately 15% say dying is something that concerns them "a great deal" or "quite a bit," while another 30% indicate it troubles them "somewhat." We're talking about close to one in two people.

Contrary to popular thinking, concern about dying does not increase as one gets older. The concern level is 43% for those younger than 35, 47% for 35- to 54-year-olds, and 40% among people older than 55. The key variable is not aging, but rather *health* combined with age. When one is young and health is a major personal concern, anxiety about dying is understandably higher than when one has had the chance to live a fairly long life and then experiences failing health. These words, delivered at the funeral of a 21-year-old Ontario woman, sum up the prevalent perplexity that is felt:

> *When death strikes the very old it may break our hearts, but when death strikes the very young it's enough to break our spirits. We want to scream our protests about all that could have been and should have been.*[8]

- Some 31% of adults under 35 say they are very concerned about their health, compared with 27% of those 35 to 54, and 40% of people 55 and older.
- Regardless of their age, people who are worried about their health are more anxious about dying than others (60% versus 35%).
- But among those Canadians younger than 35 who are concerned about their health, 37% are very troubled about dying, compared with 29% of 35- to 54-year-olds, and just 23% of those people 55 and over.

There is another crucially important issue in the 1990s surrounding death. Technology that prolongs life is not making decisions about dying any easier. "Fifty years ago," writes religion journalist Nestor Gregoire, "great-grandmother never had to face some of the difficult moral questions that we must confront today. When there was a serious illness, pneumonia was often the old man's friend. Death was natural. There was nothing anyone could do."[9]

TABLE 5.2. **FEELINGS ABOUT DYING BY AGE**					
% Indicating Concerned About Dying					
	N	Great Deal/ Quite A Bit	Some-what	Little Or None	Totals
NATIONALLY	1044	15	29	56	100
18–34	432	17	26	57	100
35–54	365	14	33	53	100
55+	247	13	27	60	100
Health Concern	333	30	30	40	100
18–34	132	37	24	39	100
35–54	97	29	36	35	100
55+	97	23	32	45	100
Health Not a Concern	711	7	28	65	100
18–34	295	7	27	66	100
35–54	261	9	31	60	100
55+	144	7	24	69	100
SOURCE: PROJECT CAN85.					

Today life can exceed our desire for it. Consequently an increasingly important question for many is the question of how they can die with dignity — including the right to die when they choose. Highly publicized Canadian cases have included those of Nancy B., the paralyzed woman in Quebec, who won the right to be removed from a respirator that was keeping her alive, and Sue Rodriguez of Victoria, whose pursuit of the freedom to die in the face of her incurable neurological disease led her all the way to the Supreme Court of Canada.[10] On a visit to Vancouver in mid-1993, world-renowned British cosmologist Stephen Hawking, suffering from a disease similar to that of Rodriguez, had this to say when asked to comment on her situation: "People should have the right to die if they want to. It is one of the few rights severely ill people have left." Yet, beyond rights, Hawking added, "I don't think one should do it."[11] Expected to be increasingly common are controversies involving doctors, such as that surrounding a highly regarded Timmins, Ontario, physician, who pled guilty in 1993 to giving a lethal injection to an elderly patient.[12]

Here the very question of *when* we are to die becomes in itself a complex and agonizing issue. As Muriel Duncan, editor of the *United Church Observer*, reminds us:

We live in a time when medicine's ability to prolong our lives is forcing us to look at difficult questions. I know that living can seem much harder than dying. And sometimes pointless. Yet I know someone may badly want to die at night and fight for life in the morning. I know that doctors, trained to sustain life, sometimes do that simply because they can. But others take compassionate risks for their patients. I know too that relatives and friends have a hard time separating their own pain from the patient's and may confuse their own inability to suffer with the patient's. Or they may want them to linger because they can't face life without them. I'm not sure I'd want too much decision-making left to relatives alone.[13]

Doctors, for their part, are hardly of one mind. A 1992 University of Calgary survey of some 1,400 physicians in Alberta found that 44% felt it would be "right" in certain cases to take specific action to end a dying patient's life — a step beyond doctor-assisted suicide such as Rodriguez proposed. Yet only 28% said they themselves would be willing to take part. About one in five doctors said they had been asked at least once to assist in active or intentional euthanasia.[14]

In a joint written intervention to the Supreme Court of Canada, the Canadian Council of Catholic Bishops and the Evangelical Fellowship of Canada expressed their opposition to physician-assisted suicide, asserting, "Our living together in community requires a basic trust that human life and dignity will be respected and protected. Euthanasia and assisted suicide erode this trust and undermine the community's commitment to life and responsibility to care and comfort."[15]

Arguing for palliative care over euthanasia, Dr. John F. Scott, the head of palliative medicine at the University of Ottawa, voices this alarm: "The overall effect of sanctioned euthanasia in our society will be to give more power to the powerful and thereby increase the powerlessness of the very sick." Continues Scott, "Legalized euthanasia would not relieve the fear and pain of the dying. Instead, it would open a floodgate of death in Canada."[16]

But others, like Rodriguez, believe that human dignity is only possible when one's power to control the termination of life is also accepted and protected. Most people are currently leaning in that direction. A November 1992 Gallup poll asked Canadians if they are in favour of competent doctors being allowed to end a patient's life if the patient has "an incurable disease that causes great suffering" and the patient has made a formal request in writing. Some 77% said yes, considerably above the 1968 figure of 45%.[17]

Scott Peck was right: "Life is difficult."[18] So, we are discovering, is death.

Life After Death

Apart from worrying about dying, Canadians do not particularly want to see life come to an end. But given that it will, about 90% of people across the country say they have given some thought to what happens after death. It's hard to imagine, by the way, what has been holding back the remaining 10%! As well-known journalist Tom Harpur points out in his book *Life After Death,* the question is age-old, universal, and centrally significant. "Surely," he writes, "the most momentous personal question of our day — or indeed any other — is, having once died, is that the end or do we somehow live again?" Our surveys also provide Canadian support for his contention that "there has seldom been a time in history when more men and women held some form of belief in survival beyond the grave."[19]

- The 1990 PROJECT CANADA survey has found that about 70% of people across the country say they believe there is life after death, with only 14% ruling out the possibility altogether — compared with 16% back in 1945 and 19% in 1960.[20]
- The same proportion — 70% — think there is a heaven, and almost 50% believe in hell. (No, that's not a typo — the figure is 46%, to be precise.) In 1969, the earliest poll I have uncovered so far that probed the same areas, Canadians who said they believed in heaven came in at about 70%, while hell was endorsed by 40%.[21]

The steadiness of these belief levels over time undoubtedly has been due, at least in part, to the extensive publicity given to near-death experiences, channellers, and claims of reincarnation.[22] Among an exploding number of metaphysical authors has been Seattle-based Betty Eadie, author of *Embraced by the Light.* In 1993 she toured Canada, telling people about her near-death experience in 1973, when she allegedly left her body, saw Jesus, and was told to return to Earth with a message of love. Indicative of the broad market appeal that such people aspire to have, Eadie said in an interview during a stop in southern Alberta that she's equally comfortable being identified as either a born-again Christian or a New Ager.[23]

These growing number of sources, however, have not enhanced Canadians' understanding of what life after death is actually like. Asked in the 1980 PROJECT CANADA survey, "What do you think will happen to you after death?" about 50% of them said they really didn't know, 20% said they would "simply stop existing," and a further 20% maintained that they would "go to heaven." The remaining 10% suggested they would be reincarnated (7%), go to purgatory (2%), or end up in hell (1%).

The 1990 survey did not probe all such possibilities. But it did find that no less than 26% of Canadians are now maintaining they will be reincarnated — a remarkable jump from the 7% figure of just a decade ago. It doesn't appear to be a fluke; the 1992 figure for the country's 15- to 19-year-olds is even a bit higher, at 32%.

It's a somewhat bizarre situation: despite the fact that close to 75% of Canadians define themselves as Christians,[24] those who believe they will be reincarnated appear to outnumber those who believe that they are heaven-bound. Reincarnation, for many people, seems to be easier to swallow than resurrection. The misgivings of the lead character in novelist John Irving's *A Prayer for Owen Meany* seem to be shared by more than a few people: "I find that Holy Week is draining; no matter how many times I have lived through his crucifixion, my anxiety about his resurrection is undiminished — I am terrified that, this year, it won't happen; that, that year, it didn't."[25]

	N	Yes, Definitely	Yes, I Think So	No, I Don't Think So	No, Definitely Not	Totals
In Life after death	1249	40	28	18	14	100
In Heaven	942*	38	32	17	13	100
In Hell	1187	24	22	28	26	100
That you will be reincarnated	1185	9	17	38	36	100

TABLE 5.3. **BELIEFS ABOUT LIFE AFTER DEATH**

In %'s

"Do you believe . . ."

SOURCE: PROJECT CAN90.

- Some three in ten Roman Catholics and two in ten Protestants maintain they will be reincarnated, as well as two in ten "nones." The level for people from other world faiths, some of which advocate reincarnation, is only slightly higher, about one in three.
- Some three in ten people younger than 55 hold such a view, but that's only marginally above the two-in-ten level for Canadians 55 and older.
- Indicative of mix-and-match theology, about 30% of those who believe in either heaven or hell also maintain they will be reincarnated — presumably to give them another shot at the top postlife prizes.

The mystery of death and what lies beyond it creates a huge market for answers. The findings suggest that, during the past decade, advocates of reincarnation have been making impressive market gains.

GOD AND THE SUPERNATURAL

Faced with mystery, including the mystery of death, Canadians are inclined to look to the gods for answers. In doing so, they of course find themselves in the company of many others across the country whose beliefs in supernatural powers and entities — including God — have not necessarily been based on either mystery or intellectual struggle. In the course of their religious socialization, many have come to take God and possibly other entities such as angels, spirits, and Satan pretty much for granted. For them, the gods have had a long-standing place in how they put reality together.

Whether grounded in the experience of mystery or assumed to be normal from childhood, acceptance of the explanatory place of God and the supernatural is widespread in Canada.

The Old and the New

The vast majority of people across the country continue to believe in the existence of God. The figure today is just over 80%, with the proportion of blatant atheists around 8% — up slightly from 5% in 1945, but unchanged from the 8% level of 1969.[27]

But Canadians don't just stop with static belief. Almost half the population maintain they have actually experienced God's presence. What's more, for large numbers of Canadians, "God is real." Some one in two say they pray privately daily to weekly. Only about 25% indicate that they never pray. To the cynics who say that prayer is often just a ritualistic rote-like experience with little sense of an actual living God out there, I would agree that it's undoubtedly true in some and perhaps many cases. Nevertheless, it's also clear that, for at least very large numbers, God — however conceptualized — is a *living* reality.

And, unlike the case with organized religion, God's popularity is not diminishing. At a time when only 26% of Canadians are saying that religion is "very important" to them, about 90% maintain that God either continues to be "important" or is becoming "more important." Make no mistake about it: God is doing well in the polls.

In addition to their acknowledgment of the ongoing presence of God, significant numbers of Canadians embrace ideas about reality beyond the everyday world of touch and sight and sound. Take angels, for example. Gordon Legge, the religion editor at the *Calgary Herald,* has been among those who have noted a resurgence of interest in what many had thought to be a near-extinct religious species. Legge writes: "Angels are everywhere, whether or not you believe in them, in books, movies, mugs, and ornaments." Authorities with angel-related organizations, such as the AngelWatch Network in New Jersey, he says, are claiming that "guardian angels are turning up in individual lives with increasing frequency."[28]

In late 1992 Legge invited readers to tell him about "their angelic encounters." Here's a quick sampling of some of the responses, the first told by Legge, the rest by the readers.[29]

- Twelve-year-old Richard awoke from his sleep at the home of his foster parents in Montreal to a figure at the end of the bed, dressed in a long white gown and glowing in the darkness. She told him, "Do not be afraid. I am an angel from God. I'm here to tell you that your mother is in heaven with Jesus." He went back to sleep only to be woken by the sound of the telephone. Minutes later, his foster mother entered his room and said, "I have some very bad news." The boy stopped her and said, "I know. Mommy is dead."
- They say angels watch out for drunks and fools. In August 1983 I'd been drinking beer for three days straight, and I decided it was time to get some sleep. It didn't take me long to pass out. I had no plans and no job to go to. Next thing I knew, someone had grabbed my leg and pulled me on to the floor. Surprised as I was, I couldn't help but notice black smoke pouring into my bedroom. I then saw

three wispy-looking shapes pushing against the smoke. I then realized the building was on fire. Stunned, I saw the shapes flying toward the bedroom door, as if to tell me I should follow. I did. I will never forget the three friendly shapes who saved my life.

- My son was in an accident and received a bad concussion when he was 17 years of age. I prayed, "Lord if you are going to take him, let me talk to him," praying he would become conscious. The next day it seemed life was leaving him and all colour disappeared. I bent low to catch any breathing when three or maybe four small angels appeared and circled his head. I saw them and heard the whir of their wings. Then his colour began to return. He awoke and is alive today.

- In the 1970s I was into the drug scene. One day while high on LSD I was so depressed I considered suicide. I was standing on the Granville Street bridge in Vancouver and made up my mind that this was it. As I started to climb upon the guardrail, I remember saying to myself, "If there's anyone up there, you'd better get ready, because I'm going to meet you in just a few seconds." Suddenly, someone grabbed my arm, pulling me from the rail. When I turned around, I expected to see a cop. Instead what I saw totally shocked me. A man in a long white robe stood before me, and a sense of peace overwhelmed me. He touched me on the shoulder and said, "Go home." That's all he said; then he just vanished. I still battle with depression, but I have never considered taking my life again.

- I was in Bradford, England, two months ago because my mom-in-law was dying of cancer. We had discussed that she give me a sign after death that she was okay. After getting word of her death at 5:10 a.m. on a Sunday morning, I went back to sleep around 6 a.m. I was having a normal dream when there was a quick change. Mother came down fast like a ball from the sky, touched me, and shot right back in the air. I knew she was free and happy. Who cares if people think I'm nutty as a fruitcake? I don't doubt for a moment we are all surrounded by these beings. They take good care of us.

- I made friends with a group of Christians in Salmon Arm, B.C. One afternoon, a terrible pain seized my chest. I felt it was a heart attack. Soon my body felt heavy. I looked down at my chest and to my surprise I saw a pair of hands, in the attitude of prayer, cupped around my heart. The hands parted as I watched and a beam of brilliant white light came from above and entered through the opening to strike my heart. . . . I have experienced angels in my life. Indeed, I would be dead several times over if it were not for their direct, loving and divine intervention.

The experiences and interpretations of these people may not be as exceptional as you think. Large numbers of Canadians believe that a spirit world exists, seemingly alongside or overlapping with reality as we know it. Some four in ten maintain "we can have contact with the spirit world," while more than two in ten go as far as to say that "it is possible to communicate with the dead." Beyond encounters with angels, experiences verifying such "a supplementary world" do not appear to be particularly uncommon. Nor, according to prominent sociologist Thomas Luckmann, should they be particularly rare. "Subjective experiences of transcendence are universal," and come in a variety of forms. "It can hardly be doubted," he writes, "that human beings have had and still have such experiences everywhere."[30]

I myself haven't heard a disembodied voice, or encountered something in the way of a ghost-like figure. But I have met others who have.

- I was a guest on an open-line show in Hamilton when a business executive called. He related the experience of having awoken one morning to a male figure standing at the foot of his bed, a person he had never seen before. "Suddenly, he just disappeared," said the bewildered caller.
- A Prairie farmer wrote me, relating how he stopped his tractor, seeing a figure standing in the field. Getting down, he approached the person; but she "faded away." He believed that the figure had been his wife — who had died a number of years before.
- A nephew of mine, then five, nonchalantly told his mother that a woman came down the hallway of their house, walked into the kitchen, and then "just disappeared." Unknown to him, the description he gave fit that of a woman who had previously lived in the house for two decades and had died of a heart attack in that same kitchen a number of years earlier.

The point is not that all these claims are valid. They probably aren't. Sociologically, however, they represent experiences that an extremely large number of people in Canada believe they have had. As such, it would be irresponsible, academically and otherwise, to simply dismiss them without carefully considering the obvious: they may be pointing to a reality or realities that are beyond the myopic eye of the scientist and citizen who limit what is to what can be proved empirically.

In addition to beliefs about God and the spirit world, we saw earlier that no less than about 50% of the population claim to have personally experienced precognition and telepathy. Clearly many don't think that what happened to them was simply a coincidence. Six in ten Canadians openly acknowledge they believe in ESP, with approximately the same proportion maintaining that some people have special psychic powers. As with God, the experiential coexists with the cognitive; belief and experience are intertwined.

TABLE 5.4. **GOD AND THE SUPERNATURAL: ADULTS**

In %'s

"Do you believe . . ."

	Yes, Def-initely	Yes, I Think So	No, I Don't Think So	No, Def-initely Not	Totals
GOD					
That God exists	56	26	10	8	100
Have personally experienced	21	23	31	25	100
SPIRIT WORLD					
Can have contact with it	13	25	36	26	100
Can communicate with the dead	7	16	37	30	100
ESP					
It exists	23	36	22	19	100
Some have psychic powers	19	40	26	15	100
Have experienced precognition	21	26	28	25	100
ASTROLOGY					
Its claims are true	8	26	36	30	100

SOURCE: PROJECT CAN90.

Astrology is another explanatory offering that has a noteworthy following. Approximately one in three people across the country say they believe in the claims of astrology. But that's only the true believers. No less than a solid 88% of Canadians just happen to know their astrological signs, with half the nation admitting they read their horoscopes at least once a month — outnumbering readers of the scriptures, incidentally, by two to one.

God and the spirit world, ESP, astrology — it all adds up to a lot of Canadians putting a lot of stock in a lot of supernatural phenomena.

The Young and the Old

Supernatural beliefs and practices are not about to go out with hoopskirts — or the twentieth century. Our surveys of young people have shown conclusively that, if anything, the fascination they have with supernatural phenomena exceeds that of older generations. Teens tend to give credibility to just about every-thing — from the conventional to the unconventional, from God to astrology, from the divinity of Jesus to psychic powers, from life after death to reincarnation.

They also don't limit their beliefs to the immediate vicinity. The 1984 survey found that 69% believed that "there is life on other planets." And why shouldn't they? Forget the sci-fi videos, the *ETs*, the sightings, and the UFO abduction tales. Credible agencies and scientists have contributed to the belief.

In late 1991, for example, the 41st International Astronautical Congress in Germany gave its attention to ensuring that, if aliens ever show up on telescopes or doorsteps, we will be prepared. The congress, which annually reviews progress in space exploration, evaluated efforts to invent a new language for communicating with creatures from another planet. Said one delegate from the NASA-funded Search for Extra-Terrestrial Intelligence Institute in California, "There's nobody who writes international greeting cards, but we have to find one for the world." NASA launched an $80-million project in 1982 to transmit signals to aliens in outer space; now more money is needed to pick up the long-awaited responses.[31]

Believe it or not, that wasn't a particularly eccentric event. The U.S. *Voyager* space probe that was spun off into outer space in the 1970s carried pictures depicting life on Earth and a recorded message from then UN secretary general Kurt Waldheim — just in case aliens were encountered.[32]

At minimum, interest in UFOs and the possibility that aliens have visited our planet in the past twigs a sense of curiosity and deep-felt mystery. Maybe, however, there's even more involved.

A Toronto-made documentary of the 1985 book *In Advance of Landing*, by Canadian Douglas Curran, suggests that interest in UFOs and aliens may point to a kind of spiritual yearning, "masked under varying degrees of eccentricity." One Vancouver woman in the film, who has taken photos of flashes of light she believes are tied to her encounters with aliens, puts things this way: "I think we all know, deep down inside of us, that we didn't really originate on this Earth. Maybe that's why we're always looking up." The documentary is "only tangentially concerned with the question of outer space," notes reviewer Salem Alaton. "Its real subject is the nature of human aspiration and belief."[33]

Some clarification and caution is needed here. What is the religious significance of interest in the supernatural and the unknown, including worlds beyond? Gregory Baum, in discussing the occult and Eastern spirituality, reminds us there may be little or none. Both expressions, he says, may be largely self-serving, unlike the "great religions" that are "powerful, culture-creating movements." Nevertheless, writes Baum, "the turn to the irrational is a significant protest against the highly rational, technological and bureaucratic society of the West and as such deserves to be taken seriously."[34]

Following Baum, I suggest it is not the intrigue with mystery in and of itself that is religiously significant. What's important in these findings is that they signal unrest and receptivity to some of the key themes religion historically has addressed. The accelerated openness to a better understanding of previously taboo subjects, including sexuality and injustice, has brought with it a new willingness to openly explore such issues as spirituality and death. With that openness has come a growing recognition of the rightful place of supernatural ideas.

Now, as the end of the millennium draws near, beliefs in the paranormal are increasingly being held without apology by virtually everyone and are viewed as worthy of the attention of scientist, journalist, and filmmaker alike. And don't forget the policeman. One recent study in the U.S. found that a full one-third of police forces in the 50 largest American cities have made use of psychics.[35] Canadian police departments have also made use of their "gifts." Young people, along with others, are consequently giving such beliefs as much if not more credibility than Canadians of previous generations.

TABLE 5.5. **GOD AND THE SUPERNATURAL: TEENAGERS**

In %'s

"Do you believe . . ."

	Yes, Def-initely	Yes, I Think So	No, I Don't Think So	No, Def-initely Not	Totals
GOD					
That God exists	47	34	12	7	100
Have personally experienced	13	21	41	25	100
SPIRIT WORLD					
Can have contact with it	14	31	37	18	100
Evil forces exist	28	36	24	12	100
Supernatural forces exist	25	41	25	9	100
Can communicate with the dead	9	27	42	22	100
ESP					
It exists	15	39	33	13	100
Some have psychic powers	20	49	22	9	100
ASTROLOGY					
Its claims are true	13	40	32	15	100

SOURCES: PROJECT TEEN CANADA surveys, 1984, 1988, and 1992.

Those embracing the supernatural even include the occasional convert from the clergy. One mainline minister recently commented, "I had to decide if I actually believed in the supernatural." He tells of coming in contact with a series of stories about strange coincidences — Joe Carter of the Toronto Blue Jays saying that God used a dream to inform him to stay with the team; an ABC anchor awakening from sleep at precisely the same time his daughter was seriously injured in a car accident; a cancer patient believing she was healed by an unknown visitor. "At one time, while finishing my Bachelor of Science degree, and believing supremely in what was provable in a laboratory," he writes, "I might have dismissed it all as hallucination and self-hypnosis. I don't anymore." He says he has seen "too many things that can only be of God, for they are beyond human explanation," adding on a more conventional note, "I am convinced that God raised Jesus because I've felt Him in my life."[36]

The Wrong and the Right

It's hard to believe that just three decades ago, "wise men" in theological schools were telling us that modern men and women could no longer think in supernatural terms. Rationality, they maintained, precluded such outdated mental outlooks. They were wrong.

Also suspect is the kind of caution expressed by *United Church Observer* columnist Karen Toole Mitchell, when she quips, concerning the biblical account of Jesus' ascent into heaven, "Let's face it, the resurrection is hard enough to defend without adding the ascension." She continues, "All too often the church has interpreted the ascension as Jesus' getaway plan. Artists have depicted it as divine star-trekking with Jesus being beamed up by God."[37] For better or worse, Karen, the survey findings suggest that kind of wild imagery may not actually be all that hard a sell with Canadians these days. While Christian Reformed writer Bert Witvoet likewise expresses reservations about how literal the account should be taken, the way he puts the question is, I think, in touch with the mood of curiosity characterizing our times:

> When Jesus said farewell to his disciples and rose up in front of their eyes, he went up, up . . . until a cloud came between him and the squinting and gaping disciples. . . . What happened to Jesus after a cloud hid him from sight? Did he continue his journey into space? Did he fire a rocket to speed him up past Mars and Jupiter out of the Milky Way into the heavenly spheres? I don't think so. . . .[38]

Intrigue with mystery is not merely resulting in belief in God and supernatural phenomena persisting in Canada. Belief is flourishing! If the apostle Paul were to take a cross-country tour, he might well be heard to repeat the words he used in Athens some 2,000 years ago: "I perceive that in every way, you are religious."

Of great significance, the findings suggest there has not been a particular increase in supernatural interest and belief over time. Levels of belief in God and life after death, along with psychic phenomena, haven't really changed all that much. In April 1993 a *Maclean's* cover story triumphantly declared to the nation that "God Is Alive." Queen's University historian George Rawlyk exuberantly "broke the news" that "Canadian religion [is] changing fundamentally before our eyes." The results were supposedly so shocking, says Rawlyk, that when seasoned pollster Angus Reid saw them, "the top of his head blew off because he realized the results were very, very important."[39]

A little history is worth recalling, indicative of the stability of belief patterns over time. In December 1977 the widely distributed national newspaper magazine insert *Weekend* published the results of its poll on religion. It noted that beliefs were high, but that membership and attendance were low. "As might be expected," the summary read, "the overwhelming majority of Canadians are professed Christians." The title of the story? "God Is Alive and Well in Canada."[40]

Everyone's research, including mine, comes up with a consistent finding: over the years, a rich market for supernatural and spiritual matters has persisted in Canada. The news is not that God is alive. God has always been alive. The news is that interest and intrigue persist, in spite of the problems of organized religion. The result may well be a very sizable, ongoing spiritual vacuum because, to recall Stark's language, the key religious firms are failing.

If that's the case, then the 1990s are a time when the Canadian market is ripe for institutions, groups, and individual entrepreneurs who have something to bring. Fortunes can be made. Faith can also be shared.

6

THE SEARCH FOR MEANING

Canadians are also looking for meaning. That quest, which provides a second indicator of the interest that people have in the spiritual dimension of life, is hardly a new one. What does seem new is the extent to which individuals in the 1990s are publicly engaging in its pursuit.

In part reacting to excessively technocratic, rational, and materialistic tendencies, sizable numbers of North Americans are being flagrant in their attacks on organized religion and in their flirtations with new religious possibilities. In Alvin Toffler's words, there is "a sky-darkening attack on the ideas of the Enlightenment."[1] John Naisbitt sees the trend as global: "At the dawn of the third millennium," he says, "there are unmistakable signs of a worldwide multidenominational religious revival." Naisbitt points to a number of North American indicators — New Age thought, channelling, charismatics, "scandal-prone TV preachers," the success of Bill Moyer's "Power of Myth" television series with Joseph Campbell, and Campbell's own best-selling book of the same name.[2]

Similar signs of spiritual unrest also exist in Canada. Journalist and author Ron Graham spent two years travelling the country attempting to "discover the soul of God's dominion." He concluded that "for all the talk of Canada as a secular and materialist country there seems to be more and more attention to spiritual issues." Says Graham, "All across Canada . . . I found religion trying to get back to Truth."[3]

While Graham relied heavily on observation and interview, the hard data of survey research provide some impressive support for his conclusions. In Canada, the search for meaning takes many forms, perhaps most noticeably people's need for fulfillment, their raising of questions of meaning and purpose, and their desire to have God brought in on life's pivotal passages.

LOOKING FOR MORE

Canadians, like many people in other highly advanced societies, have two primary preoccupations: relationships and resources. We spend much of our lives pursuing good relationships with family and friends, along with a comfortable life. When we think we have both, we try to find time to enjoy them — and hope that our health holds. People, money, time, and health. Nothing concerns us more.

Is This All There Is?

Except, perhaps, the feeling we are still somewhat empty, that life is being lived and time is passing, yet our achievements still leave us only partially fulfilled. Approximately one in three people say they are troubled by the sense that they "should be getting more out of life." While the sentiment is particularly pronounced among younger adults, it also characterizes about three in ten people between the ages of 35 and 54, and some two in ten of those 55 and older. Among the younger cohorts, "getting more" undoubtedly also has a strong material component. However, for others who are fairly satisfied with what they have attained and acquired, "getting more out of life" seems to point to a vacuum that continues to exist.

	N	Money	Time	Health	Children	Marriage/ Relation- ship	Getting More Out of Life
Nationally	1249	50	38	30	18	17	34
18–24	107	77	52	30	4	24	61
25–34	344	60	39	22	12	16	40
35–44	249	53	41	28	27	23	34
45–54	174	43	34	30	27	15	29
55–64	139	30	33	32	15	13	18
65+	185	28	26	49	23	9	19

TABLE 6.1. **SELECT PERSONAL MAJOR CONCERNS**

"How often do these common problems bother you?"

% Indicating Concerned About "A Great Deal" or "Quite a Bit"

SOURCE: PROJECT CAN90.

On the whole, Canadians have fared pretty well. The material has been widely circulated: in May 1991 the United Nations released data on a large number of quality-of-life indicators for 160 countries worldwide. Canada, declared the U.N., ranked second only to Japan as a place to live. The United States, for example, placed seventh. Said one U.N. official, "I don't think Canada realizes how fortunate it is."[4] As of 1992 Canada was still doing well, ranked second only to Japan.[5]

Many interest groups, of course, were not happy to get the good news and were quick to debunk the report. After all, when your business is telling people how bad things are in the course of jockeying for scarce resources, carriers of good news become the enemy. Problems create jobs; the elimination of problems can be tough for some sectors of the economy.

Obviously there are people in Canada who are experiencing unhappiness and pain, discrimination, and a wide variety of forms of deprivation. Life for many such people is not particularly good; much of their energy is being given to sheer physical and emotional survival.

Yet, subjectively and collectively, Canadians are a remarkably happy and content lot. Some 90% say that, all in all, they are either "very happy" or "somewhat happy"; only about 2% say they are "not happy at all." The figures today are higher than the level in the so-called "happy days" of the late 1950s, and easily above those reported for virtually any country in the world — including the U.S.

Most of us claim to be receiving considerable gratification from our relationships in the form of family and friends. Further, things are reasonably good financially. Satisfaction with one's finances increases markedly after the age of 35, even though there might not be a comparable rise in actual income, especially for people older than 65. Over time, we seem either to increase our incomes or lower our expectations.

The kicker for many Canadians isn't relationships or money or even health. It's time. Having found that partner, having had those children, having found that job, and having procured that income — without losing our health in the process — we fight for time to enjoy it all. And what's worse, the months and years are flying by. One is getting older, the children are no longer children, the fireplace is gathering dust, the holidays seem all too short. Success that was supposed to make life easier has brought with it ever escalating demands and expectations, which require more and more of that precious commodity — time.

TABLE 6.2. **RELATIONSHIPS AND MONEY**				
% Indicating High Satisfaction				
	N	Family Life	Friends	Financial Situation
NATIONALLY	1249	91	92	70
18–24	107	76	96	62
25–34	344	93	92	61
35–44	249	90	93	68
45–54	174	91	87	72
55–64	139	93	93	81
65+	185	94	95	84
SOURCE: PROJECT CAN90.				

Think I'm exaggerating? The 1990 national survey asked Canadians, "How often do you have time on your hands that you don't know what to do with?" A whopping 4% said "quite often," 29% indicated "now and then," and a majority of 67% responded "almost never." Further, when asked, "Do you find that you have time to do the things you want to do?", 21% said "usually," 44% "for the most part," and 35% "not really."

The feeling that one is short on time is particularly acute among those older than 35 generally and between 35 and 44 specifically. Yet even retirement doesn't bring an end to the time problem: six in ten people older than 65 say they "almost never" have extra time on their hands, while almost two in ten say they don't really have time to do the things they want to do.

TABLE 6.3. **CONCERN ABOUT TIME**			
In %'s			
	N	Almost Never Have Extra Time	Don't Have Time to Do the Things I Want to Do
NATIONALLY	1249	67	35
18–24	107	53	34
25–34	344	63	39
35–44	249	75	44
45–54	174	71	38
55–64	139	71	36
65+	185	63	17
SOURCE: PROJECT CAN90.			

For many Canadians, time is more important than money. A late 1987 national survey carried out by Decima Research found that when it comes to charitable or nonprofit organizations, for example, 78% of Canadians would rather donate money than volunteer their time.[6]

Almost Content

What these findings add up to is a situation where Canadians are pursuing relationships and resources with a fair measure of success. They don't lack for pressure: marriages and other relationships are known for their ups and downs, and children have been known to grey the heads of a parent or two. Finances might be improving but, given unstable economies and the lack of job security, they require constant surveillance.

Still, for most people across the country, with the passage of time an interesting switch in priorities takes place. Asked to what extent various themes have become "more important," "less important," or remained about the same in their own lives "with the passage of time," Canadians exhibit some very clear patterns:

- Physical issues — such as material comfort, sexuality, and physical appearance — become less important.
- Relational issues — family life, parents, marriage, and children — also become less of a priority, along with friendships and social concerns.
- Intellectual growth also ceases to know the importance it did earlier in life.
- The one area where there is a shift in the direction of increased importance with the passage of time? God.

And so it is that a Toronto couple, in an interview with Kim Zarzour of the *Toronto Star,* acknowledged that the material world just didn't fulfill their needs. Doug, 31, recalls, "We were pulling in good salaries and living in the Forest Hill area and both had interesting jobs, could go downtown for the nightlife anytime we wanted — but there just had to be more out there." Along with his wife, a lapsed Catholic, he has returned to church.[7]

Let's not get confused here. It's not that Canadians cease to value physical comfort and good relationships, along with intellectual development. It's just that, as those issues are taken care of, a residual area of life that still seems to need nurturing is spirituality.

These findings do not suggest that everyone from British Columbia to Newfoundland is restless for the gods. The data do, however, point to the fact that a sizable number of people feel a need for something more out of life. As an editorial writer for the *Anglican Journal* has put it, "A spiritual vacuum exists at the centre of society and at the centre of people's lives . . . people today are searching for an undefined 'something else' to fill this vacuum."[8]

TABLE 6.4. **PRIORITIES OVER TIME**

% Indicating Have Become "More Important" to Them
"With the Passage of Time"

	PHYSICAL					RELATIONAL				MENTAL		SPIRITUAL
	Suc-cess	Sex	Mat. Comf.	Appear-ance	Frd-ship	Fam. Life	Soc. Iss.	Mar-riage	Par-ents	Child-ren	Intel-ligence	God
18–24	71	61	52	49	66	64	54	52	50	48	71	23
25–34	41	36	43	22	53	74	46	47	53	72	54	21
35–44	33	25	35	24	51	72	49	43	47	68	45	31
45–54	23	13	28	17	42	61	42	40	40	58	36	29
55–64	15	9	30	19	48	55	43	32	29	46	36	29
65+	10	6	34	18	45	50	36	31	34	53	31	39

SOURCE: PROJECT CAN90.

LOOKING FOR ANSWERS

One of the most basic characteristics that separates us from other living things is our ability to reflect. That ability is stimulated in turn by the need to make sense of our existence — in Max Weber's words, by an "inner compulsion to understand the world as a meaningful cosmos and take up a position toward it."[9] Noted anthropologist Clifford Geertz has written that it appears to be a fact that at least some people, and in all probability most people, are unable "just to look at the stranger features of the world's landscape in dumb astonishment or bland apathy without trying to develop . . . some notions as to how such features might be reconciled with the more ordinary deliverances of experience."[10] Luckmann states it this way:

> *Every human being is aware of the limits of its experience and of the boundaries of its existence. There is a "before" and "after" and "behind"*

one's ongoing actual experience, and there is a "before" and "after" one's own life. . . . Our common sense tells us that we are part of a larger world to which there is much more than merely our own selves, our own body, our own awareness.[11]

The argument is not just academic. We have already seen how death and the possibility of living beyond it is a mystery that's of great interest to people. But it's only one of the big questions people are asking.

The Questions Generally

Some 85% of Canadians say that, in the course of living out their lives, they find themselves reflecting on three questions: How did the world come into being? What is the purpose of life? And how can I find real happiness? The people who think they have found the answers to these seemingly universal questions are in the minority; only about 15% to 20% indicate they have been able to lay these three questions to rest.

A fourth big question, raised by more than eight in ten people, is, "Why is there suffering in the world?" Suffering, of course, continues to be very much a reality — personally, locally, nationally, and globally. It also remains something that perplexes Canadians. Somehow, suffering is seen as unnecessary, even unnatural. If its sources are human, we are inclined to think that problems causing human pain can be and should be alleviated. If the sources are seen as chance events — such as a child being killed in a car accident or a friend dying in his prime — we invariably find ourselves asking, "Why?" The absurdity of what seem to be needless events calls out for explanations.

Henry Morgentaler, for one, says he cannot believe in God because of his experience in Nazi death camps: "I don't look for absolute truths any longer. In Auschwitz, all around me, tens, hundreds prayed daily to their God. I was an atheist and I lived."[12] Reflecting on the Nazi situation, sociologist Peter Berger comments that what happened is among the "deeds that cry out to heaven."[13] The suffering and the silence were too much for Morgentaler.

Patricia Clarke, a United Church journalist, recently recalled how she wondered in her Sunday School days how, "if God made everything, and saw that it was good, who made evil?" She says she never got an answer that satisfied her, and the questions have not gone away: "Does a good God do bad things? Does God allow Bosnia and Somalia, earthquakes and tidal waves? Doesn't God care? Or is the power of evil stronger than the power of love?" She writes that we believed that "every day we were getting better and better, building the Kingdom of God on earth. But something happened on the way to the Kingdom. The Depression, two world wars, Hiroshima, Auschwitz, Mount Cashel, Marc Lepine. Evil was alive and well and dwelt among us."[14]

On a deeply personal level, there are the stories of people like George Campbell of Powell River and Lesley Parrott of Toronto. Campbell tells us that on a warm spring day in early May 1982, his youngest son committed suicide. "He was 18 years old. There was no warning. We had no signals that anything was amiss. I will not try to explain the black, hollow days following our son's death, because it is too painful. Such a thing is unexplainable, except perhaps to those who have gone through this desolate despair."[15] In July 1986, Parrott's 11-year-old daughter was abducted, raped, and murdered. The killer has never been found. Parrott writes, "Prior to losing Alison, although aware that evil was a force in the world, I had never truly had to ponder the meaning or impact of its existence. I found myself suddenly identifying with concentration camp survivors, with mothers who had lost their sons to needless wars."[16]

The cry of suffering raises the question of meaning, not only for those who are forced to experience it directly, but also for those who care about them. As a friend of mine so simply summed it up, "If we love someone, we don't want to see them suffer."

TABLE 6.5. **REFLECTION ON MEANING**

% Indicating Raising Versus Resolved

	How did the world come into being?	What is the purpose of life?	How can I find real happiness?	Why is there suffering in the world?	What happens after death?
Nationally	61–24*	70–17	61–22	83–10	73–16
18–24	87–8	80–4	75–18	91–1	79–12
25–34	56–28	73–17	66–23	84–12	78–14
35–44	55–30	63–24	62–24	79–16	66–24
45–54	62–24	70–15	63–16	79–11	72–15
55–64	68–18	72–12	49–26	84–7	73–16
65+	63–14	63–19	50–23	82–8	69–12

*The first figure refers to those who raise the question, the second to the % who no longer do. The remainder haven't asked the questions.

SOURCE: PROJECT CAN80.

Purpose Specifically

It's one thing to note that people over their lifetimes are asking questions about meaning and purpose. The *urgency* of those questions, however, has often been downplayed by observers, myself included. Skeptics point out that most of us are so preoccupied with our immediate concerns about such matters as relationships, money, time, and health that we put questions of abstract "meaning" on the back burner. According to the experts, these mega questions are dusted off primarily during times of major crises, which may be years or even decades apart.

The argument has some merit. In the 1990 PROJECT CANADA survey, we asked Canadians about the extent to which wondering about the purpose of life is a current concern for them. Some 25% said the question is one that troubles them either "a great deal" (9%) or "quite a bit" (16%). In keeping with the "major crisis" argument, people who are looking for purpose are somewhat more likely to be unhappy with life (24%) than those who are not pursuing purpose (5%). However, this finding also means that about 75% of people who are concerned about meaning are essentially happy with life. They nonetheless appear to be looking for more.

For most of these Canadians, the issue of life's purpose is far from a back-burner issue. And their numbers are sizable. To put the figures into perspective, the 25% level of high concern about purpose

- is only slightly below that of health (30%);
- is similar to the levels for job (29%), along with looks and loneliness (24%);
- is greater than the levels of concern associated with sexual life, marriage, children getting older, and boredom (all around 20%).

Moreover, a further 25% of the population say that they are "somewhat" concerned about the purpose of life, bringing the total percentage of Canadians troubled about purpose to around 50%. But let's keep our balance. Purpose is not a burning issue for everyone; the remaining 50% of Canadians indicate they have little or no concern about the question. My point here is that the purpose of life *is* an important matter for as many as one in two people.

And it's not just religious folk who are trying to work out theological details, or older people or women. Concern about resolving the question of life's purpose is higher among those Canadians who do not place a high value on religion than those who do, among younger rather than older adults, and is only marginally higher among women than men.

Such a need also appears to exist on the university campus. Rev. Paul Ellingham, a United Church chaplain at the University of Waterloo, comments that his encounters have led him to conclude that students "need more than just education. They need spiritual and emotional support and a vision that university is not everything."[17]

These findings indicate that a sizable market exists for those who have something to say about life's purpose. Younger adults appear to be particularly receptive.

Presbyterian minister Dennis Oliver is among those who are convinced of receptivity to a faith that speaks to personal and social meaning. Oliver recently wrote that people outside the church are among those who are "seriously seeking a better life for themselves and others. They want love, justice, peace, and freedom in the here and now," and where human example, books, preaching, and prayer "prove relevant to such goals, they will listen."[18]

I agree.

	N	Great Deal/ Quite A Bit	Some- what	Little Or None	Totals
Nationally	1096	25	25	50	100
Religion:					
Not Very NB	823	27	27	46	100
Very NB	262	21	22	57	100
18–34	421	30	27	43	100
35–54	391	22	26	52	100
55+	244	22	22	56	100
Women	548	28	25	47	100
Men	550	22	26	52	100

TABLE 6.6. **CONCERN ABOUT PURPOSE**

% Indicating They Are Bothered by the Question of Life's Purpose

SOURCE: PROJECT CAN90.

LOOKING FOR RITUAL

If religion has ceased to have significance for Canadians, they should find themselves able to do very nicely without it, particularly when they are facing life's key passage events. Such is not the case.

Get Me to the Church . . .

I recall a friend of mine who surprised me a number of years ago by casing out the city I was living in when his child was born, looking all over for someone who would perform some kind of "birth ceremony." He didn't seem clear about what it was that needed to be done; he was simply convinced that something needed to happen.

He's in familiar company. Approximately nine in ten adults say they plan to turn to religious groups when they need weddings, funerals, and birth-related ceremonies carried out — if they haven't already done so. The pervasiveness of this desire for religious ceremonies can be seen in the fact that there is very little difference by attendance level: those who don't attend regularly are almost as likely as weekly churchgoers to turn to religious groups for such rites. There also is very little variation across the country, or between women and men.

We're also not just talking about older Canadians. An analysis of the desire for rites of passage by age shows that younger adults are no less likely than older people to be looking to religious groups to carry out such rites.

TABLE 6.7. **DESIRE FOR RELIGIOUS RITES OF PASSAGE**

% Indicating What Ceremonies Performed in the Future

| | Adults 25 & Over | | | 15- to 24-year-olds | | |
	Birth	Marriage	Death	Birth	Marriage	Death
Nationally	26	29	60	75	82	85
B.C.	21	20	54	57	78	81
Prairies	25	30	70	71	79	83
Ontario	24	29	60	75	81	85
Quebec	35	30	53	87	88	90
Atlantic	22	29	65	71	78	82
Female	29	30	60	77	81	86
Male	24	28	59	73	82	84
25–34/15–19*	40	34	56	76	88	87
35–54/20–24*	19	22	67	74	76	83
55 & over	18	20	59	—	—	—

* Refers to 15- to 24-year-olds side of the table.

SOURCES: PROJECT CAN90; PROJECT TEEN CANADA 88.

Our 1988 PROJECT TEEN CANADA national survey found that some 75% of 15- to 24-year-olds said that they anticipate turning to religious groups in the future for birth-related ceremonies, 80% for weddings, and 85% for funerals. These findings are remarkable when one remembers that only 17% of these same young people maintained they were attending religious services on a weekly basis and just 14% indicated they highly value religion.

More Than Just for Mom

When reflecting on the desire for church weddings and child christenings and dedications, it's easy to dismiss such expectations as having little or no religious significance. Many cynics see such requests as primarily the product of rather prosaic factors, including the pressures of parents and grandparents, cultural tradition, and even less virtuous factors. One Calgary clergyman told me his church was a wedding favourite "because it has one of the widest centre aisles in town." A Roman Catholic parish worker in Nanaimo says some people who want to circumvent the preparation process state emphatically, "I just want to get the kid done."[19] I personally knew of a couple in rural Indiana who chose one church over another because the building had air-conditioning.

There's little doubt that the desire for rites of passage commonly reflects coercion, cultural habit, and the seeking out of the appropriate professional to do such jobs. But there's more to be said. Clergy who are "out there in the field" comment that frequently the desire for these passage ceremonies also reflects a sense, however poorly articulated, that "God needs to be brought in on this." The symbolism of the minister who is present can be significant in itself. Having been in that place, Kenn Ward, a Lutheran minister and journalist, puts it this way: "What we sometimes disparagingly call hatching, matching, and dispatching are very important moments in people's lives — moments when the presence of . . . the ordained person reminds those people of God's presence."[20]

The scene of the marginal affiliate at the wedding, funeral, or christening can be an important indicator of the presence of latent spirituality in Canadian culture. If the cynic has difficulty with weddings and christenings, he or she needs to reflect on funerals. In his novel, *Paradise News*, British author David Lodge has Yolande offering these reflections following Ursula's death:

> *It's funny, this dying business, when you're close to it. I always thought of myself as an atheist, a materialist, that this life is all we have and we had*

better make the most of it; but that evening it seemed hard to believe that Ursula was totally extinct, gone for ever. I suppose everybody has these moments of doubt — or should I say, faith?[21]

The message of limitation is particularly pronounced when the person who dies is young, the departure unexpected. Faced with the reality of such irretrievable losses, Canadians find themselves receiving little solace from the institutions that fill their lives on a day-to-day basis — the media, education, business, government. Even family and friends can at best offer only sympathy. Yet into this very large void steps religion — the previously ignored cultural dark horse — addressing, with unexpected strength, authority, and uniqueness, the question of what lies beyond death.

For too long, religious leaders have been underestimating the significant "meaning" role that faith brings to life's pivotal passages. They have been fooled by what they have seen as a consumer approach to rites, and in some instances have responded in kind. Ceremonies have been handled in a rote detached manner by people who seemingly have adopted the "hatch, match, and dispatch" mentality. The spiritual significance of requests has been grossly underestimated.

It seems strange to say it, tragic to say it, but it needs to be said: there is good reason to believe that, in their pursuit of rites of passage, large numbers of people have been wanting far more spiritually than what religious leaders have been providing. Clergy have confused spiritual quest with crass request. It is not uncommon for ministers and priests, triumphantly declaring to others that they, after all, have upheld the standards of the church, to turn people away. Some have even proclaimed that these vacuous requests should fall into the domain of civil types, such as justices of the peace. Such clergy need to have their cultural eyes checked. Opportunities for ministry are being lost.

Indicative, perhaps, of the extent to which Canadians rely on religious groups to interpret life is the aforementioned finding that the loss of confidence in church leaders has not affected the desire for rites of passage. People who say they do not have much confidence in religious leaders nevertheless *are no less inclined than others* to continue to look to religious groups for baptisms, weddings, and funerals.

The day may come when credibility problems will have severe

consequences. People could reach a point where they begin to believe that the spiritual benefits of having ministers perform baptisms, weddings, and funerals are neutralized by the problems of the religious organization themselves. To the extent they do, religious groups will be rid of the nuisance of having to service consumer-minded affiliates. But they also will say goodbye to an invaluable link with their nominal adherents.

Fortunately for religious groups, that day has not yet come.

7

RELIGIOUS
MEMORY

I love music. Apart from the music itself, I have always been fascinated by the way a song coming over the radio waves from yesteryear carries with it so many memories — of another time, younger family members, other friends, other feelings, other loves. As a pop song in the late 1970s poignantly put it "Love songs last longer than lovers ever do."[1]

In like manner, religion lasts longer than involvement with organized religion ever does. The reason is not complex: religion is something that is learned and sustained, rejected or rekindled primarily in family contexts. Consequently it is invariably interwoven with memories of family life.

Consider these fast facts concerning people who do *not* attend services regularly:

- Some 78% say they attended monthly or more when they were growing up, accompanied by 66% of their mothers and 54% of their fathers.
- Close to 90% who have come from Protestant, Catholic, or other-faith homes have retained the religious ties of their parents.
- Almost half the irregular attenders regard their religious-group heritage as either "very important" (20%) or "somewhat important" (28%); only one in five say their religious group backgrounds are "not important at all."

These findings are consistent with the argument that we learn what religion we are from our parents and mirror their involvement in their traditions when we are growing up. The cultures of those religious traditions — in a wide array of quantities — become part of our family's culture, sometimes complete with symbols such as family Bibles, family pianos, and family burial plots.[2] They also become part of our personal cultural repertoire. We learn certain choruses and hymns, worship styles, language, theological ideas; we are exposed to particular role models and lifestyles. We subsequently come to have feelings of familiarity in the presence of our religious cultures.

Obviously those feelings are not always positive. For some people, the religion of their parents is associated with memories and emotions that are unpleasant, sometimes painful. Winnipeg free-lance writer Joan Thomas, for example, writes in the *Globe and Mail's* Facts and Arguments page, that her fundamentalist upbringing was something she has had to spend a lifetime recovering from. "When I stopped identifying myself with the church," she says, "I felt the relief of someone who has been balancing large and unwieldy objects on her head for a prolonged period, and has finally set them down."[3] The fact that the self-help group Evangelicals Anonymous exists suggests that Thomas is certainly not alone. Likewise there are many people who have broken decisively from probably just about every other kind of religious group.

Yet even for so-called apostates, what is "normal" religiously is hard to shake — as evidenced by the fact that many are inclined to view all religious cultures through the eyes of the one in which they were raised. A Presbyterian minister friend of mine tells me how, from time to time, he receives "a four-letter noncompliment" from a hostile ex-Catholic who mistakes him for a priest. Misplaced aggression betrays the depths of many a person's religious socialization. Their religion often goes with them on their flights to freedom.

Our religious identity — our sense that we are United or Roman Catholic or Alliance or Jewish — is acquired through our families and additional significant others. It carries with it a religious culture that, in turn, is typically fused with family culture.

That's why religion continues to be part of the lives of Canadians long after their active involvement in the churches has ceased. It, too, outlives the romance, the disenchantment, and the breakup. As such, in many and perhaps most cases, its persistence signals an enviable opportunity for those who value faith.

THE PSYCHOLOGICAL LINK

The pervasiveness of "identity remembered" can be seen in the apparent paradoxical finding that, while only about two in ten people across the country are currently attending services every week, close to nine in ten nonetheless continue to identify with a religious group. For all the talk about people not seeing themselves as having a religion, the most recent, 1991 Canadian census reports that a mere 12% explicitly say that's the case.

Approximately 45% of Canadians continue to think of themselves as Roman Catholics, while some 35% think of themselves as Protestants. Almost another 5% identify with other world religions. Only 12% do not identify with any religion. And as we have just noted, there is nothing vague about the intergenerational patterns — some 90% are identifying with the religion of their parents. Even a solid majority of about 80% of teenagers identify with a religious group. It's true that the number of "transitional nones" are up, particularly at the expense of the United Church — reflecting there and elsewhere both age structure and the lack of exposure to church life. Still, given that only 18% of teens across the country are regular weekly attenders, the ongoing ID level is impressive.

TABLE 7.1. **RELIGIOUS IDENTIFICATION: ADULTS AND TEENS, 15 TO 19**

In %'s

	Adults		Teenagers	
	1981	1991	1984	1992
ROMAN CATHOLIC	47	47	51	41
PROTESTANT	41	37	34	28
United Church	16	12	10	4
Anglican	10	8	8	6
Baptist	3	3	3	2
Lutheran	3	2	2	1
Presbyterian	3	2	2	1
Pentecostal	1	2	2	1
Other/Unspecified	5	8	7	13
OTHER FAITHS	5	4	3	10
Jewish	1	1	1	1
Other/Unspecified	4	3	2	9*
NONE	7	12	12	21

*Buddhist, Hindu, Muslim, Native, Sikh: 1% each; unspecified 4%.

SOURCES: Adults, Statistics Canada; teens PROJECT TEEN CANADA.

What is particularly striking are the high levels of identification right across the country. Even in British Columbia, some 70% of residents identify with a religious group. In Quebec, the figure is a remarkable 96%! Mark Twain's wry observation about people not being able to "stand on a street in Montreal and throw a brick without breaking a church window," might have renewed significance. Given the great demand for rites of passage, there's still a need for many of those buildings.

The anomaly is disturbing: regardless of their participation levels in religious groups, most Canadians still include religion as part of how they define themselves.

Not Going but Not Gone

If it weren't so tragic, it would be almost funny — a humorous commentary on the foggy perception religious leaders have of the current religious scene. At a time when groups think they are losing people, those apparent defectors, for the most part, haven't gone anywhere. They're still very much at home — maybe not showing up much to eat with the rest of the family, but they're still somewhere in the house.

What's more, even when groups would *like* to get rid of a few, the truth is, if anything, that these nominal affiliates are hard to shed. They can be chastised, ignored, and removed from church lists — and frequently are. But they don't really leave. They go on thinking that they are Roman Catholics, Anglicans, Baptists, Buddhists, or whatever. Here groups thought they were losing everybody; but in fact they can't get rid of them!

University of Saskatchewan researcher Marc Mentzer has carefully compared what Canadians tell the census taker they are, versus how many show up on membership lists. He found that, as of the early 1980s, the ratios of census to roll were ranging from about 5:1 for Presbyterians, through 4:1 for Mennonites, and 3:1 in the case of Anglicans, Baptists, and Lutherans, to around 2:1 in the case of the United Church and Pentecostals. There was little variation between the census and membership counts for groups like Eastern Orthodox, Christian Reformed, Mormon, and Christian and Missionary Alliance. Roman Catholics and Jews, incidentally, take their membership counts from the census.[4]

In 1985 and again in 1990, we asked these alleged dropouts to respond to the following statement:

Some observers maintain that few people are actually abandoning their religious traditions. Rather, they draw selective beliefs and practices, even if they do not attend services frequently. They are not about to be recruited by other religious groups. Their identification with their religious traditions is fairly solidly fixed, and it is to these groups that they will turn when confronted with marriage, death, and frequently, birth. How well would you say this observation describes YOU?

What we have found in both surveys is that some 85% of these marginally involved affiliates say the statement describes them either "very accurately" or "somewhat accurately." For all the alarm about defection, they are still in the camps of the groups with which they are identifying. In the now fairly famous words of the late Anglican archbishop, Lewis Garnsworthy, "It's not that they're leaving; it's just that they're not coming."

TABLE 7.2. ACCURACY OF IDENTIFICATION STATEMENT: 1985 AND 1990		
In %'s		
	1985	1990
ROMAN CATHOLIC		
Quebec	90	94
Outside Quebec	82	91
PROTESTANT		
United Church	91	92
Anglican	84	92
Presbyterian	82	84
Lutheran	82	83
Conserv Protestant	85	81
OTHER FAITHS	75	71
SOURCE: PROJECT CANADA Survey Series.		

It's important to note that, because religious identification is grounded in family and friendships, it's not easy — socially, psychologically, and emotionally — to switch. As we saw in Part I, it really doesn't take place as much as researchers like Posterski and Barker think. In fact, they themselves acknowledge that their findings indicate that switching, when it does take place, is not done flippantly; people usually move elsewhere with great reluctance and with considerable strain.[5] And they are only talking about people moving from congregation to congregation, not from one entire religious tradition to another.

As mentioned earlier, from a sociological point of view, switching — of Protestant to Catholic or mainline to conservative — is a form of deviance. Like any other such variations from norms, switching is resisted by relatives and friends, not to mention the dissonance caused by the wide range of beliefs, values, and memories that the switchers themselves have already internalized.

Skeptics need to take a look at Tim Heaton's examination of religious intermarriage in Canada, based on the 1981 census and published in 1990. What he found was that only 22% of all Canadian marriages at that point in time were actually of the interfaith variety. While that's up from less than 10% in the 1920s, it nonetheless is, in Heaton's words, "remarkably low," supporting "the claim that ties between religion and family remain strong." The tendency to marry outside one's faith was lowest, at about 10% for Roman Catholic, Jewish, and Eastern Orthodox individuals. Consistent with my argument that "nones don't stay nones," it was highest among people with no religious preference (45%).[6] Perhaps some clarification would be helpful.

The None Exceptions

Some think that the obvious variation from the tendency to retain identification is what sociologists call "religious nones." This category tends to receive a disproportionate amount of publicity, in large part because its significance is largely misunderstood.

In June 1993, for example, the national media gave major play to Statistics Canada's release of the most recent (1991) national census on religion. What particularly intrigued reporters was the disclosure that the percentage of Canadians now saying they have no religion is 12%, up from only 7% in 1981 and 4% in 1971. Illustrative of the media's focus, Jack Kapica of the *Globe and Mail* began his story on the census findings with these words: "A record number of Canadians do not have a religion."[7]

The census figures that seemingly documented the increasing move on the part of Canadians toward no religion have received noteworthy corroboration. As we have just seen, our 1992 PROJECT

TEEN CANADA survey of 4,000 15- to 19-year-olds across the country found 21% of teenagers saying they had no religious preference — up dramatically from 12% just eight years earlier.

What is not well recognized, however, is what these "no religion" figures actually mean. As I attempted to show in *Fragmented Gods,* people who carry the "none" label tend to wear it for fairly short periods of time. They're usually younger people who claim no religious tie until such time as they marry, have children, and experience death in the family. As they move through those stages in their late 20s and 30s and call on religious groups for a number of rites of passage, most reaffiliate, typically identifying with the religion of their parents.

- A simple age analysis of the no-religion category reveals that it is top-heavy with younger Canadians. According to Statistics Canada's own release summary, 42% of the "nones" are under 25, and 81% are under 45. Complementary PROJECT CANADA findings show that, as of late 1991, some 35% had not yet married, and 46% did not have any children.[8]
- A cohort analysis of nonaffiliates since they began to officially appear in census data in the 1970s suggests that, rather than the "nones" constituting a permanent category, close to one-half deserted the category during the past fifteen years. In 1975 16% of 18- to 34-year-olds claimed no affiliation; by 1990 the figure for 35- to 54-year-olds — absorbing most of those people in that 18 to 34 cohort of 1975 — had shrunk to 9% (see TABLE 7.3).

In short, at least to date, residence in the "none" category continues to be temporary for many and probably most people. As my colleagues Merlin Brinkerhoff and Marlene Mackie recently pointed out in their detailed analysis of "nones" in Canada, "particular individuals move in and out of that category at different points in their lives." Generalizations about such people, they say, "should be made very cautiously."[9]

What seems to have changed in the 1990s is the size of the pool of temporary "nones," but not the pool of permanent "nones." A larger number of young adults and teenagers are saying they have no religious preference. That is hardly the same, however, as saying they have no religious culture. All it takes is an event to bring it to the surface.

TABLE 7.3. **NONES BY AGE: 1975–1990**		
In %'s		
	1975	1990
NATIONALLY	8	10
18–34	16	19
35–54	5	9
55+	2	4
SOURCE: PROJECT CANADA Survey Series.		

THE CULTURAL LINK

It's intriguing to talk to people on planes who apparently have no interest in religion, let alone commitment to it, only to find, in the course of an extended conversation between, say, Toronto and Calgary, that they have religious histories.

Latent Commitment

I might make a playful comment about the Pope, for instance, only to find that an eyebrow is raised — and the passenger in the next seat is a covert Catholic. Subsequent conversation reveals he attended church a fair amount as a young person and still catches the occasional mass. He tells me he wouldn't dream of wandering randomly into a Pentecostal church, what with "all that emotional stuff" going on. Unknown to both of us, another eyebrow goes up in the seat behind us. A woman, who was raised Pentecostal but hasn't attended church in years, surprises herself by suddenly feeling defensive and whispering loud enough for the latent Lutheran beside her to hear, "As if I'd get euphoric about the prospect of having to sit through a Catholic mass."

Because most of us have been immersed in family cultures that have invariably included religion, its presence and even its influence is often not as far away as we think. No, for most Canadians, religion is not as explicit as their gender or place of residence, their occupation or their marital status. But it's still there, and if it doesn't come out fairly early in the extended conversation with the person on the plane, it nonetheless surfaces at certain times, such as when:

- the census taker asks the question outright;
- a death, a birth, or marriage takes place;
- we turn away a canvassing Jehovah's Witness;

- a moral issue, such as abortion, is being discussed;
- our children want to attend the Mormon church.

Recently two friends, Grant and Linda, told me about attending a wedding a week earlier where the mother was incensed that her daughter was marrying someone who wasn't a Roman Catholic. What they found hard to comprehend was that the mother hadn't gone to mass in years. No matter. The family was nonetheless Catholic and her daughter should certainly have known better!

I also was amused — as they were when I drew it to their attention — by their reaction when I made the mistake of referring to Linda as a defunct Anglican. She, like Grant, hadn't been actively involved in any religious group for about two decades. "I was Baptist!" she exclaimed with more than a little vigour. Seems that some people get more upset about being linked to the wrong group than they do about being called "defunct."

Linda's reaction serves as a reminder that even when people see themselves as *former* Baptists or *former* Presbyterians or *former* Catholics, such identities in no way minimize the memory or preclude the legacy of such religious histories.

Familiar Strangers

The number of people who are identifying but not attending every week works out to about 65% of the Canadian population — translating into close to 18 million people when their children are included. It looks like an awful lot of religious dropouts. But what's badly misunderstood about these people is that the *majority* actually show up in church buildings from time to time — maybe because it's Easter, or Christmas, or a time when they feel they want more out of life, or maybe because Mom and Dad have come to visit for the weekend.

TABLE 7.4. **ATTENDANCE LEVELS OF NON-WEEKLY ATTENDERS**

In %'s

	N	2–3 Month	Once Month	Sev a Year	Once a Year	<Once a Year	Never	Totals
NATIONALLY	779	7	8	26	23	18	18	100
Roman Catholic	336	5	11	34	24	14	12	100
Protestant	406	9	4	19	22	22	24	100
Other Faiths	37	5	11	34	24	19	7	100

SOURCE: PROJECT CAN90.

Regardless of the particular reason at the time, just 18% of these nonweeklys say they *never* attend services at all. Let's get the facts straight: most Canadians do attend services; they just don't attend regularly.

Their unpublicized presence can be readily observed if we're careful about how we read attendance polls. Gallup annually informs us how many people attended services "in the past seven days"; in 1993, the figure was 36%.[10] The 1993 *Maclean's* Angus Reid poll told us 23% of Canadians say they attend services every week. A discrepancy? Not at all. Listen carefully. What follows is extremely important:

- In any given seven-day period, people show up who are not necessarily there every week.
- On a given Sunday, nonweeklys add about 13% to the 23% of weekly churchgoers; that's how we get up to 36%.
- Put another way, in any given week, roughly one in three of the people who are present at services are *not* weekly attenders.

Their appearance in a specific church setting is no accident. When they choose to attend a service — or have their children attend — they typically opt for the group with which they identify. Such a pattern holds for about 85% of nonweekly mainliners, close to 80% of nonregular conservative Protestants, and no less than 97% of nonweekly Roman Catholics.

TABLE 7.5. **RELIGIOUS IDENTIFICATION BY WHERE PEOPLE ATTEND: WEEKLYS AND NONWEEKLYS**

In %'s

Identification	N	Where Attend Mainline	Cons.	RC	Other	Totals
MAINLINE						
Weeklys	40	97	1	2	<1	100
NonWeeklys	178	85	3	12	<1	100
CONSERV PROT						
Weeklys	32	5	95	<1	<1	100
NonWeeklys	31	13	76	11	<1	100
ROMAN CATHOLIC						
Weeklys	160	<1	1	99	<1	100
NonWeeklys	300	1	1	97	1	100

SOURCE: PROJECT CAN90.

What these findings suggest is, for many people who identify but are not highly involved, the inclination to attend is not necessarily far from the surface. In fact, most of them are already making occasional — if not frequent — appearances. When the mood hits them, they won't randomly choose a church to attend that morning. They know full well where they'll be heading — in the direction of the church of their childhood.

Suggestive of the latent salience of their religious identification is the additional finding that 49% of these nonregular attenders say religion is either "very important" (15%) or "somewhat important" (34%) to them. While 33% report religion is "not very important," only 18% maintain it's "not important at all" to them.

It doesn't add up to a picture of people who have abandoned the country's religious groups, let alone religion.

Familiar Styles

What often is underestimated is the extent to which religious cultural content is transmitted from generation to generation. If people have stopped attending regularly, the common assumption is that religion's influence is over. In reality, the cultural imprint — however fragmented — has been made long before.

- She thinks she has retained little of her Roman Catholic background until she enters a Pentecostal church for a wedding and finds herself in a strange religious environment, complete with robust singing and prayers where congregational members spontaneously and noisily join in.
- Although he remembers the United Church services of his childhood, he feels at a loss as he enters the Roman Catholic sanctuary. People are making signs, kneeling, and chanting on cue. It's hard to know when to do what; and some are just now filing out of their pews and heading up to the front of the church for communion. Should he go, or should he stay put? Would anyone know the difference?
- She thinks she can slip quietly into the back pew, engage in familiar worship, and not be noticed. Unfortunately, the new Lutheran pastor has attended a seminar where they stressed the importance of "visitor friendly" worship; he has decided to try the idea out. And so now the liturgy is not taken from the book of worship, some gospel songs are used in place of the standard hymns, and visitors

are greeted so warmly that for a moment she fears she might be singled out. What's happened, she wonders, to my church?[11]

- And what's going on in Sunday schools these days? They send the kids to a church in the neighbourhood with the same denominational banner as the family's. But the songs their offspring come back humming are different from the ones they used to sing, and the lessons don't seem to have quite the same emphases. And did they say that the new minister who wants to drop by is a woman?

In a recent article in the *Presbyterian Record,* Mary Lee Moynan, a Roman Catholic, told of her first visit to a Presbyterian church — seemingly not requiring a particularly long bridge. "As I crossed this Protestant threshold," she writes, "I was sure one of two things would happen: the roof would cave in or I'd have a heart attack." Entering the sanctuary, she whispered to her Presbyterian husband, "Bob, someone has stolen all the statues. . . . Greetings at the door had been a surprise too. . . . The second surprise was the absence of silence." The person sitting beside her struck up a conversation. "I knelt down to give thanks and cracked my chin. Whoever had stolen the statues had taken the kneelers too." Moynan says she found herself beginning her prayer with the sign of the cross — alone; she notes she heard the best choir she'd ever heard sing and a novel children's sermon; and she wondered "if the invitation to receive communion would be extended to a visitor." She concludes her article by indicating she continues to do most of her worshipping in the friendly confines of her Roman Catholic cathedral.[12]

If Mary Lee found that service hard to handle, I wish she had accompanied me to an evening service of Lethbridge's Victory Family Church this past May. Victory is a grassroots Pentecostal congregation that has grown from a handful of people to some 500 in about a decade. That night there were about 400 present. As I told a gathering of Pentecostal ministers a few days later,

> *Frankly, it was the closest thing to a religious pep rally I had ever attended. Remember the old camp-meal grace, "Rub-a-dub-dub, thanks for the grub, yea God!"? Well, that was the tone. Good grief — they even raised one hand in the air and cheered, "Praise God! Praise God!" Now, looking around at you, I can see that some of you are saying, "So? What's wrong with that?" Hear me well: nothing. If you find that meaningful, then fine. But*

understand something: that kind of worship you think is great is something that a visiting Anglican will probably regard as downright blasphemous.

Religious cultures — our groups have them, and we all, to varying degrees, have been touched by them. It therefore is not surprising that we feel a measure of awkwardness when we are in the service of a different group. It's also why Canadians who attend sporadically don't wake up on a given Sunday morning and arbitrarily decide where they will catch this month's service.

For many people who haven't been actively involved in religious groups for some time, the high level of affinity they have with their religious subcultures has been forgotten. It is not, however, gone.

As some readers may be aware, through about grade 11, I was involved — along with my parents and the rest of the family — in a very conservative Baptist denomination. I haven't been involved with that particular group for some 35 years. In early 1985, I developed two important new friendships with people who, coincidentally, were both in the television business. One was a 35-year-old advertising salesman, the other a 25-year-old TV anchorwoman. Both had graduated from Bible schools on the Prairies. What I realized fairly quickly — to my surprise — was that a major component of our rapport was that, although none of us was now involved in such groups, we all had been significantly influenced by our former religious cultures.

For instance, we could make plays on words that we, as the culturally initiated, understood, such as, "Go and sin some more," or, in expressing disgust about some committee, quip, "Father, forgive them, for they know not what they do." We readily agreed that the effort to live out simple interpersonal norms and values from that conservative evangelical subculture — fairness, trust, politeness, low-keyness — had, in fact, functioned to make it very tough to survive in our respective professional worlds. And we also understood why some of our evangelical peers from earlier decades had struggled to retain faith and why some had succeeded, while others had not. If you recognize that kind of religious culture, you help to illustrate my point. Come to think of it, if what I'm describing seems foreign, you still support my point.

Today in Canada, there are millions of Canadians who continue to have a link of cultural commonality with the country's religious groups. Observers are quick to note the link in situations where the so-called ethnic link is pronounced, such as with Jews, Hindus, Muslims, Sikhs and, in the Christian case, groups including Mennonites and Quebec Catholics. Usually the experts speak of a close tie between ethnicity and religion. Such a tie between religion and culture also characterizes many additional individuals. The religious component of group and personal culture is found wherever people see themselves as United or Anglican or Lutheran or Baptist. Significantly it also is present to varying degrees when people insert the word "former" before their religion, or the prefix "ex." The tipoff of the existence of the latent religious culture is a person's naming a religious group as his or hers. Whether the tense is present or past may matter little.

TABLE 7.6. VALUE ACCORDED RELIGIOUS HERITAGES: NONWEEKLY AND WEEKLY ATTENDERS		
% Indicating "Very Important" or "Somewhat Important"		
	Nonweeklys	Weeklys
ROMAN CATHOLIC		
Quebec	50	87
Outside Quebec	47	87
PROTESTANT		
Lutheran	41	**
Conserv Prot	35	94
United	32	91
Anglican	31	86
Presbyterian	23	**
OTHER	67	99

**Numbers insufficient to compute stable %'s

SOURCE: PROJECT CAN90.

THE TRADITION CONTINUES

Invariably there are those who ask, in view of the fact that Canadians aren't attending churches regularly, won't religious identification soon be a thing of the past? And without involvement, what will there be to remember? These are important questions.

The Secondary Source

These concerns, however, seem based on the assumption that the tendency of people to think that they are Catholics, Lutherans, Sikhs, Bahai, or whatever, is based on their having a grasp of the content of their faith and then proceeding to make a logical decision to align themselves with that group.

There's little reason to believe this is usually the case. Surveys in Canada and the United States, for example, have documented an incredible ignorance of the basics of religious content, regardless of whether or not people are marginal affiliates or active members. The 1975 PROJECT CANADA survey, for example, carried out when participation and identification were higher than now, found that only about 50% of Canadians felt they could cite the gist of the Ten Commandments, identify some of the better-known Old Testament prophets, or identify Peter as the person who denied Jesus — even though some 85% viewed themselves as Protestants or Roman Catholics. My 1985 survey of close to 1,800 Anglicans in the Toronto diocese revealed that only 20% of those who described themselves as "actives" and 8% who viewed themselves as "inactives" knew that Thomas Cranmer was the author of their beloved Book of Common Prayer.[13] As of 1990, just 29% of Canadians were able to identify "Exodus" when asked if they could name the second book in the Bible. The Quebec bishops, in their analysis of Catholicism in the province, lament that, even though people say they are Roman Catholics, "it is as though the Christian faith were nothing more than a vague belief in God coupled with the desire to be honest in one's relationships with others."[14]

TABLE 7.7. **RELIGIOUS KNOWLEDGE: 1975–1990**

"Do you happen to know who denied Jesus three times?"

	% Correct	
	1975	1990
NATIONALLY	51	43
18–34	50	34
35–54	48	44
55+	55	52

SOURCES: PROJECT CANADA Survey Series.

As attendance declines, along with personal commitment, it should surprise no one that knowledge about religion is diminishing. Sure there are some functional alternatives that are picking up some of the slack. Roman Catholic schools and private schools have been growing in number, while religious studies programs at universities have known a post-1970 era of expansion. Still, the net effect for the population as a whole is hardly a religiously literate nation. As of the 1990s, the answer to the simple "Who denied Jesus?" question still eluded large numbers of Canadians, both old and young, with the numbers of those in the dark up significantly from the mid-1970s.

Yet, when it comes to religious identification, all of this doesn't seem to matter all that much.

The Primary Sources

What seems to be far more important to religious identification and religious memory than the rational response to content are two factors: *family history* and *rites of passage*. When a relative of mine, who was not attending any church with regularity, was asked by his mother where he planned to get married, he surprised her by responding, "the Baptist church." When she asked, "Why Baptist?" he stunned her with the blunt response, "Well, you're Baptist — so I must be Baptist." A quick scan of our friends and ourselves will probably tell a fairly consistent story: latent identification follows intergenerational patterns, and comes to the fore when rites of passage are being carried out — a wedding, a christening, a funeral.

And so it is that a 22-year-old who has not been attending services with any frequency whatsoever is powerfully reminded that he *is* an Anglican when his grandfather's funeral is carried out in an Anglican church. Family history, in combination with passage rites, instils identification. As for content, it is largely an irrelevant variable. What else is new? There is good reason to believe that content, while forever a great cause for concern and debate among theologians and leaders, has never been all that important to the average person. To recall sociologist Jay Demerath's phrase, "Religion is more often the product not of urgency but of imitation."[15]

Religious identification is largely learned through significant others, notably our parents and friends. The old line of John Wesley — "I learned more about God from my mother than from all the theologians in England" — describes a very old, but nonetheless ongoing pattern.

Identification is transmitted from parents to children and reaffirmed through rites of passage. It receives additional support from special services that are typically associated with key family events, particularly Christmas. Ironically the common putdown to the effect that "he only goes to church for weddings and funerals and at

Christmas and Easter" misses a critically important point: *he is there and something is happening.* Identity is being reaffirmed; life is being given meaning; memories are being constructed. These are far from trivial events.

Ongoing identification, latent commitment, and cultural legacies all point to the fact that religion continues to be a very real part of the memories of Canadians. They might be out of sight, but their religion is not out of mind.

8

THE RELIGIOUS MARKET

The findings add up to nothing less than a fascinating religious situation. Most Canadians exhibit receptivity to the things religion historically has addressed. The vast majority continue to have links to the churches. The situation seems almost ideal for those who value faith.

THE GENERAL PICTURE

Involvement Patterns

To make sense of the findings, there is value in looking at Canadians in terms of their identification and involvement tendencies. What emerges are some fairly distinct patterns:

- While a core of close to 25% of the population are highly involved in the nation's religious groups, just over another 25% are "marginal affiliates." These people continue to identify with the groups and to appear in the churches from two or three times a month to a few times a year.
- Almost a further 40% are "inactive affiliates" who identify but attend about once a year or less.
- Only about 10% of Canadians have actually said goodbye to organized religion. Yet even here, caution needs to be used in assuming that the churches have been permanently rejected. About eight in ten of these "nones" are what might be termed "disaffiliates," in that their parents identify with a religious group. Just two in ten of them are "nonaffiliates," who come from homes where both parents are "nones."

TABLE 8.1. **INVOLVEMENT CATEGORIES**

In %'s

Category	Size	Description
ACTIVE AFFILIATES	24%	Identify; attend nearly every week or more
MARGINAL AFFILIATES	27	Identify; attend 2–3 times a month to several times a year
INACTIVE AFFILIATES	39	Identify; attend once a year or less
DISAFFILIATES	8	Don't identify, parents do; 93% attend < yearly
NONAFFILIATES	2	Don't identify, nor do parents; 96% attend < yearly

SOURCE: PROJECT CAN90.

Pervasive Receptivity

But the significance of ongoing identification — even when someone is a former disaffiliate — can be seen when the findings concerning mystery, meaning, and memory are viewed through the five involvement categories.

- Both marginal affiliates and inactive affiliates exhibit very high levels of interest in mystery and meaning, are following in parental identification footsteps, and are not inclined to turn to other groups. In fact, the marginals closely resemble the actives in many ways.

- The inactives stand apart from both actives and marginals in not seeing the relationship between their spiritual interests and what the churches have to offer; most inactives don't place high importance on either religion or religious-group heritage.

- The disaffiliates and nonaffiliates show fairly high levels of intrigue with psychic phenomena, spirit-world contact, and reincarnation, but lower levels of interest in more conventional supernatural ideas about God, Jesus, and life after death. Meaning, however, appears to be very important to people in both of these "religious none" categories — including the desire for at least some rites of passage. Religious memory among the disaffiliates and non-affiliates, however, at least at present, is seemingly not contributing to a favourable predisposition toward religion.

The findings point to a culture that is anything but hostile or, for that matter, indifferent toward issues that historically have been of central importance to religion. Quite the opposite. Our key idea sources, such as the media, have recognized the intrigue Canadians have with mystery, and have provided large amounts of material — programs, movies, rock groups, videos, books, articles, and merchandise — that have been both a response and a further stimulant to such interest.

	NAT	ACTIVE AFFILS	MARG'L AFFILS	INACTIVE AFFILS	DIS- AFFILS	NON- AFFILS
	(1171)	(282)	(319)	(459)	(80)	(30)
INTRIGUE WITH MYSTERY						
Psychic powers	60	49	65	65	52	42
Spirit world contact	39	32	43	43	29	16
God's existence	82	97	95	78	26	23
Have experienced God	43	75	53	27	6	2
Divinity of Jesus	75	96	90	67	14	9
Life after death	68	84	76	62	31	29
Will be reincarnated	26	17	27	31	20	13
THE SEARCH FOR MEANING						
Concerned about purpose	51	41	53	52	62	67
Wanting more from life	68	56	70	73	79	72
Want birth ceremonies	26	20	30	29	15	32
Want wedding ceremonies	28	20	34	32	13	24
Want funerals conducted	61	65	64	61	42	46
RELIGIOUS MEMORY						
Same ID group as mother	86	92	95	91	10	100
Same ID group as father	83	89	93	85	17	100
Not inclined to leave group	80	N/A	90	89	N/A	N/A
Relig somewhat important	56	97	75	31	5	6
Relig gp heritage important	48	89	66	24	2	6

TABLE 8.2. **MYSTERY, MEANING, AND MEMORY BY INVOLVEMENT CATEGORIES**

In %'s

SOURCE: PROJECT CAN90.

As well, ours is not a culture that suppresses reflection about the meaning of life and the possibilities surrounding death. In days past people have lamented the reluctance to discuss death and dying. Today, in a period where few topics are taboo, the meaning of death — and life — are increasingly being brought into the open. It's not that our culture is short on skepticism, or long on answers. But it does give a green light to people exploring questions of death and the beyond.

Nor does our culture attempt to obliterate specific forms of religious culture. Multiculturalism and the Charter of Rights and Freedoms provide us with enormous freedom to live out our lives and express our religions in almost any way we want. Ours is a society in which religious traditions can be instilled and sustained.

For too long, religious leaders have been blaming culture for religion's problems. These findings provide strong support for the argument that, unconsciously or not, Canadian culture actually has been contributing to a market for mystery and meaning, while encouraging the preservation of religious memory. In many ways, then, the conditions are excellent for religion.

A PROFILE PREVIEW

From the standpoint of both descriptive information and policy implications, it's worthwhile to provide a quick preview of what involvement and receptivity look like for religious groups across the country and within some key social categories.

TABLE 8.3. **INVOLVEMENT CATEGORIES BY RELIGIOUS GROUPS**					
In %'s					
	N	Active Affiliates	Marginal Affiliates	Inactive Affiliates	Total
NATIONALLY	9143	28	31	41	100
ROMAN CATHOLIC					
Outside Quebec	2438	33	35	32	100
Quebec	2545	27	35	38	100
MAINLINE PROT					
United Church	1355	16	33	51	100
Anglican	889	14	32	54	100
Presbyterian	255	18	31	51	100
Lutheran	244	20	33	47	100
CONSERVATIVES					
Baptist	247	43	26	31	100
Others	721	57	15	28	100
OTHER FAITHS					
Eastern Orthodox	114	11	60	19	100
Jewish	99	25	42	33	100
Other	250	34	31	35	100
SOURCE: Computed from Statistics Canada, *General Social Survey,* 1991.					

Religious Groups

Among the some nine in ten Canadians who identify with religious groups, about 30% are active, 30% marginal, and 40% inactive. Variations between groups, however, are extensive:

- Roman Catholics tend to follow a "one-third, one-third, one-third" pattern, with actives being slightly higher and inactives lower outside of Quebec.
- Mainline Protestants have roughly a 20–30–50 pattern, with little difference between the country's four primary groups.
- Conservative Protestants are the reverse, at around 50–30–20, with various evangelical groups — not identified explicitly by Statistics Canada — tending to fare a bit better than Baptists in particular.
- Other faiths vary considerably, with newer groups such as Hindus and Sikhs[2] mirroring the one-third pattern of Roman Catholics outside of Quebec, Jews having an involvement level similar to Quebec Catholics, and a group such as the Eastern Orthodox at about 10–60–20, with few actives but also relatively few inactives.

Region and Community Size

Active affiliates tend to be proportionately highest in the Atlantic region, at 40%; elsewhere, the actives make up about 20% of regional populations. Marginal affiliation decreases from east to west, dipping to just 11% in B.C., with inactive affiliation increasing from east to west. Both disaffiliation and nonaffiliation are higher in B.C. than anywhere else.

The findings underline what earlier analyses of service attendance by region have shown concerning the unique aversion to organized religion in British Columbia. A core of about 20% of people in B.C. are actively involved in religious groups. But after that, the situation departs from the patterns in other regions. Only an additional roughly 10% of the people in that West Coast paradise are even marginally involved with the churches — well below the levels elsewhere. The rest are either inactive or not affiliated.

Active involvement is definitely lower in the larger cities than in the smaller communities. In Montreal, Toronto, and Vancouver the proportion of active affiliates is about one-half the figure for communities with populations smaller than 10,000. However, it's interesting to note that the proportion of marginal affiliates is similar, regardless of community size, as are the figures for inactive affiliates. The percentage of people who claim no affiliation is twice as high for the country's three largest cities (14%) as it is for cities and towns with populations of under 100,000 population (7%).

Keeping in mind our regional findings, we need to use caution, however, in assuming that urban size, as such, has a negative impact on religious involvement. A peek at the participation patterns for Montreal, Toronto, and Vancouver show that Vancouverites easily lead people from the other two Canadian cities in their apparent detachment from organized religion. Other cultural factors beyond sheer city size are clearly involved.

TABLE 8.4. **INVOLVEMENT CATEGORIES BY REGION AND COMMUNITY SIZE**

In %'s

	N	Active Affiliates	Marginal Affiliates	Inactive Affiliates	Dis- affiliates	Non- affiliates	Totals
NATIONALLY	1171	24	27	31	7	3	100
B.C.	141	22	11	50	12	5	100
Prairies	197	23	25	43	7	2	100
Ontario	418	21	29	42	6	2	100
Quebec	309	23	31	35	7	4	100
Atlantic	106	42	34	21	3	0	100
1 million-plus	297	15	28	43	8	6	100
999–100,000	326	22	27	40	8	3	100
99–10,000	171	28	23	43	5	1	100
under 10,000	377	30	29	34	6	1	100
Montreal	127	15	30	43	5	7	100
Toronto	126	14	34	41	6	5	100
Vancouver	65	18	14	47	16	5	100

SOURCE: PROJECT CAN90.

Gender and Age

Nationally, women differ very little from men in their involvement patterns. Both sexes are almost equally likely to be actives, marginals, inactives, disaffiliates, and nonaffiliates. The pool sizes differ little.

When it comes to age, as expected, the active affiliates are drawn disproportionately from people older than 55. However, the proportion of marginal affiliates is actually slightly higher among those younger than 55, even though the percentages of inactives and those not affiliated are higher for younger adults. The significant finding here is that the marginal affiliate pool for the 18 to 34 and 35 to 54 age cohorts is substantial, and that the proportion of these younger Canadians who have opted to drop out of religious groups altogether is not very high — only 7% and 16% respectively.

	N	Active Affiliates	Marginal Affiliates	Inactive Affiliates	Dis- affiliates	Non- affiliates	Totals
NATIONALLY	1171	24	27	31	7	3	100
Female	599	26	28	36	7	3	100
Male	572	22	26	42	7	3	100
55+	293	41	25	31	2	1	100
35–54	406	22	29	42	6	1	100
18–34	426	13	27	44	11	5	100

TABLE 8.5. **INVOLVEMENT CATEGORIES BY GENDER, AGE, AND EDUCATION**

In %'s

SOURCE: PROJECT CAN90.

REALISTIC EXPECTATIONS

Taken together, this preliminary examination of involvement categories suggests that the market for religion in Canada is sizable. The highly involved constitute a numerical minority of only about 20%. Yet, across the country, among both men and women and within all age cohorts, large numbers of Canadians are still showing up in the churches. Relatively few are cutting their ties altogether. Religious memory is almost everywhere.

Further, the vast majority of these people, along with many of those who have no affiliation, are continuing to exhibit interest in mystery and meaning. Religious groups could hardly ask for a better opportunity.

What Do People Want?

I believe these findings indicate a substantial market for the supernatural — for a "product" that speaks to the unexplained and the unknown by offering answers that lie beyond the human plane. Such a contribution is needed, because many of the questions people raise require answers that transcend what we can know empirically. In the words of sociologists Stark and Bainbridge, "Some common human desires are so beyond direct, this-worldly satisfaction that only the gods can provide them."[4] As Canadians live out life, complete with its elements of mystery, they are open to explanations of a supernatural variety. An opening for those who have something to say.

Canadians are also trying to figure life out. Many feel that what they are doing with their lives doesn't seem to have much significance. Their sense that there has to be something more seems to be particularly acute during times of passage — marriage, birth, death, and, presumably, other transition and adjustment points — children leaving home, divorce, retirement, and the "big" decade birthdays of 30, 40, 50, and so on.

Such efforts to understand life more completely are highly personal. It's as individuals that we pursue answers concerning the unexplained and the unknown. It's as individuals that we raise questions about purpose because we want to be able to experience personal fulfillment. Our needs as individuals are basic to spiritual quest.

But our efforts to address mystery and find meaning also are interlocked with social considerations. So much of life is lived out in relationship to other people that it becomes almost impossible to ask, "What does it all mean?" without dubbing in any number of substitutes for "it all," including, "my career" or "my family" or "my children" or "my friendships" or "my group involvement." Ethical and moral questions are essentially questions about how we should relate to others. Even such a personal question as, "Will I live after I die?" often is asked because we find ourselves wondering, "Will I ever see my mother/father/child/friend again?" Similarly, many of our queries involving the unexplained — such as apparent psychic experiences — commonly involve other people with whom we seem to be "connecting."

And so it is that our efforts to deal with the issues of mystery and meaning invariably involve a blend of the supernatural, the personal, and the social. Or, to return to the language of *Fragmented Gods,* the spiritual quest encompasses three centrally important features — *God, self,* and *society.* Successful attempts to respond to Canadians' intrigue with mystery and quest for meaning will be solidly in touch with all three.

How Much Do They Want?

An obvious question that arises for those who aspire to bring religion to Canadians has to do not only with the quality of religion, but also with the quantity. Those of you who are familiar with the fragmentation argument I offered in 1987 will recall that I joined many others in maintaining that a major problem facing organized religion in this country is that Canadians are highly selective consumers. They want only specialized fragments of what the country's religious groups have to offer. The problem, I have been saying for almost a decade, is not that people want so much; rather, it's that they want so little. Fragments are relatively unimportant consumer items, chosen over systems because they are more conducive to life in our present age.

Such a "consumer report" obviously represented bad news for people who maintain that religion should speak to the entirety of one's life.

My indictment was premature. It assumed that Canadians are adequately aware of what religion has to offer and have proceeded to make highly selective choices. They allegedly have scanned the religious smorgasbord and taken only the things they want. The argument also assumed that religious groups are, in fact, adequately presenting the key elements of religion.

The recent survey findings bring both assumptions into question. There is good reason to believe that a considerable number of Canadians are failing to associate their interest in mystery and meaning with what religion historically has had to offer. To continue with the analogy, they aren't even checking out the smorgasbord, because they don't expect to find the kind of food they want. For their part, religious groups are commonly giving their primary attention to matters that are only marginally related to the gods and what they have to say about the spiritual quests of the populace. Tragically the gods are often unknown to both customer and company.

What seems clear is that the majority of Canadians want little of what the churches have to offer. What is far less clear is that they want only limited amounts of what religion has to say about their fundamental questions pertaining to life and death. In other words Canadians are not in the market for churches. They are, however, very much in the market for the things that religion historically has been about.

POSTSCRIPT: A HOLY INCOMPREHENSIBLE SITUATION

It's all rather bizarre. Organized religion in Canada is in serious trouble. Membership and attendance have been steadily declining since at least the early 1950s. The inclination of Canadians either to place high value on religion or see it as having a significant impact on life has been dropping in the past 50 years. Differences in involvement and commitment by age suggest that the problems facing organized religion will only get worse in the immediate future.

TABLE 8.6. **RECEPTIVITY OF TEENAGERS TO SPIRITUALITY**	
In %'s	
IMPORTANT: *"Very"* or *"Somewhat"*	
The quest for truth	86
Harmony with nature	83
Spirituality	62
Religious Involvement	33
BELIEVE: *"Definitely"* or *"I think so"*	
How we live will influence what happens to us after we die	64
I myself have spiritual needs	58
For detailed options, see notes.[5]	
SOURCE: PROJECT TEEN CANADA 92.	

A common — and convenient — response is to say that people just aren't that interested in religion anymore, that religious groups are having to operate in very difficult times. What we've been finding lately, however, suggests that such an observation is a false reading. In the midst of the apparent demise of faith, there are signs that the market for religion remains substantial.

For the sake of argument, imagine a Canada where:

- people no longer are intrigued with mysterious happenings or wondering about death and beyond;
- supernatural beliefs are regarded as outdated, religious practices ridiculed as signs of superstition;
- people no longer reflect on life's significance;
- almost all marriages are conducted by civil authorities; few people want children baptized or dedicated; funerals are nonexistent;
- hardly anyone has memories of religions past — most indicate they have no religious preference.

Such a culture would be a place where organized religion would find the going tough. *But just the opposite is true.*

- intrigue with mystery is almost everywhere;
- people are fascinated with the supernatural;

- they want to find out how to make life more meaningful;
- they seek out the churches for rites of passage;
- almost all continue to identify with religious traditions;
- their biographies typically are characterized by religious memories.

It all adds up to an incredible paradox. Precisely at a time when the cultural conditions seem ideal for religion to have an important place in the lives of Canadians, religious groups across the country are in a state of decline. It's as if McDonald's and Wendy's and Burger King are all going under at a time in history when Canadians love hamburgers; or that television manufacturers cannot sell TV sets at a time when Canadians want a set in every room in the house.

The situation calls for more people who think their faith has something to bring to culture to ask the obvious question, as one Unitarian member has in a recent letter to his paper's editor: "Why does a denomination with so much going for it grow so slowly in what can only be considered fertile times?"[6] Reflecting on declining United Church membership figures, Tom Bandy, the staff person for congregational mission and evangelism, similarly acknowledged recently: "We're not hearing the needs of people. The public is very religious. But mainline churches simply aren't meeting the needs."[7]

Reflecting on the situation in B.C., the most secular of Canadian regions, veteran United Church Minister Gordon Pokorny recently commented, "I haven't seen more visible evidence of people searching for spiritual well-being in the past 50 years."[8] Highly respected *Vancouver Sun* religion and ethics writer Douglas Todd says he continues to be "amazed by [widespread] spiritual feeling" and by "how many great spiritual people there are out there."[9]

Something is seriously wrong. Given what seem to be excellent "market conditions," the time has come to put aside niceties and ask the obvious question: "Why is organized religion floundering instead of flourishing?"

PART III
WHY THE CHURCHES
ARE FAILING

R eligious groups are failing in what appear to be spiritually prosperous times. The intrigue that Canadians have with mystery, their desire for meaning, and their ongoing experience of religious memory add up to a great opportunity in our day for faith to be shared. Yet, it's not happening. The churches are going broke and the population is going hungry. It doesn't make sense. Or does it?

Some of the key reasons for the apparent paradox of "failure in prosperous times" may be organizational. Even though religious groups claim to deal with the gods, they nevertheless are also social organizations that are subject to the same problems as their secular counterparts. To be effective, organizations have to be sound structurally, be clear on what they do, identify their potential markets, and deliver their products. On all four counts, religious organizations are found wanting. It wouldn't be so serious if new religious groups could come in and fill the void, similar to how new businesses arise to give new life to failing economies. Unfortunately the religious firms that are failing in Canada also have a lock on the market. Canadians are the losers.

9

STRUCTURAL PROBLEMS

hen companies fail, we assume their failure has something to do with them. Bankrupt operations, be they local, national, or multinational, exhibit some fairly obvious characteristics. Finances, personnel, product, price, promotion, delivery, customer relations, reputations, change, and competitiveness are among the factors to which people point in explaining what went wrong. Few observers are inclined to look at the demise of the local restaurant, the regional grocery chain, or the national airline and suggest that their problems were the inevitable result of the economy or changing times. Our assumption is that the best companies find ways to stay alive when conditions are unfavourable. And when they do, we assume it was far from an organizational accident.

All of which is to say religious groups that not only survive but thrive don't do so by chance. Conversely it's no secret why others are on the verge of collapse, in effect winding down their operations with ever-shrinking remnants. For all the efforts that the gods go through to create and stimulate and resuscitate groups, the fact is that religious organizations tend to be very fragile organizations.

- In the long run they have a tendency to change in the direction of becoming more secular. So it is that people like Max Weber and H. Richard Niebuhr drew attention to the cyclical pattern noted earlier — where denominations give birth to reformist sects that, in turn, eventually evolve into denominations, only to spawn renewal sects that become denominations, and so on.
- In the short run religious groups are extremely vulnerable

organizations, because they are so highly dependent on their members and because they constantly have to contend with society's influence. Many groups are consequently relatively ineffective; others don't make it.

In the United States, organizational fragility appears to be offset to a large degree by at least two important interrelated factors. The first is the presence of an unregulated religious market. The second is the relative proficiency of the groups that are successful.

Many observers have described the U.S. "religious economy" as one with a very high level of vitality. Groups compete with each other for truth and market shares. I'm not being flippant. Stephen Warner, in an article just published in the *American Journal of Sociology*, maintains that "the new paradigm" being used to understand religion in the United States has as its key "the disestablishment of the churches and the rise of an open market for religion." Warner points out that disestablishment in the U.S. "did not occur overnight," but "was the fruit of an ironic alliance between deistic political elites and insurgent evangelical firebrands." Disestablishment did, however, have two profound implications for religion: it provided freedom to exercise religion in general and it provided no protection for any group in particular. "For the churches, says Warner, "it was sink or swim" with the long-term result of disestablishment being "a far higher level of religious mobilization than had existed before."[1] According to J. Gordon Melton, the director of the Institute for the Study of American Religion, Santa Barbara, there were about 800 religious denominations in the U.S. in 1965; today, with a number of the mainline groups faltering, Melton estimates there are about 1,600.[2]

Consistent with Niebuhr's argument, Finke and Stark maintain that as some religious groups fail, others arise to take their spots, picking up their defaulted shares of the market. The net result over time — from 1776 through the 1990s, say the two sociologists — is that overall levels of religious-group participation grew steadily up until the 1920s and has remained at about the same level ever since. What's important to keep in mind here is that the process is not something magical, more or less the inevitable result of "what Americans are like." Rather, as Warner has emphasized in his extensive review of the use of the marketing model in the U.S., what is distinctive about American religious institutions is that they have worked extremely hard over time to bring people into churches. "Despite the impression on the part of today's conservative Christians that the United States was founded as a Christian nation," writes Warner, "the early decades of American independence were times of eclectic spiritual ferment but thinly disguised church membership."[3]

Quite remarkably, the secular competition of the last half of this century has not seriously affected the national level of religious involvement. Sure, mainline groups have been experiencing serious numerical and resource problems.[4] Methodists and Lutherans, Presbyterians and Episcopalians have been among the religious companies that have sustained heavy losses. But because of the vitality of the religious competition, primarily in the form of conservative Protestants, the overall level of church participation has remained stable. Consequently, to the extent that Americans have exhibited intrigue with mystery and are searching for meaning, there is good reason to believe the country's religious companies, both older and newer, have serviced and are still servicing them fairly well.

In Canada, on the other hand, involvement in the churches has dropped — dramatically. It's no organizational accident. In keeping with Niebuhr's assertion, some of our premier religious firms have been moving away from their roots. But Stark is right: a centrally important difference between our two countries is that our religious economy, unlike theirs, has not been "deregulated."

In Canada, everyone is not fair game for growth-minded groups. As I pointed out in *Fragmented Gods*,[5] that's not the way pluralism works up here. Whereas American religious groups aggressively compete with each other in their pursuit of truth, Canadian groups essentially exist to service their regular and new customers. They aren't particularly encouraged to recruit affiliates of other groups, for that sort of thing smacks of bigotry and exploitation, especially if the people involved are immigrants, aboriginals, members of disadvantaged groups, children, or the elderly. Aggressive proselytizing of such people conceivably might be seen by some critics as a violation of the Charter of Rights and Freedoms.

Compare Canadians' cautious approach to the expression and dissemination of faith with that, for example, of that great American, uh, journalist — yes, you're reading it here — Ann Landers. In a column distributed across the continent on February 11, 1993, Landers responded to a letter from America's best-known atheist, Madalyn Murray, which complained that Landers insults thousands of people daily with her "Judaeo-Christian" advice. Landers, using Murray's own data to point out that 90% of her 90 million readers are *not* atheists, had this to say:

> *If you do not believe in God, Madalyn, it's perfectly all right with me. I am not trying to force religion on anybody. But I'll be darned if I will stop advising my readers to seek help from their spiritual leaders just because some atheists don't like it.*

Definitely not the words of a Canadian.

Our apprehension about any signs of coercion leads us to be wary of enterprising new sects and cults — especially in light of the stories we've heard over the years about new religious movements, David Koresh kinds of cults, over-zealous Jehovah's Witnesses, Scientologists, Mormons, and the like. We are also uncomfortable with religious hard sells and soft sells, be they in the form of the television preacher, the touring evangelist, the door-to-door campaign, or a March for Jesus.

As a result — although the long-established religious groups in Canada have been experiencing the secularization tendencies of which Niebuhr spoke, and despite Canadians' intrigue with mystery and search for meaning — in contrast to the U.S. situation, the market slack has not been picked up by new and vigorous religious firms. To make matters worse, the older companies that have continued to monopolize Canada's religious market have been experiencing some very serious organizational problems.

In at least the immediate future, "religious deregulation" is not going to take place in Canada. The religious mosaic — complete with its ideology of respect for diverse expressions and its disapproval of assimilation efforts — is well entrenched. Hope for the sharing of the gods consequently lies in the reformation of existing groups. However, if reform is to occur, it's extremely important to have a clear understanding of some of the organizational reasons the gods are not being shared with Canadians.

RESOURCES

We have already seen that Canada's religious groups are facing serious resource problems because of the ongoing decline in the level of participation. Increasingly, there will be fewer people and fewer dollars with which to work. Ministry in Canada, however, is being further hampered by the nature of the religious work force, as well as by the fragmented organizational structures that characterize many of the country's groups.

Volunteer Work Forces

At a time when organizations in the private and public sectors are drawing on the burgeoning human resources field to fine-tune their selection, training, and use of personnel, religious groups somewhat amazingly continue to rely primarily on volunteers. That's not to say they can't make themselves look good on paper. They can readily produce elaborate flowcharts delineating division of command as it's found at the local, regional, and national levels.

What's more, volunteer efforts can be applauded and treated as both necessary to and synonymous with effective ministry. As one Lutheran advertisement in a denominational magazine puts it, "Do you know what makes the world go round? Volunteers like you! Because of you, the daily ministry of the Gospel is extended around the world."[6]

The problem, however, is that volunteers don't exactly make the world spin. In fact, the churches frequently are little more than paper organizations.[7] Obviously they vary greatly in structure, ranging from the extensive bureaucratic hierarchy of the Roman Catholic Church through the somewhat more democratic systems of the Anglican and United churches and to the congregational autonomy-styles of groups like Baptists and Pentecostals.[8] Yet, at the point that laity become involved at local, regional, national, and even global levels, what religious groups have in common is that most of the laity are volunteers. Out of the commitment they have to the faith and the church, people are asked to occupy vitally important organizational roles and fulfill them effectively.

This heavy dependence on lay volunteers makes religious groups painfully vulnerable as organizations. Their volunteer work forces are neither hired after careful screening, nor fired when they perform ineptly. For their part, some volunteers would like to quit, but feel they can't. As the Assembly of Quebec Bishops research report stated, "Committee and group leaders work to the point of exhaustion; yet they often have to continue in their tasks for many years." Still, if members — and I use the term loosely — are not treated the way they think they should be, they can simply quit. On occasion the disgruntled stay, sometimes to the detriment of both morale and mission.

Consider the problems frequently associated with religious volunteers:

- Since they need to be willing to offer their time, availability is often a more important criterion for appointment than competence.
- Where elections are involved, there is no guarantee that the best candidates fill the positions.
- Most can give their roles only a limited amount of time.
- Many are not particularly well trained for their positions.
- They are highly mobile; their congregational roles, for example, are almost always secondary to other considerations, such as a job transfer to another part of the country.

This doesn't quite add up to the dream situation advocated by the human resources expert. The problem is not that organizations in our society cannot function well if they have volunteers. Not at all. Volunteers obviously can enhance them if they are used to complement a stable core work force. But if the organization becomes top-heavy with volunteers, it can start to teeter and have considerable difficulty functioning efficiently and effectively. The "priesthood of all believers" might be a virtuous theological concept. But operating in religious-group situations, it has the potential to make ministry anything but easy.

In many if not most instances, Canada's denominations and local congregations find themselves running on volunteers. The Roman Catholic Church, in large measure because of a shortage of full-time employees in the form of priests and other members of religious orders, is gradually following suit. Such excessive dependence puts religious groups in a position that is the envy of very few secular organizations. Imagine a hospital trying to function well with 99% of its staff comprised of volunteers, let alone a department store or a restaurant. Yet, that's what a typical Canadian congregation or parish tries to do, only sometimes the ratio of paid staff to volunteers is not 1 to 99 but more like 1 to 300! It's a pipe dream.

Such organization tends to exclude religious groups from high-flying corporate circles. Decima Research's 1987 national survey for the Canadian Centre for Philanthropy found that religious groups are the number-one place where volunteers give time (35%), followed by minor sports, the Cancer Society, and community centres (7–10%), along with Guides/Scouts, the Red Cross, the United Way, and the Heart and Stroke Foundation (5% each).[9]

For organizations with the dream of transforming Canada, that's mighty strange company to keep.

Autonomous Franchises

Companies with operations that are spread out nationally and globally clearly require well-developed co-ordination. Good communication among their various parts — not to mention the companies with which they are interdependent, as well as their customers — is of critical importance. At the consumer level, for example, the toll-free number has become a commonplace means of direct and fast contact with a company, to make inquiries, receive clarification, complain, and so on.

On an international level, co-ordination is a complicated matter. Harvard Business School professor John Quelch points out that businesses that go global have to resolve an array of issues that involve a delicate balance between centralized control and decentralized autonomy. Quelch writes: "The least threatening, loosest, and therefore easiest approach . . . is for headquarters to encourage the transfer of information between it and its country managers."[10] Still, even for the top corporations, co-ordination of its various parts is difficult, to say the least.

If religious groups find effective ministry difficult at the local level, they find it incredibly taxing regionally and nationally. It's far more than a communication problem. To their credit, a number of groups are connected electronically through an array of interactive North American, national, and regional computer networks, such as UChug, Anglinet, Lutherlink, Ecunet, and Francisnet. Hundreds of Canadian churches are believed to be hooked into one network or another.[11]

No, the problem is greater than being able to make contact. Blame it on the Protestant Reformation. Or maybe accelerated individualism in our time. But an ongoing problem that groups face — be they Protestant, Roman Catholic, or another faith — is that individual congregations have been making a virtue of the autonomy of the local church.

Simply put, many a local congregation or parish insists on having freedom over its own affairs. Known, not coincidentally, as a "congregational" form of government, the concept has long been explicitly popular among denominations that I, along with other sociologists, have been dubbing "conservative Protestant" — including Baptist,

Christian and Missionary Alliance, Pentecostal, Mennonite, Nazarene, Evangelical Free, Reformed, and Plymouth Brethren groups. It also is frequently implicit in other religious groups as well.

However theologically admirable the concept may be regarded, in practice it frequently translates into an organizational nightmare. Predictably, the co-ordination of co-operative ventures by the parent national bodies of such autonomous churches is, in the euphemism of the day, challenging.

THE CASE OF THE CANADIAN BAPTIST FEDERATION

Baptists are illustrative. In Canada, they comprise five major groupings — the Canadian Baptist Federation, the North American Baptist Conference, the Baptist General Conference of Canada, the Fellowship of Evangelical Baptist Churches in Canada, and the Canadian Convention of Southern Baptists. Historically these groups have strongly emphasized the sovereignty of the local church. The price has been considerable.

The problems of the Canadian Baptist Federation, for example, are not a secret. The CBF, founded in 1944, is comprised of western, central, and eastern conferences. Perhaps an unobtrusive indicator of its co-ordination difficulties is its inability to come up with a national magazine. The *Canadian Baptist* has served only the West and Ontario-Quebec, and in 1993 was in danger of losing the support of the West. The paper's editor, Larry Matthews, has written that in the 1990s "there's no free ride" for the denomination. He suggests that the dominant congregational creed is, "If something can't be shown directly to benefit the local church, then don't do it."[12] What's more, he says, "We are paralyzed in a crisis, ineffective in challenging, supporting or assisting other churches. The independence we prize as individuals is acted out by our churches, which seek neither to be accountable to other churches, nor to come to the aid of churches in difficulty."[13] He adds, "All of us who draw paycheques from the donations of Canadian Baptists had better produce demonstrable results — or we're history."[14]

Richard Coffin, the general secretary-treasurer of the CBF, similarly acknowledges, "For churches, the bottom line is their return. They want to know what their contribution to the denomination will do for their particular church." While Coffin does see an upside to congregational freedom, he adds, "Local church autonomy is our weakness when we think that our leaders shouldn't have any authority in denominational life." Coffin quips, "Someone once said when introducing me that I have the most prestigious and powerless position in Canadian Baptist life."[15]

William Brackney, the principal of the CBF-affiliated McMaster Divinity College, maintains that the time has come, not only for the Canadian Baptist Federation, but for all five major Baptist denominations to come together. "What Baptists in Canada need is a good national funeral service to which only the family would be invited," he said in 1992. "At that service, we need to commit the 'remains' to the historians and get on with the future of the church."[16]

It's an interesting thought, Bill. But given the value that Baptists place on autonomy at the personal, local, regional, and national levels, excuse me for not setting a day aside just yet to catch the collective rite of passage.

* * *

A fairly common organizational problem for all of Canada's religious groups is that members of local churches have been known to withhold their financial support of the national bodies when they don't agree with their programs and pronouncements. In recent years, groups suffering from such tendencies have included the United Church, when it was embroiled in its controversy surrounding homosexual ordination, and the Evangelical Lutheran Church in Canada, whose birth in the 1980s, through a merger of the Lutheran Church in America-Canada Section and the Evangelical Church in Canada, was greeted with muted enthusiasm by many rank-and-file members. In the Anglican instance, whether because of disenchantment with the national church or not, in the past 20 years giving to parishes has increased by 38% in real dollars and giving by parishes to dioceses is up by 23%. However, excluding special appeals, giving to the national General Synod has increased by only 3%.[17]

As a result, rather than Canada's religious groups being able to marshal their collective resources in ministering to regions and the nation, they often are hamstrung by disagreement and division. And too few, it seems, have toll-free numbers with customer-relations people standing by.

Even the Roman Catholic Church in Canada, writes University of Waterloo sociologist Kenneth Westhues,[18] historically has had its national influence weakened considerably because it has been regionalized and polarized into English- and French-speaking camps.

Gregory Baum comments that the problem extends to the church's theologians: "I always regret that the Catholic theological literature of Quebec is almost unknown by Catholic theologians in English-speaking Canada."[19] Beyond theology, consensus is frequently lacking, neutralizing the ability of even this largest of national religious groups to have a concerted co-ordinated impact on Canadian life.

In reflecting on his near-decade as national Lutheran bishop before stepping down in 1993, Donald Sjoberg observed that people at the congregational level often consider the national office remote. Some, for example, would like to tie their individual churches more directly to things like missions and decentralize the denomination. "Rather than working through the synod or the national church," he said, "they want to do it directly. They want to cut out the middle man." Sjoberg noted that such a pattern reflects debates happening all over the world about central power and local autonomy, adding that Canada's unity debate — with church language dubbed in — would not be all that different from his denomination's debate.[20] Sjoberg probably receives little consolation from the fact that what the Lutherans have been experiencing is common to most if not all Canadian religious organizations.

A work force that is top-heavy with volunteers, combined with autonomous congregations that are difficult to co-ordinate, does not add up to organizations with the collective resources to function effectively — locally or regionally, let alone nationally or globally.

FLEXIBILITY

It's almost a law: individuals and organizations that accomplish their goals have to stay focused. Distractions that focus or consume an organization's resources can be disastrous.

Probably since the very inception of religious groups, one factor has constantly broken their concentration, siphoned off their resources, and reduced their effectiveness: social change.

Change, of course, does not have to be an enemy. Successful organizations must constantly change, update themselves to stay in touch with the times. They ignore new demographic patterns, new technologies, and new cultural trends at their peril. At best, organizations that disregard change become peripheral; at worst, they disappear altogether. Religious groups are no exception.

Yet, for some strange reason, social change tends to immobilize religious organizations. It functions like kryptonite, that alien rock that used to transform the man of steel into a mere mortal. Here's how change does its debilitating work.

Keeping Up Without Giving Up

Faced with the introduction of things that are new — ideas, products, services, and programs — religious organizations have to differentiate between what needs to be retained in the name of integrity and what can be changed without sacrificing integrity. Since religion claims to be more than merely a product of culture — having, for example, as its focus a God who has brought the world and all cultures into being — change cannot automatically be accepted. Often the issue of authority is raised: Will religion's claims be authoritative, or will culture's? The issue is one that has received attention from many thinkers, the most prominent of which include social historian H. Richard Niebuhr[21] and theologian Paul Tillich.[22]

When both religion and culture claim authority in a given area, such as sexuality and euthanasia, *conflict* results. When religion yields to culture, as commonly happens in scientific and technological areas, the relation is one of *cultural dominance.* Conversely, when culture yields to religion, such as in addressing the question of life after death or the spiritual significance of life's key passages, *religion is dominant.* In cases where neither culture nor religion claim authority, either because the issues are innocuous or because neither is able to be very definitive — for example, in predicting the future — there is obviously *no conflict* or dominance.

FIGURE 9.1. **RELIGION AND CULTURE'S RELATIONAL POSSIBILITIES**

		Authority Claimed by Culture	
		Yes	No
Authority Claimed by Religion	Yes	Conflict	Religious Dominance
	No	Cultural Dominance	No Conflict

A major problem religious groups face is their constituents' tendency to support major cultural shifts. When change is being endorsed by our major idea-instilling institutions, namely the media, education, and government, and further supported by business, many people expect their religious groups to fall into line. After all, if sexual freedom, gender equality, multiculturalism, and environmental concern are good enough for society, so the thinking goes, they should be receiving the blessing of churches who are in step with the times. To be slow to provide such support is, frankly, to invite bad public relations.

Shaped as they are by our culture, many parishioners are understandably impatient with any sign that religion is balking at following culture's lead. Groups constantly live with allegations that they are "dragging their feet" or "living in the past." Leaders, as well as members, frequently get impatient. Ernest Howse, a pillar of the United Church through much of this century, once said of his own denomination — which hardly has lacked for taking a chance or two — "It's impossible for anything coming out of United Church headquarters to be too radical. They have built-in brakes. General Motors must envy our brakes."[23]

Change-minded religious groups also have to contend with people who want things to stay just the way they are. Prominent Anglican leader John Bothwell, in commenting recently on the controversy in his church over the introduction in the mid-1980s of *The Book of Alternative Services,* expressed exasperation. The old *Book of Common Prayer* has become, he said, "like an old comfortable pair of shoes," which some parishioners refuse to repair or replace despite its outdated language and grim view of the human soul. "They think of the church as a rock that never changes," Bothwell added. "Well, God doesn't change, but the church is for people and there has to be some growth and adaption to modern reality."[24]

Further, for religion to be too closely associated with ideologies some people regard as suspect, such as Marxism, is to run the risk of getting not only a negative reaction from within the churches but some bad publicity from the outside — as the World Council of Churches has experienced with *Reader's Digest* writer Joseph Hariss in the 1980s and 1990s. His 1982 article, "Karl Marx or Jesus Christ?" was critical of the WCC's funding of what Hariss regarded as radical groups, while his February 1993 article, "The Gospel According to Marx," accused the WCC of fusing religion and revolutionary politics, including permitting a KGB presence on the council.[25]

And then there's the problem of leaders disagreeing on the pace of change. In 1992 Canadian Council of Churches president and United Church minister Bruce McLeod wrote a *Toronto Star* column supporting the blessing of same-sex relationships. His material upset Jonathan Gerstner, the executive-secretary of the Reformed Church of Canada, a Council of Churches member. Gerstner was having to deal with some angry constituents, who wanted to apply those brakes of which Howse spoke to McLeod's position.[26]

People who don't think religious groups change quickly enough usually minimize a centrally important fact: religious leaders constantly have to filter change through a faith screen, attempting to discern when the issues involved violate the tenets of religion and when they do not. The process is not easy, nor particularly fast.

In this century in Canada and many other Western countries, the churches have had to wrestle with change in such important areas as birth control, sexual standards, gender relations, family structure, racial and cultural equality, and, most recently, sexual orientation — an issue that some say will be *the* issue for the church in the 1990s. Bob Harvey, the *Ottawa Citizen* religion editor, describes the situation this way:

> Today the Christian church finds itself in the midst of a revolution. For two thousand years Christians have believed that the practice of homosexuality is contrary to Scripture. Governments followed the churches' lead and made homosexuality a crime, and even the medical profession considered homosexuality a disease. Then in the 1960s, governments began to decriminalize homosexuality, and in 1973 the American Psychiatric Association delivered the final blow when it decided that homosexuality is not a disorder after all. . . . Suddenly it was the churches that were out of step.[27]

In the 1980s and 1990s, churches have been trying to find their sexual orientation footing amidst ongoing changes to human rights codes such as Ontario's which now acknowledges same-sex couples. In the near future codes will probably also acknowledge same-sex marriages.[28] Few if any of the country's religious groups are advocating segregation by sexual orientation, whereby gays and lesbians are restricted to their own congregations.[29] The issue has to be resolved, and groups are trying.

- In the 1980s the United Church of Canada pioneered the idea of full participation in the church for homosexuals, which created massive conflict. Having dealt in 1988 with the question of homosexual ordination, the church's General Council found itself in 1992 having to face the question of the blessing of same-gender covenants; it chose to acknowledge the lack of agreement on the issue and leave discussion to each local congregation.[30]
- Anglicans, at their triennial synod in 1992, agreed to spend $51,000 on a three-year study of homosexuality, with the findings to be brought back to the next synod, in 1995.[31]
- Presbyterians, at their 118th general assembly in Hamilton in June 1992, released an 18-page "Report on Human Sexuality." The report says that homosexual activity, as well as premarital sex and adultery, are contrary to God's will. Following considerable debate, the report was adopted as an interim report and referred to presbyteries, sessions, and congregations for study.[32]
- Lutherans, in response to a motion adopted at their national convention in Saskatoon in 1989, are conducting a study of human sexuality and its implications for the denomination.[33]
- The Baptist Convention of Ontario and Quebec passed a "Resolution on Sexual Orientation" at its annual assembly in 1988, asserting that "homosexual behaviour is unacceptable in the sight of God," yet denouncing the condemnation and rejection of homosexuals.[34]
- As for evangelicals more broadly, Professor John Stackhouse, a past president of the Canadian Evangelical Theological Association, says that evangelical churches are simply "a decade behind." They will eventually have to address the question, because "the issue is on the wider cultural agenda and because there's a coming out of homosexuals within the evangelical denominations themselves."[35] Lines are already being drawn; for example, Marjorie Hopper, a Canadian who sees homosexuality as a sin requiring a conversion experience, has formed a recovery group called Another Chance.[36]
- Jews, specifically Reform, find themselves weighing the issue of same-sex "commitment ceremonies," with rabbis currently basing their decisions to perform such ceremonies on their personal convictions. Rabbi Michael Stroh of the Temple Har Zion in Toronto is among those dissenting. "I will work with homosexual couples to help them create a Jewish home," he says, "but I cannot

marry them, nor can I officiate at a ceremony of commitment or blessing."[37]

Their positions have pleased some — and alienated many.

Case Example 1: Some Mainline Protestant Problems

Sexuality is only one area where groups have had a difficult time with change. The desire to bring about organizational change in the form of mergers, as well as the need to respond to an issue like gambling, can also tie groups in knots.

Consistent with its high-profile effort in the post-1950s to champion the freedom and equality of all Canadians, the United Church of Canada attempted in the late 1980s to address the issue of homosexuality. Tabled in 1987, its national task force report — "Sexual Orientation, Lifestyles and Ministry" — recommended the recognition of homosexuals as full-fledged members of the church; of particular significance, homosexuals would also have the right to be ordained as ministers. At a stormy national General Council held in Victoria in 1988, a "Membership Ministry and Sexuality Statement" was accepted.

The controversy, however, was divisive and costly. University of Toronto sociologist Roger O'Toole and his associates have suggested it was so intense it "threatened the denomination with the first major schism since its foundation in 1925."[37] On one side were those who felt the United Church was abdicating the historical Christian view that homosexuality is a sin. On the other side were advocates of the position who saw the effort to embrace homosexuals as prophetic, a forward step in making the church truly inclusive. O'Toole and his colleagues write that the latter camp saw the development "as a far-sighted, loving expression of a socially relevant progressive theology," while the other viewed it "as the last straw in liberal theological appeasement of the forces of sin and evil."[38]

During the debate, the denomination's national magazine, *The Observer*, was deluged with mail, with opponents of the proposal outnumbering its supporters approximately six to one.[39] A national organization known as the Community of the Concerned sprung up within the church, lobbying for the defeat of the proposal. Summing up the uneasiness many members felt, well-known evangelical author Maxine Hancock, a member of a United Church congregation in northern Alberta at the time, put it this way: "A good many members of the United Church of Canada feel like back-seat riders in a fine old car which has been commandeered for a joy-ride."[40]

In the aftermath of the General Council's 1988 acceptance of the recommendation, almost half of the church's 4,000 congregations submitted opinions on the statement to the 1990 General Council in London. One analysis claims that 75% of the churches disagreed in one way or another with the policy, with only 6% indicating clear support.[41] As noted earlier, about ten congregations and an estimated 25,000 people left the denomination. A levelling off in donations to the church's Ministry and Service Fund — which pays for programs administered by the national church — was attributed in large part to many members registering their dissatisfaction with the Victoria decision by closing their chequebooks.

In attempting to make an adjustment in light of what the leadership saw as theologically and culturally appropriate, the United Church received the accolades of some and the derision of many. Prophetic? Maybe. A sellout to culture? Maybe. The point is that, in groups like the United Church where in 1993 an estimated one in three regular attenders were maintaining that the denomination has become "too liberal,"[42] flexibility is a two-edged sword. At the customer level, it has significant costs, as well as rewards.

Of particular importance, dealing with issues of change can divert a group's attention from other matters that perhaps are more pressing and, frankly, more important. Maintaining that the state of the country has warranted primary attention in recent years, well-known Winnipeg minister and politician Bill Blaikie says of the sexual controversy, "The United Church of Canada was tragically distracted in 1988 by the issue of gay ordination when the powers and principalities launched a major offensive on the United Church's Canada. It must not be distracted again, or history will judge it harshly for its complacency in the face of its own destruction."[43] Stan McKay, who was elected moderator in 1992, has expressed a similar concern about his "great sense of loss in the lengthy time we spent discussing homosexuality while there were so many things in the periphery of our membership, like the abuse and harassment issue, and other areas of pain and suffering that we were willing to leave aside."[44] Minister Tom Stevenson put it much more bluntly at the height of his inability in early 1993 to become the first openly gay man to join the Christian clergy: "We've got a world in great trouble. People are starving. Rivers and forests are dying. But there's a group of people obsessed about what I do with my genitals."[45]

TABLE 9.1. **UNITED CHURCH HOMOSEXUALITY ATTITUDES: BEHAVIOUR, RIGHTS, ORDINATION ELIGIBILITY**				
% Approving				
	N	Homosexual Relations	Same Rights as Others	Eligible for Ordination
ALL: Canada	1249	34	81	36
United Church	187	31	85	37
UC MEMBERS				
18–54	23	48	83	45
55+	39	11	81	32
UC NON-MEMBERS				
18–34	32	30	95	46
35–54	57	42	87	39
55+	28	28	71	31
UC ATTENDANCE				
Weekly	27	22	85	39
Less than Weekly	153	32	85	36
SOURCE: PROJECT CAN90.				

In the mid-1980s Lutherans appeared to be coming together when the two disparate groups — the Lutheran Church in America-Canada Section and the Evangelical Lutheran Church of Canada — merged to form the new Evangelical Lutheran Church in Canada. Yet, in October 1992, the Canadian Association of Lutheran Congregations was founded in Calgary, headed by the Rev. Vernon Roste. He, along with his church in Kamloops, B.C., had already left the ELCIC over disagreements on issues including abortion and sacramental practices. As many as 15 Lutheran congregations on the prairies were expected to join Roste's new association.[46] This has all been happening at a time when the relatively new ELCIC has been short of the necessary funds to put a number of important programs in place and has also been trying to grow. It has to be extremely discouraging.

And then there's the intriguing problem emerging with aboriginal peoples and Christianity. The Anglican and United Church denominations have been leading the way in attempting to right past wrongs and embrace First Peoples as equals. But across the country, natives want to establish gambling on reserves as a way of raising much-needed revenues. Gambling, however, is strongly opposed by both denominations. Consequently the two groups are caught between trying to champion the principle of self-government, while feeling the need to insist on conformity to church positions.

In some parts of the country, church officials are voicing their opposition to gambling on reserves; in others, they are reluctant to speak out. Anglican Bishop George Lemmon of Fredericton has expressed things this way: "There is a dichotomy, but what the church is doing is taking a moral stand. We involve ourselves out of a pastoral concern and as the conscience of society." Some native leaders are willing to listen to the churches, but others are very impatient with the churches' involvement. Chippewa Chief Del Riley of the Thames band near London, for example, says, "I'll hear what the churches have to say, but I have other considerations. When you have nothing else to grasp on to, you make tough decisions." Wilma Wessel of the United Church's Saskatchewan Conference admits that the church is in a "ticklish situation."[47]

Case Example 2: Roman Catholics

Changes that directly affect family life have created considerable turmoil within the Roman Catholic Church during the last half of this century. The sexual revolution, gender equality, and divorce have been among the most difficult issues with which the church has had to deal. Through it all, the official position of the church has remained firm: sex outside marriage is forbidden. Women are not allowed to be ordained. Divorce is not permitted.

Accordingly, the Vatican doesn't hesitate to sanction apparent dissenters, including Father André Guindon of St. Paul's University in Ottawa. The views he expressed on premarital sex, homosexuality, and contraception in his 1986 book, *The Sexual Creators,* have been attacked for opposing church doctrine. Subject to acceptable clarification, he faced the possibility of losing his right to teach as a Catholic theologian. Lines in his book such as, "When you preach a sexual ethic based on marriage and procreation, you're talking to a minority of people," have not worn well with Rome.[48]

Likewise, Matthew Fox, the founding director of the Institute of Culture and Creation Spirituality in Oakland, California, was officially dismissed from his Dominican order in early 1993. Fox joined the Dominicans in 1960 and became a priest in 1967. He remains a priest, but cannot exercise his ministry without the permission of a diocesan bishop. His problems with the Vatican began before he founded the institute in 1977. According to Vatican spokesman Joseph Cardinal Ratzinger, Fox's thinking — which combines Christian mysticism with creation-centred spirituality — is out of touch with the church's official teachings.[49]

Lest anyone be confused, there is little ambivalence about orthodoxy on the Roman Catholic side. A steady stream of documents are released from the Vatican covering almost every imaginable aspect of life. In late 1989, for example, the Pope's so-called "guardian of orthodoxy," the Congregation for the Doctrine of the Faith, issued a 23-page document warning Roman Catholics that Zen, yoga, and Transcendental Meditation can "degenerate into a cult of the body." Increased attempts to fuse Eastern and Catholic meditation, said the church, can pose "dangers and errors," including the syncretistic merging of practices. Congregation president Ratzinger said the report was not condemning Eastern methods, but elaborating on guidelines for genuine Christian prayer. "The fundamental affirmation of the document is very simple," he told a news conference. "Christian meditation is not submersion in an impersonal divine atmosphere, in an abyss without face or form."[50]

In late 1992 the Church released its new catechism — the first since the Council of Trent in 1566. It has been hailed by Pope John Paul II as one of the major events in the recent history of the Roman Catholic Church.[51] Included in this summary of the Church's beliefs are the following:[52]

- *Birth control* associated with self-discipline and infertile periods is acceptable; any action taken to make procreation impossible before, during, or after the conjugal act, however, is not acceptable.
- *Ordination* is limited to baptized men, in keeping with Christ's own example; ordination of women is not possible.
- *Homosexuality* goes against natural law; while homosexuals should be treated with compassion and fairness, they are urged to be chaste.

There's not a lot of room for negotiation. Pope John Paul II, in a 1990 synod address, had this to say about the problem of the shortage of clergy being met by ordaining mature married men: "This solution must not be taken into consideration. Other solutions must be found to this problem." According to the Pope, the vocation of the priest is to be a complete self-offering; to ordain married men would be equivalent to acknowledging that complete self-offering is too much to ask.[53] As for women, the Pope told Quebec bishops in a 1993 meeting in Rome that the church "does not consider [itself] authorized to admit women to priestly ordination," although it recognizes "the great importance of their participation in community life."[54] Upon their return to Quebec, Bishop Bernard Hubert acknowledged the dilemma they feel: "As bishops, we experience an uncomfortable situation because we want to live in a dual solidarity: to be united with the leaders of the universal church and to welcome, at the same time, that which is positive."[55]

Concerning divorce, in addressing a group of visiting bishops from France in early 1992, the Pope described people who have divorced and remarried as "men and women who live in irregular situations." They require "spiritual assistance and the full aid of the church's affection and care," he said, but reiterated the Catholic policy of banning such people from receiving communion.[56]

In some ways, such defiance of dominant cultural trends is commendable and certainly more sociologically interesting than blatant cultural acquiescence. The Roman Catholic Church is clearly not being led by culture — at least, as critics would be quick to remind us, by *today's* culture. Still, whatever may be laudatory about such a position, it's clear that the church's defiance is also carrying a very heavy price. And as Susan Mader Brown of King's College notes, the problem is being compounded by the fact that "lay people are more theologically literate than they used to be, and therefore less inclined to accept what authority says simply because authority has said it."[57] Large numbers of Roman Catholics simply do not or cannot reconcile official teachings with everyday life. For example:

- A majority of Roman Catholic adults reject the church's position on sex outside of marriage, along with divorce and abortion.
- About nine in ten favour the use of artificial birth control methods.[58]
- Some three in four feel that women should be eligible for ordination as priests.
- A slightly higher proportion maintain that priests should be allowed to marry.
- Teenage Roman Catholics not only tend to reject the church's

sexual teachings, they also are receptive to people who are not married both living together (91%) and having children (73%).

TABLE 9.2.	**SELECT ROMAN CATHOLIC ATTITUDES BY ATTENDANCE AND AGE**						
% Approving							
	N	Premarital Sex	B.C. Info	Abortion: Health	Abortion: on Demand	Ordination of Women	Priests Marrying
ALL: Canada	1249	80	95	95	38	–	–
Rom Caths	505	82	94	93	27	70	77
Weekly Attenders							
18–34	31	87	99	93	6	62	72
35–54	53	72	91	81	15	65	77
55+	68	47	74	80	9	48	61
Less than Weekly							
18–34	157	98	99	99	39	86	79
35–54	123	91	98	95	34	70	81
55+	46	69	90	97	21	60	78

The last two items read, "Women should be eligible for ordination as priests"; "Priests should be allowed to marry." Responses were obtained for Roman Catholics only.

SOURCE: PROJECT CAN90.

Roman Catholic leaders must find such obvious disparity between official church teachings and attitudes of the laity extremely discomfiting. Sizable numbers of Catholic women and men must also find the disparity not particularly life-enriching. Some members — laity, priests, and others — have been abandoning the church altogether. The defectors, however, appear to constitute a small minority. As embroiled Ottawa professor André Guindon recently expressed it, "I've had heart attack after heart attack trying to do my job well. This is my church, why the hell should I leave?"[59]

Most of the dissidents appear to be staying within the boundaries of the church and seem to fall into three camps — the passive, the troubled, and the militant.

Those taking a *passive* position see a dichotomy between life and faith. They view the church's proclamations as unreasonable, irrelevant, and impractical, and therefore ignore them. Some undoubtedly experience a measure of guilt; most at minimum feel a measure of alienation. Others, while certainly placing a high value on faith, don't choose to be confrontational. They appear to have found ways of articulating the dichotomy in ways that minimize potential conflict. For example, in a recent interview with *Maclean's*, Suzanne Scorsone, the director of the office of family life for the archdiocese of Toronto, was quoted as saying that the church has a hierarchy of values, with the core teachings and central mysteries more important than certain issues of sexual morality.[60]

The *troubled* take the teachings of the church at face value and accept Rome's authority over matters of faith and life. These people consequently experience considerable agony as they attempt to reconcile the church's position with what they encounter in everyday living. They, along with many other Canadians — personally or through family and friends — know the realities of sexuality and divorce, not to mention cohabitation, abortion, and gender inequality. As one woman who went through a marital breakup put it, "My husband's infidelity broke my heart but divorce crushed my spirit."[61]

The third camp, the *militant,* are not content to be either passive or troubled. Some are on the outskirts of the church, retaining affiliation but not overtly involved. A high-profile American example is Pulitzer Prize winner Anna Quindlen, a journalist with the *New York Times*. In 1990 she wrote that the "men at the top [of the church] are uniquely unqualified to face the most pressing issues of their time. Birth control, the ordination of women, permission for priests to marry, abortion — all rise from sexuality and femininity. The primacy of the priesthood rests upon celibacy and masculinity."[62]

Other militants, however, are working within the church to bring the Roman Catholic Church, as they put it, into the twenty-first century:

- In 1990 the Coalition of Concerned Canadian Catholics endorsed a full-page ad in a March issue of *USA Today,* urging the church to ordain women and "to discard the medieval discipline of mandatory priestly celibacy." The Canadian branch held its fourth annual conference in Toronto in May 1993, drawing 350 people to its two-day event. Present with Professor Guindon were American Speakers Virginia Hoffman *(The Co-dependent Church)* and Michael Crosby *(The Dysfunctional Church),* who implored Catholics to pursue reform.[63]
- Professor Mary Malone of St. Jerome's College in Waterloo said in

mid-1993 that women are making important contributions to the church, and "if they stopped working for the church, the church would close down." But, she added, their involvement has come as a result of their own initiative and not because of a change in attitude on the part of the church. "I think there is still a great deal of chauvinism and discrimination and inability to deal with women," claimed Malone. "People don't know what to do with them."[64]

- Excluded to date as full members at world synod gatherings, the national board of the Leadership Conference of Women Religious asked the church to include women as full participants in deliberations at its 1994 world synod on religious life. The U.S. board said that it is "reflecting aspirations of women religious throughout the world."[65]

- In 1974 Mary Jo Lamia, a divorced woman, and Sister Josephine Stewart, a family counsellor, founded the Beginning Experience Inc. in Fort Worth, Texas, to help Catholics deal with divorce. It has since spread across the world, reaching such countries as Ireland, Singapore, and Canada.[66]

Some Catholics, while advocating change, call for a measure of patience in the light of current structural realities. Following the November 1992 decision of the general synod of the Church of England to ordain women to the priesthood, the Vatican announced that the move constituted "a new and serious obstacle" on the path toward reconciliation of Anglicans and Roman Catholics.[67] Responding to both decisions, Margaret Brennan, a professor in the Pastoral Department at Regis College in Toronto, had this to say: "No matter how varied the personal desires of women in terms of ordination, exclusion from priestly ministry has been — and is — perceived as a profound public and symbolic statement of inequality." Yet, cautioned Brennan, given that "the present clerical structures [might] succeed in neutralizing the new gifts that women have to offer our church, [it] just might be that these gifts can flourish, and make a greater contribution to the transformation that is sorely needed, through the continued participation of women in those areas where they are already actively involved."[68]

In some cases, great effort is being made on the part of church leaders to engage the laity, to reflect on possibilities, and pursue effective ministry, even though collisions with the Vatican may be inevitable.

An example is what is referred to as the People's Synod in the diocese of Victoria that took place between 1986 and 1991. Convened by Bishop Remi De Roo, it was charged with the task of "discerning how best to renew and strengthen the faith of the people of the Victoria diocese."[69] Several thousand Catholics and numerous non-Catholics participated in identifying key issues, developing proposals for action, and making specific decisions concerning action. Decisions were reached by consensus rather than by voting.

Of the 90 actual delegates, 71 were lay members, 46 were women, with all but six laity. (At the previous diocesan synod a century before, the delegates were all clergy and therefore all men.) Well-known Roman Catholic Grant Maxwell was among the participants who came away from the synod "challenged"; commentator Mader Brown was among those who applauded the effort, while reminding the diocese that patience will be required in their attempts to implement some proposals — including the ordination of women — that are in conflict with Rome.[70]

As with the mainline Protestants — and most of Canada's religious groups, for that matter — Roman Catholic leaders face the dilemma of needing to be sufficiently flexible to accommodate members who believe that certain changes are necessary, while at the same time reaffirming the position of the tradition when it is believed that proposed changes violate the integrity of the faith. It's neither an easy nor enviable task.

How Change Divides and Debilitates

The effort to distinguish between "the appropriate new" and "the appropriate old" is more than merely strenuous; it also places religious leaders in what amounts to a no-win situation. The problem they face is that both flexibility and inflexibility invariably carry with them personal casualties.

The argument isn't only theoretical. People who, in the face of change, come away satisfied on the one hand and dissatisfied on the other are everywhere to be seen in religious organizations. The subsequent morale problems among the paid and unpaid staff critically affect the way they relate to each other as a human community, and how well they can carry out ministry as a religious organization. Moreover, in the process, the overall attention that change requires consumes enormous amounts of organizational energy.

And so, to return to where I began, change functions to break the focus of religious groups, turning them inward rather than outward — as it has the United and Roman Catholic churches in recent years. The diverse flexible and inflexible responses of leaders and members to proposed innovation almost invariably produce division, absorbing organizational resources as they debate the age-old question of whether this is "of God" or "of man." In the words of John Congram, editor of the *Presbyterian Record,* "The tragedy of our lives is that too often we allow secondary issues to create unwarranted hostility and division while the essentials get lost in the sound and the fury."[71]

The flexibility issue is centrally significant for religious organizations and always will be. The reason? The change problem never goes away because change itself never ends. The ongoing arrival of new issues produced by a changing culture serves to keep religious groups in a perpetual state of tension and division. Division and diversion of resources seem almost unavoidable correlates.

IMAGE

In what seems like a previous incarnation, I was the minister of a church that had experienced some difficulties prior to my arrival. To my chagrin, I quickly discovered that the community's perception of the church and its previous minister was not very positive. A brother-in-law suggested I hang a big banner on the front of the church that read:

UNDER NEW MANAGEMENT

Not something I would do, of course, but still a pretty good piece of advice.

Contentious Connotations

In the 1990s Canada's religious organizations have a serious image problem. Newly arriving clergy and newly arriving members discover that association with religious groups frequently carries with it certain stereotypical characteristics that aren't especially flattering. Pastoral rookies and congregational neophytes can be forgiven for likewise secretly wishing, as they attempt to experience a "new day," that they could hang out an UNDER NEW MANAGEMENT sign.

Ask the average person in this country what first comes to mind when she or he thinks of organized religion, and any number of the following will undoubtedly be mentioned: sexual abuse, TV evangelist scandals, ordination of homosexuals, sexism, rules, lack of enjoyment, money, old people, weddings, funerals.

The associations have not been derived in a vacuum. Let's shoot straight:

- The highly publicized sexual-abuse cases involving Roman Catholic priests and other clergy have made it difficult for anyone who wears a clerical collar to so much as smile at a child, let alone stroll past playgrounds. Some nervousness was apparent, for example, when in early 1993 a former Jesuit priest — who said he wanted to "help heal the wounded" — was named chairman of the Alberta Human Rights Commission.[72]
- TV evangelist scandals have fed the age-old stereotypes about hypocritical clergy who are more interested in money and sex than ministry. The culprits may have been primarily American, but Canadian clergy in every religious group have suffered a serious public relations setback.
- The controversy over the ordination eligibility of homosexuals has, at minimum, left many Canadians wondering what's happening in the churches — especially in light of the fact that the majority of the population continues to disapprove of homosexuality. Rightly or wrongly, many had assumed that the church was the last place where homosexuality would be condoned.

Sexual scandals and sexual controversies are never all that great for any business, but when you're in the religion business they can be disastrous. The developments of the past few years have made the tough task of ministry even tougher. The churches hardly needed all the negative publicity. And it just seems to keep on coming:

- In July 1992 a Toronto United Church organist of 25 years was sentenced to six months in jail and two years probation for having a sexual relationship with a boy who'd been only 11 when the six-year relationship began. The man was fired from his job as a high school teacher, but forgiven and eventually reinstated by his congregation.[73]
- The same month a Lutheran pastor in Calgary pleaded guilty to six counts of indecent assault and one count of sexual assault

between 1971 and 1985. The acts consisted mainly of touching and fondling.[74]

- The minister of Montreal's Roxboro United Church, 31-year-old Christopher Bowen, was suspended — with pay — in November 1992 for appearing nude in *Malebox,* an Ottawa-based gay magazine. He had been minister of the suburban congregation for less than six months. Bowen subsequently took the Montreal Presbytery to court, seeking reinstatement.[75]

- James Ferry, an Anglican priest, made national headlines in 1992 when he was fired by Toronto Bishop Terence Finlay for his refusal to end a noncelibate relationship with another man. The bishop's actions were upheld by a diocesan bishops' court. Ferry's autobiography has contributed to the case's receiving ongoing attention.[76]

- Rudy Pohl, a Baptist minister in Ottawa, was barred from his pulpit early in 1992 for allegedly ignoring his board and denouncing homosexuality from the pulpit. The fact that one of the most active members was a homosexual was well-known to the congregation. The board members said they were shocked, not by the content of what Pohl said, but by the timing, which represented Pohl's refusal to "take counsel from the leaders of the church on an important and sensitive issue." The highly publicized incident gained a predictable polarized response.[77]

- In May 1992 Tim Stevenson was ordained into the ministry of the United Church of Canada. A graduate of the Vancouver School of Theology, Stevenson was the first openly gay man to be ordained by the UC. However, despite the official position of the church, whereby gays and lesbians are entitled to full membership and participation, placement proved difficult — and embarrassing for the denomination. In July 1993 Stevenson was finally placed, becoming the minister of Burnaby's 40-member St. Paul's United Church. Coincidentally, another gay clergyman, the previously married Gary Paterson, became the new minister of Ryerson United Church in the Vancouver community of Kerrisdale, moving from Vancouver's First United Church.[78]

These kinds of events have kept the public eye on the sexual side of religion. Child abuse has been devastating; the homosexual controversy has, at minimum, called for education, information, and an effort to maintain good public relations. For the most part, religious groups have not been able to fend off extremely negative publicity. In the sexual abuse instance, as Anglican primate Michael Peers has pointed out, the typical response of groups has been denial and control, where control takes the form of silence.[79] The result has been a further deterioration of image.

What is perhaps especially telling about the organizational ineptness that frequently plagues religious groups is that they have been poorly prepared to respond to possible "product" and "personnel" problems. For example, despite the Roman Catholic Church's elaborate division of labour, it "has always had difficulty communicating with the press," says Father John Pungente, a specialist in media literacy. He suggests that one only has to look at the church's inability to deal with the media in the aftermath of the Mount Cashel charges to see the severity of the problem. Religion writer Jack Kapica notes that in Toronto, the media hub of Canada, the Roman Catholic Church finds itself led by an archbishop who is extremely uncomfortable relating to the media.[80] Rather than making good use of the media, Archbishop Ambrozic has found himself embroiled in controversy for comments deemed inappropriate.[81] It hasn't been a match made in heaven.

If religious groups are ill-prepared for normal ties with the media, one can hardly expect them to be ready for journalists and cameras and microphones when the going gets rough.

No company wants bad publicity. But it sometimes happens. Problems need to be anticipated, so that a measure of damage control can be implemented.

- In 1982 and 1986 Johnson and Johnson faced a major problem when it was found that Tylenol bottles had been tampered with. The company responded quickly with new tamper-resistant packaging, advertising that asked people to continue to trust Tylenol, rebates for bottles that had been thrown away, and — the second time around in 1986 — the replacement of capsules with caplets. The company was highly successful in retaining customers.[82]
- In June 1993 Pepsi-Cola faced a temporary credibility crisis. In a span of one week, more than 50 people in 23 states claimed they had found hypodermic needles in Pepsi cans. By the end of the week, the Food and Drug Administration had found no evidence for the claims, and there were more than a dozen arrests for false reports. Meanwhile, Pepsi rushed to reassure the public that every-

thing was all right. An ad in more than 200 Saturday newspapers proclaimed, "As America now knows, those stories about Diet Pepsi were a hoax. Plain and simple, not true."[83]

In contrast to such immediate responses in the corporate sector, the churches typically act as shocked as everyone else when a scandal breaks. I'm not sure why. These kinds of problems have beset religion throughout its history; they're hardly new to the 1980s and 1990s. Deviance involving sex and money are virtually inevitable given the nature of the "morality business."

No, I'm not for a second saying that denial is in order, when it's unwarranted. Quite the opposite. In late June of 1993, for example, the Vatican committed a terrible public relations error when, on the heels of Pope John Paul II's condemnation of clergy sexual abuse, chief spokesman Joaquin Navarro-Valls was quoted by Reuter's as saying that child sex abuse by U.S. priests wasn't primarily their fault. "One would have to ask if the real culprit," he said, "is not a society that is irresponsibly permissive, hyper-inflated with sexuality and capable of creating circumstances that induce even people who have received a solid moral formation to commit grave moral acts." Not content to stop there, Navarro-Valls accused the media of sensationalism, saying that the number of priests implicated in the U.S. — about 400 so far — is little more than 1% of all American priests, and probably less than that found in other sectors of the general population.[84]

Such defiance is only going to further reduce the value of Roman Catholic Church holdings on the North American religious stock exchange. Damage control may sometimes require admission of guilt, followed closely by a clearly articulated remedial plan. That message, quite obviously, has not got through to the Vatican.

Beyond playing defence in the face of charges, there are times when the churches should also be playing offence. They need, for instance, to publicly distance themselves from events done "in the name of God" that have the potential to seriously damage their image and thereby severely hamper their ability to minister. Well-known evangelical John Redekop of Wilfrid Laurier University says, "We watch with both revulsion and understandable fascination, and usually without public comment, as the Branch Davidians or some other outlandish deviants create deception and havoc." The church, he continues, has "waited for government and the secular press to expose and oppose evil done in the name of God" before raising its voice. The church has traditionally been silent, he maintains, when "people who claimed to be Christians" mistreated aboriginal Canadians, sexually abused children, and "made a mockery of Christianity" by exploiting people through television.[85] The silence of which Redekop speaks not only is ethically irresponsible, it is organizationally disastrous.

Playing offence with image also means that religious groups need to speak out when they are being unfairly represented. Brian Stiller, for example, did what I think groups need to do when, in early 1993, he objected to a Leon's Furniture advertisement. The ad used a caricature of an American televangelist and made use of the word "miracle" in playing on the hucksterism many associate with televangelism. Stiller, the executive director of the Evangelical Fellowship of Canada, said that while EFC is not interested in defending American televangelists, the ad amounted to Leon's use of its "economic muscle to ridicule a particular expression of faith." In his letter to the company, Stiller asked, "Would you allow your advertising agency to develop a commercial built on the ways and styles of . . . the Hasidic Jews? Or a particular movement within the Hindu faith or Canadian native spirituality? I think not." He asked that Leon's discontinue the advertisement.[86]

Similarly, when the *Winnipeg Free Press* published a series of 14 articles from May 1 to 4, 1993, linking Mennonites to drug trading, charging that "Mexican Mennonites are smuggling large amounts of marijuana into Canada," the Manitoba Mennonite community did not sit back. Groups of Mennonite leaders, including well-known religion journalist Harold Jantz, met with editors of the paper to challenge the stereotyping and with the RCMP to clarify the situation. Editor Duncan McMonagle gave Mennonites space in the *Free Press* to put the smuggling issue into perspective, while the RCMP acknowledged the very limited level of Mennonite involvement. Winnipeg's Jewish Community Council was among those offering support, with one spokesman saying he was "very much disturbed" by the articles and the prominence they gave to the ethnic backgrounds of those involved.[87] It seems to have been a good effort at damage control.

For a Good Time, Don't Phone the Churches

Organized religion's image problems are not limited to its credibility crisis. There's an ongoing problem with how religion tends to be viewed. Survey after survey documents what we all know well: first and foremost people want to enjoy life. What's up for debate is how they can find happiness. Here's where religion does not come in.

When Canadians think of spontaneity and fun, few think of religion. For most, religion is perceived as synonymous with rules, rigidity, and righteousness. Take, for example, the Salvation Army. It has managed to escape the wrath that the public has been reigning on religious leaders. George Gallup recently commented that, when it comes to respect shown charitable groups, his extensive polls have found that the Army "has always been right at the top of the list."[88] Nonetheless, the Army is well aware it has a serious image problem. It might be associated with kindness, but it isn't very often associated with fun — the very name "Army" precludes levity. Further, most people don't even know that the Salvation Army is a denomination, complete with buildings, worship services, and congregational programs. The net result is that many Canadians would be happy to give the Army a few bucks. Few, however, would be inclined to join it.

The PROJECT CANADA surveys of adults and teenagers clearly document how religion is ranked when Canadians think of the things that make them happy. Relationships, music, and one's home are near the top, followed by career, television, sports, and even their pets. *Right at the bottom* — viewed as an important source of happiness by only about 30% of adults and 15% of teenagers — is one's religious group.

TABLE 9.3. **SELECT SOURCES OF ENJOYMENT FOR TEENAGERS AND ADULTS**		
% Indicating Receiving "A Great Deal" or "Quite a Bit" of Enjoyment		
	Adults	Teenagers
Friendships	92	93
Your marriage/relationship	88	69
Music	81	89
Your own home/room	79	68
Job/school	57	43
Television	53	61
Sports	45	67
Your pet(s)	41	48
Your religious group	32	15
SOURCES: PROJECT CAN90 and PROJECT TEEN CANADA 92.		

But surely, you say, weekly attenders get a great deal of enjoyment from church life. Not really. To be fair, if we add the "great deal" and "quite a bit" figures together, we come up with 78% for adults who are weekly churchgoers, and 50% for teenagers. But let's really be fair: if we stop with those who exuberantly say they get a "great deal" of enjoyment from church life, the level for weekly attending adults dips to 43%; in the case of teens who are there every week, it falls to 24%.

Beyond quibbling about the feelings of the faithful, what is perhaps most important about the enjoyment findings is what they say about the image that people on the margins have of what's taking place in the churches. It's hard to imagine that many people, young or old, look forward to services with the keen anticipation accorded a rock concert, *Phantom of the Opera,* or a major sporting event. Speaking to 1,400 people who gathered for a conference in Hamilton recently, Paul Cain of the Kansas City Vineyard Fellowship didn't beat around the bush: "The church of the New Testament scares people to death," he said, while "the church of the twentieth century bores people to death."[89]

As for organized religion's appeal to teenagers specifically, Tony Plomp, a well-known Presbyterian, acknowledges that "most of our congregations have not discovered how to appeal effectively to contemporary youth. Our music is not particularly attractive to the Much Music generation. Our messages from the pulpit require concentration and thought and the discipline of listening, a skill few develop as they watch easy-to-absorb, flashy, fast-paced television shows." Plomp further notes that sermons are frequently out of touch with young people, while services are often too formal and "lack the excitement which many crave."[90]

People who value faith have maintained historically that religion, for all the demands it may make, nonetheless enriches life. Presumably, such enrichment translates somewhere along the line into an enhanced sense of happiness and well-being. If such is still the case, religious groups have been doing a very poor selling job. They haven't delivered the message that "faith can be fun."

Find yourself recoiling at the phrase? Some people do. On occasion, I've had critics suggest to me that religion is a serious matter, that enjoyment is hardly something people should expect from the churches.

Too bad. If that's the case, then the churches have little to bring to Canadians who want to be able to laugh and enjoy life, especially when they have to endure some things that aren't all that great. If the image the committed want to sell is one of seriousness and solemnity, they have done their work well.

Hopefully, though, there are still a good number of church people out there who believe that, while religious faith is demanding, it also can enrich life and make people smile. Dr. Arthur Van Seters, the principal of Knox Theological College in Toronto, has written recently that a group like Presbyterians should be among them. "Enjoying God doesn't exactly have a Presbyterian ring to it — at first," he says. "But the Westminster Catechism does say, in fact, that our chief purpose in life is to 'glorify and enjoy' God. This is more than knowing; it is a feeling, an emotional expression out of a deeply personal relationship."[91] People like Van Seters, however, have a major public relations job in front of them.

The popularity of Jack Kapica's frequent columns on religious jokes in the *Globe and Mail* suggests that there are a good many Canadians who both feel a measure of affinity with religion and also enjoy a good laugh.[92] And yes, that Fellowship of Merry Christians I wrote about in *Fragmented Gods* is still going strong, at last count distributing its monthly *Joyful Noiseletter* to some 20,000 members.[93]

It's not all just a laughing matter. Palmo Carpino, a part-time Catholic youth minister in Calgary, has been on the comedy club circuit for more than a decade. In making use of humour in ministry, Carpino comments that it "is a way of breaking down barriers and feeling comfortable with people." It helps them to get away from the belief "that a person's faith is something that's only done for one hour on Sunday and is very straitlaced."[94]

Peter Berger makes the further point that one of the functions of humour is that it allows us to "bracket" even the painful and tragic experiences of life and in so doing imply that "the imprisonment is not final but will be overcome."[95] The late British writer Malcolm Muggeridge wrote shortly before his death: "There is a close connection between clowns and mystics. Laughter is indeed God's therapy."[96]

It would be most fortunate if, in the course of their preoccupation with issues such as justice and peace, religious groups could not also show battle-weary Canadians that life is lived most enjoyably and productively when we keep our balance with good amounts of humour. Societies need it; souls need it. To the extent that religion puts the temporary into perspective and knows that life and history are never out of control, it should be associated, not only with strength and confidence, but also with much joy.

The Marginalizing of Women

It's not a new problem, but women's inferior place in religious groups still has not been clearly resolved. In the 1990s the churches continue to be viewed by many as sexist patriarchal organizations. Unfortunately the perception is true in more than a few group instances — beyond, incidentally, the Roman Catholic Church.

- An editorial in the October 1992 issue of the *Anglican Journal* stated: "Within the Anglican Church of Canada there are disconcerting signs that the voice of women — never very strong — is diminishing." According to the editorial, women were sitting on fewer rather than more national committees than just three years earlier. "Without a quota," the writer argued, "it is entirely probable that, even though they are a majority in the pews, women will remain a minority voice in the church."[97]
- Many Baptist women in Western Canada, says active lay member Janet Atwood, "are frustrated, angry, and hurt by their male-dominated homes and churches," and are losing hope.[98] Among them is Ann Adrian, a Vancouver lawyer and Baptist church member, who writes: "I bear the scars of the struggle, as do many of my sisters of my generation. My concerns have been patronized, trivialized. Today I no longer actively participate in the life of the church. I still attend the worship service." She adds, "However, I'm tired."[99]
- Two Canadian Mennonite conferences, the Brethren and Evangelical, do not allow women to be ordained, while two do — the Mennonite Church and General Conference.[100] Some ten to 15 Winnipeg women, calling themselves "post-Mennonite survivors," have formed a support group for women who have left the church because of abuse they have suffered at the hands of Mennonites. One member said she could not distinguish between the rigidity and judgmentalism of the church and the abuse she experienced personally at home.[101]
- A Lutheran lay person has recently complained that her church has not been sufficiently vocal in condemning sexual abuse, tending instead to opt for silence and the protection of the gender status quo. It's time, she says, for the church to treat women with the dignity it shows men.[102]
- As of the 1990s, Christian Reformed leaders were still debating whether women should be allowed to hold the church's highest offices, including elder, minister, and evangelist. Indicative of the

ambivalence, its North American all-male synod — about 25% of which is Canadian — tentatively approved inclusion by a close vote of 95–88 in 1993. Prior to the vote, anticipation of official approval had already contributed to a defection of members; an acceleration of secessions was consequently anticipated.[103]

- An official recently informed me that women who graduate from Pentecostal theological colleges have great difficulty finding congregations that want them as pastors. The ministers and boards of many Pentecostal churches, along with grassroots evangelical congregations, continue to be disproportionately male — in sharp contrast to the makeup of their memberships.

- Even at the United Church's 1992 general council in Fredericton, it was noted: "Women were still going later than men to the microphones, and going in half the numbers." One female delegate from Halifax suggested: "It has a lot to do with the traditional roles women have played in the church."[104] An ordained minister, Gloria Miller, says there are still subtle signs of condescension toward women in the denomination, with women often among those most resistant to change.[105]

Further, women's groups that have been an organizational asset to denominations, such as United Church Women and Evangelical Lutheran Women, are frequently seen as things of the past. Gwen Hawkins, the editor of the ELW's national women's magazine, noted recently, "As older women pass from the scene, we have to have something to offer younger women."[106] Dorothy MacNeill, a charter member of the 30-year-old United Church Women, comments that the UCW has an increasingly old membership, has not been at the forefront of the inclusive language struggle, and is often viewed as synonymous with serving food and selling baked goods. The recruitment of equality-minded women, she suggests, will be increasingly difficult.[107] And Alexandra Cyngiser, who has been active in the Women's League for Conservative Judaism in Calgary, comments, "We, as women, approach the future confidently and unafraid," adding, "I have defined my own stance regarding Judaism." But the question, she says, is how to pass that feeling on to the next generation.[108]

Obviously, many changes have been taking place. As early as the 1930s, a woman, Evangeline Booth, held the highest existing rank in the Salvation Army worldwide. From 1986 through 1993, a second woman, Eva Burrows, held the same position of General.[109] Responses to the need for gender equality can be seen in such areas as inclusive language and the acceptance of the ordination of women, along with heightened sensitivity to women performing similar roles to that of men in denominations and local congregations.[110] Symbolic of the goals of some groups, the Bloor Street United congregation in Toronto chose a black woman to play Jesus in its 1993 Passion Play presentation. The reason, said minister Robert Oliphant, was to present the story in a more universal light to break through gender and colour barriers.[111]

Individually and collectively, religious groups have denounced violence against women. In March 1992, for example, the four major mainline Protestant groups joined forces with the Canadian Conference of Catholic Bishops and the Evangelical Fellowship of Canada, as well as other organizations, to present a submission to the federal government's Canadian Panel on Violence Against Women.[112] The World Council of Churches has declared the years 1988 to 1998 the "Ecumenical Decade of Churches in Solidarity with Women in Church and Society."[113]

But at this point in time, the image that many and perhaps most women in Canada have of religious groups is far from that of social organizations where upwardly mobile, successful, and equality-minded women can feel at home. Feminism and faith are still a questionable match. Ann Adrian describes her feeling of discouragement:

> I am tired of church services led exclusively by men; I'm tired of hymns, readings and sermons which exclude over half the congregation because we are female; I'm tired of nobody caring that we feel excluded; I'm tired of the church espousing traditional values while ignoring today's realities; I'm frustrated that women are often limited by their sex rather than by their abilities; I'm disillusioned by a theological interpretation of Scripture which offers liberation on one hand and unilateral subordination on the other. Is there hope for the future? I must truthfully answer that, from my experience, I feel there is very little."[114]

Perhaps her feelings are shared by only a minority of women who attend church. But the fact that such feelings still exist in the early 1990s reveals that gender equality is still an elusive dream in at least some religious settings.

It also needs to be pointed out that steps such as ordination do not necessarily eliminate sexism. A recent study of about 125 Mennonite women pastors in the two North American denominations that ordain them came up with some disturbing news. The study was conducted by Renée Sauder, who carried out the research before returning to the pastorate in Waterloo. She found that most of the women in reality are serving as co-pastors with their husbands — 70% said they would not have been hired without their spouses. While the women were reasonably successful at finding entry-level positions, subsequent upward mobility tended to be difficult. Further, 24% of all women pastors and 34% of those not co-pastoring with husbands said they had been sexually harassed in their church settings by congregational members, usually on Sunday mornings.[115] These kind of findings hardly signal the arrival of gender equality.

Nancy Nason-Clark, a sociologist at the University of New Brunswick, sums up what churches would actually look like if women and men were equal partners:[116]

- The gender breakdown of the local church board or governing council would not differ from the nursery school roster.
- The proportion of women on the platform would approximate the proportion of women in the pews.
- The language and liturgy of worship and instruction would be inclusive of the diversity among believers.
- The full expanse of the church's ministry would have men and women serving as partners on the basis of talent, willingness to serve, and spiritual maturity.
- The programs offered to the congregation and community would represent the full range of needs and experiences of ordinary women and men, boys and girls alike.

Many women clearly can't be bothered with it all; this side of revolution, change takes a lot of time. Despite whatever progress has been taking place in the churches, the research finding is perhaps telling: to the extent that Canadian women believe they do not have enough power in our national life, they are less inclined than women who are not concerned about insufficient power to bother with religious groups, value religion, or have confidence in religious leaders (see TABLE 9.4).

Perceptions of Women's Power	N	Attend Weekly	Religion Very NB	Confidence in Relig Leaders
"Too Little"	406	22	24	33
"Right Amount"	172	29	37	37
"Too Much"	17	56	58	55

TABLE 9.4. RELIGIOUS CORRELATES OF PERCEPTION OF POWER: CANADIAN WOMEN

In %'s

SOURCE: PROJECT CAN90.

To be successful, organizations have to be structurally sound. I am maintaining that Canada's religious groups have a number of structural problems that make it difficult for them to function effectively:

- They rely on volunteers and frequently emphasize the local outlet over the national company.
- They are extremely vulnerable to the debilitating effects of social change; their assessment of innovation tends to be slow and divisive, which is often costly, in distracting them from their ministry goals.
- Their image as religious organizations has not been very positive, especially in light of the negative publicity they have received in recent years, the ongoing disinclination of people to associate religion with enjoyment, and the tendency of religious groups to be seen as patriarchal and sexist.

The problems, however, go much further than personnel, flexibility, and image.

10

PRODUCT PROBLEMS

I n her best-selling book about cultural trends and their impact on the economic marketplace, Faith Popcorn proclaims the prevalent rule of the day: "Ask not what your consumer can do for you but what you can do for your consumer." Winning over the consumer, she says, depends on how much extra you can actually deliver: the "Product, plus, plus, plus."[1]

Popcorn is describing, of course, what has come to be known as the marketing concept. According to the concept, the key to business success is determining the needs and wants of target markets and proceeding to deliver products more effectively and efficiently than competitors. The central element is customer satisfaction; the buzz word is "consumer sovereignty."

By way of background, the marketing concept is seen by observers as representing the third era in North American business.[2] The first was the *production* era, extending from the late 19th century into the early part of the 20th. Its emphasis was on the efficient mass production of goods. An old line ascribed to Henry Ford sums up the uniformity mood: "The customers can have any color car they want as long as it is black."[3] Between the 1920s and early 1950s, there was a shift to the *sales* era. Here the prevalent thinking was that products needed to be *sold*. It was a time when salespeople and advertising were seen as the key players in persuading people that they needed what was being offered.

With the early 1950s came the beginning of the *marketing* era. The efficient production and extensive promotion of products, so the new thinking went, provided no guarantee that customers would buy them. What companies had to do was find out what customers wanted and go out and produce it — a total reversal from the sales era's emphasis on producing a product and then trying to convince people they wanted it.

The starting point for proponents of the marketing concept is the consumer. It's where everything begins. Well-worn expressions sum up the outlook: "Find wants and fill them"; "Make what you can sell instead of trying to sell what you can make"; "Love the customer — not the product."[4] In the words of management theorist Peter Drucker, "The aim of marketing is to make selling superfluous. The aim is to know and understand the customer so well that the product fits . . . and sells itself."[5] Successful organizations in the 1990s know their clientele and know what they are delivering.

What does all this have to do with religion? This: the disparity between Canadians' apparent receptivity to spirituality and their lack of interest in organized religion reveals that the country's religious groups have not done a particularly good job of getting in touch with people's wants and needs. As United Church minister Gordon Turner, the denomination's former head of evangelism and new church development, has put it, "Right now, we're just not scratching where they're itching."[6]

RELEVANCE REVISITED

On the surface, the formula for getting in touch looks fairly simple. Marketing professors like American Philip Kotler and Canadian Gordon McDougall advise us, "The company must make sure that its objectives and product lines remain relevant to the market," adding, "Alert companies will periodically re-examine their objectives, strategies, and tactics."[7]

Relevance, however, is an elusive goal. A topic that intrigues one person often bores another; a cause that stirs one group brings out nothing but apathy from another. Relevance is highly relative.

Consequently any organization that tries to be relevant to many people has to develop a highly diversified product line to appease its highly diversified clientele. Unfortunately, in doing so, the organization runs the risk of spreading itself too thin. Instead of doing one thing or a few things very well, it may end up doing a large number of things with remarkable mediocrity — and so lose customers to the specialist who offers superior quality and efficiency.

In case you missed it, department stores are facing a tough present and a tougher future. They are losing market shares to specialty outlets of the small and warehouse variety. The percentage of total retail sales claimed by department stores dropped from 10.8% in 1981 to 7.2% in 1991. In 1992 the figure slipped to around 6.5%. "If it continues," says Toronto retail analyst John Winter, "there aren't going to be any department stores left."[8]

What's true of the department stores is also true of the local congregation. When it comes to relevance, it's hard to please everybody. An attempt to do so can be fatal. A TV commercial has expressed the need to be specific this way: "Like grandma always said, do one thing and do it better than the other guy."[9] Whether or not Grandma actually said it, the line is worth taking seriously. Gordon Turner, in applying the principle to the United Church, writes: "The church is in a highly competitive marketplace. If we are to survive we need to be deeply aware of what it is we are offering." He adds, "And we must offer it well and with credibility."[10]

Irrelevant Relevance

Peter Berger made the observation that relevance is at best "a very fragile business."[11] In the case of religious groups, it's not just a matter of relevance being elusive. Since groups claim to take their cues from sources other than culturally grounded customs, relevance may be largely irrelevant.

This is where religious groups have to modify the marketing concept. The companies involved with snacks or footwear might start by asking the potential customers what new chip dip or running shoe they would like — and then manufacture them and put them in the stores. But religious groups presumably don't determine what they will offer simply in response to market research.

Rather, the devout ideally have a clear sense of what it is that they are *supposed* to bring to culture. To cater to whims or fleeting interests is to succumb to culture and provide a religion that is nothing more than a response to consumer demand. Ron Rempel, editor of the *Mennonite Reporter*, sums up the situation this way: "If the church does not meet people's needs, it may find itself with no people. However, if the consumer approach takes over completely, the church could lose its distinctiveness in the long run."[12] The message of the churches is not consumer-driven; in theory, at least, it's driven by the gods.

Relevance Rediscovered

But that doesn't mean there is necessarily a contradiction between what people say they want and what religion has to bring. On the contrary, one would like to believe that if in fact religious groups have received their lines from gods who care about people, the message that's passed on — be it "to comfort or to challenge"[13] — would strike a responsive chord with the needs of a good many of the populace.

What's required are careful readings of where people are — what they want and need. And then, with integrity, groups need to draw on religion's resources and respond to those wants and needs, at minimum as a starting point in sharing their faith with Canadians.

In the midst of our preoccupation with empty pews, it's important to keep in mind that *not all churches are empty.*

- Sitting at that religious pep rally I referred to earlier, I found myself looking around at the 400-plus present on a Sunday night and concluding, "They must be in touch with something, even if I'm not sure what it is."
- In highly secular Vancouver, where Sunday mornings are made for relaxation and Sunday evenings for still more relaxation, an Anglican church — yes, an Anglican church — is drawing about 500 people to its Sunday evening services. St. John's Shaughnessy features "a contemporary service with lively music" and is packing the church with people whose average age is estimated to be 29. Stephen James, the former minister, observed, "We found that people really want to know about God. They're incredibly hungry."[14]

These two snapshots, set alongside those of empty cathedrals with small elderly congregations, lead to at least one modest conclusion: the products are very different. In the packed churches, a responsive chord is being struck. Sometimes it may mean little more than the fact that the best religious show is being staged, and the saints are coming out in droves.

It could mean a great deal more.

Historically, religion in its diverse forms has had much to say about that part of reality that lies beyond what can be comprehended by the senses. Religion has also given considerable attention to the question of how individuals can find personal fulfillment. Still further, it has given no little play to the topic of interpersonal relations.

In short, as I argued in *Fragmented Gods,* faiths generally and Christianity specifically have traditionally focused on three major themes — God, self, and society. Religion has assumed that all three are relevant, indeed, centrally important, to the human condition. As such, they constitute the heart of religion's message. To emphasize only one or two of the themes is to dilute what faith can bring to culture. To offer them in integrated form is to offer Canadians a powerful religious package.

SOME QUESTIONABLE PRODUCT LINES

As we have seen, to look at Canadian culture is to observe clear signs of extensive interest in all three of these areas. Yet to varying degrees, in their attempts to be relevant, Canada's religious groups have failed to be three-dimensional. Somewhat ironically, in the process they have become largely irrelevant to the vast majority of Canadians. Here are some examples.

Playing Down God

Canadians are interested in God. They not only believe in God in overwhelming numbers, 40% to 50% think they have experienced God. God is extremely popular, even if religion is not. The same goes for supernatural questions generally.

Rather than decreasing, intrigue with the supernatural seems to be on the rise. Supernatural ideas have gained considerable credibility in recent years. They've been the subject of top-grossing films, the focus of media features, and the object of scientific investigation.

It therefore is strange that organized religion has been so inept at capitalizing on such a blatant opportunity. A quick scan of the emphases of Canada's religious groups provides us with some clues as to the apparent ineptitude. It's easy to oversimplify here; nonetheless, I think we can readily spot some fairly distinguishable patterns. You be the judge.

- Many mainline Protestants are cautious when it comes to explicit talk about supernatural realities and possibilities. Yet there are telling contradictions. Some clergy, I suspect, would not be particularly comfortable talking about being possessed by the Holy Spirit. But they would willingly engage in a conversation about a person having an out-of-body experience. They might not get excited about discussing the prospects for a literal heaven, complete with streets of gold. But they'd be fairly at ease discussing the possibilities surrounding reincarnation.
- Roman Catholics and conservative Protestants are quite comfortable

discussing God and life after death; however, they cringe when someone murmurs about being able to communicate with the dead or claims to have psychic powers.

Between the mainliners being suspect of supernatural emphases and Roman Catholics and conservative Protestants being wary of unconventional ideas, the collective result is that Canada's religious groups are doing at best only a partial job of responding to the market for the supernatural. Little wonder that Canadians turn to quasireligious organizations in order to supplement their religious diets.

Illustrative of what is possible yet what is actually occurring are the recent observations of two Presbyterians, former moderator John Cameron and Carleton law professor Margaret Ogilvie. Cameron has written that the Christian faith continues to be well equipped to speak to the widespread search for meaning. "The message of Easter and the resurrection," he says, can "add a new vision of life and a new quality to life's experiences."[15] Yet Ogilvie has been pointed in suggesting that Presbyterians need to do a better job of focusing on this unique "God" dimension, as opposed to other programs and issues. "Where a barbecue attracts 60 members and a Bible study group only six," she says, "there are one too many activities offered and the barbecue must go." She continues, "Nor, I hasten to add, is the purpose of Bible study 'to have a great time and meet new people' as announced by an elder recently. . . . We must restore the sense that a Christian community is Christian first and last; otherwise, community activities are simply secular gatherings — the congregation as social club." Similarly, she says, the social concerns to which the church gives its attention need to be "determined strategically in accordance with doctrinal identity. Jumping on every politically correct bandwagon should be avoided." The church should have something unique to say, in contrast to sermons that are "indistinguishable in substantive content from the previous week's newspaper editorials."[16]

Her critique may be overly harsh. Then again, maybe not.

Obviously, people who value faith are free to ignore supernatural phenomena if they so choose. Many do. They opt for rationality and empiricism and regard the sheer exploration of the supernatural as inappropriate — both for themselves and others. In lieu of viewing topics like the gods, a spirit world, and life after death as acceptable areas of exploration, some assume that highly subjective inward journeys are the stuff of religious quest.

The result of such a choice, however, is a limited connection with Canadians, both young and old, very large numbers of whom say they are puzzled about the purpose of life, think a spirit world may exist, and increasingly believe in reincarnation. Reflecting on the issue of life after death, for example, Tom Harpur writes that there's "a major paradox in the fact that, while more people than ever are concerned about dying and what may lie beyond, fewer and fewer turn to traditional religion to find the answers they seek." Not only, he says, do people find limited help in what the churches teach, but many of the churches avoid the topic altogether. His indictment needs to be taken seriously: "Indeed, in many ways the present spiritual searching in our culture is a rebuke to organized religion and suggests that its essential message is failing to communicate reasonable answers to life's most basic and most urgent concerns."[17]

Michael Steinhauser of the Toronto School of Theology states the importance of the "God" issue this way: Canadians "are searching for the supernatural and spiritual dimension of their lives" that has been "lost in the complexity of modern society." Their voices need to be heard by people who, in turn, are "in contact with the supernatural and spiritual in their own lives." He adds, "Only through contact with one's own spiritual depths can one hope to minister to the void of others."[18] In many instances, the experience and the response of which he speaks seem to be missing.

Many people in religious circles may not know it, but one of the most outstanding contemporary champions of justice in Canada is a person by the name of Aziz Khaki. Since coming to Canada from Africa in the 1970s, this Muslim minister has worked tirelessly to enrich life for all Canadians. He has given his life to the pursuit of a more just country, serving on national and regional task forces. He also has attempted to bring people of diverse faiths together, organizing and presiding over the Pacific Interfaith Citizenship Association of British Columbia, while also being a founding member of the North American Interfaith Network.

In his diverse roles, Khaki has befriended prime ministers, premiers, and cabinet ministers, along with Pope John Paul II and the Dalai Lama. He told me recently that one of the puzzling characteristics he finds about many Christian clergy is that they are reluctant to talk explicitly about God — as if it somehow involves an overstepping of interfaith boundaries. "I talk about God," he says, "but even though it's clear that they think in terms of God, many of them don't openly refer to God." He added, "We have to talk about God; otherwise, we're not any different from anyone else."[19]

M. Scott Peck makes a similar point. In attempting to bring the idea of God and community to the world of business, he says he is "profoundly aware of how strange" words like God and the Holy Spirit must sound to most executives. Even those who are most deeply religious, he suggests, haven't typically "thought of what it would be like to let God into their organizations." However, writes Peck, "there is no other way for me to talk about it. [We] struggled to develop some sort of marketing language that would not have to use such words as 'God' or 'love.' Eventually we gave up. We have to call a spade a spade."[20]

Canadians, like people everywhere, think in terms of the gods. They need to hear more about them from the churches. The problem in Canada, however, is summed up in Thomas Luckmann's critique of religion in the Western world: "Although the specialized religious institutions have not entirely abandoned traditional Christian rhetoric, this rhetoric increasingly expresses reconstructions of transcendence that have only a tenuous relation to the traditional Christian universe."[21]

Playing Down Self

Since the publication of *Fragmented Gods,* I've had to put up with a lot of critics troubled that I've had the audacity to suggest that religion has some good things to say about self. Schooled, in many instances, in theological thinking that deprecates the individual, they literally have accused me of sounding like TV evangelist Robert Schuller or someone who unconsciously has been co-opted by the New Agers.

I get more than a little upset with the criticism. My point in 1987 was the same as it is today: large numbers of Canadians want to be able to feel good about themselves. There's a lot of pain and suffering and anguish out there. If religion has something to say to these people that can result in their finding resources and hope that translate into their feeling better about themselves, others, and life, then religion needs to say it.

If, on the other hand, religion has little or nothing to offer when it comes to self-affirmation and personal hope, then the last person for the committed to get upset with is the sociologist. He's simply saying there's a tremendous opportunity in our day to respond to the widespread need for self-affirmation. If those who value faith have nothing to say, that's unfortunate. The business they could have had is headed elsewhere.

I, for one, am naive enough to believe that religion generally and Christianity specifically have much to say about self-affirmation. I think of biblical ideas such as our being created "in God's image" or our having the potential to become "children of God." Perhaps I'm missing something, but it seems to me that imagery like that provides powerful affirmation concerning what people can become, why they can feel good about themselves, why they can have hope.

In the area of self-affirmation, some of Canada's religious groups seem to be doing a better job than others:

- The mainline groups appear to score reasonably well here, if not always. Reflecting on the three themes in the summer of 1987, the late Toronto archbishop Lewis Garnsworthy said to me, "We Anglicans are doing a pretty good job when it comes to God and society. But we're still not doing a very good job when it comes to self. We're still singing hymns about, 'Such a worm as I.'"
- Roman Catholics and conservative Protestants have both known traditions where self-denial has been a dominant theme. Any semblance of self-affirmation has been commonly equated with pride and the glorification of self. It has not always been easy for Catholics and evangelicals to feel good about themselves.

A few years ago at an evangelical conference where I spoke on this theme, an attractive young woman rose to her feet during the response period. With considerable emotion, she said to the audience:

Look at me — I'm an example of what he's been talking about. For years I haven't been able to feel good about myself. I've felt guilty for my looks, my talents, my energy. As a result, I've been in therapy for the last four years trying to straighten out my life.

It's not easy to be an active part of a Protestant group that stresses self-denial, citing such role model biblical verses as "I am crucified with Christ; nevertheless I live — yet not I . . ." without feeling some effects. Similarly, it's not a breeze to be a part of a Roman Catholic parish where one is constantly being reminded of the ongoing need for forgiveness of sin without feeling that one is constantly falling short.

Regardless of the specifics of a person's theology, surely the flip side of sin is the message of forgiveness, new beginnings, newfound strength, hope. It's not just that one's sins have been taken care of; it's also that a person can literally find new life.

Religion has the potential here to make a major contribution in the instilling of hope — the belief that the page will turn and that one's spirit and life will be renewed. The old insightful cliché, "Where there's hope, there's life," still holds. It's a message religion over the centuries has been able to bring to people. At its best, it has been accompanied by a caring religious community. Now is hardly the time to suppress either the message or the support.

I spoke earlier, in chapter 6, of George Campbell and Lesley Parrott, who had tragically lost their children. In the aftermath of his son's suicide, Campbell wrote: "My wife and I clung to each other. Our sons and our parents held us and tried to comfort us. But it wasn't enough." He went on to say, "In the depths of our grief and despair we were led, literally by the hand, to a man who was able to help us. His name was Tom Kidd. He was the pastor of the local Lutheran church. . . . Through Tom and that little Lutheran church, our family found the promised comfort and peace of Jesus Christ."[22]

Parrott, whose daughter was murdered in 1986, acknowledges that the goodness of those who have supported her has not taken "the pain away" or diminished "the evil that has been done." Yet, she says, in part, because of a warm and loving Christian upbringing, she has "been able to recognize, accept and embrace goodness when I have needed it." A member of Bloor Street United Church in Toronto, Parrott offers these powerful words: "I believe we cannot wait till tragedy strikes to reach out and show that the power of love is more pervasive than the power of evil. Let's make sure that love, caring and joy are so strong that when we confront evil, we are able to survive and emerge as victors."[23]

Canadians, like people everywhere, are in need of hope that affirms life and affirms self. Sometimes it's because they need a new chance; at other times, it's because they need to be freed from debilitating emotional pain. The message of the possibility of new beginnings is one that needs to be heard. It not always is.

One final observation. I believe that religion has the chance to do something different and highly significant in the area of self-affirmation. By calling people to go beyond viewing themselves as victims in traction, own their biographies, and go forward with life, religion can make an invaluable cultural contribution.

Stimulated in part by the 1992 publication of Charles Sykes's *A Nation of Victims: The Decay of the American Character,* there's a growing realization that we, like the Americans, are in danger of creating a "society of victims" in which everyone feels that their problems have been created by someone or something else.[24] The list of these seems endless — world and national history, economics, politicians, fathers and mothers, ethnicity, gender, age, physical characteristics. . . . The growing range of abuse possibilities goes far beyond severe physical and sexual forms. "Abuse" is in danger of becoming a catchall term assigned indiscriminately to any and every form of perceived negative influence.

Last week a friend told me about a co-worker who had been "abused." The woman felt abused because her parents had been Jehovah's Witnesses, and she had grown up exposed to their narrow and rigid view of the world. If we are allowed to so liberally interpret our biographies, all of us can see ourselves as the victim-products of something.

Not surprisingly, increasing numbers of self-described victims are showing up in the churches, mainline and conservative alike. Baptist official Don Anderson, for example, has commented that, in conformity with evangelical entry requirements, many new congregational members claim that their lives have been transformed. In reality, however, many "seem to live in 'the old' as abused victims, injured parties, or helpless addicted individuals. The church," he says, "is cluttered with chronic-care patients" who demand tremendous amounts of "time, care and energy from an overloaded pastor, or from me."[25]

As a sociologist, I have more than an average appreciation for the effects of social environment on people. But somewhere along the way, it became rather obvious to me that while it's fine to chronicle its influence in our lives, we have to assume some personal responsibility for what happens. More important, if our lives are to be raised to a new level, we have to decide what we will do from this point on. The alternative is stay in a perpetual state of paralysis. *Vancouver Sun* writer Douglas Todd suggests that while it's not inappropriate for people to point out that they've suffered unfairly, "the challenge for all of us is to avoid the blame game — to get beyond self-interest and build up character and integrity." Ideally, he says, people "acknowledge they've had tough knocks, find someone who believes in them and move on to become productive, compassionate and creative citizens."[26]

Christianity has always been concerned about the need to enhance social environments. But it also has stressed the importance of our personal response to the environments in which we find ourselves. Of particular importance, it has stressed the possibility of redemption — the chance for new beginnings, personally and socially.

In our victim-oriented society, the message of social and personal accountability needs to be recovered, along with the motivation for new beginnings that comes from the belief — the hope — that a better existence is possible. Religion, with integrity, can offer such a message. It's a voice that needs to be heard.[27] To date, however, it's not at all clear that the country's religious groups are sold on the idea that they are in the self-affirmation business.

Playing Up Society

Social life is of central importance to Canadians. Individually, there is nothing we value more than good relationships and family life. Nationally, in the post-1960s, we have been focusing attention on the pursuit of a just and fair society, adopting the key intergroup policies of bilingualism (1969) and multiculturalism (1971), and passing the Charter of Rights and Freedoms (1982). Aboriginal issues have also become prominent concerns. Internationally, recent decades have seen a significant increase in global awareness, stimulated by communication and transportation advances and the movement toward a worldwide economy, as well as our having a common stake in environmental matters.

Religion, in speaking to the everyday concerns of Canadians, has needed to address relational issues — beginning with primary interpersonal ties, then extending outward to community, region, nation, and world. In the words of Nobel Peace Prize winner Rigoberta Menchu of Guatemala, "It is not enough to just believe and have faith in God. . . . Very many people believe in God, but they don't believe in humanity; and they don't give parts of their lives to build a better world for the rest of humanity."[28]

It's a task religious groups can carry out with total integrity. Religions have had much to say about how we are to relate to one another on all these levels. The Judaeo-Christian tradition has been among those that have emphasized relational ideals such as love, compassion, equality, peace, and the responsible use of resources.

How well have Canada's religious groups fared in the social realm? The general consensus seems to be that they have fared reasonably well.

The **Roman Catholics and mainliner Protestants** — led by the United Church — have made social issues a very high priority in recent years. To varying degrees, they have been directly involved in responding to social concerns both in Canada and abroad. Further, the two groups have been lobbying and speaking out on issues through a number of structures — the Canadian Council of Churches, the Canadian Conference of Catholic Bishops, and the World Council of Churches. Statements from Bishop Remi De Roo, for example, attacking "socially irresponsible capitalism" as "immoral and a distortion of what should be a creative partnership," have become familiar to Canadians.[29] Catholics and mainliners have co-operated in such initiatives as PLURA in addressing poverty, and programs including Ten Days for World Development in responding to global concerns.[30]

The **conservative Protestants** have had a mixed record. Some denominations still seem to follow the edict that the only way to change society is to change individuals. Consequently they continue to target personal salvation as the primary pathway to the alleviation of society's ills. Other evangelicals, however, are committed to combining an emphasis on changing individuals with tackling social concerns head-on:

- The Salvation Army had its origins in social ministry and continues to make extraordinary contributions in Canada and some one hundred other countries; its well-known outlets for serving people exist from British Columbia to Newfoundland, and number almost 20,000 worldwide.[31]
- Mennonites have attempted to respond to conditions worldwide through their highly acclaimed Mennonite Central Committee, with close to 1,000 people working in extremely diverse types of ministry in more than 50 countries; Canadian groups gave $16 million to MCC in 1992.[32]
- The high-profile para-church organization World Vision also has been engaged in international development and relief programs, including working with refugees arriving in Canada.

- Concern about Canadian social issues has resulted in the formation of organizations such as Citizens for Public Justice, headed by
Gerald Vandezande. The organization "seeks to promote justice in
Canadian public affairs," responding "to God's call for love, justice
and stewardship through research, education and advocacy."[33] As
Vandezande expressed it on one occasion, "We should not privat-
ize the Christian faith but communicate its radical relevance
through deeds of justice, love and mercy that bring healing and
hope to our wounded world."[34]

- The umbrella organization for conservative Protestants, the Evangelical Fellowship of Canada, has consciously attempted to increase social awareness, in large part through the efforts of its
executive director, Brian Stiller.[35] Illustrative of the emphasis is this
recent EFC ad in its national magazine, *Faith Today:*

> *When* parliament *debated whether to protect the unborn* . . . EFC *was
> there. When* legislators *considered Sunday shopping* . . . EFC *was there.
> When a* court *decided that a board of education could not teach religious
> curriculum* . . . EFC *was there. When a civil servant tried to get our*
> judicial system *to redefine the family to include homosexual unions* . . .
> EFC *was there. And when* media *attacks* (sic) *or distorts* (sic) *evangelical
> beliefs* . . . EFC *is there."*[36]

Particularly in view of their fairly dismal past records, it needs to
be pointed out that both mainliners and conservatives are exhibiting
a growing openness to better understand Canada's aboriginal peoples and to draw upon their spiritual insights and work alongside
them.[37] For example:

- The Canadian Council of Churches designated 1992 as a year of
repentance to mark the 500th anniversary of Columbus's arrival
in the Americas, a time to reflect on the history of Canada from
the perspective of native people and listen to their stories.[38]

- The United Church has followed up its 1984 Sudbury apology with
the establishment of the All Native Circle Conference and the 1992
election of a Cree Indian, Stan McKay, as its moderator. The
previous moderator, Walter Farquharson, told the 67th annual
Alberta and Northwest conference in 1991, "Just as the church was
enriched with feminism in our church, we are enriched with native
spirituality and cross-cultural theological insights."[39]

- Roman Catholics, who one abhorred any sign of religious syncretism, are among those who are incorporating traditional native and Inuit objects, practices, and beliefs into their churches' liturgy. Drums and sweetgrass are sometimes a part of mass; the Bible, crucifix, and candle share space with tobacco, cedar, and stone.[40]
- While Presbyterians and Lutherans have stopped short of official apologies, the executive council of the Anglican Church of Canada in 1993 endorsed a call for an apology to aboriginal people "for the violence done to them as individuals, as cultures and as societies" through residential schools. Its northern diocese of Caledonia, according to Anglican journalist Bill Glisky, "remains a leader in ministry with native peoples," pursuing ministry of the laity, being "in the forefront of support for native land claims," and attempting to make the church as a whole "more aware of the problems facing first peoples."[41]
- Baptists are showing a new willingness to listen to what First Nation peoples have to say, inviting their input in the course of attempting to understand the past more clearly, and to pursue an enhanced future.[42]

With respect to social concerns more generally, **other faith groups,** typically associated with cultural minorities, have tended to focus their social-action efforts on improving the situation of their own people. Among the more prominent have been the Jewish organization B'nai B'rith, and the Committee for Racial Justice, headed by Aziz Khaki. Both organizations have been championing religious freedom and improved interfaith relations in Canada.

All in all, Canada's religious groups have shown a willingness to come to grips with social issues,[43] with even the conservative Protestants making up a fair amount of ground in recent years.[44] Moreover, the country's major groupings are showing a willingness to work together, forming coalitions when their concerns are similar. For example, representatives from the Roman Catholic Church, the Mennonite Central Committee, and the United Church have been among many groups working to help resolve the impasse between the Lubicon Cree in Alberta and the federal and provincial governments.[45]

In the admirable process, however, are unmistakable signs that the country's churches have frequently fragmented their three-dimensional package.

Reconnection's Elusiveness

To be effective, religion has to address *all* three themes at the heart of religion — God, self, and society — starting with God. It's not the sociologist's job to proof text, but for the record, to quote the founder of Christianity, no less, the summation of law and faith lies in "loving God with all our being, and our neighbour as ourself." A Hindu teaching stresses the same three themes — worship and rituals "are only the first step towards realising God. The second is to love and serve our fellow beings. The third is to enlighten and educate ourselves."[46] Anything less than an emphasis on all three themes results in a fragmented, emaciated expression of religion.

- To stress *God* and leave out self and society is to end up with a head-in-the-heavens kind of religion that fails to address one's personal needs, as well as those of others.
- To emphasize *self* without God or society is to run the risk of basking in a narcissistic kind of religion that is neither informed by an authoritative source beyond ourselves, nor inclined to care very much about others.
- To focus on *society* alone is to have a religion that is people-oriented, yet both lacks a spiritual dimension and fails to adequately look after self.

Archbishop Ted Scott, the retired primate of the Anglican Church of Canada, has written that the integration of these emphases is essential both for ministry and for those who seek to minister: "If we fail to care for our own health, and the health of our relationships with nature, with other people, and with God, then God's task and ours become that much more difficult."[47]

Eleanor Barrington, a United Church member from Ottawa, has summed up the importance of this balance well. Active for years in the environmental and parenting movements, she writes: "I came back to the church for a last-ditch antidote to postpolitical depression — a disillusioned activist in search of energy and inspiration." She says she "experienced preaching that offered me genuine personal and political reinforcement. I found a spiritual community that extended itself to outsiders and to the outside world of our needy downtown neighbourhood. People tend just to keep on giving till they give out. It's called burnout, but perhaps it's really spiritual starvation." She makes this succinct observation: "We who do ministry on the very personal and very political fronts get our needs met by a supportive congregation, so we can go out and meet others' needs. Being together in faith aspires us to take on the challenges of social change — one act at a time, one week at a time. It's a vital formula."[48]

The "product" problem that characterizes Canada's major religious groups is that of fragmentation. Groups have been having considerable difficulty putting the three pivotal themes together in the manner of which Barrington speaks. Tom Harpur offers this terse observation:

> [The] search for justice and the "preferential option" for the poor as opposed to a religion of "pie in the sky when you die by and by" — all this is praiseworthy and long overdue. But instead of dealing with both sides of "what God hath joined together," the rush to social justice has left out the matter of personal, spiritual concerns virtually altogether.[49]

In broad strokes:

- Roman Catholics have scored high on God and society — low on self.
- The United Church has been strong on society, acceptable on self — weak on God.
- Anglicans have been solid on society and God — spotty on self.
- Conservative Protestants have been strong on God, terrible on self — weak on society beyond the evangelical community.

An exploration of such patterns among Canadians, using data on the perceived importance of the three themes over time among regular attenders, provides some preliminary support for such impressions (see TABLE 10.1).[50] The analysis reveals that

1. *God* is highly valued by a particularly large number of conservative Protestants, with regular mass attenders in Quebec a distant second.
2. The theme of *self* is given the highest ranking by Quebec Catholics and receives the lowest endorsement from active Anglicans and conservative Protestants.
3. *Society* is most enthusiastically embraced by Quebec Catholics, followed by people who are active in the United Church.

Relative to people involved in Canada's other religious groups, churchgoing Catholics in Quebec show signs of exhibiting a fairly robust God-self-society balance. It may reflect the fact that they are involved in a religious company that has a fairly well-integrated product — at least compared with everybody else.

As we will see shortly, having the best product is an encouraging start. But that by itself isn't enough.

We've been describing only the four main Canadian religious groupings. Are Presbyterians, Lutherans, Mormons, Unitarians, Jews, Hindus, or Bahais faring any better? You who are involved with those groups are in a much better place than I am to say. If any groups are scoring high on all three themes, they are without question clear exceptions to the rule.

TABLE 10.1. **IMPORTANCE OF GOD, SELF, AND SOCIETY THEMES FOR REGULAR ATTENDERS***

% Indicating Have Become "More Important" Over Time.

	N	God	Self	Society
NATIONALLY	346	57	40	55
ROMAN CATHOLIC	180	52	42	61
Outside Quebec	109	48	38	56
Quebec	71	59	47	69
PROTESTANT	150	61	37	51
Anglican	31	46	32	50
United Church	27	55	42	58
Conservative	53	78	34	54

*Regulars = attend twice a month or more.[51]

SOURCE: PROJECT CAN90.

The Indispensable Starting Place

I mentioned that religion, in addressing all three areas, has to start with God. The point is critical to the argument of this book. Following the thinking of Rodney Stark, articulated first with colleague William Bainbridge[52] and later with Roger Finke,[53] religion finds its unique place in representing the gods. Issues such as the meaning of life and what, if anything, lies beyond death cannot be resolved without looking beyond the human and empirical plane. "Some common human desires are so beyond direct, this-worldly satisfaction," Stark has written, "that only the gods can provide them."[54] Phillip Berman, in his book *The Search for Meaning,* has expressed our dilemma this way: "We arrive here, after all, with few clues as to where we came from and with even fewer clues as to where we are headed. Here on earth, between time and eternity, ours is but a fleeting little stopover, the only certainty before us being death."[55]

Consequently a faith that proclaims the gods without addressing self and society may be an *incomplete religion.* But a faith that addresses self and society without addressing the gods *ceases* to be a religion. It has disposed of the "supernatural referent" that distinguishes religious interpretations of life from strictly humanist ones.[56] As such, it is unable to speak to the mysteries of life and death. In time, such expressions will, in fulfillment of Stark's prophecy, be "headed for the sideline."[57]

To be unique in modern cultures where uniqueness is largely an elusive dream, religion has to have the gods as its starting place and proceed to interpret self and society through their eyes. As John Naisbitt puts it, "Science and technology do not tell us what life means. We learn that through literature, the arts, and spirituality."[58] Church-growth expert Leith Anderson is more direct: "The churches of the twenty-first century that flourish among those seeking the supernatural will be the ones that talk about and offer authentic supernatural experiences."[59]

Religions that start with the gods and proceed to embrace self and society provide their host societies with a powerful product. Those that start somewhere else find themselves in trouble. For example an extensive research project carried out on Presbyterians in the U.S. by three highly regarded researchers — Benton Johnson, Dean Hoge, and Donald Luidens — concluded that somehow during the twentieth century, Presbyterian "churches lost the will or the ability to teach the Christian faith and what it requires" to its younger cohorts. The result has been severe membership losses, with the remaining remnant feeling "at home" in churches that do "not seem very important to them." As for the future, they write that "the prospects that [the current members'] offspring will make a serious Christian commitment are even dimmer than their own prospects turned out to be."[60] Similarly, American Rabbi A. James Rudin has recently written that "Rabbis around the country constantly report that each time they preach or teach about spirituality, their synagogues are packed with ardent listeners." He notes that Christian clergy also find that "congregations are eager for guidance on how to find God and, in the process, themselves," while seminary faculty describe "the intense spiritual hunger of their students."[61]

In Canada and elsewhere, the evidence is that God- and spiritual-oriented religions are in touch with what Canadians indicate they want and need. However, to the extent that groups decide either to minimize the gods or to solely embrace them, they grossly devalue their religious product and jeopardize their own futures.

THE EROSION OF TRADITIONAL CUSTOMER BASES

In the 1990s two major Canadian retailers that fell on hard times were Woodwards and Birks. Among the reasons cited for their problems were the companies' efforts to alter their dominant clienteles. Woodwards, after years of being the department store of the common people, attempted near the end of the 1980s to upscale its operation. Analysts say that the chain proceeded to lose many of its original faithful customers, while failing to gain its hoped-for share of the upscale market. Birks, on the other hand, tried to move in the opposite direction, downscaling its previously elitist jewellery stores. But in making the switch, Birks is said to have lost many of its previous high-income customers, while being unable to gain a satisfactory share of somewhat lower-income earners. Both companies in effect lost large chunks of their traditional customer bases.

When religious groups decide to make major changes in what they have to offer, the revisions similarly can have important implications for their own "customer bases." The post-1960s have seen Canada's two largest groups — the Roman Catholic and United churches — make significant changes in their "product lines." From the vantage point of the 1990s, one wonders what has been gained — and what has been lost.

The Roman Catholic Case

Vatican II was supposed to renew the Catholic Church by bringing it into the modern world. Convened by Pope John XXIII, the Council met in Rome from 1962 through the end of 1965. By the Council's end a number of changes had been put into motion. They included celebration of the mass in the vernacular instead of Latin, revised catechisms, and greater consultation between leaders and laity in the governing of the church at all levels. The Council also encouraged the whole of the church — including laity — to become more active in mission. That mission was to be directed to the secular world, with training to be geared not only to understanding faith but understanding culture.[62]

The subsequent reviews have been highly positive. Bishops called to Rome to reflect on post–Vatican II developments maintained in their final report that the recommendations had known a "zealous" response; liturgical changes specifically had been allegedly received "joyfully and fruitfully."[63] In Canada, a 1986 survey that the bishops conducted found that 86% of practising Catholics maintained that the changes in the church since Vatican II had been "mostly for the better."

To be sure, some observers have not been quite as enthusiastic about Vatican II's positive reception. As I reported in *Fragmented Gods,* Anne Roche Muggeridge maintained that the Council had undermined the Church's authority. Writer Robertson Davies, an Anglican, argued that the end of the Latin mass also marked the end of "splendour and beauty" that carried significant mystique. "Rome," he said, "turned her back on the poetry in which lay much of her power." As for the 1986 bishops' survey, it had a severe methodological shortcoming: the sample consisted of active Catholics. Some 95% of those polled were attending mass once a week or more. Of course the people still involved were acting pleased, but the survey results said nothing about the large number of Catholics who ceased to be as active between the 1960s and 1980s; as noted earlier, 85% of Roman Catholics were attending weekly in 1965, compared to a current 40%. The sources of decline undoubtedly are many. At minimum it's safe to say that the Vatican II "product modifications" appear to have done little to halt the decline in participation.

Let's get things in perspective. If General Motors had undertaken a major product change and proceeded to have a dramatic drop in sales, it would have sounded ludicrous to hear top executives acting excited about the results.

The hope of the Roman Catholic Church was that *aggiornamento* — updating — would make the church more attractive and more meaningful to people around the world — including Canada. In this country, at least, it hasn't happened. In their comprehensive study of what has been happening to religion in Quebec in the past two decades, the research committee of the Assembly of Quebec Bishops wrote:

Communities have invested a great deal of effort and resources in the liturgy and the sacramental preparation, especially of children. . . . Several new activities have been developed: family masses, youth masses, shared homilies, celebrations, linked with special events or themes. . . .

Now, however, communities are less creative, for many of these experiences have yielded poor results: those for whom they were intended, young people and those who have drifted away from the church, have not returned to the community. Several of the new activities have now been abandoned. People are exhausted.[64]

Looking at the carnage, Gregory Baum acknowledges that Catholicism has become "more visible in memories, architecture, public symbols and the saints' names given to villages, towns and organizations" than in the number of practising Catholics.[65]

Jean Hamelin has offered this terse summation of the Quebec situation: There has been genuine renewal, "but the noise of the things that are dying still drowns out the voice of the things that are coming to birth."[66]

Obviously some will argue that it's not the international church's fault — that the numerical decline would have taken place anyway, and without the Vatican II changes, losses would have been even more severe.

Maybe. But the harsh reality is that the updating program has been, for the most part, a flop. Canadians in large numbers continue to say they are Roman Catholics and to express interest in God and meaning. The fact that they are not bothering to pursue such interests by looking to the Catholic Church suggests that another international board meeting to update the church is urgently needed.

The United Church Case

At about the same time in the 1960s the Roman Catholic Church was looking to Rome, the United Church of Canada, it could be argued, was looking to Ottawa. Always socially conscious, the country's largest Protestant denomination set its sights on championing equality and justice. Not by chance it found itself in sync with some pivotal government policies.

In the late 1960s and early 1970s, coinciding with the passing of the Official Languages Act in 1969, the United Church began to package itself as a bilingual denomination. As one walks east from Yonge Street, Toronto's main artery, toward the national head office on St. Clair Avenue, the sign L'Église Unie du Canada informs the stranger that this is the place. The English version of the sign, incidentally, appears on the other, less travelled side of the building.

The denomination has also solidly endorsed the federal government's multicultural ideal and has attempted to be a church that reflects the cultural diversity of the country.

One of its past three moderators was a Korean, Rev. Sang Chul Lee, and another an aboriginal, Rev. Stan McKay.

The United Church has also championed the rights of the disadvantaged — women, cultural minorities, aboriginals, the poor, the powerless, the exploited, the abused. Its effort to be an inclusive church has sometimes been costly, most notably in the controversy generated by its willingness to accept homosexuals as full members of the church. Canada has been making progress in the direction of greater equity and improved living for all people. Accordingly, this often maligned denomination deserves credit for the contribution it has made.

There is, however, an important question that needs to be addressed. Allowing for the fact that the United Church has chosen to have a pronounced social-justice emphasis, to what extent has it been offering a product that Canadians — including those with United Church backgrounds — actually want from a religious group?

There is good reason to raise this question. For all its efforts to deal with pressing Canadian issues, the United Church has had little success in attracting young Canadians. The denomination might be prophetic. It might be ahead of its time. It might be paying the necessary price of not being a popular church in the course of confronting culture. But the fact remains that it is being bypassed by more and more people.

No, I'm not talking merely about the disenchantment of people within the church, represented by such organizations as the National Alliance of Covenanting Congregations with its 100 or so member congregations, the Community of Concern with its focus on structural reform, the evangelically oriented United Church Renewal Fellowship, or the conservative-minded Church Alive. Their existence in itself suggests noteworthy alienation.[67]

I'm also not talking about its declining membership, which is even more indicative of the fact that the United Church may not be in touch with the religious needs of Canadians. The denomination has sustained membership losses every year since about 1960 and has seen its total membership fall from a high of some 6% of the Canadian population in 1960 to a current 3%. Further, age structure realities, as we have seen, point to a very severe drop in the next two decades. Empty buildings on a Sunday — like empty grocery stores on a Saturday — say something about the fit between the product and the customer. When Vancouver's St. Andrew's–Wesley cathedral has 300 people in a 1,500-seat facility, Lethbridge's Southminster United can only find 250 people for its 1,200 seats, and Montreal's St. James United draws an average of just 150 people to its sanctuary designed to hold 2,000, one has to wonder to what extent these three outlets are in touch with the religious needs of the populace.[68]

Playing the role of prophet might well be a noble organizational or personal ambition. But all people are not prophets and few churches are schools for prophets. Across Canada, there currently are some three million people who "think" that they are United Church. Most of them hopefully have some sympathy with at least some features of the church's justice agenda. Noteworthy numbers of them, however, are saying they also have an interest in God and spirituality.

Research carried out by Clair Woodbury's Centre for Research and Training in New Church Development in Edmonton, for example, has found that the dominant reason people started attending new United Church congregations — cited by 30% of newcomers — was "out of a desire to be nurtured spiritually."[69] That finding, however, speaks only to those who *are* attending. Perhaps a more sobering finding is that, among 15- to 19-year-olds who indicate they are United, 13% claim to attend services just about every week, and a mere 7% say religious-group involvement is "very important" to them. Yet 19% give that same rating to spirituality. Further, three times the number who place the "very important" tag on group involvement — 21% — acknowledge they "definitely" have spiritual needs.

What is clear in the United Church instance is that the strong justice agenda is not, by itself, hitting a distinct and unique responsive chord with many Canadians. More seriously, the effort to focus so heavily on social issues may have resulted in relatively little being left for those who are actually in the pews.

It seems significant that the very people who are the most active in United Church congregations across the country are also people who value God and spirituality, hold fairly conventional beliefs, pray, and

regard their religion as important to them. Justice issues alone probably brought few of them in — or keep them there.

The research findings support the argument that, while justice
attempts are highly commendable, if they are not accompanied in a
high-profile way by a strong emphasis on things spiritual, large numbers of people are left feeling empty. In the interview with the *United
Church Observer* I mentioned in Chapter 4, Duke theologian and
pastor William Willimon — who, according to the magazine, is widely
read within the denomination — had this to say about mainline
groups generally and the United Church specifically: "There is no
sense that our political statements come peculiarly from the Gospel
and the Gospel's odd way of our looking at things. To me the United
Church of Canada made the disastrous assumption that somebody
had asked it to run Canada. We don't have to make this country work,
we don't even have to make it turn out right. God might not even care
if it turns out right."[70]

From a marketing perspective, there is an obvious problem with
focusing so heavily on justice matters. The issue has been well defined
in terms of "market positioning." If businesses are to succeed, they
have to make sure that a product occupies a clear, distinctive, and
desirable place in the market and in the minds of target customers.[71]

Justice issues are being promoted by a wide variety of Canadian
institutions and interest groups. People consequently need to be able
to find a clear fusion of God and society when they deal with religious
groups. Otherwise, to again cite Lutheran theologian William
Hordern, religion is unable "to tell the world something that the
world is not already telling itself."[72] Willimon puts it this way: "One of
the problems of mainline Protestantism is that we don't really have
much interesting to say." In particular, "we seem to lack something
interesting to say that can't be heard elsewhere. That's deadly. It's
usually interesting advice but the worst thing is that it's not any
different advice than they could get at Rotary."[73]

Significantly, there has been extensive dissension in the United
Church over the failure to achieve an adequate justice-spiritual syn-
thesis. That conflict perhaps provides an important tip-off as to why
so many Canadians with mainline roots, who are open to the God
dimension of life, are not bothering much with the churches.

Somewhat ironically, in the course of championing justice and
frequently assailing white Anglo-Saxons for their racism, bigotry, and
sexism, the United Church has been relating to a membership whose

ancestry, in close to 80% of cases, has been British. It's a precarious way to relate to one's customers, especially when you depend on their participation and money to operate successfully.

One has to wonder to what extent such passion for justice, including the instilling of guilt for past collective sins against aboriginals, for example, has been matched with some good news, some hope, some vision of a better life in Canada for everyone, including WASPs. If it hasn't, what's remarkable is not that so *few* people are attending United Churches, it's that so *many* still are.

Similarly, while going to bat for inclusive families, whose structures and functions seem to have no limit, one can be forgiven for asking — as *Observer* writer Mike Milne does — if "in its rush to be inclusive, the United Church may be leaving behind . . . the two-parent, opposite-sex couple with kids." While being appropriately sensitive to change and diversity, says Milne, "we may be failing to celebrate the many happy, traditional-looking families who still make up the vast majority of all families."[74] To the extent that the celebration has not been taking place, the church's constituents have been left dangling.

Keith Spicer, in a searing article written a few years back for Southam News, raised many of these same issues.[75] Critical of United Church and Anglican officials for describing the U.S.-Canada free trade pact as an "empty and meaningless ceremony," Spicer spared few thoughts. In the wake of Pierre Berton's admonition that churches should abandon their comfortable pews, Spicer wrote that churches "opened doors and windows on the world, broadened their social action to embrace neglected needs and minorities, to become (as every tired Sixties institution had to) relevant. In the past quarter-century, "our mainstream churches have placed themselves in the hands of political ideologues, bureaucrats of the self-congratulatory left who think that compassion and half-baked 19th-century Marxism make perfect substitutes for clear thinking." He continued:

> *Here is what clear thinking might produce for the muddled ayatollahs at United and Anglican HQs: Our membership continues to plummet; we can't even attract the young people whom "relevance" was supposed to attract; yet churches such as the Pentecostal grow dramatically — while emphasizing pure faith, salvation, and decent living. Is it possible we are barking up the wrong tree?*

He concludes that if they wish to see "empty and vain ceremonies," they should go to their own churches. That visit, he says, will reveal declining flocks that are in a state of disarray:

They will see an elderly and declining membership mystified by their chief pastors' off-the-wall preaching against "transnationals" and the evils of free trade. Congregations wondering why, in God's name, they should be tithing for the ideologues' pet obsessions about big business, lesbian priests, and Nicaragua. The smugness of these ecclesiastical busybodies carries them serenely through any and every politician and economic issue. But their know-it-all pride blinds them to the very reason for their calling: to help the little, ordinary people find God.

Before mainliners dismiss Spicer's hotheaded comments and burn this book, they should listen to the sociologist with his hand up at the back of the room. Knowing his style, I suspect that Rod Stark would say something like, "Now Keith, there's no reason to blow everybody out of the water. But you do have a point. Most of the people who bother with the churches come there for the gods; the rest are add-ons. People want a religion capable of miracles, that brings sanity and order to life. If those kinds of things are missing, you're right — the churches' days are numbered."[76]

* * *

The cases of the United and Roman Catholic churches serve to remind us that, like Woodwards and Birks, religious groups have traditional customer bases. When they make substantial revisions in their products in the name of progress or prophecy, they need to be clear on the people to whom the new religious merchandise is being marketed. The Roman Catholic Church might have made significant adjustments. But it's unclear who, if anyone, has reaped the benefits. The United Church might have become an advocate for social justice. But it also may have abdicated its spiritual leadership of white Anglo-Saxon Protestants, and thereby lost access to very large numbers.

Structural problems and questionable products would by themselves almost guarantee the ineffectiveness of any kind of organization. Religious groups, however, are characterized by a third significant hurdle that makes ministry to Canadians difficult.

11

PROMOTION PROBLEMS

L et me begin by giving you who value religious faith a breather, while I take a shot or two at my own profession . . .

Academics tend to be very poor entrepreneurs. Most see the end in all of their research activities as lying solely in the publishing of articles and books. And so it is that deans and salary committees sit around tables and note that Professor So-and-So published *x* number of articles, and perhaps even a book in the last year. Seldom do academic peers ask the obvious question: "To what extent were the articles and books read?" Certainly no one would be so crass as to ask how many copies of the book were printed, let alone sold. Sometimes research is well-disseminated; usually it's not. Even when findings are published, the articles are often not read very widely. For most short manuscripts, the final resting place is the professional journal. In the case of more extensive expressions of research, the burial grounds are unread books.

As I pointed out in *Mosaic Madness,* so extreme is the aversion to dissemination of information beyond the academic community that a book that sells more than, say, 2,000 copies is regarded with suspicion. If average people could be interested in the book, so the academic thinking goes, it surely must contain "pop" material. Media appearances — outside of one's offering the occasional political or economic observation in the *Globe and Mail* or on the national news — are also viewed with reservation. Rewards for any flirtation with the media are sparse.

These observations are not sour grapes. I have been a full professor since the mid-1980s, and my involvement within my discipline is extensive. But while some colleagues spend their careers talking to each other, I myself prefer to expand the circle of conversation to include people with an interest in the topics at hand. Hence my conscious effort to write books that are academically respectable, reasonably comprehensible, and, I hope, enjoyable.

The transition to popular interpreter has not been an easy one. I have learned that to reach the point where you — yes, *you* — are actually reading this book, a number of things have had to happen. First, the book has to be written, which is the easiest part. Second, you, the potential reader, must become aware that it has been written. Third, it has to be made available to you. Beyond sheer production, promotion, and distribution are indispensable to dissemination. One might write a great book. But if no one knows it or the publisher doesn't get the book onto the store shelf, it just doesn't matter. It sounds cynical but it's true: how good a book is has little to do with how well it sells. I have no doubt whatsoever that some great published manuscripts have never been discovered, just as many mediocre ones have received unwarranted praise.

Which brings me back to religion. The three-dimensional product of God, self, and society is potentially powerful. If it can be brought to Canadians in an integrated way, there's reason to believe it will receive a favourable response. Not everyone will get excited. But some — maybe many — will.

TARGETING THE AUDIENCE

When it comes to life, there are few unanimous votes. Individual tastes, whims, inclinations, and dispositions result in diverse preferences and pleasures. Consequently, successful companies and organizations have to figure out *who* their market is — who potentially will be interested in what they have to offer.

Marketing Segmentation

In the business sector, an important change in marketing strategy has been taking place that has important implications for religious groups. After attempting for years to mass market — to promote one product to all buyers — companies moved to product-differentiated marketing, varying the product in terms of size, style, and so on. Toothpaste, for example, came in various flavours, with or without fluoride, in tubes and pumps.

Increasingly, however, the name of the game is "target marketing" in the form of what is called "market segmentation." The so-called "total market approach," whereby a company directs a product at an entire population, is sometimes still used. But it only works when the product is something that almost everyone buys, and where variations don't make much difference — such as salt, sugar, and unleaded gas.

What is increasingly recognized is that markets tend to be extremely heterogeneous. People want different kinds of food, cars, houses, clothes, entertainment, and vacations. Therefore, to market to those diverse wants, research is carried out that divides potential customers into categories on the basis of common characteristics. Those traits presumably are linked to relatively similar product needs.[1]

Using such a segmentation approach enables an organization to bring its full marketing arsenal of product, price, promotion, and placement to bear on a specific target group.[2] And so, Canadians are segmented on the basis of:

- demographical variables, such as age and gender;
- geographical variables, such as community size and region;
- psychographic variables, including personality (gregarious, competitive), consumption motives (durability, economy), and lifestyle (boomer, achiever).

Even religion is sometimes viewed as a useful variable for market segmentation. As three Canadian marketing professors note, "Some religions encourage or discourage the use of various goods or services, among them birth control pills, some meats, or certain types of clothing."[3]

So far, religious groups have been slow to catch on to market segmentation trends. To the extent that they do try to relate to people outside their own ranks, they are inclined to engage in what University of Waterloo sociologist Robert Prus reminds us are "cold calls," which are efforts to involve prospects with whom there has been no prior contact. "As situations wherein strangers are approaching strangers, cold calls denote ambiguous contexts fraught with potential rejection," says Prus.[4] Such contacts are sometimes necessary, even if they are not particularly enjoyable. At minimum, however, it seems wise at least to supplement such uncomfortable encounters with those involving people who are not total strangers.

One of my greatest frustrations since the publication of *Fragmented Gods* has been my inability to convince many expansion-minded leaders that they need to stop trying to reach all of Canada. To retrieve some pertinent data from Part II, in addition to the 20% to 25% of Canadians who currently are weekly attenders, some 70% of the total population continue to identify with religious groups. What's more, most — close to 80% — say they have no intention of heading elsewhere.

As I have been emphasizing, these kinds of findings suggest that religious groups make a serious analytical and tactical error when they equate low attendance with desertion. Two widespread assumptions simply aren't warranted: (1) the tendency of leaders to treat their own inactives as dropouts and, in effect, give up on them, and (2) the tendency to treat every Canadian who is not in someone's church on a given weekend as a potential recruit.

At the level of policy and program, such false assumptions have led groups wanting to grow to use a total market approach — trying to reach virtually everyone who isn't actively involved in some congregation. As far as I am aware, no one has ever had much success using this fish-net approach, in large part because the resources required to go after everyone simply are not there. In the course of failing to reach everybody, the danger is that groups run the risk of failing to reach virtually anybody. In this futile process, they dissipate both their resources and morale.

A far more productive strategy, it seems to me, is to go the route of market segmentation. The place to start is religious identification. As a writer for the *Orthodox Church* newspaper recently put it in light of a U.S. Gallup finding that 1% of the U.S. population think they are Orthodox, "If there are so many *unchurched* Orthodox, should not efforts be made to reach them before attempting to convert the other 99% of the country?"[5]

Earlier when we were looking at the way religion might influence life, I pointed out that a person's identifying with a given group might not represent a primary status, if she or he is nominally involved. But that doesn't rule out religious ID as a secondary status with significance for an individual. At minimum, one's belief that one is a Presbyterian or Anglican or Lutheran or Jew is a tip-off to the presence of a specific kind of religious history. In turn, that history and memory have implications for how they will relate to the various religious groups they encounter.

It therefore seems rather obvious that, initially at least, if a person thinks he or she is a Presbyterian, then the Presbyterians have a better chance of relating faith to that person than any other group in the country. The same can be said of people who think they are Roman Catholics, Baptists, Mormons, or whatever. In some situations, past experiences might be associated with antagonism toward the group, in which case another group may have a better opportunity than one's religious alma mater. In most instances, however, our findings suggest that the task will be that of cultivating interest, rather than running for cover.

To date, religious groups have done worse than not merely think along religious-identification segmentation lines. They have been engaging in a bizarre self-annihilating tendency to deny that religious identification even exists. When they do concede its existence, they proceed to minimize its significance if people are not also actively involved in their churches. For instance:

- A retired Anglican priest, Clifford Evans, recently told readers of the *Anglican Journal* that "discussion should begin throughout the Anglican church toward the surrender of all civil licences to marry." Evans maintains that "those who may have sought to be married in church should first contract a civil marriage with a view to later consecration or blessing of their union." He argues that "the church should confine itself to the consecration or blessing of the union of couples who seek it."[6]
- His thoughts mirrored those expressed by well-known Atlantic Presbyterian minister, Robert Steele, a short time ago, who said that it's high time wedding ceremonies involving inactive affiliates were turned over to civil authorities.
- Not to be outdone, the Assembly of Quebec Bishops' 1992 report on religion in the province included the observation: "The Church is still asked to provide the great rites of passage in the lives of individuals and families. This demand, which is frequently independent from any faith process, doesn't seem likely to stop any time soon." The response to this good news? "In the long term, it could reduce the Church's role to that of a mere folk tradition."[7]

Presumably the above would welcome the news that Edward and Ruth Simmons formed a company called Weddings a few years back and opened chapels in Hamilton and Burlington, Ontario. A former Protestant minister and later probation officer, Simmons views his company as meeting the needs of people who want a spiritual component to their wedding, yet aren't involved in a religious group. He makes use of the services of a number of ministers and organists, who are paid on a per-wedding basis. His company offers a variety of different ceremonies, both religious and secular. Fairly early in its existence the company expanded its range of services to include dedications.[8]

Let's clear up this issue once and for all. The data are not in any sense vague: as of the latest (1991) census and endless opinion polls, close to 90% of Canadians continue to see themselves as religious somethings. Moreover, even when they are not actively involved, religious memory is a reality for the overwhelming majority. Because of the Canadian emphasis on pluralism rather than assimilation, the mosaic rather than the melting pot, religious identification remains remarkably stable across generations. The religious market is regulated ideologically if not legally.

As a result, people simply are not switching all that much. Their ongoing identification, coupled with the ongoing desire for rites of passage, translates into a great opportunity for religious groups. They have readily identifiable clienteles with which they can work.

Anglicans, Presbyterians, Roman Catholics, and others who occasionally call for the churches to stop carrying out marriages because of inadequate commitment levels need to realize how self-destructive such declarations are. Having grown up with a father who spent a good chunk of his life in the insurance business, I can say with some certainty that such "leads" would be the envy of more than a few thousand companies and their reps right across the country. Rather than decrying ongoing identification, groups need to find creative ways of making good use of it.

Predictable Objections

Some people invariably say, "But it still is tough." Of course it's tough. But if you think you have it rough as a Presbyterian when you are dealing with a woman who "thinks" she is Presbyterian, imagine what it's like for a Jehovah's Witness in the same spot. Similarly, it's no song for an Alliance pastor to recruit the expired Roman Catholic, or for the Catholic priest to get the defunct Pentecostal out to church. In working with individuals who identify with them, groups won't always succeed. But they'll usually have a better chance of engaging in ministry than anyone else.

There also are some who object to the idea of focusing on one's marginal affiliates for other reasons, including concern that the denominational target group may be too small a challenge. A few years back, one leader told me with much emotion at a U.S. conference, "Our mandate as Mennonites is not to reach Mennonites — it's to 'go into all the world.'" I found myself immediately responding:

> *I'm not trying to tell you where to stop; I'm just trying to tell you where to start. Start with people who think they are Mennonites. When you are through with them, move on to your religious cousins — Baptists, Alliance, Pentecostals, Reformed, and so on. And when you are through with them, move on to the Episcopalians, Presbyterians, Methodists, and Lutherans. But don't stop there — next, work with inactive Jews and Hindus and Muslims. And when you have no other worlds to conquer, take on the toughest category of all — the lifelong "nones."*

My argument would probably draw applause from the marketing crowd. The experts in that field tell us that businesses and other organizations don't necessarily have to stop with a market segment. But they suggest there is wisdom in starting with the segment and moving outward. Kotler and McDougall, for example, write that "most companies enter a new market by serving a single segment, and if this proves successful, they add segments." They suggest that a number of Japanese companies have done just that in North America with such products as automobiles, cameras, watches, and electronics. The companies carefully entered what they considered a neglected part of the market, built a name by satisfying those customers, and then spread to other segments.[9]

No one is saying where the thing has to stop. Lots of companies want full market coverage. But the starting point is crucial. Successful marketing requires a clear identification of who might have an interest in the product. In the religious sector, what's needed is a strategy for outreach that starts with the people a group has the best hope of attracting — the people who identify with the group. This careful targeting may be the key to turning the religious situation around.

To date, Canadian religious groups continue to try for everyone. In 1992–93 the evangelistic rage among some conservative Protestant groups in more than 35 cities took the form of delivering a free video entitled *Jesus* to households. Co-ordinated by Campus Crusade for Christ, the campaign's goal was to take the gospel via video to every Canadian home. Buoyed up by what they said had been extensive and positive media coverage, organizers expected another 40 to 50 cities to be on line for 1994.[10]

To their credit the evangelicals are getting in on the ground floor of what Harvard professor John Quelch says may be the wave of the future — where catalogues are replaced by video discs or "discalogs."[11] Unfortunately, by their own definition, the video giveaway — at $10 a pop — was defined as a "saturation campaign." There was little sign that the distribution was tied in any way to the religious identification of the recipients.

As usual, despite the enthusiastic "guesstimates" of immediate conversions, the results of such nontargeted efforts can be expected to be less than awesome. In Regina, organizers said that one in four homes took the video, with an average of three people watching it fairly soon, and one in five joining in the "sinners' prayers" at the end of the video. An Edmonton volunteer, Art Mulder, wasn't as enamoured. "Out of 40 people we visited on our route, we distributed seven videos. One of the recipients turned out to be a United Church member," he said. "Two more watched the video and showed no interest in Christianity, and the other four have still not got around to watching it."[12] A minimal criticism of such a saturation approach is that it is far from cost-efficient.

And in Toronto, another Crusade for Christ venture saw Christians from more than 225 churches spend a day in December of 1992 distributing copies of the book *Why Am I on This Earth?* to 150,000 homes. According to *Why* organizer Marilyn McRae, the primary goals were to deliver a book to every family in greater Toronto — a task calling for an estimated one million books — and to get 25,000 people praying for other people by name. McRae said that the million-books goal became less and less of a focus, adding, "There's certainly a movement going on."[13]

Here again, significant resources were expended. But for all the efforts to be upbeat, there's little doubt that such an unsegmented blanket approach — regardless of the successes involved — ensures a considerable and unnecessary waste of money and time.

Perhaps the day has come to give segmentation by identification at least an experimental try.

CREATING AWARENESS

Companies that have identified their markets typically make use of the media — primarily television and radio, newspapers and magazines — to make contact with potential consumers. Their commercials and ads have been carefully tailored to the demographic and psychographic profiles of the people they are targeting. It's all part of what is referred to as the "marketing mix."

In the book business, they aren't usually quite so elaborate. There may be some ads in newspapers and a fair number of pamphlets and brochures circulated to potential buyers. But we authors are largely at the mercy of the media for interviews, reviews, and articles that will make people aware that a new book is on the shelves.

What we authors do have in common with the corporations, however, is our dependence on a process that media analysts refer to as the "two-step flow of communication." Most people, the experts tell us, receive large amounts of their information not directly from the media but from other people who saw it or heard about it. When it comes to product information, a key source is people who talk to each other.

Current Strategies

In view of the fact that the country's religious groups have not, for the most part, clearly identified their target markets, they understandably have not developed particularly good strategies for making their product known to their nominal affiliates.

The primary method of many groups has been to encourage their members to share the church and faith with others on a one-to-one basis. In relying on people, religious groups have been in good company. According to marketing professors William Zikmund and Michael D'Amico, personal contact "is the most widely used means by which organizations communicate with their customers. . . . In its various forms, [it] is the most commonly used promotional tool."[14] As Presbyterian minister Laurence DeWolfe puts it, "We don't need to produce another magazine, or sell crystal crosses, or offer meditation courses on tape. Just show the world around us people who live in this world with confidence, hope and humour. Perhaps more than anything else these days, humour."[15] An overstatement, perhaps, but DeWolfe makes the relational point.

Yet, the personal contact method is not without its shortcomings. First, a safe assumption is that some of the faithful take it seriously, while most do not. Second, religious organizations face the same problems as other groups and companies when they rely heavily on what amounts to — dare I use the phrase? — sales reps who are human. Being a good sales representative requires, of course, a wide variety of skills, including such traits as the ability to establish rapport, present information, and handle objections. It also calls for one's organization to do considerable work in the areas of administration, training, motivation, and compensation. Careful recruiting and ongoing monitoring are essential. A demanding task for resource-rich companies who can hire and fire, it's herculean for low-budget churches that find themselves having to rely on volunteers.

In addition to emphasizing personal contacts, Canada's religious groups have tended to engage in promotion efforts of the undifferentiated blanket variety:

- Door-to-door canvassing, neighbourhood pamphlet blitzes, newspaper advertisements, and occasionally local radio and television programs speaking to their own people, as well as to Canadians generally who happen to tune in, by means of the national cable channel, Vision TV.[16]

But religious groups are scarcely tapping into television, that major mind-maker of the 1990s. Professor Brian Joseph writes of the Roman Catholic Church, for example, "Historically, the Catholic church came late to the print medium, to modern scripture scholarship, and to the electronic mass media. It still does not take television seriously."[17] The reluctance of Canada's religious groups to use television is showing in the viewing figures.

- Only about 2% of Canadians say they watch religious programs on television "several times a week or more."
- Another 8% say they catch such programs "about once a week."
- A further 8% watch religious programming "about once a month."
- The remaining 82% of Canadians say they "hardly ever" or "never" tune in to such programs.

What's particularly interesting to note is that the 18% figure for current viewers is down dramatically from 75% in 1957, when the question was first asked. As might be expected, the dropoff has been enormous across all regions, ages, for women as well as men, and for both Catholics and Protestants. About 60% of the weekly-plus viewers, incidentally, are also weekly churchgoers.

TABLE 11.1. **RELIGION TV PROGRAM VIEWING, 1957 AND 1990**

% Indicating Watch at Least Sometimes*

	1957	1990
NATIONALLY	75	18
Roman Catholic	77	22
Protestant	74	18
B.C.	64	12
Prairies	83	17
Ontario	73	14
Quebec	74	25
Atlantic	78	27
Under 30	67	6
30–39	71	9
40–49	81	15
over 50	80	34
Women	80	18
Men	70	18

*1957: Included religious programs on radio.

SOURCES: 1957: May Gallup poll; 1990: PROJECT CAN90.

Strangely, at a time when television is shaping Canadian minds to an unprecedented degree, compliments of the arrival of cable,[18] religious groups have been engaged in a semimasochistic effort to limit their TV exposure. In what is most certainly a shortsighted battle, some evangelical groups have been working hard to convince the CRTC that they should have their own channels, while others — mostly mainliners — have fought to limit them to the CRTC-mandated multifaith Vision TV. The whole controversy is largely irrelevant, of course, as technology will result in hundreds of channels becoming available over the next few years.[19] Do we really care if "The Bread of Life Church" occupies channel 212?[20]

Significantly, in June 1993, the CRTC made some modifications on its long-standing ban on single-religion broadcasting, opening the door to such broadcasts, while retaining strict guidelines.[21]

Even with the possibility of having their own channels, religious groups must come up with large amounts of cash to get on the air, stay on the air, and, most important, be seen. As Reginald Stackhouse, an Anglican and former MP, points out, television is an expensive medium to sustain, "like a monkey on your back."[22] Historian and journalist Desmond Morton comments, "Real access to the media is tightly restricted." Says Morton, "Only a billionaire like Ross Perot can afford enough TV time to deliver his message. Major productions cost millions of dollars." Those who spend that kind of money are few.[23]

Ironically, while technology is expanding the number of channels and making it possible for religious groups to go on television, the number of channels will make it extremely difficult for their programming to be seen, especially if people have to pay for the privilege. The danger is that religious channels will have a sort of in-house rather than outreach function, of some value to the initiated but of limited value in relating faith to people outside the churches.

As a result, religious groups serious about promoting the gods to Canadians beyond their boundaries may find that a better strategy is to follow the lead of the top companies and buy time on the channels that most people are watching.

Primarily, it seems, because of cost, advertising on major television networks that is aimed at nonactive affiliates seldom appears. Notable but limited exceptions are Salvation Army, Church of Jesus Christ Latter-Day Saints, and Seventh-day Adventist television and radio commercials, which are made in the U.S. and aired in Canada. They tend to deal in a soft-sell way with the themes of self and society.

Describing such ads, Ronald Alsop, writing in the *Wall Street Journal*, has noted that "religious advertisers increasingly are injecting slice-of-life themes into commercials that might be confused with advertisements for Kodak, Pepsi-Cola, or Coca-Cola." In Canada and the U.S., a Latter Day Saints commercial features three muddy farm kids having a water fight when their parents pull up in a truck. Instead of reprimanding them, their parents take a picture. The commercial is capped by the message "Don't let the magic pass you by." Only in the last three seconds is the Mormon Church sponsor identified. Canada is not quite at the point of the Episcopal Church's U.S. ad on forgiveness a few years back that featured the line "In the church started by a man who had six wives, forgiveness goes without saying."[24]

Overall, Canadian religious groups don't exactly score high on promotion. Not that they necessarily fare any worse than some of their American counterparts. In research Phillip Cooper and George McIlvain carried out about a decade ago in a major midwestern city, emphasis on promotion was found to be lower among religious organizations than any other public groups. The level was somewhat behind health care, public service, and professional organizations, still further behind cultural and human service groups, and far behind education and political organizations.[25]

Increasing the Exposure

If our findings are accurate — that Canadians want and need what religion has to offer — then it is essential that the churches find better ways of marketing both who they are and what it is they have to bring. It's time for religious groups "to go public." Some are.

THE DIOCESE OF NEW WESTMINSTER CASE

In 1990 the Anglican diocese of New Westminster, centred in greater Vancouver, embarked on a five-year $550,000 advertising campaign aimed at supporting evangelism. The brainchild of communications officer Lorie Chortyk, the program has as its primary target groups lapsed Anglicans and people with a spiritual interest who have no formal religious ties (remember that, according to the 1991 census, some 31% of B.C. residents say they have no religion). A series of posters has been created, based on input from target groups and surveys of inactive Anglicans. About a dozen variations exist, all carrying the slogan "Show your spirit. Come back to church." People wanting more information are given both a Vancouver number and, yes, a toll-free number (see FIGURE 3.1). Those receiving enquiries have been given training and information by the communications office, so that they are able to process the calls.

The posters have been distributed throughout the diocese for posting wherever possible and advantageous, such as in schools and stores. They also appear as quarter-page ads — outside the church directory sections — in some 20 community newspapers about 10 times a year. Brief additional information concerning local parishes is often added. A Christmas poster ad is also placed in the *Vancouver Sun*.

Chortyk told me the campaign met with some apprehension at first, summarized in the objection of one member who protested, "You're trying to sell the church like Coca-Cola — it's disgusting!" But the general response has been positive, with people increasingly realizing that the campaign stimulates conversation, contributes to a more positive image of the church, and overall supports efforts to share faith interpersonally. Incidentally, the idea of distributing coffee mugs, T-shirts, and key chains is also being explored.[26]

FIGURE 3.1. **PROMOTION, ANGLICAN STYLE**

當你踏入新環境
教會大家庭歡迎你
使你賓至如歸
歡欣鼓舞

When you arrive in a new place it's nice to know God already has a family waiting for you.

Sometimes things are so different it's hard to feel like you really belong. But at church you do belong, because your family is part of our family – God's family. And we're waiting to welcome you this Sunday.

Show your Spirit. Come back to church.

The Anglican Church

For information about an Anglican parish in your community, call 684-6306 or outside Vancouver 1-800-665-1105

境遇變遷，人地生疏，不易產生歸屬。但因禰之內皆兄弟，基督的教會歡迎你，因為你也是我們家庭的一員。本星期日，我們將如展雙手，恭候尊駕閣府參加主日崇拜。

激發愛主熱誠，請來一同敬拜
加拿大聖公會

有關鄰近聖公會禮拜堂梁會詳情，請致電：872-1884。歡迎查詢。

Does the thought of going to church still give you a pain in the neck?

You may be surprised to see how much the church has changed. The way of dressing for services is more comfortable and so is the style of worship. So come prepared to relax, free from life's restrictions, and let the most important part of you breathe again.

Show your spirit. Come back to church.
The Anglican Church
For more information call 684-6306

It's an interesting start. The possibilities are limited only by imagination and finances — and a lack of humour. St. Mark's Lutheran Church in Kitchener, for example, plugged into Ontario's Sunday shopping controversy by posting a sign in front of the church that read Open Sunday 9–12![27] As it stands, by the way, some of the better eye-catching advertisements are probably of the accidental, typo variety. A recent ad in the *Sudbury Star* for St. Peter's United Church indicated that the service would feature "consummation and baptism." As one minister commented, "Some churches will do anything for ratings!"[28]

Given the long and even great traditions of groups, the wealth of raw material that exists is nothing less than incredible. "Stars and stories" from the present and past can be co-opted, entertainers and athletes among them.[29] For example, the *Presbyterian Record* ran an article in early 1993 entitled "The Presbyterian Who Invented Basketball." The story featured James Naismith who "designed basketball to promote clean living and Christianity." In light of the tremendous popularity of basketball among today's Canadian youth — Michael Jordan, as of 1992, was our teens' favourite athlete[130] — one doesn't have to be overly creative to envision some of the things that could be done with that kind of legacy.[31] Presbyterians need to start their promotional engines. So does everyone else.

An important word of caution, however: the product needs to be in place. Yes, good promotion might work. Targeted inactives might give a congregation a look. But before Canada's religious groups embark on programs for increasing awareness of faith and ministry, they need to be sure they can deliver the "God, self, and society" product. It's not at all self-evident that, currently, many congregations can.

12

DISTRIBUTION PROBLEMS

Successful authors do not sit on their books. They make the world aware of them and see that they are in the stores. A lot of churches have been sitting on their books. One grouping that doesn't claim to be, and isn't perceived to be, warrants a closer look. I'm thinking of the conservative Protestants.

Evangelical Protestant groups typically give strong play to the God dimension of the faith and talk a lot about outreach. As we have seen, however, for all the commotion, they've been less than a phenomenal success.

WAREHOUSE RELIGION

A major reason proselytizing fails has been known for some time. To the novice it sounds incredible, but it nonetheless happens, and often: evangelicals don't take the gospel outside their buildings. They proclaim the good news from the safety of their sanctuaries. Insiders have referred to it as preaching to the converted. Outsiders, such as the well-known Oxford sociologist Bryan Wilson, suggested a number of years ago that it's tied to the tension many evangelicals feel in believing they should be separate from the world, yet actually having to go into it and preach the gospel. "Evangelism," wrote Wilson, "means exposure to the world and the risk of alienation" from one's group.[1]

One way to resolve the dilemma is not to bother to count very carefully. Or, as I have politely suggested in a few evangelical settings — hard though it may be to say it, it needs to be said — evangelicals haven't always been honest. Many leaders conveniently don't bother to differentiate between "real live sinners," who have come from outside the evangelical community, and "homegrown sinners," who are their very own sons and daughters. More than a few pastors stock their pews with the latter and pretend that they have fulfilled the Great Commission.

Reflecting on our Calgary research on evangelicals some 20 years ago, Merlin Brinkerhoff and I asked why, if outsiders are not being brought in by the churches, congregations continue to use the same means of outreach year in and year out. "Why, for example," we asked, "do churches continue to hold weekly evangelistic-type services in their buildings when few if any outsiders are ever present?" We continue to stand by our response to the question we raised:

> One obvious explanation is that, on the surface, such evangelistic programs do work. Many family members, including relatives, are responding to the evangelistic appeals and are being converted. Until such time as someone does some counting . . . it is easy to believe that evangelistic programs are being successful. . . . Holding evangelistic services even when the audience is predominantly Christian gives a church the appearance of "preaching the gospel to the lost," allowing a member to feel that he/she belongs to an evangelistic church. . . . It may thus well be that religious groups are organizationally defective with respect to the explicit goal of proselytism, precisely because, with respect to latent functions, it is advantageous to be so.[2]

Even worse, as Ted Mann pointed out way back in the 1950s after studying groups in Alberta, some evangelicals take the outreach masquerade a step further: they use it for personal entertainment.[3] They sit back in fairly comfortable pews and take in their favourite preachers, prodigals, and — of course — singers.

Sound cynical? Marianne Meed, *Faith Today* news editor writes: "Evangelicals have an addiction — the Sensational Testimony. We love a good sinner-to-saint saga, the more spectacular the better." Meed says that the ST has spawned an entire industry of books, records, videos, and conferences. It also has produced such high-priced entertainers as Mike Warnke, with his stories of drugs and sex, and Betty Maltz, who purportedly visited heaven between being declared brain dead and being brought back to life. Both of these stars, Meed notes, have now been discredited.

Meed is candid in her assessment: "The ST is a sanctioned form of entertainment for evangelicals — the same ones who would reject many of the stories if they were to come via an R-rated movie, explicit book or TV talk show. We get the same voyeuristic thrills from the ST but without the risk of appearing less than holy." She maintains that such a preoccupation can keep evangelicals from facing their own problems and helping each other with their struggles.[4] In addition to not motivating people to look at themselves, ST's also do little to motivate evangelicals to look beyond their own religious boundaries.

It's also not readily apparent that collective efforts to witness necessarily involve a significant transcending of group boundaries. Take, for example, the annual March for Jesus event, that appears to have particular appeal to evangelicals. The 1993 march took place on Saturday, June 12, and organizers claimed that more than 100,000 Christians in some 40 Canadian cities participated — joining 1.5 million people in 80 countries. The marchers numbered about 10,000 in Toronto, Winnipeg, and Edmonton, along with an esti-mated 15,000 in both Ottawa and Vancouver. Co-ordinator and family lawyer Marty Klein of Toronto maintains that it's "not just a one-day event" but has the lasting effect of "bringing people together." Ottawa co-ordinator Marny Pohl said she sees the march as an "amazing declaration that Jesus is King of righteousness."[5]

Co-operation might be enhanced and morale boosted. What is hard to believe is that the marching (which ends in prayer) in and of itself communicates very much of anything with much clarity to onlookers, let alone the message that "Jesus is King." Such a massive emergence of "the church into the world" may make it seem that witnessing is taking place. In reality, ironically, marches might provide further evidence of the reluctance of evangelicals to actually go into the world and share the gospel with average people, one on one.

Evangelicals have a good book. But often it doesn't leave their warehouses.

They're not alone. As we have seen in detail, no religious group is showing signs of being very adept at touching Canadians who are outside the churches. Cliff Reinhardt, for example, has this to say about his denomination: "We Lutherans lack a sense of mission. All too often, we indeed just sit and wait . . . not for lack of love for God or neighbour, but because we're just not sure what to do."[6] Roman Catholic Bishop Bernard Hubert, the president of the Assembly of Quebec Bishops, told 600 delegates from the province's dioceses in late 1992, "Our fear of leaving our familiar environment to meet with confidence those who are different from us reveals a profound malaise in our Church. . . . It is difficult for us to leave the cocoon of Christendom to become an effective minority in a pluralistic milieu."[7]

When it comes to sharing the religious product, it appears that a good many church buildings across the country have a lot of unopened crates. The stock is not getting out of storage.

Doing Well but Forgetting Why

Organizations in general run the risk of suffering from a common malady known as "means-end inversion." Simply put, the organization continues to operate, but few people know why. A company, a service club, a school, or a government department can miraculously live on indefinitely, with little sense of where it came from or why it continues — something like a stray toboggan on an endless hill. The old joke sums it up well: As the couple bomb down the highway, she looks up from the map and says, "Honey, we're on the wrong road." "I don't care," he replies. "We're making great time!"

In an influential article published some three decades ago, Theodore Levitt used the term "marketing myopia" to describe sellers who liked their products so much they lost sight of the needs of their customers — liking trains more than transportation, for example, or liberal arts programs more than education. "Selling," he wrote, "focuses on the needs of the seller; marketing on the needs of the buyer."[8]

In view of the propensity of people in religious groups to become fond of the familiar, it's extremely easy for them to experience this marketing myopia. Take programs, for example. There still are a few churches around that lament the death of the evening service. In late 1992 Rick Hiebert of the Pentecostal Assemblies of Canada asked, "Why won't believers support the Sunday evening service? What's wrong with people's commitment?"[9] A nationally distributed Canadian Press article a few months later began with the line "God isn't dead but his flock is dwindling, thinned out by the lures of television and secular society." The article's message was that television had killed off the evening service.[10]

The question that arises is this: Does it really matter? A 1990 Statistics Canada survey found that 40% of Canadians are regular weekend workers. Among two-income couples, one person is working weekends in more than half the cases. With the easing of Sunday shopping restrictions in provinces like Quebec, that figure is only going to rise.[11]

These findings only confirm what most groups have known for

years: Sunday — let alone Sunday night — is increasingly a tough time to get everyone together. However, wise groups will remember that "the Sabbath was made for man, not man for the Sabbath" and adjust their schedules accordingly. As the head of a Salvation Army task force examining Sunday evening services, Major Denis Skipper, commented, "My vision is for an Army that's more, not less, in the years ahead — not more meetings for meetings' sake, but more commitment to Christ and obedience to the Great Commission."[12] The death of old forms is hardly synonymous with the death of a congregation's program, let alone religion.

Marketing myopia can also characterize entire congregations and, for that matter, denominations. It happens when groups become turned in on themselves, losing sight of the reality that ministry to the world requires that they and their products be a means to an end, and not just an end in themselves. Observers since at least sociologist Max Weber have drawn attention to what is referred to as "routinization."[13] Groups that originally were characterized by enthusiasm, spontaneity, and commitment to ministry become, over time, preoccupied with themselves as organizations, losing touch with the original reasons they came into being.

Canadian religious groups frequently exhibit routinization, giving an inordinate amount of attention to themselves as organizations.

- Ask religious leaders about the problems facing religion today, and chances are good that most will bemoan numbers and finances — rather than their failure to minister effectively to the Canadian population.
- To the extent that leaders talk about marketing, they are inclined to take the lead of people like George Barna in aspiring to "market churches" rather than trying to market faith; the emphasis is on appealing to the initiated who are "choosing churches," versus finding ways of sharing faith with outsiders.[14]
- Primary concerns often centre upon "church growth" and "church planting," rather than addressing the spiritual needs of the people across the country.
- The effectiveness of churches is often measured by how many people they put into a physical building so many days a month, and their ability to get them to subscribe to appropriate belief and behavioural norms — and, of course, to give fairly generously of both their time and their money.

Don Posterski and Irwin Barker's findings, I think, provide considerable support unfortunately for the "in-turned club" argument. What their sample of some of the most highly involved members in the country has told them is that the things they value first and foremost about their churches is not social service or the sharing of faith with others who need it. Rather, those active members want a church that serves them, along with their families, first and foremost. True, they want their churches to be officially engaged in "local evangelism," especially if they are involved in conservative Protestant churches. It's part of the evangelical creed — what else can they say? But when push comes to shove, 27% openly admit they want a congregational focus while only 14% think their congregations' ministry should be aimed primarily at the community; the rest want both.[15]

TABLE 12.1. IMPORTANT FEATURES OF CHURCH LIFE: VIEWS OF CANADA'S MOST ACTIVE MEMBERS

% Viewing as "Very Important"

"A church that . . ."

gives people a sense that they belong	82
places strong emphasis on the family	74
creates a sense of self-worth among members	69
meets the emotional needs of those who attend	58
demonstrates strong understanding of today's culture	46
gives equal status/opportunities to men and women	39
places strong emphasis on healing/miracles	28

SOURCE: Derived from Posterski and Barker, 1993: 241–242.

Such self-absorption might make for solid congregations. But it doesn't result in religious groups sharing faith with Canadians outside their physical boundaries. Unfortunately it's very easy for the warehouse to become a clubhouse, a gathering place for the initiated, in some instances scarcely extending beyond one's own extended family and its close friends.

M. Scott Peck sounds a warning concerning what might happen to such churches. "We get in serious difficulty whenever we attempt (as we often do) to exalt our human institutions," he writes. "God actively loves, blesses, and nurtures" those organizations that suit God's purpose. But, unlike God's love for individuals, "God's love for organizations is fully conditional." Peck adds, "If the organization is sufficiently sinful, God will dump it, desert it, even if it is a church supposedly operating in God's name."[16]

Churches as Family Shrines

As a student minister in rural Indiana in the late 1960s, I was taken by the interesting symbiosis that existed between seminary students and small churches. Some 2,000 congregations are said to lie within a 75-mile radius of nearby Louisville, Kentucky. Most are tiny. Their existence is made possible by a large labour supply of seminary students who serve them on a part-time basis. In reality, many congregations are what we might almost call family shrines. They are typically dominated by a few families who staff the boards, the Sunday schools, the choirs, and even the keyboards. In such instances the family of God actually consists of a number of godly families.

Officially the churches claim to be committed to evangelism. They want the gospel to be preached and usually expect an "altar call" at the end of each service. They even have revival meetings every spring and fall, when, as a seminary student friend of mine sacrilegiously put it, "They book the Holy Spirit twice a year and crank up the level of emotion." These are what John Stackhouse, a religion professor at the University of Manitoba, has called "high days in the evangelical church calendar" when "people raised in such traditions [commit] their lives to Christ 'on schedule.'"[17]

For all the external signs of engaging in outreach, I increasingly had great difficulty being convinced that the people in my small church really wanted things to change. New people would have upset the organizational applecart. It may have meant changing the makeup of the board, subtracting a teacher or two, putting someone new on the piano (who, to be perfectly honest, could actually play it well). Evangelism could have been divisive — maybe even brought on a church split. Incidentally, speaking of splits, in such situations family harmony was closely related to congregational harmony. In my own Indiana situation, a serious family falling-out a few years earlier had resulted in our losing two families and the Methodists, by mere coincidence, gaining two.

Neal Mathers, a Presbyterian minister, is blunt in his assessment of the prevalence of such tendencies, especially in smaller congregations. He writes that congregations often have their leadership structures in place, with people in power liking things that way. "Because church growth would bring in new people who could upset this balance of power," says Mathers, "the present power brokers may support the vision [of outreach] in principle, but they will find ways to frustrate it in practice."[18] Larger churches also tend to have mixed feelings about the infusion of new people. Speaking about congregations generally, Stackhouse comments that people with authority "have a deep vested interest in maintaining things as they are." He adds, "A little revival, a little freshness within the established order, can be tolerated and even welcomed. But any disruption of the defining ways and means of the group will be stoutly resisted."[19]

Canada, of course, does not lack for denominations and congregations that are socially, culturally, and theologically homogeneous. Such groups are particularly prone to turning their warehouses into clubhouses. It is relatively easy to live with the illusion that one's congregation is reaching out to others when, if all were known, growth is heavily internal, consisting largely of geographically mobile members and their children — with denominational ties often going back generations.

Given that we officially have a Canadian cultural mosaic, religious leaders like to claim that their groups are socially and ethnically diversified.

- Presbyterians inform readers of their national magazine that their people come in a wide "variety of shapes and sizes," "walks of life," and "range of backgrounds."[20]
- We read that, at the United Church's biennial national meeting in Fredericton in 1992, "at least 11 languages were spoken during Council, including Cree, German, French, Spanish, Korean and Swahili."[21]
- The 1992 Anglican General Synod in Toronto, says the *Anglican Journal,* "passed a slate of motions which increase the church's commitment to multiculturalism." An internal report that was received says that "people from all cultures and races should be welcomed into church fellowships."[22]
- Mennonite Brethren leader Paul Hiebert told a church conference in 1993 that the group is a diverse, multi-cultural denomination, with 95% of new growth consisting of non-whites and baby boomers.[23]

Posterski and Barker offer such groups the supportive observation that "community does not mean sameness," either socially or culturally. Canadian churches, they maintain, have shown an "openness to ethnic diversity," in keeping with Canadians' "proud tradition of accepting the subcultural and ethno-cultural differences among them."[24]

Who are we kidding?

Posterski and Barker's own data don't even support such grandiose claims.[25]

- When they asked their lay sample — allegedly comprised of the most active church members in the country — if switching to a different congregation is warranted when "people more like yourself in areas such as age, family composition, education and income" are wanted, 60% said yes!
- When asked pointblank if switching to a different congregation is warranted when "more people like yourself in terms of ethnic background," are wanted, virtually the same proportion of Canada's blue-ribbon laity — 46% — said yes!

Keep in mind that such survey data merely tap ideals; I personally am amazed that such high proportions of people would openly admit to such blatant homogeneity preferences. The actual *behavioural* figures may well be even higher.

Beyond attitudes and values, it's fairly easy to probe what is going on in practice by taking a quick peek at religious identification through the eyes of basic social variables. One is cultural-group ancestry. A thorough examination requires work at congregational levels, since national aerial shots obviously can fail to detect local variations. Still, if churches are really becoming cultural blends, the faces should be showing up in the national family portraits.

They don't, at least not in sufficient numbers to justify all the rhetoric. An examination of religious identification by cultural background reveals striking patterns that are persisting into the 1990s:

- Just 7% of Roman Catholics have non-European roots, despite the global nature of Catholicism.
- All but about 2% to 8% of the people who identify with the mainline Protestant groups continue to trace their backgrounds

either to Britain or to European countries other than France; the links remain specific to certain countries, such as Anglicans to England, and Lutherans to Germany and Scandinavia.

- Only the conservative Protestants can claim — and only barely so — that more than 10% of their affiliates have cultural roots that are neither European nor North American.
- The backgrounds of people identifying with Eastern Orthodoxy and Judaism continue to be overwhelmingly continental and Eastern European.
- Over 90% of Canadians who identify with other faiths trace their cultural ancestry to countries other than Europe and North America — Asia and Africa in particular.

Keep in mind that we're not just talking about the relative inability of religious groups to cross into non-European sectors of the population. We're talking about the lack of success that groups have had over time, in simply recruiting people from various parts of Europe! When one glances at the background of the population nationally versus the makeup of the country's religious groups, we find that

- Roman Catholics have few people of British background.
- Anglicans, Presbyterians, and the United Church haven't got very far beyond British boundaries.
- Lutherans have failed to make headway among people with British and French roots.
- Conservative Protestants, like their mainline counterparts, have had little success recruiting French Canadians.
- People of other faiths have shown little sign of including Canadians located outside their very limited cultural-group boundaries.

More accurate than broad claims about cultural heterogeneity, it seems to me, is the recent observation of Presbyterian minister Gordon Fish. He comments that the Scottish and Irish accents that used to be heard in many of Canada's urban neighbourhoods are being replaced by the voices of people from places like Portugal, Vietnam, and Korea. The response of the churches? "We have no idea how to minister and make the gospel relevant to them," says Fish, "although for years we were comfortable in sending our missionaries to their lands. But here in Canada? That's another matter."[26]

TABLE 12.2. **RELIGIOUS GROUP IDENTIFICATION BY CULTURAL GROUP ANCESTRY: 1991**

In %'s

	British	French	Other Europ.	North Amer.	Other	Totals*
NATIONALLY	40	31	29	4	8	112
ROMAN CATHOLIC	23	59	23	3	4	112
MAINLINE PROT.						
Anglican	82	7	19	4	2	114
Lutheran	20	5	83	1	1	110
Presbyterian	79	5	20	4	1	109
United Church	73	6	29	6	2	116
CONSERVATIVES						
Baptist	60	5	29	4	14	112
Other Evangelical	45	8	45	6	11	115
OTHER RELIGIONS						
Eastern Orthodox	2	<1	85	<1	12	100
Jewish	7	4	91	4	7	113
Other Faiths	5	2	6	1	91	106
NONE	50	13	37	7	11	118

*NOTE: In 1991, more than one cultural group could be cited by each respondent; that's why totals exceed 100.

SOURCE: Derived from 1991 General Social Survey, Statistics Canada.

Echoing the same refrain, Roland Kawano, the multicultural ministry specialist, has written, "Curiously, the churches in the host society have always been the initiators of spiritual movements in societies in other parts of the world. But when people from those other countries come to the host country, the church in the host society frequently becomes afraid. It is unable or unwilling to cross the barriers in its own multicultural society." He adds, "The churches in the host society too often remained locked in their own ethnic culture." He reminds everyone that much of the problem lies in the fact that the mainline churches in Canada are themselves, "ethnic churches, dominated by English speakers and English culture."[27]

Also sobering are the reflections of Canon John Erb, the rector of Toronto's St. Michael and All Angels Anglican Church, a parish that, according to *Anglican Journal* writer Vianney Carriere, is "the most racially diverse congregation in the city." Erb estimates that slightly more than half of the congregation is black, and includes Jamaicans,

Barbadians, Trinidadians, St. Lucians, Guyanese, West Indians, Africans, black Canadians, and a sprinkling of native people and Orientals. "We are," he says, "the founding parish answering black needs."

But a problem exists. The racial groups tend to cluster, reminding him that his work is not done. As he looks out on his congregation on Sunday morning, he sees — not individuals — but all-white groups sitting next to all-black groups. "It is very much a racial thing and it is absolutely infuriating," Erb says. He acknowledges that the parish's programs and activities also split along racial lines: the dances are all black; the cribbage group is all white. There is, however, one place where things are mixed that points to hope — the Sunday school. "Kids: that is where the best integration takes place," Erb says.[28]

Even ethnic churches are not exempt from this problem of excluding outsiders. A University of Lethbridge student from Hong Kong, for example, told me she felt like a marginal member in the local Chinese Alliance church. She, along with a number of friends, plans to return to Hong Kong after graduation. As a result, she said, "All of us students have limited involvement in our Chinese church because many positions require citizens or Canadian-born Chinese. We lack a feeling of being at home in the church."

To the extent that congregations are homogeneous because of history or class or ethnicity, it's not surprising that they're not particularly attractive to outsiders. Equally important, this side of the uninitiateds' looking "like us" or behaving "like us," it seems clear that they haven't been particularly embraced.

It's no coincidence that many evangelical groups, for example, encourage people to make a "profession of faith," yet typically have what amounts to waiting periods before new converts are actually invited to join their churches. Little subtlety is involved. As Bryan Wilson has observed, there is a reluctance "to accept into the [group] new members who are incompletely socialized from the [group's] point of view."[29]

Newcomers have to give evidence of being socialized into the theology and lifestyle of their new groups — sometimes, for example, abstaining from alcohol use — before they are allowed to have their names placed on the membership rolls. As one member of the initiated put it in a recent letter to an evangelical magazine, "Don't people realize that the church has a code: You must be born again! We are tired of hearing how unloving the church is. Let people repent, set their lives in order and we are more than willing to fellowship with them."[30]

Statements like that underline the fact that the appearance of outsiders frequently threatens the religious status quo, upsetting the familiar, complete with memories of days past. Here again, Neal Mathers, drawing on church growth research, notes that growth "will mean strangers in 'my' pew, people who don't understand 'our story,' demands for new programs, perhaps even a building program that will alter, or even replace 'our place.'" He adds, "The cost of growth is simply far higher than many people are willing to pay."[31] Similarly, Ron Geddert, editor of the *Mennonite Brethren Herald*, raises the question of whether church members really want an infusion of new people. A major renewal, he writes, "might mean an influx of people different from those we are accustomed to seeing in our pews." Geddert asks, "Are we open to accepting people of all social, cultural and economic positions? Are we prepared to incorporate people with checkered pasts, even if they carry physical evidences of that past or are still struggling" with previous lifestyles?[32] He obviously has some doubts.

The net result of all this homogeneity is means-end inversion. In the Canadian '90s, collectively speaking at least, organized religion has not particularly succeeded in aiming its resources at Canadians who need ministry. When they have, the motive has often been membership recruitment. Even then, such outreach has taken second place to the recruitment of insiders. Frankly, "internal evangelism" is far more cost-effective. Going after "sinners" is not only extremely difficult, it also is a precarious investment with limited returns. It's hard on resources, yet provides no guarantees that outsiders will (a) be recruited, (b) fit in particularly well, or (c) stay.

For these reasons, among others, religion in Canada frequently does not get out of the warehouse. Some readily acknowledge the failure. David Webber, who leads a house church ministry for the Presbyterians in the Cariboo region of British Columbia, recently wrote: "If I look at my church's practice in Canada, I see an almost total emphasis on perpetuating the church institution — church growth, successful and attractive church programs, church extension and the like." He asks, "Is mission in Canada limited to the self-perpetuation of the institutional church?"[33]

THE ILLUSION OF SUCCESS

What's the point behind trying to reach outsiders? What's the reason in back of the city-wide crusade or the free video tapes or free books? What do leaders have in mind when they want to make their churches more effective? If the primary or even secondary motive is to put more pants in the pews, religious groups are going to find the going tough.

What's a Good Church?

Posterski and Barker's recent book is entitled *Where's a Good Church?*[34] It's an interesting question, but it reminds us all of the importance of first answering the critical preceding question, namely, "What's a good church?"

If a good church is a church that satisfies the 20% of Canadians who are already involved and has little to say to the 80% who are on the outside looking in, then it's little more than a club for the religious elite. When such people actually ask, "Where's a good church?" the question can become little more than a smug line off the lips of circulating saints who want to know, "Where's the predictable and comfortable subcultural action?"

I suggest that we have too many such churches in Canada. What the national surveys indicate is that the majority of Canadians don't want a lot of what those kinds of churches have to offer. But in light of their great interest in the mysteries of life and death, God and the supernatural, meaningful living, and spirituality, Canadians are in need of effective ministry from extremely good churches. It would be a tragedy if all such Canadians found when they responded to the country's religious groups is that

- their name was wanted on the membership list;
- their money was wanted for the church budget;
- their time was wanted for the church programs; and
- the name of the game was strengthening the religious corporation.

What's needed today in Canada is so much more.

On Drill Bits and Holes

In the marketing lore is the story of the company that made drill bits and went out of business. The company was dismayed — after all, they made the best drill bits in the whole world. What the company didn't realize is that people didn't want drill bits — they wanted a hole. And when another product came along that made a better hole for less money, the customers were history.[35]

Again I remind you that the surveys indicate Canadians don't want more organized religion. They don't want better drill bits. But they do want the things that religion historically has been about. For these people, a good church might be one that

- sees its declining numbers as a sign that it is out of touch with Canadians;
- recognizes that if it is top-heavy with the initiated, it probably is not adequately reaching nominal affiliates;
- will integrate God and the supernatural, hope for the individual, and optimal social life; and
- will exist not only to nurture its members but also to share its faith with others who are in need of it.

Historically religious groups have been called to be more than communities in which faith is experienced. They have also been expected to be the means by which faith is shared with outsiders. The Judaeo-Christian tradition, for example, is replete with the word "go": ". . . and the Lord said go . . ."; "Go into all the world . . ." While being a resource to the initiated, the religious group ideally also ministers to others — addressing issues concerning the supernatural realm, helping those who are raising questions about existence to find meaning, bringing significance to life's pivotal passages. In the words of Harold Percy of Wycliffe College, "The church exists for mission. The church exists for the sake of the whole world. The church exists to bear witness."[36] James Dickie, the well-known Presbyterian, expresses it this way: "If the church tries to hide in an ecclesiastical ghetto, peering out at the world through stained-glass windows, rather than address the changes or find meaning in all this flux, then it deserves to wither."[37]

What is disturbing about the present situation is not that organized religion is withering — any more than one would worry about the deteriorating condition of a taxi on the way to the airport. What is disturbing about the state of Canada's religious groups is that large numbers of Canadians who are receptive to the major themes of religion may miss the flight — will never be introduced to what religion can bring to life.

Because of the failure of organized religion, the gods may remain unknown.

POSTSCRIPT: IS GOD BEING REDUCED TO A CEO?

Invariably someone in the audience raises the question "But where is God in all of this? You're relegating religion to a business. What about prayer and the Holy Spirit and spiritual factors?"

Perhaps it is important to unmask some further biographical details. For the record, I personally have strong feelings and pretty clear beliefs about the reality of God and the ways in which God works in life, both through us and despite us. Prayer is an important part of my day-to-day existence. I further believe that as part of responsible stewardship, we are called to make good use of what God has given us, including our time and money, our bodies and minds, our technology and information.

If the gods are to be adequately served in the 1990s, it's incumbent on those who value faith to make the best possible use of the resources available. Terry Winter has put it this way: "Methodology is certainly secondary to the message, but we must indeed use all measures available to us today." He adds, "Let's be as professional, thorough, and self-critical as we can be. There is no excuse for halfhearted, poorly executed programs."[38]

Religious groups, as organizations, need to aspire to be absolutely the best organizations possible, to the end that ministry might be carried out effectively and efficiently.

Through such stewardship, the gods are not being exempted; they are being exalted.

CONCLUSION

Organized religion is in serious trouble. The paradox is that the problems are occurring at a time when Canadians give considerable evidence of being receptive to the areas of mystery and meaning that religion historically has been able to address, and when religious memory is still very much alive across the country. Yet, the limited success that Canada's religious groups have had in responding to that market is no accident. They have tended to be highly precarious organizations, have offered questionable product lines, haven't carefully targeted their audiences, and have had weak distribution systems. In addition, because religion has not been deregulated in Canada, it has been difficult for the slack to be picked up by new religious "firms." Consequently, the overall result of companies floundering in the midst of a rich market should surprise no one.

Can the situation be turned around? It's possible. But it will require nothing less than a dramatic transformation in how religious groups view themselves and the culture, a willingness to change, and the imaginative pursuit of the strategies that are needed. In the face of those kinds of requirements, the prospects of religious groups sharing the gods with the culture are not good. Still, the situation is not without hope.

TOWARD TURNING
THINGS AROUND

The person who values faith and believes in the church is asking the obvious question: "What can be done?" As a sociologist whose primary expertise lies in description and explanation, I have shied away from trying to lay out specific policies and programs aimed at resolving religion's problems. You who are working out there on the lines are in a much better position than I am to think through the implications of what I've been finding. You are located in a wide variety of organizational contexts that vary greatly in both their receptivity and abilities to change.

Nevertheless, since I, too, am interested in seeing a much better connection between the gods and the culture, I want to wander slightly outside my officially defined boundaries as a sociologist and attempt to provide interested readers with some ideas concerning what needs to happen. You will have to fill in the specifics.

For those readers who aren't exactly in an upbeat mood at the moment, in light of what has been said so far, let me begin by pointing out that for all its problems, organized religion has demonstrated remarkable resilience in the face of social change over the course of history. Contrary to the expectations of the early secularization advocates, including Auguste Comte, Sigmund Freud, and Karl Marx, religion is hardly in its death throes. Proclamations of religion's imminent demise, such as those of the "death of God" movement of the 1960s, have also proved to be inaccurate.[1]

Even such highly respected observers in our time as Thomas Luckmann, Peter Berger, and Bryan Wilson have underestimated the recuperative powers of existing churches. Established groups haven't just rolled over and died. The Roman Catholic Church is a rather powerful, long-established multinational corporation. The same can be said of the Anglican, Presbyterian, Lutheran, and Baptist churches, as well as many other smaller denominations, not to mention three or four major world religions. A few upstarts, such as the Mormons and Jehovah's Witnesses, have also been involved in global-expansion programs. Religious groups don't readily die. They retreat, retrench, revamp, and resurface.

The story is far from over. Religion remains a part of Canadian life. Resources are not yet depleted and constituents continue to be numerous. The possibilities have few limits. Trends can be altered and emphases can be switched. There still is time for the gods to be rediscovered by the churches and unveiled to the populace. The camera is still running.

For the record, to an extent well beyond what I felt when *Fragmented Gods* was released in 1987, I for one believe that the current religious situation in Canada should be providing those who value faith with considerable hope. The critical practical question is how religion's current poverty might give way to the tapping of its potential. Four central features, it seems to me, will be associated with faith being shared with culture: a rethinking of the church, a re-examination of culture, the renewing of old minds, and the replacing of old strategies.

RETHINKING THE CHURCH

Observers such as McMaster's Alan Roxburgh and journalist Tom Harpur maintain that religious groups urgently need to rediscover why they have been called into being if they are ever to move beyond current widespread self-absorption and address the spiritual needs of Canadians. Maintaining that a new world calls for a new church, Roxburgh writes that the church "remains focused upon itself. Until this is changed evangelization will continue to look like forays into the world in order to recruit members for our clubs. We must refocus the life of the church from the inside to the outside."[2] Harpur is widely perceived — especially by evangelicals — to be attacking organized religion. Yet his critiques stem from his strong sense that Canadians desperately need what religion has to offer; however, he points out, because of the means-end inversion of the churches, those needs are not being met.[3] Accordingly, from time to time, he has reminded me as well that I, too, have been "too soft" on the churches. For Harpur, the crisis is now.

I believe both men are right. There is a great need for religious groups to rethink what they are for and proceed to rework their views as to what's worth pursuing and what counts as success.

What Business Are We In?

In June 1989 I had the opportunity to speak at the national gathering of a small religious organization known as the Danish Church Abroad. One of the things I found intriguing about the DCA was its clarity of purpose. It was founded in 1919 by several established church people within the Danish Lutheran Church. Its purpose was to serve thousands of Danish workers who, at that time, were stranded in Berlin. Within a few years, it had spread to several European countries and now supports close to 50 pastors in more than a dozen countries, including six in Canada.

The DCA doesn't do missionary work, but rather has as its primary goal the provision of church services for Danish emigrants in their mother tongue for as long as they have an interest in it. Congregations make donations toward expenses, but the typical deficit balances are made up by the voluntary contributions to the DCA by Danes in Denmark. Organizationally, churches are not only expected but almost encouraged to fade away or become indigenous Lutheran churches, sometimes with a measure of pain for those involved. Benny Grey Schuster, the pastor of the Granby congregation in Surrey B.C., wrote in a letter to me:

> It's one thing what our mother organization in Denmark is foreseeing. It's quite another thing how the individual congregations feel about it. It is difficult — not to say psychologically impossible — to literally pour blood, sweat, and tears into the ongoing life of a small church if you haven't got the hope of survival after your own generation.[4]

The organizational experts keep telling us today that we need to be asking ourselves, "What business are we in?" The DCA is explicit about its goal: to service Lutheran emigrants from Denmark on a transitional basis. When its service is no longer needed, it will move on.

Other Canadian religious groups need to ask themselves the same question: "What business are we in?" Once more, the observations of Carleton University law professor Margaret Ogilvie are helpful. She recently told Presbyterians, for example, that "self-definition is vital to identity and survival in the rough and tumble of an international free market in religion as it never was in the Old Christian Canada. If we do not know what we believe, we can hardly expect others to know, or to care." She makes the point that "feeding the hungry and sheltering the homeless" are common to myriad religious and secular groups. "Without a firm doctrinal identity," she suggests, "our congregations are little more than lower middle-class social clubs or social welfare agencies."[5]

Such a serious raising of the "What business are we in?" question would undoubtedly reveal that, not unlike the Danish Church Abroad, many groups:

- have considerable ethnic homogeneity;
- give limited effort to recruiting outsiders;
- provide varied services to members;
- decline when no longer used by the people for which the group came into being;
- essentially follow their own people when establishing new congregations.

Disparaging though it may sound, in reality many groups are religious "clubs," existing nationally and even beyond to serve geographically mobile members. They are usually insular and isolated, both socially and culturally. That's why in the 1990s, we continue to have churches lining up like retail outlets on single city streets or within a few blocks of each other. They all claim to be open to the entire world. But their clienteles are typically highly specialized.

Such organizations develop programs that are particularly attractive to the initiated. Success invariably is measured by the turnstile count — the number of people who come through the doors, complete with their human and financial resources. Problems and crises for such congregations and denominations are related to concerns about insufficient numbers and insufficient resources, since both are major threats to organizational viability.

It's what some call a maintenance mentality. Mathers argues that it can be seen everywhere — when leaders "talk about more programs for 'our' people, and never ask themselves what they can do for the unchurched"; in board meetings where hours are spent "arguing about the plumbing, without any thought of a world that needs to hear the gospel"; and even "in the mission group that sees mission as 'over there' when it really should begin right outside our church doors."[6]

Strictly from the standpoint of personal preference, there's nothing wrong with churches' wanting to function as clubs. We have a variety of service clubs, golf and country clubs, private clubs, and professional clubs; why not religious clubs as well?

Further, some religious groups — Unitarians, Hutterites, and Jews, for example — make no claim to being engaged in the proselytizing business. Private sharing of faith among existing believers is centrally valued. In the Jewish instance, when sociologist Robert Brym informs the Jewish community that 50,000 of Canada's 370,000 Jews regard themselves as "cultural" rather than "religious" Jews — especially in secularized British Columbia — the response is to talk about the need for "outreach to the unaffiliated," and to "increase education about intermarriage."[7]

Let religious groups be cultural enclaves and clubs, if that's what they want. What's important, however, is for groups to recognize what they are doing, so that they can proceed to do it well. Like the Danish Church Abroad and some other groups, let's have no pretence of outreach. Let's be more intentional about recruiting geographically mobile members and learn how best to serve them.

The difficulty I personally have with the club concept is that it runs the risk of giving only lip service to the pressing need and exciting opportunity that exists today for Canada's religious groups: relating faith to the 70% to 80% of the population who don't have their membership club cards — and may never want them.

To be healthy, an organization clearly requires a committed core of members who will provide the resources needed for it to function. No one disputes that. The question is this: To what extent will religious groups also define themselves as bridges to the people outside the church doors, not for the purpose of producing bigger churches, but for the purpose of sharing faith with people who need it? Can they go beyond a preoccupation with maintenance to a preoccupation with mission?[8] Put another way, is it possible for churches to define themselves as being not in the church-building business, but in the faith-sharing business?

Such a redefinition of primary purpose, you see, is needed if those Canadians who are open to spirituality are to come in contact with the "unknown gods" that religion historically has had to offer. Well-respected and thought-provoking McGill theologian Douglas John

Hall reminds us that "for all intents and purposes, we have measured Christian faithfulness by the same criteria of success as are applied by the other institutions of our host culture." Spiritual vitality, says Hall, tends to be gauged by such quantitative factors as economic viability, membership growth, property holdings, and community influence.[9]

What's Worth Pursuing

If churches are, in fact, in the faith-sharing business, then priorities will commonly be reworked. People who already value faith will continue to come together and share faith with each other. Worship and experiencing of the gods, mutual sustenance and education, will all be important. Solid organizations, complete with sound human and financial resources, will unquestionably be necessary.

But the primary focus of religious groups that really are in the faith-sharing business will not be inward but outward. People involved in such settings will work to find ways to bring the gods to the populace.

The goal, however, is not as trivial as merely getting people out to church. As Harold Percy puts it, "Evangelism is not about trying to find more workers and more money for the church, nor is it about trying to conscript new members to ensure the church survives."[10]

That would be a hollow victory. The goal is to share faith. And if it should happen that those people who find faith want to come together with others in a formal physical building, so be it. More important, however, is that they are introduced to what faith has to say to life and death, and that they meet with other people who share that pursuit — wherever and whenever they find they wish to do so. It's been said so many times in so many ways. But it needs to be said again: structure must be secondary to content. Remember that the apostle of old who reminded the people of Athens about "unknown" gods also was clear about where they were to be found . . .

> What therefore you worship as unknown, this I proclaim to you. The God who made the world and everything in it, he who is Lord of heaven and earth, does not live in shrines made by human hands.[11]

Believe it or not, there are a good many religious folk in Canada whose view of faith is so narrow that they make a virtue of putting people into buildings or homes at regular times and for set time periods. They see sheer physical placement as the culmination of commitment — people in buildings, regularly. Against the opportunity I am observing in the culture, it isn't much of a vision.

What's Worth Counting

But it's easy to count. "About 180 out to church this morning, up 20 from last week, down 30 from last year," reads a typical summation. "The offering for last week was $900, month to date, $2,300, down $200 from last year at this time," proclaims the church bulletin.

The central place that church figures have for some who value faith can be seen in the primary importance that the first section of this book has to most readers. "What's happening in the churches?" is the question that's foremost on many minds. "What's happening in the culture because of what is happening in the churches?" is a question that's largely overlooked.

What's worth counting? It depends on what business religious groups are in. If they are in the church-building business, it makes sense to count heads and dollars. If they are in the faith-sharing business, it makes sense to count heads and dollars in order to get a sense of organizational health, as well as what kind of faith-sharing might be going on *within* the local outlet or the national corporation.

It doesn't take an expert in evaluation research, however, to point out the need for the counting to go much further:

- What kind of efforts are being made to bring faith to outsiders?
- What kind of success is being experienced in bringing faith to outsiders?
- What is their subsequent relationship to others in the faith community?
- What more needs to be done?

When these sorts of statistics are added to the annual head counts of average attendance, baptisms, and members in and members out, it will be possible for the skeptical outsider to begin to believe that religious groups are in the faith-sharing business.

Consider these types of things appearing in the annual report:

- Number of informal sessions at Cactus Clubs: 89.
- Number of New Age services and coffee times attended: 34.
- Number of human development courses enrolled in: 18.

- Average number of hours per week members gave to discussing faith: 2.3.
- Number of religious alumni contacted: 142; number in ongoing contact with: 27.

Religious alumni? you ask. More about that shortly.

RE-EXAMINING THE CULTURE

Peter Berger, one of my favourites in the field, has written that sociology involves "looking at old things in new ways."[12] There is a great need for religiously committed people to take such a posture toward culture. For too long culture has been seen as the enemy, whose influence is both pervasive and negative.

Co-opting Culture

Long before I was introduced to the complex and obscure definitions of culture offered by sociologists, my grade eight teacher informed me that "culture is the way of living of a group of people." If we want to understand the people with whom we come in contact, it's essential we understand their cultures — the way they live. Culture is not the enemy; it's our critically important guide to how people live — their values, their ideas, their lifestyles. If we don't like what we see, a constructive attack doesn't involve slaying the culture, but rather confronting the culture makers, notably the media, education, and government.

Culture also can serve as a reminder of the opportunity religion has. Professor Gordon Harland acknowledges that we are living in a secular consumer culture where religion has been fragmented and approached as a consumer product. But, says Harland, it would be a mistake to simply "deplore the secular society or bemoan a consumer culture." What we need to do is "approach the situation as a great opportunity, for the limitations of contemporary secular culture call us to a fresh remembrance of the treasures of the Faith and of the need to articulate and make them available for a searching age."[13]

Effective ministry will involve a co-opting of culture, using it as a map to locate the minds and behaviour of Canadians. For those committed to social and cultural change, such an approach will do more than provide a clear understanding of the *human products* of culture. It will also make it possible to begin to understand the *institutional producers* of culture. To the extent that the religiously committed are unhappy with culture, understanding its nature and sources enables them to play offence rather than defence, to assess the role our key institutions play and determine what needs to be done differently.

Co-opting, whereby existing culture is utilized by religion, may sometimes take the form of making good use of what is found in the culture, including media forms. For example, rather than decrying "that New Age newspaper," the Kitsilano Christian Community took out an ad in Vancouver's *Common Ground* in the summer of 1993. Obviously having reflected on what business it was in, the congregation had itself listed under "Spiritual Practices," sharing a page with such options as Johrei, Shambhala Training, the Sufi Order, and the Zen Centre. The ad read as follows:

> *WARRANTY. Many people are attracted to Christ — it's Christians who give them trouble. If you attend our church, WE PROMISE not to tell you how to dress, feel, think, or vote. We won't discourage your questions or insult your intelligence. WE PROMISE to welcome you in Christ's name, involve you in our community if you like, or leave you in peace if you'd prefer. WE PROMISE to smile now and then, experiencing with you the joy of life in Christ. If we breach this promise, you are entitled to reclaim your misgivings about "organized religion." Kitsilano Christian Community meets Sundays at 9:30 at 1708–West 16th Ave., and in small groups all over the place during the week. Phone. . . .*[14]

The co-opting of culture will also mean, in the Canadian setting, understanding the nature of our "regulated religious economy" and learning how to work more effectively with it. The regulated economy seems to have two dominant features: (1) established religious groupings and (2) pluralistic rules that discourage both truth claims and aggressive recruitment of outsiders. Such a situation means that there is a wariness of new sects and cults, as well as a preference for servicing one's own people rather than engaging in evangelism.

Does this cultural situation mean that religious groups in Canada cannot be effective? Not necessarily. Freer enterprise might make for a more robust religious environment. But built-in monopolies don't have to lead to ineffectiveness and stagnation. In co-opting culture, groups that are numerically dominant will seize the opportunity — the advantage, if you like. They will quit masochistically renouncing their majority and established places, and realize that the relative lack of competition means their people are "still there" and need to be reached. Concepts such as market segmentation, ongoing identification, and religious memory will all be taken seriously as these groups attempt to minister to the spiritual needs of affiliates.

As for newer and smaller groups, they, too, need to understand the implications of a regulated religious economy in Canada. The going will be tough; this is not the free-enterprise religious system of the United States. Segmentation will consequently be extremely important. "Fish-net" efforts to market religion to everyone will result in a frequent waste of resources — not to mention negative public relations. The guidelines should be fairly obvious: newer and smaller "religious companies" need to start with people who identify with them, moving outward through the concentric circles of cousins and friends and religious nothings, through people who are only nominally attached to the established groups, eventually taking on, if they so desire, the people who are religiously involved and committed. Success can be expected to be inversely related to the distance one travels from the centre to the last concentric circle.

Whether Canada's religious groups are attempting to understand trends, individuals, or the nature of the religious economy, culture needs to become their ally. It's an invaluable and indispensable resource in the effective sharing of faith.

Finding Hope in Familiar Places

If our culture is not religion's enemy, neither are the people within our society. As we have seen, most of those Canadians who are not highly committed to the country's religious groups are, through religious memory, not very far away. As researchers such as Calgary's Merlin Brinkerhoff and Wilfrid Laurier's Bruce Hunsberger remind us, there definitely are some people who are bona fide apostates who want absolutely nothing to do with religious groups.[15] But the designation applies to a fairly small number of Canadians.

The question is not how such people can be reached. Our findings make it very clear that most of the people on the edges of organized religion surface for occasional services and rites of passage. Over time, they will make an appearance. If one is less patient, they can be identified almost immediately through community surveys. Such surveys are hard work, time-consuming, and require a good number of people. As a result they are ideally conducted in co-operation with other religious groups in the areas that also recognize the merits of gathering such data. The work will result in immediate psychological and practical benefits: almost overnight, the pool of people congregations have an opportunity to relate to will grow exponentially.

The really tough question isn't contact. It's purpose. What do religious groups want to do with them? What do they want to accomplish? If their goal is simply to add outsiders to the church roster, to have them become more involved, then (they) probably will have limited success. The reason is that we find virtually no support for the argument that Canadians, in large numbers, are in the market for religious groups. On the contrary, organized religion is embraced with enthusiasm by a maximum of about one in five. Most people, the research says, want God, self, and society emphases. To return to our earlier analogy, they want a hole, not a drill. If the committed are primarily interested in selling them on their churches, they are going to win some and lose many.

Consequently, if religious groups aspire to be more than just religious clubs, ways have to be found to respond with integrity to people's spiritual needs, rather than selling them on churches *per se*. But let's be very clear. Thanks to religious memory, religious organizations are in an extremely unique and enviable position: they have a ready-made and highly stable clientele.

I would be remiss if I didn't quickly tell you a pertinent story about what I have proclaimed to be a rare phenomenon — a person who actually takes my research seriously. A minister in Calgary, Mary Thomas, told the *United Church Observer,* "We have to start seeking out" people who belonged to the church but gradually slipped away. "Reginald Bibby has said our United people haven't left us. They're just sitting out there. And to me, our mission is to be out there finding them."

She meant what she said. Thomas single-handedly blitzed the area surrounding her church. Here's how the *Observer* described her approach:

> The red-haired woman in the bomber jacket sprints up the front steps of a house in north Calgary and punches the doorbell. "Hi!" she smiles and looks directly into the eyes of the woman who answers. "My name is Mary Thomas. I'm the United Church minister in this area and I'm looking for my United Church people. Are you one of them?" It's a phrase [she] has uttered 4,000 times in the past year.[16]

Thomas's efforts resulted in 11 new families being brought into the church. She also uncovered people of other religions with an interest in having interfaith dialogue.

To put it mildly, I was impressed to hear about Thomas. But I have to say she did things the hard way — incredibly valiantly, but nonetheless, the hard way. A community survey identifying United Church folk would have saved her a lot of time.

But in some situations — and hers may have been one of them — going out into the highways and byways to round up the sheep may not even be a good use of resources. The truth is that if clergy and congregational leaders keep their wits about them and are patient, the sheep will eventually show up.

The data indicate that very large numbers of Canadians will, *on their own*, make contact with the nation's religious groups for marriages, baptisms, funerals, and the like. To use a crude analogy, in time, the gophers will come out of their holes. Further, as we have seen, on any given Sunday approximately one in three people who are present for worship are not regular weekly attenders. My surveys, along with Angus Reid's and Statistics Canada's, have all pegged the proportion of weekly churchgoers at about 23%, down from the previous years. Gallup, meanwhile, has been finding that people attending services over given seven-day periods — comprising the weeklys and others — has increased from a low of 27% in 1990 to a 1993 level of 36%.[17] This means that the percentage of Canadians who attend services at least occasionally is actually up. What's significant is that the finding signals the fact that there has been a slight increase in the number of people who seem willing to give the churches a chance.

TABLE C1. **WEEKLY ATTENDANCE AND WEEKLY ATTENDERS.**		
	In %'s	
	1990	1993
Weekly Attendance	27	36
Weekly Attenders	23	23

It's crucial here that denominations and local churches be prepared for their encounters with these marginal affiliates, and maximize their opportunities for ministry. If these people on the outskirts of the churches find that their core spiritual needs are being addressed, there is good reason to believe that a significant number will be responsive.

The apparent stranger in church on a given Sunday, the late-night caller enquiring about getting married, the couple asking to have their baby baptized, the troubled wife wanting advice about her failing marriage, the family attempting to deal with a sudden death, the young person fascinated with psychic phenomena, the university student who is intrigued with channelling — all signal spiritual quest and an opportunity for significant ministry.

Anglican Archbishop Michael Peers has observed that "even in a highly secular society like ours, there are profound and inarticulate perceptions about what is sacred."[18] Picking up on the same impression, John Congram, editor of the *Presbyterian Record,* has recently drawn attention to the fact that ridiculing so-called "Christmas and Easter Christians" is a popular seasonal sport in the churches. He wisely suggests that many of those who make their appearance believe and have deep feelings, but perhaps are wounded, alienated, confused, and uncertain. "Their appearance," says Congram, needs to be "respected instead of being patronized." Such events should be times when, if anything, "we invite all of these to come home — and to stay home, permanently."[19]

The end result may not always be a new member or a new envelope user. In all these cases, however, the door is being opened for religious groups to share faith. One hopes they will possess both the vision and the resources to respond effectively.

To return to Berger's phrase, what's needed here is the ability to see old things in new ways, to recognize the widespread receptivity to spirituality. And then respond.

RENEWING OLD MINDS

It has been apparent throughout this concluding section that a major transformation is required in the prevalent thinking about what organized religion is all about. It's not a modest request.

Considering New Possibilities

Many readers undoubtedly are already on the defensive.

- Asking what kind of business the churches are in will sound audacious to some, who will assume they are already very clear about what they are attempting to accomplish.
- Asking leaders to rethink their goals and their criteria for success, including what they are bothering to tally, will be unsettling for more than a few.

- Asking the committed to rethink the virtues of church attendance, regular or otherwise, is asking an awful lot.
- Asking people to co-opt culture connotes a sellout to many who are wary of culture and feel it has little to say to them.
- Asking clergy and others to look for opportunity in familiar places is to run the risk of being greeted with cynicism about why people want rites of passage, drop in occasionally, or are intrigued with the mysterious.

So be it. Unless Canada's religious leaders are willing at least to consider such possibilities, things are going to continue pretty much the way they are. Organized religion will continue to decline, while the majority of Canadians who are receptive to God and spirituality will remain essentially outside the churches. Such unnecessary closed-mindedness will further debilitate religion's effectiveness.

For those involved in the Christian tradition, I remind you that the apostle Paul, no less, calls you to rise above the normal ways culture puts reality together and see things from a different angle — to not be "conformed to this world but be transformed by a renewing of your minds." That kind of renewal of outlook is what the sociologist is calling for.

Who Will Be First?

My good friend and colleague, Dr. Bud Phillips, the principal of the Vancouver School of Theology, has reminded me that there are a number of stages that organizations — including churches — go through before they are willing to change. Only the most astute make changes when things are going extremely well, for why change a successful formula? Other organizations are willing to make alterations when problems begin to set in; leaky boats need to be attended to. But in still other organizational instances, it takes a full-blown crisis before change is seriously considered. The responses have been summarized by Phillips and others as tuning, adaptation, reorientation, and reformation.[20]

To scan the landscape of organized religion in Canada is to see a handful of groups at stage one, a large number at stages two and three, and a growing number at stage four. Among those in the last category are Quebec Roman Catholics. In their report, the Assembly of Bishops' research committee wrote:

Many community members have become much more conscious than 10 or 15 years ago of the urgency to do something drastic. They now realize clearly that by continuing on their current course, communities are simply heading for gradual extinction. Therefore, they are prepared to try something new and to take risks. This consciousness is an asset to be emphasized.[21]

Eventually almost every group that wants to survive will likewise have to open its mind. It's only a matter of time. The wise groups will recognize that the sooner they consider looking at old things in new ways, the better their chances of both effectively touching the lives of Canadians and flourishing as organizations. Drawing on the concept of metachurch, or changing church, Pentecostal Assemblies minister Robert W. Jones offers the observation that, over time, the church has survived and thrived on change. "Churches that are in touch in the '90s," he suggests, "may be small or large or mega-large, but they must be meta-large in their approach to ministry."[22] They also, as Presbyterian Robert Bernhardt reminds us, will do more than voice the rhetoric of the day about the need for change, new paradigms, and the like, "without deciding what actually has to be different" and proceeding to take some significant chances.[23]

Religious organizations that close their minds to new possibilities and new necessities will soon be relegated to history. Those that insist on remaining religious clubs, relying on recruiting the initiated and closing their minds to new possibilities, will see their numbers dwindle as fewer and fewer Canadians opt for religious clubs in the face of the secular social competition. And the religious groups that remain set in their old ways — feigning evangelism and outreach from the safety of their buildings, measuring success in terms of membership and finances — will likewise find that oblivion is not a great distance away.

There are, however, some very viable options to fragility and death.

REPLACING OLD STRATEGIES

A Quick Recall

In thinking of specific strategies that can be used to more effectively share faith with Canadian society, we have already emphasized a number of themes. To briefly recap:

1. A mind-set aimed at church-building needs to be replaced with a mind-set of faith-sharing.
2. In reaching out to Canadians on the fringe of religion, groups must locate those people who identify with them; this can readily be done through community surveys and by a careful, collective cataloguing of both occasional attenders and people who request rites of passage.
3. Relatedly, because geographical mobility is a fact of Canadian life, groups need to develop means of keeping track of their mobile members and affiliate "leads" as they move from place to place.
4. People who identify with Canada's various groups should be carefully targeted with an integrated religious message that addresses God, self, and society.
5. There needs to be a clear recognition that the goal is not to put people in the pews; the goal is to minister to Canadians who want spiritual answers far more than they want church involvement.
6. The subsequent relationship of these people to the church needs to be left largely to the gods, to evolve naturally.

Such emphases must be supplemented with old strategies that have proved helpful. In addition, there is a great need for innovation. Personally, I love imagination, creativity, and risk-taking, and find myself smiling when I hear a catchy commercial, an insightful line, a perceptive bit of humour, a student who takes a chance with a wild thought.

Today's most successful organizations have great amounts of all three traits, especially if they are newer entries in the highly competitive marketplace. Canada's religious groups are deeply in need of those qualities. They need leaders who are clear on what their groups want to accomplish, and then must be wonderfully imaginative and uninhibitedly creative in laying out an array of possibilities in the areas of policy and action.

Some Personal Brainstorming

The job is not mine; it's yours. But I've never been lost for a wild idea or two. Some probably should be trashed; others might have some promise. In any event, what's needed are lots of ideas. So here are a few of mine.

1. THE WORSHIP SERVICE–CENTRED CHURCH

We've been accustomed to creating churches that cater to entire families, complete with a complex range of activities. Given such factors as time constraints and diverse family structures, what is also needed is a church that both offers little and asks for little. Many people would simply like a superb worship service, complete with good music and a centrepiece sermon, offered by a person who has deep faith in God and attempts to relate that faith to everyday life.

No, they don't want the frills — the coffee after the service, the Wednesday night potluck, the Saturday social, even the Sunday school. They have neither the time nor the inclination. They do, however, want to worship, reflect, hear what God has to say about life.

I'm thinking here, ideally, of a church service where people hear a skilled and compelling preacher — a Presbyterian like Peter Marshall; a Baptist turned Episcopalian like John Claypool; the former London, Ontario, United Church pulpiteer Maurice Boyd. A sociologist friend of mine who doesn't claim to be particularly devout, surprised me a few years ago by telling me nonchalantly that his biggest regret about having to return to Montreal from London upon the completion of his study leave was that he wouldn't be able to hear Maurice Boyd preach anymore. He wanted little more than worship and a sermon, was receiving it, and it was changing his life.

On the basis of my research, combined with extensive conversations with average people across the country, I am convinced there is a tremendous market for such a specialized church. Maybe it would be a new church; maybe an outlet operated by an existing congregation. Perhaps a group of people who understand such a concept could begin to put together a chain of such specialized churches, renting some of the country's best old and empty physical structures for an hour sometime between 8 a.m. and 1 p.m., bringing in a superbly trained preacher and music team.

Regardless of the precise shape, the worship service–oriented church would be a welcome addition to the Canadian religious scene.

Several years ago, the frozen food giant Stouffer Food Corp. conducted research that showed that a significant proportion of their sales were to families with two or more children. In response, Stouffer developed the "family casserole" line and marked the dinners in packages containing meals for four or more people. The line flopped. Why? Because Stouffer's research failed to detect "split-menu dining" — the growing trend among larger active families to neither always eat together, nor necessarily eat the same things. All food manufacturers, say the experts, are having to adjust to the decline and possible ultimate death of the family meal. Consequently they are continually developing products that will appeal to diverse eating habits.[24]

Similarly, religious groups need to adjust to the realities of women with or without children[25] working outside the home, seven-day work schedules, divorce, remarriage, cohabitation, and demands on time that spread family members in every direction. The religious version of the family casserole line at minimum needs to be supplemented. The worship-centred church might be a valuable addition.

Such a possibility requires a "renewal of minds," a rethinking of what a church is for. But if that mental hurdle can be cleared and new steps taken, this specialized church form would provide an opportunity for people who want to find God intersecting with life, yet are not particularly excited about traditional churches and their programs.

A footnote: for those who think religious commitment means far more involvement, keep in mind that for some people this may well be only a first stage of renewed participation. It is, however, an attempt at ministry, beyond just sheer recruitment. Many may not want anything more. Others might. It seems to me that people who believe they are in the faith-sharing business will be content with either outcome.

2. HUMAN RESOURCE DEVELOPMENT

Earlier, I made the point that the efforts of churches to be effective organizations are hampered by their excessive reliance on volunteers. Undoubtedly a need exists for more paid staff, or at least for people willing to offer themselves to churches full-time for given periods at little or not cost — as is done, for example, in the case of the Latter-Day Saints.

In 1986, for example, the Anglicans started a program called Volunteers in Mission, through which people serve the church in various parts of the world for periods of up to one year at their own expense. In 1991 the Lutherans also began to participate in the VIM program.[26] In the late 1980s, the Canadian Baptist Federation established Canadian Baptist Volunteers, a similar program that church journalist Larry Matthews notes has been in need of funding, yet is "thrilling for the churches and a potent force for Canadian Baptist unity."[27]

The positive news about voluntarism in Canada is that religious groups are the main benefactors of such giving of time and talent. In documenting that fact in its 1987 survey on the subject, Decima Research noted that "volunteering is an accepted, if not expected part of being a member of many religious organizations."[28] A recently published analysis by University of Waterloo sociologist James Curtis and his colleagues found that one in four Canadians who do unpaid voluntary work give their time exclusively to religious groups.[29] Potentially religious groups have a lot of volunteers who can make significant contributions.

But better tapping of that volunteer work force is needed. A starting point is to recognize its tremendous diversity. When I was attending seminary almost three decades ago, I was introduced to the analogy of the church as a locker room — the place where people go at half-time after playing their hearts out. There they get a rundown and a pep talk from the minister-coach (significantly, there was not a coach *and* trainer). Refreshed, they charge back out through the doors and resume the game of life.

Following graduation, it didn't take me very long in the pastorate to realize that a more appropriate analogy perhaps was the hospital. Some members of the congregation were quite elderly; others were hurting emotionally; others simply trying to cope with life. They didn't want to blast onto the field. May I be forgiven for often admonishing them to "come alive" and be "the church in the world." As a patient parishioner kindly said to me on one occasion, "I enjoy your sermons, but I need to be fed." At the time I was puzzled, even a little annoyed. Somewhere along the way, the light finally went on.

Effective churches need to be in touch with their human resources. Not everyone can become actively engaged on the front lines of faith-sharing. Some people have retired and want to stay that way; clergy should leave them alone if that's what they want. Others are sick or injured; leaders need to quit admonishing them to take up their beds and work. But the rest of the committed bring diverse abilities and talents. A good organization lets some teach, others carry out administration, some deal with youth, others look after the music, and so on.

Then, there are those bent on reaching outside congregational life and engaging in Cactus Club conversations and other contacts with the culture. Good use can be made of them as well.

The point here is that, contrary to the claims of observers like Posterski and Barker, not every member is up to the "four pillars" of orthodoxy, community, relevance, and outreach. They either can't or won't embrace all four.

- Some members primarily need to be nourished; presumably churches can respond to them.
- Others want to become more able at what they are doing; hopefully human resource development possibilities are available to them.
- Then there are others whose vision of the church is primarily one of faith-sharing. They, too, need to be recognized, equipped, and supported.

The diversity of the religious volunteer work force can be a strength, not a weakness. But for more effective ministry to take place, there is a great need to recognize that diversity openly and proceed to work with it.

3. THE RITES OF PASSAGE MINISTER

Yes, of course I realize there already are specialty ministers who deal with religious education, visitation, music, youth, and so on. But for some time I've had something else in mind. In view of the fact that such large numbers of Canadians are going to be making contact with the nation's churches requesting rites of passage, why not be consciously set up for the onslaught?

Specifically, denominations — and in some cases, large congregations — would be wise to have personnel in place trained to deal with such people. As things stand, requests for marriages, baptisms, christenings, and even funerals are often treated as nuisances, unwanted interruptions in already busy and stressful ministerial schedules.

I'm not suggesting clergy try to rival the late United Church minister, Irvin Gordon Perkins, who performed 6,430 marriages in 56 years of ministry in Ontario — an average of about 115 a year or two each week, including about ten a week for more than 25 years in Toronto! Perkins, by the way, deservedly won the title of "Canada's Marrying Minister."[130] Many clergy have more pressing concerns on their minds than how to minister to marginal affiliates who want ceremonies carried out.

As I have been arguing, these contacts, at minimum, are invaluable leads. It seems like a good use of resources to have specialists in place who can consciously and productively respond to them. For example, the Anglican Church in Halifax might hire a diocesan "passage specialist." When a person who is not involved in the parish makes a request to be married, the minister who receives the inquiry — having received some basic public relations training in theological school and beyond — might politely say, "the Anglican Church appreciates your making contact," and proceed to inform the person that the church has someone who deals with situations in which a person is not actively involved in a particular parish. At that point, having received the permission of the enquirer, the minister would pass on his or her name to the "passage specialist," who would contact the couple and, on the basis of the screening, decide what should happen next.

Lest the idea sound rather extreme, readers need to know that the Unitarian Church has been practising something akin to it since 1970. Because the small number of Unitarian clergy couldn't keep up with the demand for weddings, memorial services, and infancy-naming ceremonies, the Canadian Unitarian Council established a chaplaincy program, in which lay persons who are trained as chaplains by the CUC, which is legally responsible for their registration with provincial authorities.[31]

No one is saying, by the way, that religious groups should have such specialty ministers simply to meet the rites demands of the customers; obviously it will be up to the religious group to decide how requests should be handled. But my point is that the demand for rites of passage is and will continue to be enormous. People will appear. The stewardship question that religious groups have to answer is how will religious groups respond? Merely to turn people away is less than a trivial triumph; it also misses an opportunity for significant interaction. To handle the situation superficially is to fare little better. What's needed is a focused attempt to deal with people on the edges of the nation's churches. A rites-of-passage minister could be one answer.

Churches have a wide range of specialty ministries. If denominations can have chaplains for students and even for air travellers,[32] surely the need for ministry to people seeking rites isn't too tough a sell.

4. RELIGIOUS ALUMNI

In a city even the size of Lethbridge (population 60,000), I constantly run into people who were previously highly involved in one religious group or another, but are not now. Consistent with the national patterns, these "religious alumni" continue to view themselves as "Anglican" or "United" or "Baptist" or "Roman Catholic." At worst, they insert the prefix, "former" or "ex."

Curiously, many say they have never been contacted by their groups. They had moved away from another place and that was that. Reminiscent of an American study of Presbyterian dropouts, where two-thirds said that no one had even enquired about their absence,[33] no one wrote, no one called. Typically, these people are not especially interested in submerging themselves in congregational life, complete with social entanglements and time commitments, but it's worth noting that most are not upset with religious groups, nor are they negative about participating in meaningful worship. They are prime candidates for the worship-centred church.

Moreover, my discussions with religious alumni here and elsewhere lead me to believe they are not at all reluctant to contribute some of their time, expertise, and even money to their alma maters. Four such good friends in Alberta who value Christian faith, yet are not involved in local churches, include: a city human resources director, a media advertising rep, the executive director of a major alcohol and drug abuse organization, and a highly regarded history professor.

Most would benefit from some ties with organized religion, notably worship opportunities. They also have much to bring. More important, they have informed me that they would make their services available if asked. I'm reminded of a story that Brian Fraser, the Dean of St. Andrew's Hall at the University of British Columbia, told me about a multimillionaire who died and left behind millions to various charities, but only about $10,000 to the church where he had been an elder for years. When the dismayed and disappointed minister pointedly asked the man's son why his father had not left the church a larger amount, the son is said to have replied, "Because no one ever asked him."

In most communities, even large cities, many of the people who have been involved in religious groups in the past but are not at present can readily be identified. How? Through such a simple exercise as people in a given congregation sitting down from time to time and systematically offering and organizing their collective information about religious alumni. The next step is for the church to figure out what is reasonable to ask and proceed to make contact.

The religious alumni constitute a rich, latent resource pool. They not only require ministry. They also have much to contribute to it.

5. A FACILITY PHILOSOPHY

A good case can be made — and probably has been since the first religious group was formed — for not having any permanent physical facilities at all. Of course we can readily recite the reasons church buildings are necessary, which boil down to needing a place to hold activities. Yet, given the role that facilities seem to play in literally grounding congregations, turning them inward and contributing to means-end inversion, an equally convincing case can be made for dispensing almost altogether with physical facilities. Some congregations, not usually by choice, straddle the issue by renting or leasing space, by the decade, by the year, or by the hour.

In the course of making the gods better known to Canadians, religious groups that bother to use facilities at all need to be highly flexible and creative. In the past, groups have typically thought in terms of large downtown churches and community satellites, with resources determining how large and lavish the structures will be. Roman Catholics and Protestants have had the notion that there should be a facility in virtually every community, with groups like the conservative Protestants commonly adopting neighbourhood names. These days, the fad among some growth-minded groups is "church-planting," where the assumption is that, if a congregational core can be established almost anywhere whatsoever, new members will gradually follow.

And now as we approach the end of the millennium, Roman Catholics cannot find enough priests to cover their numerous parishes, while Protestants find themselves overstocked with anaemic neighbourhood congregations. Compliments of current church-planting efforts, various evangelical groups will not lack for a new batch of small fragile congregations for some years to come. Other faiths have been more fortunate. Mercifully their numbers only warranted the construction or purchase of a small number of sites.

Their members usually had to drive to the synagogues, temples, and mosques.

Facilities logically have to match philosophy. That's how successful corporations work. It would be strange if religious groups thought they should be any different.

For example, if groups are in the religious club business, then I suppose they would be wise to aspire to build the best place in town, geared primarily to nuclear families and capable of hosting a wide array of activities. If they simply want to plant as many new congregations as possible, with an eye to growing as groups, then I'd imagine that the accompanying facilities that would emerge to house the budding churches would follow a fairly predictable prefab style, with variations based primarily on available finances.

If, however, religious groups are in the faith-sharing business, a bit more imaginative diversity is needed when contemplating structures. The primary issue would not be "how many" we should have but "what kind." The results of such reflection would result in the recognition that facilities for ministry need to be of all shapes and sizes.[34]

A. *THE REGIONAL CHURCH MODEL.* These days, very few viable congregations draw all their people from one neighbourhood. As attested to by the maps on the wall of many a minister's study, a healthy congregation invariably includes people from right across the city and countryside.

Such a demographic reality needs to be explicitly acknowledged. When I was growing up in Edmonton in the 1950s, people walked everywhere. Accordingly we had a neighbourhood school and a neighbourhood grocery store and a neighbourhood hockey rink. My goodness, we even had a neighbourhood doctor who made house visits. Oh yes, we also had our neighbourhood church.

But today we are living in a regional era, symbolized by mega shopping centres and super stores. The tip-off is that we drive almost everywhere — to school, to shop, to the recreational complex, to the doctor, and to church.

This, then, should also be the era of the regional church, not built to serve one neighbourhood but to serve much broader geographical areas. Cognizant of the fact that people eventually will come from all parts of the city and environs, regional churches need to be somewhat larger in size and built close to major arteries. Also cognizant of the fact that communities experience decline in vitality and prestige, regional churches will not have names that link them explicitly to communities. They don't want to live and die with the life-cycle of the areas around them.

Significantly, in monitoring our Circulation of the Saints sample of 20 evangelical churches in Calgary from the late 1960s through to the present, we have found that the congregations that have survived and thrived (a) were regional churches to begin with, (b) packed up and moved their "franchises" to newer parts of the city, or (c) were community churches that redefined themselves as regional churches, complete with new names; for example, Bowness became West Calgary, Ogden became South Calgary. Community churches as such have tended to come and go with the aging of their communities.

Regional churches have significant resource advantages over community counterparts — more elaborate facilities, multiple staffs, more people, more income. Ironically they can come into being through the merger of two or more weak community varieties — not an easy task to pull off, by any means, but still possible in theory. To those quick to say such mergers are virtually impossible, given the loyalties people have to their churches, I would tend to concur. But I would also suggest that the solution is not to continue to keep fragile congregations alive by providing denominational funding. And, for heaven's sake, groups need to be wise enough not to mindlessly create more such small congregations that will have to be dealt with in the future.

The regional proposal invariably draws two criticisms. One is that congregations are impersonal because of size. Large congregations in Canada and the U.S. are well aware of that possibility and have developed various ways of neutralizing it, such as neighbourhood study groups, occupational groups, and a variety of social events. The second is that going regional means abandoning the communities themselves. Nothing could be further from the truth. The regional concept simply means that no single neighbourhood is being asked to support a church by itself. In regional form, the church has the resources to minister to the communities. An area characterized by heavy immigration or poverty, for example, can now be better addressed because of composite resources. Here, the regional church is a far nobler response to community needs than the proverbial flight to the suburbs.

Once again, a renewal of minds is badly needed. I suggested to the Edmonton Roman Catholic diocese about three years ago that, contrary to their fears, they didn't really have a priest shortage; the problem was that they had too many parishes! If they would quit trying to provide a building for every community and enlarge their parish boundaries — in short, think regionally — many of their personnel problems would be solved. The shortage at this point in time, at least, was in large part because the means had become the ends; churches established to serve the people had become the preoccupation of the diocese.

How important are such regional churches? For what it's worth, American church planter Lyle Schaller maintains that the emergence of large churches, even "megachurches," is "the most important development of modern Christian history." He argues that such churches make it possible to offer "a broad range of choices in teaching, scheduling and programming," and goes so far as to say that one reason for the decline of mainline Protestant bodies in the U.S. has been their reluctance to foster such big versatile churches. "Like the mom and pop grocery stores, small churches can't compete with them," says the 69-year-old United Methodist. He adds, "Whether it's right or not is not terribly important. It's where we are. The churches have to live where the world is."[35]

A quick asterisk concerning rural areas. The same principle holds. For years religious groups have been providing large numbers of small religious outlets for farmers and other people living in small communities. Denominations continue to have multipoint charges, where some ministers conduct at least three services every Sunday. It's a luxury that few groups can now afford. This is the age of the car and truck and sports car. A lot of those same "ruralites" drive past their church buildings many times a week to obtain needed products and services that are most certainly not being brought to them. Good stewardship calls for a regional movement in rural Canada as well.

B. THE 7–11 MODEL. Regular church structures are good for some things, not so good for others. During my graduate school days at Washington State University in the early 1970s, I spent two years studying Skid Row missions in Seattle. The people who attempted to minister to the homeless men maintained that the appropriate facility was essentially a storefront church — a retail outlet converted into a religious outlet, readily accessible to men in the heart of the Skid Row area.

Regional churches need to be supplemented by what we might call the 7–11 or Mac's Milk model — small physical facilities strategically located in areas requiring ministry. Sometimes it might be a literal storefront; other times it might take the form of a rented gym or some other recreational facility, a coffee shop, a spot somewhere in a high-rise apartment building, maybe even space in a mall.

One highly publicized example of the last has been the Marketplace Chapel in Edmonton's shrine of North American consumerism, the West Edmonton Mall. Started by the Pentecostal Assemblies of Canada as a means of reaching out to mall employees and visitors, it now focuses on ministry to teenagers "who make the mall their second home." The chapel is supported by 16 churches and eight different denominations throughout the city.[36]

Across North America, the Salvation Army has been particularly adept at making use of on-site buildings in ministering not only to homeless men and abused women, but also to young people. In Ottawa, for example, the Army runs a Youth Resource Centre as an emergency shelter for young people described as "abused, 'throwaway' kids" who have been "victims of unstable family violence and unworkable custody situations." The centre is located in the men's hostel in the lower end of town and is usually full.[37] In Vancouver, the Crosswalk Drop-In Centre provides food, clothing, counsel, and referrals to about 8,000 people each month from its downtown, storefront location.[38] Similarly, street ministries like the Mustard Seed have been operated by the Baptists in a number of cities; Hands On is run by the Mennonites in Saskatoon.[39]

C. THE WEDDING CHAPEL MODEL. Invariably this proposal raises hackles, but it needs to be considered. We all know that properties represent significant financial investments and are the church homes of active members. Understandably there is a reluctance to make them overly accessible to people who are not congregational members. Then, incidentally, there's the couple to consider: while they may have a poorly articulated sense that they "want God brought in on this," they may not be particularly anxious to have a ceremony carried out in a church in which they are not involved.

Perhaps, therefore, it would be wise to consider alternative sites to regular church facilities. One option is wedding chapels, operated by religious groups, located in attractive places, with ceremonies carried out in a first-class manner by well-trained personnel. In some instances, the chapels may be part of a regional church complex; in others they might be found in a resort, a small park, maybe even a place like the West Edmonton Mall. Sometimes they might be purchased or built from scratch; on occasion, small fragile churches might be redefined as chapels.

What needs to be kept in mind here is that Canada's religious groups are going to be experiencing an unprecedented number of requests for weddings in the next decade or so. These contacts represent an opportunity that is the envy of any business enterprise. The critical questions that arise include: how will numerically failing churches manage to cope with demand? and how can the churches respond in a way that will maximize the opportunity for ministry?

Chapels may be part of the complex solution.

D. THE COMMUNITY CHURCH MODEL. The call for regional churches is not a call for the elimination of every community church. In some situations where, for example, there is a strong sense of community identity — based on such characteristics as history, geography, ethnicity, or social class — it may well be that the community church concept makes good sense.

I would argue, however, that such situations are the exception rather than the rule. As noted earlier, congregations that live with the community also tend to die with the community. When a community is young, it is populated with young, upwardly mobile couples and plenty of children. Such demographic realities translate into growing churches that are populated with geographically mobile church members and burgeoning Sunday school and youth programs. But the day comes when those upwardly mobile couples and their teenagers and young adults move upward and outward. And the community church finds itself beginning to wheeze and look for the fresh air and new start that the spanking new suburb offers. Regional churches can avoid such a fate.

Still, as mentioned, there are exceptions. But what's needed is the wisdom to know when and when not to go with the community approach.

Clearly some groups are going to have more difficulty than others in persuading their members and hierarchies that structural flexibility is needed. Quebec Roman Catholics are among them. The authors of the *Risking the Future* report find themselves having to question the policy that "gives buildings a disproportionate importance," and asking, "Must we really take every possible means to keep churches that are too large and too costly to maintain?"[40] The fact that the question has to be raised and debated suggests how far that action is lagging behind reflection.

6. RELIGION AND CULTURAL CRASH COURSES

Ideally when the people in the churches interact with the rest of society, the unknown gods are unveiled to the culture. Such idealism, however, makes the critically important assumption that the gods are well-known to the people in the churches. It's a big assumption — probably too big.

Let me get personal here. I myself highly value faith. I am intrigued with the maverick ways the gods work and long ago put aside any presumption about when and how the divine is interacting with things human. Faith for me is something that is deeply personal, very real, extremely important.

Nonetheless, in the midst of attempting to reflect with people who are involved in the churches about faith and life, I find that a typical response is a tolerant ear and a cautious smile, followed by enquiries about where I fellowship or whether I'm keeping up my personal devotional life. On one occasion a fairly flexible evangelical friend who I assumed knew me better told me that when he was asked by conference organizers about my spiritual condition he informed them that I had "come a long way" and "wouldn't embarrass them." The tribute was underwhelming.

Many of the religiously initiated have personal forms of faith that are products of religious assembly lines. They are clones of each other, who use the same words and phrases, think the same thoughts, act the same, and, yes, sometimes even look remarkably similar. They have clear-cut definitions of what constitutes commitment and what does not. There's not a lot of elasticity.

In short, a good number of people involved in the churches lack a religion that has *individuality* — a deeply personal faith that is the end result of the absorbing of information, serious reflection, and uncomfortable and sometimes painful struggle. For many, faith is prefabricated. Observations of others that religion is learned much like the multiplication table[41] or is the result of imitation rather than urgency[42] are not gross exaggerations. It seems particularly clear that the narrow views of spirituality and quest that are prevalent in the churches typically are blinding members and leaders to some of the blatant cultural indicators. Many "church people" fail to spot such obvious signals as the widespread fascination with the meaning of myth; burgeoning enrolments in self-actualization courses; growing interest in teachings emphasizing our oneness with nature; intrigue with the fusion of faith and physics. Such emphases are often not understood and are rejected outright.

Then there are the signals that appear in everyday social interaction:

- a young man musing about his possible encounters with supernatural forces;
- a young widow trying to understand a puzzling dream involving her husband;
- a university student maintaining there is something to reincarnation;
- a person who seldom attends church describing himself as a Lutheran;
- a nominal Roman Catholic attending an occasional mass;
- an office colleague looking for a church to be married in.

If the churches are ever to succeed in introducing the gods to culture, then the churches need to start by introducing the fullness of the gods to their own people. The thesis of J.B. Phillips's book of three decades ago, which is contained in his title, *Your God Is Too Small*, needs to be repeated over and over again within congregational settings. The narrow parameters that frequently limit what people view as valid spirituality and valid enquiry need to be blown away.

Religious groups need to ensure that explicit instruction is provided both inside and outside church settings, so that enhanced clarity concerning religion and today's cultural quest for spirituality can be adequately understood. The concept has been grasped by the authors of the Quebec bishops' *Risking the Future* report. They write that church members must learn "to recognize the signs of a quest for meaning and spirituality in the people they meet," to the end that faith can be shared by people with skills appropriate to secularized society. In ministering effectively to social needs, the authors call on committed believers to become a "creative minority" who engage in "a critical reading of modern culture."[43]

Only through such expanded vision can those who value faith see the gods clearly for what they are — the fullness that religion can bring to life — as well as comprehend the wide range of concerns relating to God, self, and society that religion is capable of addressing.

7. ENSHRINING THE SOCIAL LINK

A final strategy note is not especially wild-eyed, but of fundamental importance. Many of us who have studied the sources of religious commitment over the years have acted like Columbus in search of the New World. Assuming that religious involvement was increasingly something of a random phenomenon, we tended to explore myriad individual and structural determinants of commitment. We not infrequently mixed explanations of sect and cult recruitment with religious participation more generally, using what are referred to as "deprivation" and "processual" models as readily on Episcopalians and Presbyterians as on Mormons and Moonies.

In light of the findings on the high level of stability of religious affiliation between generations, we now know there is little mystery surrounding the sources of commitment in Canada or elsewhere. The transmission of religion follows readily identifiable social lines running from parents to children to friends to marriage partners and varied adult ties. Few religious ideas can be traced to social vacuums.

Religious organizations without adequate programs aimed at young people, such as Sunday schools and teen groups, are asking for annihilation. As a headline in a recent column on children in the *United Church Observer* put it, "They're the hope and strength of every congregation and the future of the church." The new Canadian Buddhist Bishop Y. Matsubayashi is among those who understand the reality well. In a 1993 greeting in Kelowna, B.C., he had this to say: "I wish to concentrate on the children's religious education in my first year. The future of the Buddhist Churches of Canada will depend on the shoulders of our children and grandchildren. In order to bring up fine Buddhist children, I would like to emphasize and revitalize the Dharma School and Young Buddhist Association."[44] He may not succeed. But he knows where best to put his energies.

Further, to the extent that people switch denominations, family considerations are paramount. Congregations that don't have youth programs, including Sunday schools or their counterparts, are going to be at a decided disadvantage. One particularly reputable Baptist minister and leader, Don Burke, goes so far as to say, "I have a hunch that we Baptists could exploit the strong memory of Sunday school that is part of the Canadian Protestant psyche. Most of our churches still have the structures in place for all-age Sunday schools." Burke urges Baptists to take advantage of the situation and offer Canadians "quality Christian education for all ages."[45]

Groups that want to go beyond biological growth and transmit faith to culture more broadly have to learn this relational lesson well. We have seen that outsiders who are recruited to the churches are recruited through social ties, notably friendships and marriage. Groups that aspire to make the gods known to Canadian society will have to ensure that the social link is clearly in place. Without it, the chasm between churches and culture will remain.

TWO POSSIBLE SCENARIOS

The Lost Opportunity

I'm not convinced that things are going to change all that much. The churches remain largely aloof from Canadian society, operating at the congregational level pretty much as isolated and insulated religious clubs. At their national and denominational levels, there tends to be more of an effort to communicate with the broader society. Such efforts on the part of the paid staff, however, often lack the support of the rank and file.

Meanwhile, back in the culture, spiritual receptivity is widespread. Intrigue with mystery and the search for meaning are common among Canadians. The majority are not even lost to the churches; they're just living life a short distance away.

But religious groups are slow to recognize the opportunity that is theirs. Tom Harpur sums up the situation succinctly: "Today an amazing awakening and search for a mature spirituality is going on in Canada, yet the major churches are seen as daily less and less in touch with it."[46] Scott Peck's words are chilling for those who assume that the church and the gods are immortally linked: "It occurred to me," he writes, that God has "possibly largely left the church."[47] Peck could be right; the gods could be in the midst of exploring other options.

Canada's religious groups, however, may scarcely have noticed. They are busy trying to build up their congregations, add new members, balance and increase their budgets, reach the world from the comfort and safety of their sanctuaries. They may never change significantly, never be much more than self-serving social institutions — which continue to dwindle in numbers.

Latter-day prophets, a few in sociological clothing, are as apt to be ignored or belittled as taken seriously. There are few signs that the established groups that have a stranglehold on the identification leanings of the population — the Roman Catholic, United, Anglican, Lutheran, Presbyterian, and Baptist churches — are taking advantage of what amounts to a privileged religious position. But until religious deregulation takes place — and such a development is hardly on the horizon — the very competitors that might wake up Canada's religious establishment and even reduce its market shares, have difficulty gaining credibility, as well as unleashing their resources and vitality. It doesn't seem right; much of the population is not being serviced because of the ineptness of faltering religious companies. Yet that's our current national reality.

And so in the 1990s the Canadian world goes on, churches coexisting with Cactus Clubs, with the twain seldom meeting. Meanwhile, the gods that have so much to say are only partially understood by the churches and are largely misunderstood by society.

Tragically, the gods may remain unknown in Canada.

The New Awakening

There's no reason, however, why that has to be the case. Religion historically has had so much to say about mystery and meaning, offering a powerful integrated message that speaks to the issues of God and the supernatural, individual hope and self-affirmation, societal and interpersonal issues.

People who comprehend that kind of religious faith are living in a time when the cultural conditions are pointing to high levels of receptivity to what religion has been about. Not only that, as William Stahl of Luther College colourfully puts it in his forthcoming new book, this is the age of *God and the Chip*.[48] Religious groups have in their possession the information and technological assets of the computer and electronic age, which can enable them to engage in faith-sharing with more efficiency than any previous generation.

The gods may become known through today's churches, perhaps outside of them, perhaps not at all. But let no one minimize what can be done. People can be located, latent resources can be tapped, new strategies implemented, faith shared. No, just as it was in Paul's day, not everyone will respond. "Some scoffed" then, and there's no doubt some will scoff now. Even in the robust U.S. religious market it appears that the proportion of people who want church-style religion has been coming in at a maximum of about 60%. But, as with Paul's audience when there were those who wanted to hear more, there are those who are likewise receptive today. It's incumbent on Canada's religious groups to do all they can to respond to such people.

In another era, the metaphor of the day resulted in Jesus' phrase "the harvest is plenteous." In the thought-forms of our day, it's clear that "the market is extensive." With resolve, clear-cut purpose, sound organization, and the belief that the effort to transcend personal and group boundaries pleases the gods who provide their resources, those who value faith can emerge from their religious clubs and begin to bridge the gap between the churches and the culture. It's not beyond the realm of possibility. The churches and the country may yet be awakened to the identity of the unknown gods.

It may not happen. But, then again, it can.

APPENDIX

THE PROJECT CANADA NATIONAL ADULT SURVEYS

To date, four PROJECT CANADA adult surveys have been carried out, in 1975, 1980, 1985, and 1990.

DATA COLLECTION METHOD All four surveys — self-administered questionnaires — have been conducted by mail. Each of them has used 11-page, three-hundred-plus variable questionnaires, constructed to yield extensive information pertaining to social issues, intergroup relations, and religion. The 1975 procedures of mailing the questionnaire with a front-page cover letter, sending a followup postcard, and mailing a second questionnaire have been followed, with minor variations, in all four surveys.

SAMPLING A randomly selected sample of about eleven hundred cases is sufficient to claim a confidence level of 95% and a confidence interval of four percentage points when attempting to generalize to the Canadian adult population. Gallup, for example, customarily draws a sample of just under 1,100 people in making those confidence claims.

Size and *representativeness* are the two key criteria in being able to generalize with accuracy from a sample to a population; considerable care, therefore, has been taken to ensure that both standards have been met. First, concerning size, an interest in provincial comparisons resulted in 1,917 cases' being gathered in 1975; in 1980, the sample numbered 1,482; in 1985, 1,630; in 1990 the sample size was 1,472.

Second, with respect to representativeness, the nation has been stratified by province (ten) and community size (>100,000, 99–10,000, <10,000), with the sample drawn proportionate to the national population. As resources have improved, the number of communities involved has increased from 30 in 1975 to 43 in 1980 to 104 in 1985 to 145 in 1990. Participants have been randomly selected using telephone directories (as of 1985, 98.2% of Canadian households owned telephones). Discrepancies between the sample and population characteristics have been corrected by weighting (1975: province, community size, gender; 1980: those three variables as well as age; 1985: province, gender, age). Each of the three samples has been weighted down to about twelve hundred cases in order to minimize the use of large weight factors (i.e., three or more).

As can be seen in TABLE A1, the 1975, 1980, 1985, and 1990 PROJECT CANADA samples are highly representative of the Canadian population. Samples of this size and composition, as noted, should be accurate within about four percentage points on most questionnaire items, 19 times in 20 similar surveys. Comparisons with similar Gallup poll items, for example, have consistently found this to be the case. (See, by way of illustration, findings concerning attitudes toward the courts, capital punishment, beliefs, and practices in the same survey years.)

THE PANEL COMPONENT A major interest of the ongoing national surveys has been monitoring social change and stability. Consequently, while the first, 1975, survey was a typical cross-sectional survey with 1,917 participants, the PROJECT CAN80 sample of 1,482 people included 1,056 who had also been involved in 1975. Similarly, the 1,630 PROJECT CAN85 cases included 566 people who had participated in *both* 1975 and 1980, along with 170 respondents who had filled out the 1980 questionnaire only; 894 were first-time cases. PROJECT CAN90 was comprised of 383 people from 1975, 75 from 1980, 340 from 1985, and 674 first-timers.

RETURN RATES I hold the somewhat unconventional view that return rate is not necessarily a critical issue if one can establish that a representative sample of sufficient size has been attained. With ample resources, including time and endurance, a return rate can readily be increased. However, it may be that one merely nails down the procrastinators in the population rather than gaining the participation of people who are different in some salient way from the early respondents demographically, socially, or psychologically.

Nevertheless, for a national survey, the PROJECT CANADA return

TABLE A1. **Population and Sample Characteristics: 1975, 1980, 1985, 1990**		1975		1980		1985		1990	
		Pop	Samp	Pop	Samp	Pop	Samp	Pop	Samp
Community	100,000+	55	55	51	52	52	54	53	53
Size	99,000–10,000	13	13	15	15	15	16	15	15
	<10,000	32	32	34	33	33	30	32	32
Gender	Male	49	50	49	51	49	50	49	49
	Female	51	50	51	49	51	50	51	51
Age	18–34	39	37	43	40	41	42	40	38
	35–54	35	36	31	31	32	33	33	35
	55 & over	26	27	26	29	27	25	27	27
Marital	Married	70	69	67	67	66	65	67	67
Status	Never Married	22	18	23	20	24	23	21	18
	Widowed	7	10	7	10	6	7	6	7
	Divorced	1	3	3	3	4	5	6	8
Income	<$5,000	13	16	5	6	—	—	—	—
	<$10,000	—	—	—	—	7	10	5	7
	$5,000– 14,999	49	49	23	26	—	—	—	—
	$10,000– 14,999	—	—	—	—	10	10	7	6
	$15,000– 24,999	29	25	32	32	19	25	16	14
	$25,000+	9	10	40	36	—	—	—	—
	$25,000–39,999	—	—	—	—	30	30	24	25
	$40,000+	—	—	—	—	34	26	—	—
	$40,000–59,999	—	—	—	—	—	—	24	26
	$60,000+	—	—	—	—	—	—	24	22
Education	Secondary– Less	65	61	59	52	54	50	49	45
	Post-Secondary +	35	39	41	48	46	50	51	55
Religion*	Protestant	46	46	46	50	41	45	37	44
	Anglican	12	12	12	12	10	12	8	11
	Baptist	3	3	3	3	3	3	3	3
	Lutheran	3	3	3	3	3	3	2	3
	Pentecostal	1	1	1	1	1	1	2	2
	Presbyterian	4	4	4	5	3	3	2	4
	United Church	18	18	18	18	16	16	12	15
	Other/ Unknown	5	5	5	8	5	7	8	6
	Roman Catholic	44	42	44	36	47	42	47	42
	Jewish	2	2	2	2	1	1	1	1
	None	5	8	5	10	7	11	12	10
	Other	3	2	3	2	4	1	3	3
Ethnicity	British	45	49	43	**	40	46	42	50
	French	28	20	28	**	27	29	31	26
	Other	27	31	31	**	33	25	27	24

POPULATION SOURCE: Statistics Canada. **Not available.
*Census item: "What is your religion?" *Project Canada: religious preference.*

rates have been relatively high — 52% in 1975, 65% in 1980, and about 60% in 1985 and 1990. Readers should know that the seldom-reported co-operation rates that researchers obtain in face-to-face and telephone interviews is typically around 65%. In the case of the PROJECT CANADA panels, return rates — based on questionnaires returned from people located — have ranged from about 60% to 85% (see TABLE A2). Because of the high attrition and diminishing size of the panels, no claim is being made that they are sufficiently representative or large enough to permit accurate generalizations to the Canadian population. The panels are strictly used as unique and valuable resources, assisting in the exploration of changes within the population.

FUNDING   The 1975 survey was carried out for a cost of about $14,000 and had four major sources: the United Church of Canada ($2,000), the Canadian Broadcasting Corporation ($3,000), the Solicitor General of Canada ($5,000), and the University of Lethbridge ($4,000). In 1980, the panel portion of the survey was made possible by grants from the Social Sciences and Humanities Research Council of Canada ($10,000) and the United Church of Canada ($2,000). The second phase of PROJECT CAN80, which involved filling the core out into a full national sample, cost approximately $8,000 and was funded primarily by the University of Lethbridge. PROJECT CAN85 was funded completely by the Social Sciences and Humanities Research Council of Canada ($45,000), PROJECT CAN90 by the Lilly Endowment ($65,000).

TABLE A2. **YEAR OF ORIGIN AND RETURN RATES:
1975, 1980, 1985, AND 1990 SURVEYS**

Year Of Origin

Survey Year	1975		1980		1985		1990		Totals	
1975	1917/3686	52%	———		———		———		1917/3686	52%
1980	1056/1438	73%	426/842	51%	———		———		1482/2280	65%
1985	566/793	71%	170/270	63%	894/1666	54%	———		1630/2729	60%
1990	383/453	85%	75/128	59%	340/581	59%	674/1240	53%	1472/2402	61%

RELIGIOUS GROUP SAMPLE NUMBERS   The number of cases for Canada's religious groups reported in the book are proportional to their share of the nation's population. As such, however, they clearly are not large enough to allow generalization to the groups with a high level of accuracy — especially in instances in which they fall below 100 (e.g., the conservative Protestants, Lutherans, Presbyterians). Where possible, 1985 and 1990 Lutheran and Presbyterian cases have been combined (the cases are different). Despite the relatively small size of these religious group samples, the findings at minimum suggest patterns and tendencies that need to be interpreted in the light of other available information. The survey findings offer something of a start; additional data should be pursued through individual group surveys. To my mind, an objective and fair response to what I report is not denunciations based on inadequate numbers, but rather a more elaborate examination that either corroborates or negates my findings.

Complete methodological details concerning the complementary PROJECT TEEN CANADA surveys that are drawn upon can be found in Bibby and Posterski, *Teen Trends,* 1992, pages 321–324.

NOTES

CHAPTER 1
1 Cited in Zarzour, 1989:J3.
2 Cited by Derk-Michael Strauch in *Canada Lutheran,* November 1992:12.
3 Gallup Poll, May 12, 1945.
4 Drawn from Assembly of Quebec Bishops, 1992.
5 Beaudry, 1992:14.
6 Drawn from Motz, 1990:68–69, and Ronald Kydd, personal correspondence, May 1993.
7 Motz, 1991:282. For an important analysis of such discrepancies in the U.S., see Hadaway, Marler, and Chaves, 1993.
8 Quoted in Zarzour, 1989:J3. For concern about the increase in the number of cultural versus religious Jews, see Csillag, 1993, and Lucow, 1993.

CHAPTER 2
1 This section is based on Bibby, 1991.
2 Brady, 1991.
3 Koop, 1991:1.
4 This review draws heavily on the excellent summary of research on the "post-war generation" offered by Roozen, Carroll, and Roof, 1990. The seminal work on U.S. baby boomers is Roof, 1993.
5 Roozen, et al., 1990.
6 Bibby, 1986:91; 1987:237.
7 Roof and Loeb, 1990.
8 Cited in Zarzour, 1989:J3.
9 CIPO poll #258, May 1957.
10 Gamble, *Canadian Baptist,* May 1993:23.

11 Canadian Press, Ottawa, June 4, 1993.
12 See Wan, 1990.
13 Nostbakken, 1992.
14 Baglow, 1992.
15 *Christian Week,* March 2, 1993:24.
16 Doerksen, 1992.
17 Kawano, 1992:13.
18 *Presbyterian Record,* November 1992:20.
19 Williams, 1993:22–23.
20 "God Is Alive," *Maclean's,* April 12, 1993:32.
21 Rodd, 1993.
22 *Faith Today,* March-April 1993:28.
23 Rodd, 1993:45.
24 For an exposition of the nature and goals of Vision 2000, see, for example, Motz, 1990:5–12.
25 *Christian Week,* June 22, 1993:12; Diocese of New Westminster, 1993.
26 Canadian Press, Edmonton, June 26, 1991.
27 Associated Press, Vatican City, January 22, 1991. For an important and thorough look at Roman Catholic approaches to evangelism, see *Compass,* September-October 1992.
28 Posterski and Barker, 1993:67.
29 *Canada Lutheran,* March 1993:25.
30 *Christian Courier,* May 14, 1993:2 and April 23, 1993:2.
31 Posterski and Barker, 1993:73–86.
32 Quoted in George Cornell, Associated Press, January 18, 1991.
33 The sample size here is only 31 cases and doesn't permit us to speak very definitively about those who have switched to

conservative churches. Obviously much more work, with larger samples, needs to be done.

34 Scorgie, 1993:29.
35 See, Fieguth, 1993a.
36 See Legge, 1992a, 1993; Wallace, 1993; *Faith Today*, March-April 1993:42–43.
37 Posterski and Barker, 1993:53–54.
38 Posterski and Barker, 1993:259.
39 The material in this section is based heavily on Bibby and Brinkerhoff, 1992a and 1992b.
40 Beverley, 1992.
41 Legge, 1993a:8.
42 Roof and McKinney, 1987.
43 Graham, 1990.
44 Perrin and Mauss, 1991, 1992.
45 The 1993 *Maclean's* poll finding concerning the proportion of outsiders was almost identical: "38% of those affiliated with conservative churches described themselves as converts from another faith outside the conservative realm." *Maclean's*, April 12:48.
46 This is not to be confused with the number of evangelicals, who obviously are found in other religious groups as well. The 1993 *Maclean's* poll claimed that some 15% of Canadians meet strict evangelical criteria, with 14% in fact saying they are evangelicals. These include 20% of regular churchgoing Roman Catholics, resulting in Catholics making up one-third of all evangelicals. See *Maclean's*, 1993:35,49.
47 This section draws heavily from Bibby, 1993a.
48 Durkheim, 1965:477–479.
49 Stark and Bainbridge, 1985.
50 Beverley, 1990.
51 See, for example, MacLaine, 1983 and 1985, 1992.
52 Canadian Press, April 12, 1991.
53 Cited by Canadian Press, October 25, 1989.
54 Naisbitt and Aburdene, 1990.
55 Toffler, 1990.
56 Canadian Press, April 12, 1991.
57 Naisbitt and Aburdene, 1990:281.
58 Christensen, 1993.

59 Christensen, 1991:3.
60 Naisbitt and Aburdene, 1990:280.
61 *Common Ground*, Vancouver, Summer 1993, Issue #43.
62 Vision Mountain Leadership Training Centre course calendar, 1993.
63 Motz, 1990:28.
64 See, for example, Chandler, 1988; Groothius, 1986 and 1990.
65 Canadian Press, April 12, 1991.
66 Canadian Press, April 12, 1991.
67 Statistics Canada Cat. No. 93-319:16.
68 *United Church Observer*, February 1993:10.
69 Appleby, 1990:A9. For a psychiatric interpretation of such claims, see Wright, 1993a and 1993b, as well as Bourget and Bradford, 1988. Two other helpful interpretations are Lippert, 1990 and Swatos, 1992.
70 Quoted in Appleby, 1990:A9.
71 Appleby, 1990:A9.
72 Tyler, 1993.
73 Tyler, 1993.
74 *United Church Observer*, February 1993:10.
75 Bibby and Posterski, 1992:58.

CHAPTER 3

1 Comte, 1947.
2 Frazer, 1922.
3 Freud, 1962.
4 Marx, 1970.
5 Durkheim, 1893.
6 Smith, 1937.
7 Wilson, 1966, 1979, 1982, 1985.
8 Berger, 1967, 1986.
9 Luckmann, 1967.
10 See, for example, Dobbelaere, 1981, 1987.
11 For an excellent overview of the history and nature of secularization in Quebec, see Beyer, 1993. Another important recent work is Baum, 1991.
12 Assembly of Quebec Bishops, 1992:21.
13 Weber, 1963.
14 Niebuhr, 1929.
15 Troeltsch, 1931.
16 Berton, 1965.
17 Berger, 1961.

18 For an interesting contemporary example in New England, see Demerath and Williams, 1992.

19 Wuthnow, 1976.

20 Luckmann, 1967; 1990.

21 Berger, 1969.

22 Young, *United Church Observer,* April 1993:3.

23 *Maclean's,* April 12, 1993:36.

24 Assembly of Quebec Bishops, 1992:15.

25 Cited in *Maclean's,* 1993:36.

26 See, for example, the *Catholic New Times,* February 21, 1993:5. For the response of the Canadian Church Press, see the *Anglican Journal,* March 1993:7.

27 *Catholic New Times,* February 21, 1993:5.

28 *Anglican Journal,* October 1992:7.

29 See, for example, McAteer, 1989:A5.

30 *Catholic New Times,* January 10, 1993; *Prairie Messenger,* June 21, 1993:1.

31 See, for example, Steed, 1991; *Anglican Journal,* April 1993:6.

32 Congram, 1992.

33 Slobodian, 1993:18.

34 *Primetime Live,* ABC News, May 6, 1993.

35 *Catholic New Times,* January 24, 1993:6.

36 *Globe and Mail,* June 8, 1993.

37 *Catholic New Times,* January 10, 1993:6.

38 *Maclean's,* April 12, 1993:49.

39 See, for example, the Canadian Press account from Kingston, February 28, 1993; *Anglican Journal,* April 1993:6; see also Carriere, 1992.

40 *Canadian Baptist,* April 1993:30–31.

41 See Sinclair, 1992.

42 Canadian Conference of Catholic Bishops, 1992a, 1992b.

43 Art Babych. Cited in *Christian News,* Vancouver, June 1993:6.

44 *Anglican Journal,* May 1993:3.

45 See, for example, Ray Conlogue's, March 9, 1993 review of the French miniseries *Shehaweh* in the *Globe and Mail,* (A11) which he says involves ro-

manticizing "albeit in the most up-to-date and politically correct fashion," resulting in a film that "owes more to George Orwell's *1984* than it does to *Dances with Wolves.*" For an examination of the mixed contributions of early Jesuit missionaries, see Starkloff, 1991 and Von Gernet, 1991.

46 *Globe and Mail,* February 18, 1993.

47 Editorial, *Lethbridge Herald,* July 26, 1991.

48 Lascelles, 1992.

49 Bibby and Posterski, 1992:174.

50 Slobodian, 1993.

51 Brown, 1992a:14.

52 Canadian Press, Toronto, June 7, 1993.

53 *Maclean's,* April 12, 1993:49.

54 Parsons, 1963.

55 Greeley, 1972.

56 See, for example, Martin, 1979 (Britain); Stark and Bainbridge, 1985 (globally); Hill and Bowman, 1985, and McCallum, 1986 (Australia and New Zealand); Roof and McKinney, 1987; and Chaves, 1989 (U.S.); Bibby, 1987 (Canada); Holm, 1989 (Finland); Hamberg, 1991 (Sweden).

57 Bibby and Posterski, 1992:64–68.

58 The r is .64.

59 The r here is .53.

60 See, for example, Grenz, 1993.

61 This program was introduced in the early 1980s by the Saskatchewan Pro-Life Association, with help from the former Progressive Conservative government. As of the early 1990s, support was strongest in rural communities. For an exposition of the program, see Mitchell, 1993. Concerning the Roman Catholic Challenge 93 counterpart, see Lachance, 1993b.

62 For a recent analysis of religion and life satisfaction with complementary results, see Gee and Veevers, 1990.

63 Cited in O'Brien, 1993.

64 The size of the samples of students in other private systems

are inadequate to carry out sound analyses.

65 Beyer, 1993:152–153.

66 Beaudry, 1992:14. For a stimulating discussion of the problems the Catholic Church has had in implementing social ideals more generally in Canada, see Hewitt, 1991 and 1993.

67 Congram, 1993:3.

CHAPTER 4

1 Sorokin, 1957.

2 Davis, 1949:542–544.

3 Bell, 1977.

4 Rifkin, 1980.

5 Canadian Press, Toronto, February 19, 1993.

6 *Canada Lutheran,* November 1992:L17–24.

7 See, for example, June through September issues of the *Catholic Register, Catholic New Times, Western Catholic Reporter,* and *Prairie Messenger.*

8 *United Church Observer,* January 1993:18–24.

9 Pogue, *United Church Observer,* March 1993:45.

10 Assembly of Quebec Bishops, 1992:10.

11 Cited by Victoria Drysdale in *Canadian Baptist,* April 1993:21.

12 Jones, R., 1993.

13 *Canadian Baptist,* May-June 1992:45.

14 Peck, 1993:358.

15 *United Church Observer,* November 1992:47.

16 See, for example, Hall, 1989a, and 1989b.

17 Greeley, 1972, 1989.

18 Finke and Stark, 1992.

19 Marshall, 1990.

20 Computed from Martin, 1967:44.

21 See, for example, Hill and Bowman, 1985; McCallum, 1986; for some data on membership comparisons, Curtis, Grabb, and Baer, 1992:145.

22 Decima Research, 1987.

23 Decima Research, 1987:74–79.

24 Decima Research, 1987:42.

25 *United Church Observer,* March 1993:26 and May 1993:24.

26 See, for example, the *United Church Observer,* January 1993:15.

27 Bettson, 1993.

28 *Anglican Journal,* September 1992:7.

29 *Anglican Journal,* June 1993:7.

30 See, for example, the *Presbyterian Record* advertisement, May 1993:26a-d.

31 See, for example, the *Presbyterian Record,* March 1992 and May 1993.

32 See, for example, the *Canada Lutheran,* June 1993:28.

33 See *Canada Lutheran,* June 1993:10; July-August 1992:26; April 1993:26.

34 *Canadian Baptist,* May 1993:27.

35 *Canadian Baptist,* July-August 1992 and Mackey, 1993; *Christian Week,* May 25, 1993:2.

36 Assembly of Quebec Bishops, 1992:26ff.

37 Brown, 1992a.

38 Kirley, 1992.

39 See, for example, Ryan, 1993; *Anglican Journal,* March 1993:13 and June 1993:10.

40 Marshall, 1990:11.

41 Longley, 1989.

42 Finke and Stark, 1992:274.

43 Associated Press, New York, April 10, 1991.

44 Finke and Stark, 1992:275.

45 Iannaccone, 1991:157.

46 Longley, 1989.

CHAPTER 5

1 Gallup Poll, February 28, 1979. The figure for belief in ESP was 51%, for precognition, 44%.

2 Wills, 1990:15. Cited in Warner, 1993:1046.

3 See, for example, Lett, 1992.

4 Berger, 1969:94.

5 Lupfer, Brock, DePaola, 1992. Psychologists tend to define such research under what they refer to as "attribution theory." These authors provide a good overview of this school of thought, as well as its application to religious explanations.

6 *Lethbridge Herald,* September 1, 1992:A5.

7 Bibby, 1987:146–147.
8 This was part of a euology offered by Dr. Wayne Soble at the funeral of Kara McMillan in early August 1991, in Hamilton, Ontario. *Canadian Baptist*, March-April 1992:16.
9 Gregoire, 1992.
10 See, for example, *Globe and Mail*, May 21, 1993.
11 Canadian Press, Vancouver, June 29, 1993.
12 For an example of the kind of reactions involved, see Dueck, 1993.
13 Duncan, 1993.
14 *Canadian Press*, Calgary, June 2, 1993.
15 *Catholic New Times*, May 30:2; *Christian Week*, June 8, 1993:1. For a recent exposition and discussion of the official position of the Roman Catholic Church, see Wolak, 1992.
16 Scott, 1993. For a discussion of the palliative care option, see also Haynes, 1993.
17 Gallup, November 23, 1992.
18 Peck, 1978:15.
19 Harpur, 1991:14–15.
20 Gallup Polls, May 12, 1945 and #280 January 1960.
21 Gallup Poll, January 18, 1969.
22 The literature here, especially on NDE's, is voluminous and has been covered well in Harpur, 1991. Moody's books (1975, 1988), along with Forman (1988), provide good overviews; those interested in a Christian endorsement of such experiences might consult Rawlings, 1978 — which has been re-released through *100 Huntley Street*. A stimulating critique of NDE's is offered by Alcock, 1981.
23 Leona Flim, *Lethbridge Herald*, June 6, 1993:D5.
24 *Maclean's*, April 12, 1993:34.
25 Irving, 1990:278.
26 This item did not appear in the French version of the survey. However, an August 30, 1990 Gallup poll found the national figure for belief in heaven to be essentially the same — 71%.
27 Gallup Polls, May 12, 1945 and January 15, 1969.
28 Legge, 1992b:1.
29 Legge, 1992b:B7.
30 Luckmann, 1990:130.
31 Reuter, Dresden, Germany, November 6, 1990. For a critique of SETI, see Tarter, 1993.
32 Reuter, Dresden, Germany, November 6, 1990.
33 Alaton, 1992.
34 Greeley and Baum, 1972:16–17.
35 Ayres and Drum, 1992.
36 *United Church Observer*, April 1993:20–21.
37 Mitchell, *United Church Observer*, May 1993:59.
38 Witvoet, 1993.
39 *Maclean's*, April 12, 1993:32,35.
40 *Weekend* magazine, December 24, 1977:3.

CHAPTER 6

1 Toffler, 1990:375.
2 Naisbitt and Aburdene, 1990:270–273; Campbell, 1988.
3 Graham, 1990:20,14,394.
4 Canadian Press, May 22, 1991.
5 Canadian Press, Ottawa, May 17, 1993.
6 Decima Research, 1987:97.
7 Zarzour, 1989:J3.
8 *Anglican Journal*, February, 1993:16.
9 Weber, 1963.
10 Geertz, 1968.
11 Luckmann, 1990:128.
12 Canadian Press, London, Ont., February 2, 1990.
13 Berger, 1969:82.
14 Clarke, 1993:37.
15 Campbell, 1992:9.
16 Parrott, 1993:38.
17 Culbertson, 1993:47.
18 *Presbyterian Record*, April 1993:11.
19 Fadum, 1993:5.
20 Ward, 1993.
21 Lodge, 1992:363.

CHAPTER 7

1 From "If I Sang You a Love Song," Lojo Music, BMG Music Publishing.

2 Regarding the family Bible, see, for example, Bonisteel, 1993.
3 Thomas, 1992.
4 Mentzer, 1991.
5 See, for example, Posterski and Barker, 1993; Brinkerhoff and Mackie, 1993a.
6 Heaton, 1990:366,375.
7 Kapica, 1993c.
8 Statistics Canada, 1993:7.
9 Brinkerhoff and Mackie, 1993b.
10 Gallup Canada, June 12, 1993.
11 Based on Herrig, 1993.
12 Moynan, 1993:16–17.
13 Bibby, 1985:61.
14 Assembly of Quebec Bishops, 1992:23.
15 Demerath, 1969:202.

CHAPTER 8

1 For an important analysis of people involved "marginally" and "mentally" with U.S. churches, see Marler and Hadaway, 1993. Because of the importance in Canada, at least, of identification over membership, I prefer to speak of variations of affiliation, versus variations of membership.
2 These specific groups are buried in the "Other" sub-category under "Other Faiths."
3 Figures have been adjusted to correct for under-representation of inactives because of the measures used. Details can be obtained from the author.
4 Stark and Bainbridge, 1985:7.
5 The options here for importance were: *"Very," "Somewhat," "Not very,"* and *"Not at all."* The belief options were: *"Yes, I definitely do," "Yes, I think so," "No, I don't think so,"* and *"No, I definitely do not."*
6 Letter to the editor, the *Canadian Unitarian,* March 1993:3.
7 *United Church Observer,* July 1993:33.
8 "Image" in the *United Church Observer,* May 1993:3.
9 Interview in *Christian News,* Vancouver, October-November 1992:1, 3.

CHAPTER 9

1 Warner, 1993:1051.
2 Cited in Berman, 1990:13.
3 Warner, 1993:1050.
4 See, for example, Kelley, 1972; Roof and McKinney, 1987; Wuthnow, 1988; Finke and Stark, 1992.
5 Bibby, 1987:217–219.
6 *Canada Lutheran,* April 1993:2.
7 Brannon, 1971.
8 For an excellent overview of the types of organizational arrangements characterizing religious groups in Canada and elsewhere, see Nock, 1993.
9 Decima, 1987:104.
10 Quelch, 1989:67.
11 Todd, 1991.
12 *Canadian Baptist,* April 1993:6.
13 *Canadian Baptist,* September-October 1992:46.
14 *Canadian Baptist,* April 1993:6.
15 *Canadian Baptist,* February 1993:21–22.
16 For a detailed historical examination of the voluntary principle and its relationship to "free churches," see Brackney, 1992.
17 *Anglican Journal,* June 1993:7.
18 Westhues, 1976.
19 Baum, 1991:14.
20 Koop, 1993; Friesen, 1993:8–10.
21 Niebuhr, 1929 and 1951.
22 Tillich, 1966.
23 Cited in the *United Church Observer,* March 1993:15.
24 "Old Prayer Book Still Popular," Canadian Press, Toronto: February 21, 1992.
25 See, for example, the *United Church Observer,* April 1993; the *Anglican Churchman,* March 1993:10.
26 *United Church Observer,* August 1992:15.
27 Harvey, 1993.
28 Regarding Ontario and these two issues, see the Canadian Press story of September 3, 1992, by Anne-Marie Tobin, and its news release of March 15, 1993 on the Ontario Supreme Court's rejection, by 2–1, of same-sex marriages.

29 For an exposition of gay churches, see, for example, Kapica, October 1, 1991:A1, 5; *Maclean's*, April 12, 1993:41.

30 *United Church Observer*, October, 1992:11; see also, August 1992:12–13.

31 Reported in the *United Church Observer*, August 1992.

32 See the *Presbyterian Record*, July-August 1992:24.

33 *Canada Lutheran*, March 1993:8–9; for an example of members' views on homosexuality, see *Canada Lutheran*, April 1993:6–7.

34 *Canadian Baptist*, September-October 1992:6.

35 Harvey, 1993:18.

36 Canadian Press, Vancouver, February 5, 1993; see also Jost, 1993.

37 O'Toole, et al., 1993:274.

38 O'Toole, et al., 1993:274.

39 *United Church Observer*, June 1988:10.

40 Maxine Hancock, Canadian Press, August 15, 1988.

41 *United Church Observer*, November 1992:17.

42 *Maclean's*, 1993:49.

43 Blaikie, 1992:6.

44 Interview with Joanne Helmer, *Lethbridge Herald*, February 13, 1993:A4.

45 Canadian Press, January 22.

46 *Canada Lutheran*, December 1992:27.

47 Carriere, 1993a. See also, "No Compromise on Gambling," an editorial in the *Anglican Journal*, May 1993:16 and, regarding gambling more generally, "Synod Condemns Gambling." November 1992:13. Gambling is something a number of other religious groups strongly oppose. See, for example, the Salvation Army's *War Cry*, March 6, 1993:1; the Christian Reform's *Christian Courier*, May 21, 1993:24.

48 Babych, 1993a:1.

49 *Anglican Journal*, June 1993:6.

50 Associated Press, Vatican City, December 29, 1989.

51 *Anglican Journal*, February 1993:4; *Prairie Messenger*, June 7, 1993.

52 Drawn from the *United Church Observer*, January 1993:34–35.

53 Brown, 1992a:16; *Prairie Messenger*, June 7, 1993:5.

54 *Catholic Register*, May 22, 1993:1, 15; *Prairie Messenger*, May 17, 1993:6.

55 *Western Catholic Reporter*, June 7, 1993:8; *Prairie Messenger*, June 7, 1993:6.

56 Associated Press, Vatican City, March 28, 1992.

57 Brown, 1992a:8. Baum (1991:64) maintains that in Quebec specifically, the "efforts to make the Catholic church a participatory organization have failed." For a thorough examination of the post-Vatican II conflict between lay input and institutional power for Catholics generally, see Ebaugh, 1991.

58 *Maclean's*, April 12, 1993:49.

59 Cited in Babych, 1993b.

60 *Maclean's*, April 12, 1993:49.

61 Perrone, 1992.

62 Cited in the *Canadian Catholic Review*, June 1992:29.

63 Babych, 1993b.

64 Gonzalez, 1993a:7.

65 *Catholic New Times*, April 18, 1993:12.

66 *Presbyterian Record*, March 1993:28.

67 See *Catholic New Times*, December 6, 1992:8–9.

68 Brennan, 1992.

69 Brown, 1992b:21.

70 Maxwell, 1992; Brown, 1992b.

71 *Presbyterian Record*, February 1993:3.

72 Headlines focused on his former role — even though he is a father of two and spent the last 13 years as deputy culture minister. See, for example, the *Lethbridge Herald*, March 12, 1993.

73 *United Church Observer*, November 1992:14–15.

74 *Canada Lutheran*, July-August:26.

75 See, for example, Kapica, 1993b, February 18, 1993 and the *United Church Observer*, April 1993:33.

76 See Ferry, 1993 and the *Anglican Journal*, Review of Books, April 1993:1A.

77 See Canadian Press, Ottawa, March 6, 1992; *Canadian Baptist*, September-October 1992:5–6,46.

78 Howard, 1993; *Christian Information News*, Vancouver, June 1993:1–2; for a member's response to Stevenson, see the *United Church Observer*, September, 1992:2.

79 *Anglican Journal*, May 1993:3. For details concerning the coverup attempts in the case of the Mount Cashel orphanage, see Harris, 1990.

80 Kapica, the *Globe and Mail*, May 26, 1993:A9.

81 See, for example, the *Catholic Register*, June 5, 1993:1; *Prairie Messenger*, May 31, 1993:3.

82 The case is cited, for example, in Pride and Ferrell, 1989.

83 O'Connor, 1993.

84 Reuter, Vatican City, June 25, 1993; see also *Western Catholic Reporter*, June 28, 1993:2.

85 Redekop, 1993.

86 EFC, 1993.

87 Enns, 1993b:3. See the three stories by Enns on the scam, the Mennonite response, and the protests of readers in the *Mennonite Reporter*, May 31, 1993:3.

88 *War Cry*, Salvation Army, March 27, 1993:1.

89 *Christian Week*, May 11, 1993:2.

90 Plomp, *Presbyterian Record*, May 1992:38.

91 Van Seters, 1992:30.

92 See, for example, the *Globe and Mail*, February 3, 1993:A20; May 12, 1993:A20; June 9, 1993:A22.

93 "God's Therapy," George Cornell and David Briggs, Associated Press, March 13, 1992. I've had enquiries about how the organization can be contacted: Its address is: P.O. Box 668, Kalamazoo, Michigan 49005.

94 Mayes, 1992.

95 Berger, 1969:88.

96 Cited in Cornell and Briggs, March 13, 1992.

97 *Anglican Journal*, October 1992:7.

98 Atwood, 1992:14.

99 Adrian, 1992:13.

100 *Mennonite Brethren Herald*, April 30, 1993:24. For a discussion of the issue in Mennonite Brethren circles, see Enns, 1993a.

101 *Faith Today*, May-June 1993:58–60.

102 Whyte, 1993:5.

103 Associated Press, June 25, 1993; *Christian Courier*, May 14, 1993:1–2.

104 *United Church Observer*, October, 1992:11.

105 Leona Flim, the *Lethbridge Herald*, May 17, 1992:A6.

106 *Canada Lutheran*, June 1992:30.

107 *United Church Observer*, November 1992:9–11. Other denominations report similar aging patterns for women's groups. See, for example, the Alberta Mennonite situation where the Alberta Women in Mission have an average age of 57 (*Mennonite Reporter*, May 17:13).

108 *Jewish Free Press*, Calgary, March 31, 1993:12.

109 *War Cry*, Salvation Army, June 5, 1993:2. For expositions on Burrows, see, for example, the *War Cry* issue of June 12, 1993:2–4,14; Shepherd, 1993.

110 See, for example, the Baptist Convention of Ontario and Quebec's report on women in ministry, 1993. For some current Jewish views, see Kraft, 1993.

111 Canadian Press, Toronto, April 13, 1993.

112 *Canada Lutheran*, May 1992:23.

113 See, for example, Whyte, 1992.

114 Adrian, 1992:13.

115 *Mennonite Brethren Herald*, April 30, 1993:24.

116 Nason-Clark, 1993:230–231.

CHAPTER 10

1 Popcorn, 1991:143. Her comment takes us into the whole area of marketing. The definitions of marketing are extremely varied. It has become an omnibus term not unlike a word such as "culture." However, a good

sample definition is offered by Phillip Kotler and Gordon McDougall (1985:2,9): "Marketing is human activity directed at satisfying needs and wants through exchange processes." Needs, they maintain, are part of human makeup, whereas wants are shaped by culture and the individual. They add that marketing translates into "sellers trying to find markets." William Zikmund and Michael D'Amico (1984:8) suggest that at the broadest level, the function of marketing is "to bring buyers and sellers together." William Pride and O.C. Ferrell (1989:8) illustrate the comprehensiveness many have in mind when they write: "Marketing consists of individual and organizational activities that facilitate and expedite satisfying exchange relationships in a dynamic environment through the creation, distribution, promotion, and pricing of goods, services, and ideas" (Pride and Ferrell, 1989:8).

Consistent with Kotler and McDougall (1985:7), among others, what I mean by "a market" is the "actual and potential buyers of a product."

2 See, for example, Pride and Ferrell, 1989:16.

3 Cited in Pride and Ferrell, 1989:16.

4 Kotler and McDougall, 1985:11.

5 Cited in Kotler and McDougall, 1985:2.

6 Quoted in Zarzour, 1989:J3.

7 Kotler and McDougall, 1985:27.

8 Dianne Rinehart, "Gloomy Future for Department Stores," Canadian Press, February 9, 1993.

9 Orville Redenbacher's popcorn commercial, A&E Network, March 17, 1992.

10 Turner, 1987:47.

11 Berger, 1969:28.

12 Ron Rempel, *Mennonite Reporter*, May 31, 1993:6.

13 The phrase and the dilemma is the subject of an analysis of Epis-

copalians by Glock, Ringer, and Babbie, 1967.

14 Quoted in *Maclean's*, April 12, 1993:50; see also the *Anglican Journal*, May 1993:2.

15 Cameron, *Presbyterian Record*, April 1992:12.

16 Ogilvie, 1993:28–30.

17 Harpur, 1991:15.

18 Steinhauser, 1993.

19 To get a sense of Khaki and his work, see, for example, Khaki, 1991 and 1992; *NAIN News*, Spring 1993.

20 Peck, 1993:349.

21 Luckmann, 1990:134.

22 Campbell, 1992.

23 Parrott, 1993.

24 See, for example, Richard Gwyn, *Toronto Star*, November 22, 1992.

25 Anderson, 1993.

26 Todd, 1993:C13.

27 For a brief but insightful comment on the inclination of churches to cater to a victimization model, versus offer an alternative to it, see Anderson, 1993:6.

28 *United Church Observer*, January 1993:42–43.

29 *Prairie Messenger*, May 24, 1993:1.

30 See, for example, *Canada Lutheran*, February 1992:16–18.

31 *War Cry*, Salvation Army, June 12, 1993:4.

32 *Mennonite Brethren Herald*, 1993:14–16.

33 Drawn from the *Catalyst*, June-July 1993:8.

34 Letter to *Christian Week*, May 25, 1993:13.

35 See, for example, Stiller, 1986 and 1991; Van Ginkel, 1992.

36 *Faith Today*, May-June 1993:17.

37 For an excellent overview of the relationship of the churches to native peoples, past and present, see Lewis, 1993. Ambivalence about the Roman Catholic contribution can be seen in the 1991 Starkloff and von Gernet articles.

38 Canadian Press, Camrose, May 17, 1991. For opposing viewpoints held by two evangelicals on the impact of Columbus's

arrival in America, see Pinnock, 1993 and Dekar, 1993.

39 *Lethbridge Herald,* May 23, 1991:1.

40 Lewis, 1993:249; Lachance, 1993a.

41 Glisky, 1993. However, some are calling for caution in the course of co-opting native spirituality. See, for example, Presbyterian John Sperry, 1993.

42 See, for example, Morikawa, 1993:13.

43 For an excellent "report" on leaders' perceptions of how their groups have been trying to influence Canadian culture, see VanderVennen's 1991 edited volume of papers; they were written by scholars representing mainline Protestant, Roman Catholic, and conservative Protestant traditions for an October 1988 conference. Concerning an increase in Jewish concern for problems beyond those facing the Jewish community, see William Abram's editorial in "Viewpoints," *Canadian Jewish News* supplement, July 8, 1993:2.

44 Abuse in its varied forms, for example, has been receiving considerable attention. Beyond mainline and Catholic groups, see the *Mennonite Reporter,* May 17, 1993:1ff; Sevcik in the *Free Methodist Herald,* March 1993:8; the *Christian Courier,* May 21, 1993:1ff.

45 Collins, 1993. See, also, for example, the coalition against pornography. The *Globe and Mail,* May 7, 1991:A5. Addressing social issues can also be divisive. For an example of Jewish hostility toward the United Church's position on Israel's treatment of Palestinians in the territories and Gaza, see the editorial, "Unjust Resolution," in the *Canadian Jewish News,* June 10, 1993:14.

46 Cited in *Deepanjali 1992,* Hindu Society of Calgary, p.17.

47 Scott, 1993.

48 Barrington, 1992.

49 Harpur, 1991:245.

50 It's very difficult to standardize measures of the value placed on God, self, and society in such a way as to permit us to make comparisons *between* the three — to say, for example, that "twice as many people value self as value God." We can, however, compare groups on each separate measure. That is what is being done here.

51 The precise items used were, for God, "God"; for self, an index using "material comfort" and "physical appearance"; for society, an index using "social issues" and "getting along with others."

52 Stark and Bainbridge, 1985.

53 Finke and Stark, 1992.

54 Stark and Bainbridge, 1985:7.

55 Berman, 1990:5.

56 For this distinction, see, for example, Glock and Stark, 1965.

57 Finke and Stark, 1992:275.

58 Naisbitt and Aburdene, 1990:272–273.

59 Anderson, 1992:22.

60 Johnson, Hoge, and Luidens, 1993:19,16–17.

61 In the *Prairie Messenger,* May 24, 1993:16.

62 Brown, 1992a:7.

63 Bibby, 1987:18.

64 Assembly of Quebec Bishops, 1992:23.

65 Baum, 1991:25.

66 Cited in Grant, 1988:245.

67 See, for example, the *United Church Observer,* December 1992:9.

68 See the *United Church Observer,* December 1992:17.

69 Woodbury, 1992:23.

70 *United Church Observer,* November 1992:45.

71 See, for example, Kotler and McDougall, 1985:36; Darmon, Laroche, and Petrof, 1989:177ff.

72 Hordern, 1966:46.

73 *United Church Observer,* November 1992:44.

74 Milne, 1993.

75 Spicer, 1987. The following quotations are all taken from this article.

76 Drawn in part from Finke and Stark, 1992:275. See also Ralph Milton, *This United Church of Ours*. Winfield, B.C.: Wood Lake Books, 1991.

CHAPTER 11

1 Pride and Ferrell, 1989:88.
2 See Pride and Ferrell, 1989:89ff. They define the marketing mix in terms of these "4 P's" and suggest that it represents "everything that can be done to influence the demand for a product."
3 Darmon, Laroche, and Petrof, 1989:85.
4 Prus, 1989:257.
5 *Orthodox Church*, April-May 1993:6.
6 Evans, 1993.
7 Assembly of Quebec Bishops, 1992:24.
8 Van Velzen, 1989.
9 Kotler and McDougall, 1985:33.
10 See, for example, Canadian Press, Edmonton, March 13, 1993; *Christian Week*, April 27, 1993; *Western Catholic Reporter*, May 10, 1993:6.
11 Quelch, 1989:129.
12 Fledderus, 1993:20.
13 *Christian Week*, February 16, 1993:3.
14 Zikmund and D'Amico, 1984:525.
15 DeWolfe, the *Presbyterian Record*, March:11.
16 See Wilson, 1993.
17 Joseph, 1993:7.
18 See, for example, Bibby and Posterski, 1992:60ff.
19 See Harvey Enchin, the *Globe and Mail*, February 24, 1993:B1ff; March 1, 1993:B1ff; and June 4, 1993:A1,A2.
20 For discussions of the controversy, see, for example, the *United Church Observer*, September, 1992:39–40; Kapica, 1992; Jones, W., 1993; *Christian Week*, May 25, 1993:8; Kitchen, 1993.
21 See, for example, the *Globe and Mail*, June 4, 1993:A2; *Western Catholic Reporter*, June 14, 1993:7r,

June 24, 1993:7; *Christian Week*, June 22, 1993:1,4.
22 Quoted in Kapica, 1992:A6.
23 Desmond Morton, the *Toronto Star*. Cited in *Theological Digest and Outlook*, January 1993:13.
24 Alsop, 1985:31.
25 Cited in Pride and Ferrell, 1989:769.
26 Personal interview, Vancouver, June 7, 1993.
27 *Canada Lutheran*, February 1993:33.
28 Reported in the *Christian Courier*, May 28, 1993:3.
29 See, for example, Toneguzzi, 1992.
30 Bibby and Posterski, 1992.
31 Macmillan, 1993:20–22.

CHAPTER 12

1 Wilson, 1959:11.
2 Bibby and Brinkerhoff, 1974.
3 See Mann, 1962.
4 Meed, 1993.
5 Fieguth, 1993b; *Christian Week*, June 22, 1993:1.
6 Reinhardt, *Canada Lutheran*, BC Synod News, October, 1992:B21.
7 Beaudry, 1992:14.
8 Cited in Kotler and McDougall, 1985:11.
9 Hiebert, 1992:9.
10 Canadian Press, Peterborough, March 13, 1993.
11 Canadian Press, Ottawa, October 17, 1991.
12 *War Cry*, Salvation Army, May 29, 1993:9.
13 Weber, 1963.
14 Barna, 1990 and 1992; see also Elliott, 1993.
15 Posterski and Barker, 1993:257,245.
16 Peck, 1993:60.
17 Stackhouse, 1993:18.
18 Mathers, 1992a:33.
19 Stackhouse, 1993.
20 *Presbyterian Record*, May 1993:26b,c.
21 *United Church Observer*, October 1992:11.
22 *Anglican Journal*, September 1992:Synod Supplement 3A.

23 *Mennonite Brethren Herald,* April 30:14.
24 Posterski and Barker, 1993:60.
25 Posterski and Barker, 1993:254–255.
26 Fish, the *Presbyterian Record,* January 1993:11.
27 Kawano, 1992:94,111ff.
28 Carriere, 1993b.
29 Wilson, 1959:11.
30 *Faith Today,* March-April 1993:10.
31 Mathers, 1992a:33.
32 *Mennonite Brethren Herald,* May 4, 1993:3.
33 Webber, *Presbyterian Record,* 1992:26.
34 Posterski and Barker, 1993.
35 Based on Kotler and McDougall, 1985:3.
36 Percy, 1993:13.
37 Quoted in Zarzour, 1989:J3.
38 Winter, 1993:10.

CONCLUSION

1 See, for example, Altizer and Hamilton, 1966.
2 Roxburgh, 1993:128.
3 Harpur, 1986.
4 Personal correspondence, February 28, 1989.
5 Ogilvie, 1993:27.
6 Mathers, 1992b:18.
7 Csillag, 1993.
8 Mathers, 1992.
9 Hall, 1989a:51.
10 *Anglican Journal,* April 1993:10.
11 Acts 17.23–24. New Revised Standard Version.
12 Berger, 1963.
13 Harland, 1992:14.
14 *Common Ground,* Vancouver Summer 1993:47.
15 Brinkerhoff and Mackie, 1993a; Hunsberger, 1983.
16 Bye, 1991:27.
17 The PROJECT CAN90 survey found that 23% of Canadians claimed to attend services almost every week or more, virtually the same level as found in the 1991 General Social Survey conducted by Statistics Canada, and in the 1993 Angust Reid survey carried out for *Maclean's.*
18 Cited in *Maclean's,* 1993:50.
19 Congram, *Presbyterian Record,* December 1992:3.
20 Course on the Church and Society, Vancouver School of Theology, April 1992.
21 Assembly of Quebec Bishops, 1992:26.
22 Jones, 1993:24.
23 Bernhardt, *Christian Courier,* June 18, 1993:9.
24 Cited in Pride and Ferrell, 1989:5.
25 See, for example, Manera, 1993. For Canadian research on religion and childlessness, see Krishnan, 1993.
26 Nevile, 1991.
27 *Canadian Baptist,* April 1993:6.
28 Decima, 1987:104.
29 Computed from Curtis, Grabb, and Baer, 1992:143; the comparable U.S. figure is even higher — one in two.
30 *United Church Observer,* February 1993:10.
31 Krutz-Weil, 1992.
32 See, for example, McLeod, *Canadian Baptist,* November-December 1992:24.
33 Cited in the *Presbyterian Record,* March 1993:44–45.
34 A variety of commentators have examined some of the possibilities here. See, for example, Anderson, 1992:53–65.
35 George Cornell, Associated Press, January 18, 1991.
36 Alseth, 1993:20.
37 Hammond, 1993.
38 Haggett, 1993.
39 See, for example, Rempel-Burkholder, 1993.
40 Beaudry, 1992.
41 Freud, 1962.
42 Demerath, 1969:202.
43 Beaudry, 1992:1.
44 *Bodhi Mind,* Vancouver Buddhist Church, May 1993:13.
45 *Canadian Baptist,* May-June 1992:45.
46 Harpur, 1993:B7.
47 Peck, 1993:353.
48 Stahl, forthcoming.

REFERENCES

Adrian, Anne
    1992   "What Do Women Want?" *Canadian Baptist*, September-October:9–13.
Alaton, Salem
    1992   "Spacey Raptures Mask a Spiritual Yearning." *Globe and Mail*, June 1:C1.
Alcock, James E.
    1981   "Psychology and Near-Death Experiences." In Kendrick Frazier (ed.). *Paranormal Borderlands of Science*. Buffalo: Prometheus Books.
Alseth, Jim
    1993   "Marketplace Chapel: A Beacon of Hope." *Christian Week*, April 13:20.
Alsop, Ronald
    1985   "Advertisers Promote Religion in a Splashy Style." *Wall Street Journal*, Nov. 21, 1985:31.
Altizer, Thomas J.J. and William Hamilton
    1966   *Radical Theology and the Death of God*. New York: Bobbs-Merrill.
Anderson, Don
    1993   "Are There Any Signs of the New?" *Canadian Baptist*, May:6.
Anderson, Leith
    1992   *A Church for the 21st Century*. Minneapolis: Bethany House.
Anglican Diocese of New Westminster
    1993   "Profile: The Diocese of New Westminister." Synod discussion paper. Vancouver: New Westminster Diocese, May 11.
Appleby, Timothy
    1990   "Satanism: Recurring Stories Make Authorities Believers." *Globe and Mail*, November 27, 1990:A1,9.
Assembly of Quebec Bishops
    1992   *New Directions for the Future: A Summary of the Research*. Quebec City: Research Committee of the Assembly of Quebec Bishops on Local Christian Communities.
Atwood, Janet
    1992   "Women Are Losing Hope." *Canadian Baptist*, September-October:14–17.
Ayres, Jane Sweat and Mark W. Drum
    1993   "Psychics: Do Police Departments Really Use Them?" *Skeptical Inquirer* 17:148–158.
Babych, Art
    1993a "Canadian Theologian Replies to Vatican Criticisms." *Catholic New Times*, March 7:1,17.
    1993b "Coalition Explores Idea of 'Dysfunctional Church.'" *Catholic New Times*, May 16:1,13.

Baglow, Ferdy
   1992   "Windows of Opportunity: Chinese Witness and Outreach in British Colum-
          bia." *Canada Lutheran*, February:14–15,32.
Bainbridge, William Sims and Rodney Stark
   1982   "Church and Cult in Canada." *Canadian Journal of Sociology* 7:351–366.
Baptist Convention of Ontario and Quebec
   1993   Report on the Working Group on Equality in Ministry: 1988–1993. Toronto:
          Division of Pastoral Resources, BCOQ.
Barna, George
   1990   *The Frog in the Kettle.* Ventura, Calif.: Regal Books.
   1992   *Church Marketing.* Ventura, Calif.: Regal Books.
Barrington, Eleanor
   1992   "Front Page." *United Church Observer,* August:2.
Baum, Gregory
   1973   "The Survival of the Sacred." In Andrew Greeley and Gregory Baum (eds.).
          The Persistence of Religion. New York: Herder and Herder. 11–22.
   1991   *The Church in Quebec.* Ottawa: Novalis.
Beaudry, Albert
   1992   "Risk New Future or Die, Report Warns Quebec Parishes." *Catholic New Times,*
          December 6:1,14–15.
Bell, Daniel
   1977   "The Return of the Sacred: The Argument on the Future of Religion." *British
          Journal of Sociology* 28:419–449.
Berger, Peter L.
   1961   *The Noise of Solemn Assemblies.* Garden City, N.Y.: Doubleday.
   1961   *Invitation to Sociology.* New York: Doubleday.
   1967   *The Sacred Canopy.* Garden City, N.Y.: Doubleday.
   1969   *Rumor of Angels.* Garden City, N.Y.: Doubleday
   1986   "Religion in Post-Protestant America." *Commentary* 81:41–46.
Berman, Phillip L.
   1990   *The Search for Meaning: Americans Talk About What They Believe and Why.* New
          York: Ballantine Books.
Berton, Pierre
   1965   *The Comfortable Pew.* Toronto: McClelland and Stewart.
Bettson, Bob
   1993   "The Shape of Things to Come." *United Church Observer,* April:32–33.
Beverley, James A.
   1990   "Understanding the New Age." Willowdale, Ont.: Ontario Theological Seminary.
   1992   "John Wimber, the Vineyard, and the Prophets." *Canadian Baptist,* March-
          April 1992:32–38.
Beyer, Peter
   1993   "Roman Catholicism in Contemporary Quebec." In W.E. Hewitt (ed.). *The
          Sociology of Religion: A Canadian Focus.* Toronto: Butterworths. 133–156.
Bibby, Reginald W.
   1977   "Why Conservative Churches Really Are Growing: Kelley Revisited." *Journal
          for the Scientific Study of Religion* 7:129–138.
   1986   *Anglitrends.* Toronto: Anglican Diocese of Toronto.
   1987   *Fragmented Gods: The Poverty and Potential of Religion in Canada.*
          Toronto: Irwin.
   1990   *Mosaic Madness: The Poverty and Potential of Life in Canada.* Toronto: Stoddart.
   1993a "Secularization and Change." In W.E. Hewitt (ed.). *The Sociology of Religion:
          A Canadian Focus.* Toronto: Butterworths. 65–81.
   1993b "How to Fail in Prosperous Times: An Organizational Analysis of Religion
          in Canada." Presented at the annual meeting of the Pacific Sociological Associ-
          ation, Portland, April.

1993c "The Melting Pot in the Mosaic: Religious Assimilation in a Pluralist Canada." Presented at the International Society for the Study of Religion. Budapest, July.

1993d "The Fragmented Mosaic." In David A. Roozen and C. Kirk Hadaway (eds.). *(Church and Denominational Growth.* Nashville: Abingdon.

Bibby, Reginald W. and Merlin B. Brinkerhoff

1973 "The Circulation of the Saints." *Journal for the Scientific Study of Religion* 12:273–283.

1974 "When Proselytizing Fails: An Organizational Analysis." *Sociological Analysis* 35:189–200.

1983 "Circulation of the Saints Revisited." *Journal for the Scientific Study of Religion* 22:253–262.

1992a "Circulation of the Saints: 1966–1990: New Data, New Reflections." Presented at the annual meeting of the Scientific Study of Religion, Washington, November.

1992b "On the Circulatory Problems of Saints: A Response to Perrin and Mauss." *Review of Religious Research* 34:170–175.

Bibby, Reginald W. and Armand L. Mauss

1974 "Skidders and Their Servants: Variable Goals and Functions of a Skid Road Rescue Mission." *Journal for the Scientific Study of Religion* 13:421–436.

Bibby, Reginald W. and Donald C. Posterski

1985 *The Emerging Generation: An Inside Look at Canada's Teenagers.* Toronto: Irwin.

1992 *Teen Trends: A Nation in Motion.* Toronto: Stoddart.

Bibby, Reginald W. and Harold R. Weaver

1985 "Cult Consumption in Canada: A Further Critique of Stark and Bainbridge." *Sociological Analysis* 46:445–460.

Blaikie, Bill

1992 "The United Church and Canada Sinking or Swimming Together." *Touchstone,* 10:5–8.

Bonisteel, Roy

1993 "Family History Between the Pages." *United Church Observer,* February:30.

Bourget, D.A. and J. Bradford

1988 "Satanism in a Psychiatric Adolescent Population." *Canadian Journal of Psychiatry* 33:April.

Brackney, William

1992 "The Former Things Have Passed Away." *Canadian Baptist,* September-October: 47–48.

Brackney, William H.

1992 "Voluntarism: The Dynamic Principle of Free Church." 1990 Hayward Lectures. Wolfville, N.S.: Acadia University.

Bradley, Ken

1993 "Educational Questions Christians Ask." *Faith Today,* May-June:34–36.

Brady, Diane

1991 "Saving the Boomers." *Maclean's,* June 3:50–51.

Brannon, Robert

1971 "Organizational Vulnerability in Modern Religious Organizations." *Journal for the Scientific Study of Religion* 10:27–32.

Brennan, Margaret

1992 "Is the Ordination of Women the Wrong Answer for the Present?" *Catholic New Times,* December 6:8–9.

Brinkerhoff, Merlin and Reginald W. Bibby

1985 "Circulation of the Saints in South America." *Journal for the Scientific Study of Religion* 28:151–167.

Brinkerhoff, Merlin and Marlene Mackie

1993a "Casting Off the Bonds of Organized Religion." *Review of Religious Research* 34:235–257.

1993b "Nonbelief in Canada: Characteristics and Origins of Religious Nones." In W.E. Hewitt (ed.). *The Sociology of Religion: A Canadian Focus.* Toronto: Butterworths. 109–132.

Brown, Susan Mader
1992a "The 1990 Synod in the Context of the Canadian Church." *Canadian Cath-2olic Review,* January:6–18.
1992b "Forward in the Spirit: Challenge of the People's Synod." A review. *Canadian Catholic Review,* May:21–22.

Bye, Christine
1991 "A Smile and a Hearty Welcome." *United Church Observer,* September:27–28.

Campbell, George M.
1992 "A Message of Hope." *Canada Lutheran,* December:9.

Canadian Conference of Catholic Bishops
1993a *From Pain to Hope.* CCCB Ad Hoc Committee on Child Sexual Abuse. Ottawa: Publications Service, CCCB.
1993b *Breach of Trust/Breach of Faith.* CCCB Staff Under the Directions of the Ad Hoc Committee on Child Sexual Abuse. Ottawa: Publications Service, CCCB.

Carriere, Vianney
1992 "Child Abuse Leaves Legacy of Pain." *Anglican Journal,* October:1,10.
1993a "Native Gambling Evokes Divided Church Response." *Anglican Journal,* May:6.
1993b "Integrated Parish Is Still Divided." *Anglican Journal,* June:13.

Chandler, Russell
1988 *Understanding the New Age.* Dallas: Word.

Chaves, Mark
1989 "Secularization and Religious Revival: Evidence from U.S. Church Attendance Rates, 1972–1986." *Journal for the Scientific Study of Religion* 28:464–477.

Christensen, Linda
1991 *The New Age in Focus.* Interest Ministries: Wheaton, Ill.
1993 "Beyond Belief: Understanding the New Age Experience." Presented at the annual meeting of the Pacific Sociological Association, Portland, April.

Clarke, Patricia
1993 "Casting Light on the Darkness." *United Church Observer,* April:37–39.

Collins, Stephanie Baker
1993 "Christians Speak Out About Lubicon." *Christian Courier,* April 23:1–2.

Comte, Auguste
1966 *System of Positive Polity.* New York: Burt Franklin Research and Source Works Series.

Congram, John
1992 "No Clean Hands." *Presbyterian Record,* February:16–21.

Crosby, Michael H.
1991 *The Dysfunctional Church.* Notre Dame, Ind.: Ave Maria Press.

Csillag, Ron
1993 "Jews by Faith Up 7%; 'Ethnic' Issue Looms." *Canadian Jewish News,* June 24:6.

Culbertson, Debbie
1993 "Campus Connection." *United Church Observer,* May:46–47.

Curtis, James E., Edward G. Grabb, and Douglas E. Baer
1992 "Voluntary Association Membership in Fifteen Countries: A Comparative Analysis." *American Sociological Review* 57:139–152.

Darmon, Rene Y., Michel Laroche, and John V. Petrof
1989 *Marketing in Canada.* Third edition. Toronto: McGraw-Hill-Ryerson.

Davis, Kingsley
1949 *Human Society.* New York: Macmillan.

Dekar, Paul
   1992   "Christopher Columbus: Began Earth's Destruction." *Canadian Baptist,* July-August:27, 29–30.
Demerath, N.J. III
   1969   "Irreligion, A-Religion, and the Rise of the Religionless Church." *Sociological Analysis* 30:191–203.
Demerath, N.J. III and Rhys H. Williams
   1992   "Secularization in a Community Context." *Journal for the Scientific Study of Religion* 31:189–206.
Desiato, Tonia
   1993   "Bishops Launch Residential Schools Project." The *Catholic Register,* May 15:3.
Dobbelaere, Karel
   1981   "Secularization: A Multi-Dimensional Concept." *Current Sociology* 29:1–216.
   1987   "Some Trends in European Sociology of Religion: The Secularization Debate." *Sociological Analysis* 46:377–387.
Doerksen, Alan
   1992   "Five Churches Put a New Face on Toronto Baptists." *Canadian Baptist,* September-October.
Bueck, Lorna
   1993   "Slap on the Wrist for Doctor Who Hastens Death." *Christian Week,* May 11:4.
Duncan, Muriel
   1993   "Observations." *United Church Observer,* February:8.
Durkheim, Emile
   1965   *Elementary Forms of the Religious Life.* New York: The Free Press.
Ebaugh, Helen Rose
   1991   "The Revitalization Movement in the Catholic Church." *Sociological Analysis* 52:1–12.
Elliot, David
   1993   "Choosing a Local Church." *Pentecostal Testimony,* April:24–25.
Enns, Aiden Schlichting
   1993a   "Mennonite Brethren to Discuss Role of Sisters." *Mennonite Reporter,* May 31, 1993.
   1993b   "Mennonite Community Responds to Free Press Series on Drugs." *Mennonite Reporter,* May 31, 1993.
Evangelical Fellowship of Canada
   1993   "EFC Asks Leon's Furniture to Pull Offensive Ad." EFC Press release, *Free Methodist Herald,* March:2.
Evans, Clifford
   1993   "Holy Matrimony?" *Anglican Journal,* June, 1993:9.
Fadum, Kathy
   1993   "Unbelief in Canada Today: The Sacraments Can Be Ambiguous." *Our Family,* March:14–15.
Ferry, James
   1993   *In the Courts of the Lord: A Gay Minister's Story.* Toronto: Key Porter.
Fieguth, Debra
   1993a   "PEI Churches for Island Vision." *Christian Week,* May 11:1.
   1993b   "Forty Cities Join Canadian March." *Christian Week,* May 25:1,4.
Fledderus, Bill
   1993   "Video Evangelism Reaches Thousands, Unites Churches." *Christian Courier,* May 14:1,20.
Finke, Roger and Rodney Stark
   1992   *The Churching of America, 1776–1990.* New Brunswick, N.J.: Rutgers University Press.

Forman, Joan
1988   *The Golden Shore*. London: Futura Publications.
Fox, Matthew
1988   *The Coming of the Cosmic Christ: The Healing of Mother Earth and the Birth of Global Renaissance*. San Francisco: Harper and Row.
Frazer, James
1988   *The Golden Bough*. New York: Macmillan.
Freud, Sigmund
1957   *The Future of an Illusion*. Garden City, N.Y.: Doubleday.
Friesen, Ron
1993   "He's History: The ELCIC's First Bishop." *Canada Lutheran*, June:8–10.
Gallup Canada, Ltd.
1992   *Gallup Report*. Toronto. June 6.
Gariepy, Henry
1993   *The Authorized Biography of General Eva Burrows*. New York: Victor Books.
Gee, Ellen M. and Jean E. Veevers
1989   "Religiously Unaffiliated Canadians: Sex, Age, and Regional Variations." *Social Indicators Research* 21:611–627.
1990   "Religious Involvement and Life Satisfaction in Canada." *Sociological Analysis* 51:387–394.
Glisky, Bill
1993   "Caledonia Reaches Out Despite Fiscal Restraints." *Anglican Journal*, June:10.
Glock, Charles Y. and Rodney Stark
1965   *Religion and Society in Tension*. Chicago: Rand McNally.
Gonzalez, Ramon
1993a "Chauvinism Still Rampant." *Western Catholic Reporter*, May 10:7.
1993b "Residential Schools Harmed Native People." *Western Catholic Reporter*, May 24, 1993:8.
Goodyer, Nancy
1993   "The Day the President Came to Worship." *Canadian Baptist*, May:15–16.
Graham, Ron
1990   *God's Dominion*. Toronto: McClelland and Stewart.
Grant, John Webster
1988   *The Church in the Canadian Era*. Second edition. Burlington: Welch.
1992   "Rocky Road to Church Union." *Compass*, March-April:14–16.
Greeley, Andrew M.
1972   *The Denominational Society*. Glenview, Ill.: Scott, Foresman.
1989   *Religious Change in America*. Cambridge: Harvard University Press.
Grenz, Stanley J.
1993   "Why Wait Until Marriage?" *Christian Week*, May 11:8.
Gregoire, Nestor
1992   "Euthanasia: It Is a Complicated Question." *Our Family*, September:2.
Groothius, Douglas
1986   *Unmasking the New Age*. Downer's Grove, Ill.: InterVarsity Press.
1990   *Revealing the New Age Jesus*. Downer's Grove, Ill.: InterVarsity Press.
Hadaway, C. Kirk, Penny Long Marler, and Mark Chaves
1993   "What the Polls Don't Show: A Closer Look at U.S. Church Attendance." *American Sociological Review*. In press.
Haggett, Evelyn
1993   "Crosswalk Drop-in Centre." *War Cry*, May 29:3.
Hall, Douglas John
1989a *The Future of the Church*. Toronto: United Church Publishing House.
1989b *Thinking the Faith*. Minneapolis: Fortress Press.

Hamberg, Eva M.
    1992   "On Stability and Change in Religious Beliefs, Practice, and Attitudes: A Swedish Panel Study." *Journal for the Scientific Study of Religion* 30:63–80.
Hammond, David E.
    1993   "Catch 22 in the Capital." *War Cry,* March 20:8–9.
Harland, Gordon
    1992   "Religion, Canadian Style." *Touchstone* 10:9–14.
Harpur, Tom
    1986   *For Christ's Sake.* Toronto: Oxford University Press.
    1991   *Life After Death.* Toronto: McClelland and Stewart.
    1993   "Religious Polls Miss Real Point of What's Going On in Canada." *Toronto Star,* June 13:B7.
Harris, Michael
    1990   *Unholy Orders: Tragedy at Mount Cashel.* Markham, Ont.: Viking.
Hartnagel, Timothy F. and Leo Klug
    1990   "Changing Religious Attitudes and Participation Among Catholics in the Post Vatican II Church: Some Canadian Data." *Sociological Analysis* 51:347–361.
Harvey, Bob
    1993   "A Revolution in Progress." *Faith Today,* January-February, 19–22.
Heaton, Tim B.
    1990   "Religious Group Characteristics, Endogamy, and Interfaith Marriages." *Sociological Analysis* 51:363–376.
Herrig, David L.
    1993   "Visitor-Friendly Worship." *Canada Lutheran,* March:12.
Hewitt, W.E.
    1991   "Roman Catholicism and Social Justice in Canada." *Canadian Review of Sociology and Anthropology* 28:299–323.
    1993   "The Quest for the Just Society: Canadian Catholicism in Transition." In W.E. Hewitt (ed.). *The Sociology of Religion:* A Canadian Focus. Toronto: Butterworths. 253–271.
Hexham, Irving
    1993a "Facts and Fallacies About Religious Extremism in Alberta." *Christian Week,* April 13:10.
    1993b "Canadian Evangelicals: Facing the Critics." In W.E. Hewitt (ed.). *The Sociology of Religion: A Canadian Focus.* Toronto: Butterworths. 289–302.
Hiebert, Rick
    1992   "Whatever Happened to the P.M. Service?" *Christian Week,* December 1:9.
Higgins, M., B. McGowan, D. Murphy, L. Trafford (eds.)
    1993   *Catholic Education: Transforming Our World.* Ottawa: Novalis.
Hill, Michael and Richard Bowman
    1985   "Religious Adherence and Religious Practice in Contemporary New Zealand." *Archives des Sciences Sociales des Religions* 59:91–112.
Holm, Nils G.
    1989   "Religion in Finland and the Scandinavian Model." Presented at the annual meeting of the International Conference of the Sociology of Religion, Helsinki, August.
Hordern, William
    1966   *New Directions in Theology Today.* Volume 1. Philadelphia: Westminster Press.
Hout, M. and Andrew Greeley
    1987   "The Center Doesn't Hold: Church Attendance in the U.S. 1940–84." *American Sociological Review* 52:325–345.
Howard, Keith
    1993   "A Long and Unsettling Journey: Tim Stevenson." *The United Church Observer,* January:10–14.

Hunsberger, Bruce
    1983   "Apostasy: A Social Learning Perspective." *Review of Religious Research* 25:21–38.
Iannaccone, Laurene R.
    1990   "Religion Practice: A Human Capital Approach." *Journal for the Scientific Study of Religion* 29:297–314.
    1991   "The Consequences of Religious Market Structure." *Rationality and Society* 3:156–177.
Irving, John
    1990   *A Prayer for Owen Meany.* Toronto: Ballantine Books.
Janke, Dwayne
    1991   "Boomers and Busters." *Word Alive,* May:4–7,14.
Johnson, Benton, Dean R. Hoge, and Donald A. Luidens
    1993   "Why Liberal Churches Are Declining." *First Things.* March.
Jones, Robert W.
    1993   "'Meta-Churches' Experience Change." *Pentecostal Testimony,* June:24.
Jones, William H.
    1993   "Telecommunications, Faith and Justice." *Canadian Baptist,* May:19–22.
Joseph, Brian
    1993   "*Maclean's* Report on Religion in Canada: Through a Glass Darkly." *Catholic New Times,* May 30:7.
Jost, Beth
    1993   "Out of One Closet and into Another." *Faith Today,* January-February:23–25.
Kauffman, J. Howard and Leo Driedger
    1991   *The Mennonite Mosaic: Identity and Modernization.* Scottdale, Penn.: Herald Press.
Kapica, Jack
    1992   "Praise the Lord, Pass the Chip Dip." *Globe and Mail,* October 17:1,A6.
    1993a   "How Catholic Bishops Hope to Heal Abuse." *Globe and Mail,* February1:A9.
    1993b   "Church Plays Down Nude-Photo Lawsuit." *Globe and Mail,* February 18:A2.
    1993c   "Protestant Numbers Tumbling." *Globe and Mail,* June 2:A1,3.
Kawano, Roland M.
    1992   *The Global City: Multicultural Ministry in Urban Canada.* Winfield, B.C.: Wood Lake Books.
Kelley, Dean
    1972   *Why Conservative Churches Are Growing.* New York: Harper & Row.
    1978   "Why Conservative Churches Are *Still* Growing." *Journal for the Scientific Study of Religion* 17:165–172.
Khaki, Aziz (ed.)
    1991   *Acceptance of Religious Diversity in Our Society.* Proceedings of the National Conference, October 13–14. Vancouver: The Pacific Interfaith Citizenship Association.
    1992   *Religious Expressions.* Vancouver: The Pacific Interfaith Citizenship Association.
Kirley, Kevin J.
    1992   "The Grand Seminary." A review essay. *The Canadian Catholic Review,* June:31–34.
Kitchen, Shirley
    1993   "Religious Broadcasting Needs Balance." *The Canadian Unitarian,* March:1,4.
Koop, Doug
    1991   "Are Canadians Really Going Back to Church?" *Christian Week,* September:1,4.
    1993   "Lutheran Bishop Reflects on Eight Years of Autonomy." *Christian Week,* June 22:5.
Kotler, Philip and Gordon H.G. McDougall
    1985   *Marketing Essentials.* Canadian Edition. Scarborough, Ont.: Prentice-Hall.

Kraft, Frances
   1993   "Two Canadian Women Are Ordained as Rabbis." *Canadian Jewish News,* June 24:6.
Krishnan, Vijaya
   1993   "Religious Homogamy and Voluntary Childlessness in Canada." *Sociological Perspectives* 36:83–93.
Krutz-Weil
   1992   "Chaplains to the Rescue." *Canadian Unitarian,* November, 1992:2.
Lachance, Dorothy
   1993a "Native Spirituality, Catholicism Can Blend Well." *Prairie Messenger,* May 31:3.
   1993b "Challenge '93 Group Spreads Chastity Message." *Prairie Messenger,* June 7, 1993:3.
Lascelles, Thomas A.
   1992   "Indian Residential Schools." *Canadian Catholic Review,* May:6–13.
Lazarus, David
   1993   "Homosexual Marriages on Agenda." *Canadian Jewish News,* July 8:5.
Legge, Gordon
   1992a "Churches Team Up to Accent Worship." *Calgary Herald,* January 18:E7.
   1992b "Encounters with Angels." *Calgary Herald,* December 24:1.B6–7.
   1993   "Calgary Seen as Key Centre of Revival." *Christian Week,* April 13:8.
Lett, James
   1992   "The Persistent Popularity of the Paranormal." *Skeptical Inquirer* 16:381–388.
Lewis, David L.
   1993   "Canadian Native Peoples and the Churches." In W.E. Hewitt (ed.). *The Sociology of Religion: A Canadian Focus.* Toronto: Butterworths. 235–252.
Lippert, Randy
   1990   "The Construction of Satanism as a Social Problem in Canada." *Canadian Journal of Sociology* 15:417–439.
Lodge, David
   1992   *Paradise News.* New York: Penguin.
Longley, Clifford
   1989   "Manacled to a Spiritual Corpse." *London Times,* December 2.
Luckmann, Thomas
   1967   *The Invisible Religion.* New York: Macmillan
   1990   "Shrinking Transcendence, Expanding Religion?" *Sociological Analysis* 50:127–138.
Lucow, Maurice
   1993   "Vancouver Reports Highest Rate of Intermarriage." *Canadian Jewish News,* June 10:2.
Lupfer, Michael B., Karla F. Brock, and Stephen J. DePaola
   1992   "The Use of Secular and Religious Attributions to Explain Everyday Behavior." *Journal for the Scientific Study of Religion* 31:486–503.
Mackey, Lloyd
   1993   "The BUWC Takes Its Temperature." *Canadian Baptist,* June 1993:38–39.
MacLaine, Shirley
   1983   *Out on a Limb.* New York: Bantam Books.
   1985   *Dancing in the Light.* New York: Bantam Books.
   1992   *Dance While You Can.* New York: Bantam Books.
Macmillan, Donald N.
   1993   "The Presbyterian Who Invented Basketball." *Presbyterian Record,* January:20–22.
Manera, Deborah
   1993   "What About Those of Us Who May *Never* Become Mothers?" *Pentecostal Testimony* May:32–34.
Mann, W.E.
   1962   *Sect, Cult, and Church in Alberta.* Toronto: University of Toronto Press.

Marler, Penny Long and C. Kirk Hadaway
    1993   "Toward a Typology of Protestant 'Marginal Members.'" *Review of Religious Research*, in press.
Marshall, David
    1990   "Christianity in Britain: Has the Son Set on the Empire?" *Signs of the Times*, March:8–12.
Martin, David
    1967   *A Sociology of English Religion*. London: SCM Press.
    1979   *A General Theory of Secularization*. London: Harper and Row.
Marx, Karl
    1970   *Critique of Hegel's Philosophy of Right*. Translation by Annette Jollin and Joseph O'Malley. Cambridge: The University Press.
Mathers, A.R. Neal
    1992a "Recognizing the Barriers." *Presbyterian Record*, February:32–34.
    1992b "Finding a Way Forward." *Presbyterian Record*, March:18–20.
Maxwell, Grant
    1992   "The Challenge of 'The People's Synod.'" *Canadian Catholic Review*, May:17–20.
Mayes, Alison
    1992   "Palmo Preaches Holy Humor." *Calgary Herald*, March 14.
McAteer, Michael
    1989   "TV Evangelist Suspended by Queensway Cathedral." *Toronto Star*, August 29:A5.
McCallum, John
    1986   "The Dynamics of Secularization in Australia." Presented at the SAANZ '86 Conference, Armidale, New South Wales.
McDaniel, Stephen W.
    1989   "The Use of Marketing Techniques by Churches: A National Survey." *Review of Religious Research* 31:175–182.
Meed, Marianne
    1993   "Addicted to Sensational Testimonies." *Faith Today*, May-June:33.
Mentzer, Marc S.
    1991   "The Validity of Denominational Membership Data in Canada." *Sociological Analysis* 52:293–299.
Milne, Mike
    1993   "Families: A Tradition to Celebrate." *United Church Observer*, May:21.
Mitchell, Alanna
    1993   "Faith, Hope and Chastity." *Globe and Mail*, February 18:A1,4.
Mol, Hans
    1985   *Faith and Fragility: Religion and Identity in Canada*. Burlington, Ont.: Trinity Press.
Moody, Raymond A.
    1975   *Life After Life*. New York: Bantam.
    1988   *The Light Beyond*. New York: Bantam.
Morikawa, Tom
    1993   "Listening to Native Peoples." *Canadian Baptist*, January:13–15.
Motz, Arnell, ed.
    1990   *Reclaiming a Nation*. Richmond, B.C.: Outreach Canada Ministries.
    1991   "Calling the Church to New Vision." *Yearbook of American and Canadian Churches*. Nashville: Abingdon. 281–289.
Moynan, Mary Lee
    1993   "A Roamin' Roman." *Presbyterian Record*, April:16–17.
Naisbitt, John and Patricia Aburdene
    1990   *Megatrends 2000*. New York: Warner Books.
Nason-Clark, Nancy
    1993   "Gender Relations in Contemporary Christian Organizations." In W.E. Hewitt

(ed.). *The Sociology of Religion: A Canadian Focus.* Toronto: Butterworths. 215–234.

Nevile, Donald
1993   "Volunteers in Mission." *Canada Lutheran,* March:14–15.

Niebuhr, H. Richard
1929   *The Social Sources of Denominationalism.* New York: Holt and Company.
1951   *Christ and Culture.* New York: Harper and Row.

Nock, David A.
1993   "The Organization of Religious Life in Canada." In W.E. Hewitt (ed.). *The Sociology of Religion: A Canadian Focus.* Toronto: Butterworths. 41–63.

Noll, Mark A.
1992   *A History of Christianity in the United States and Canada.* Grand Rapids, Mich.: William B. Eerdmans.

Nostbakken, Roger W.
1992   "Signs of Hope." *Canada Lutheran,* March:8–9,29.

O'Brien, Thomas
1993   "Catholic Educators Examine Catholic Education." A review. *Catholic New Times,* February 21, 1993:8.

O'Connor, Matt
1993   "Pepsi Puts the Lid on Tamperings." *Chicago Tribune,* June 20:4.

Ogilvie, Margaret H.
1993   "Living Creatively in Charterland." *Presbyterian Record,* February:27–30.

O'Toole, Roger, Douglas F. Campbell, John A. Hannigan, Peter Beyer and John H. Simpson
1993   "The United Church in Crisis." In W.E. Hewitt (ed.). *The Sociology of Religion: A Canadian Focus.* Toronto: Butterworths. 273–287.

Parsons, Talcott
1963   "Christianity and Modern Industrial Society." In Edward Teryakian (ed.). *Sociological Theory, Values, and Sociocultural Change.* Glencoe, Ill.: The Free Press.

Parrott, Leslie
1993   "When Evil Strikes Close." *United Church Observer,* April:38–39.

Peck, M. Scott
1978   *The Road Less Traveled.* New York: Simon and Schuster.
1993   *A World Waiting to Be Born.* New York: Bantam.

Percy, Harold
1993   "What Should the Churches Actually Do?" *Anglican Journal,* May:13.

Perrin, Robert D. and Armand L. Mauss
1991   "Saints and Seekers: Sources of Recruitment to the Vineyard Christian Fellowship." *Review of Religious Research* 33:97–111.
1992   "On Saints and Seriousness: A Response to Bibby and Brinkerhoff." *Review of Religious Research* 34:176–178.

Perrone, Diane C.
1992   "Annulment: Autopsy of a Marriage." *Our Family,* September:23–26.

Pinnock, Clark
1992   "Columbus: World Is Better Off." *Canadian Baptist,* July-August, 27–29.

Popcorn, Faith
1991   *The Popcorn Report.* New York: Doubleday.

Posterski, Donald C. and Reginald W. Bibby
1988   *Canada's Youth: Ready for Today.* Ottawa: Canadian Youth Foundation.

Posterski, Donald C. and Irwin Barker
1993   *Where's a Good Church?* Winfield, B.C.: Wood Lake Books.

Pride, William M. and O.C. Ferrell
1989   *Marketing: Concepts and Strategies.* Sixth Edition. Boston: Houghton Mifflin.

Princeton Research Center
1990a   *PRRC Emerging Trends,* 12:6, June.

1990b   *PRRC Emerging Trends,* 12:7, September.

Prus, Robert C.
1989   *Pursuing Customers: An Ethnography of Marketing Activities.* New York: Sage Publications.

Quelch, John A.
1989   *How to Market to Consumers: Ten Ways to Win.* New York: John Wiley.

Rawlings, Maurice
1978   *Beyond Death's Door.* Nashville: Thomas Nelson.

Rawlyk, George A. (ed.)
1990   *The Canadian Protestant Experience.* Burlington, Ont.: Welch.

Redekop, John H.
1993   "Terror in God's Name." *Mennonite Brethren Herald,* April 16:36.

Rempel-Burkholder, Byron
1993   "Miracles on Saskatoon's Drug Strip." *Mennonite Brethren Herald,* May 14:14–15.

Rifkin, Jeremy
1980   *The Emerging Order.* New York: Harper and Row.

Robbins, Thomas and Dick Anthony (eds.)
1981   *In God We Trust.* New Brunswick, N.J.: Transaction.

Rodd, Catherine
1993   "Just Like a Family: Ethnic Youth Groups." *United Church Observer,* March:44–45.

Roof, Wade Clark
1993   "A Generation of Seekers." San Francisco: Harper.

Roof, Wade Clark and Karen Loeb
1990   "Baby Boomers and Religious Change." Presented at the Conference on Changing Patterns of Belief, Queens College, CUNY.

Roof, Wade Clark and William McKinney
1987   *American Mainline Religion.* New Brunswick, N.J.: Rutgers University Press.

Roozen, David A., Jackson Carroll, and Wade Clark Roof
1990   "The Post War Generation and Establishment Religion." Unpublished paper.

Roozen, David A., William McKinney, and Wayne Thompson
1990   "The 'Big Chill' Generation Warms to Worship." *Review of Religious Research* 31:314–322.

Roxborough, Alan J.
1993   *Reaching a New Generation: Strategies for Tomorrow's Church.* Downer's Grove, Ill.: InterVarsity Press.

Ryan, Bram
1993   "A Future Together: Shared Ministries." *United Church Observer,* March:42–43.

Ryan, William
1991   "Social Teaching for Modern Times." *Compass,* November-December:35–39.

Scorgie, Glen
1993   "Clouds the Size of a Hand." *Faith Today,* March-April:27–330.

Scott, Edward W.
1993   "Focus on Central Purpose." *PMC,* May:9.

Sevcik, Irene
1993   "Child Sexual Abuse: What Can Christians Do?" *Free Methodist Herald,* March:8.

Shepherd, Victor
1993   "Eva Burrows 1929–." *Fellowship Magazine,* May-June:22–23.

Sinclair, Donna
1992   "New Policy Cracks Down on Sexual Abuse." *United Church Observer,* November, 1992:12–15.

Slobodian, Louise
   1993   "New Prince George Bishop Wants to 'Get On with Life.'" *Catholic New Times,* March 7:18.

Smith, Adam
   1937   *An Inquiry into the Nature and Causes of the Wealth of Nations.* New York: The Modern Library. Originally published 1776.

Smith, Tom W.
   1992   "Are Conservative Churches Growing?" *Review of Religious Research* 33:305–329.

Sorokin, Pitirim
   1957   *Social and Cultural Dynamics.* Revised and abridged. Boston: Porter Sargent.

Sperry, John R.
   1993   "Native Spirituality: Whence or Whither?" *Presbyterian Record,* June:17–19.

Spicer, Keith
   1987   "Our Turbulent Priests Should Get Out of Politics." *Calgary Herald,* December 10:A8. Southam News.

Stackhouse, John
   1993   "Revival and Renewal: Everybody Wants It — Don't We?" *Faith Today,* March-April, 1993:18–21.

Stahl, William
   1995   God and the Chip. Manuscript in preparation. For information contact Stahl, Luther College, University of Regina.

Stark, Rodney and William Sims Bainbridge
   1985   *The Future of Religion.* Berkeley, Calif.: University of California Press.

Starkloff, Carl
   1991   "Mission: Jesuits and Native Canadians." *Compass,* July-August:17–19.

Statistics Canada
   1993   *The Daily.* 1991 Census of Canada. June 1.

Steed, Judy
   1991   "Predatory Choirmaster Shattered Lives, Church." *Toronto Star,* September 20:A1,11.

Steinhauser, Michael G.
   1993   "Treating the Whole Person." *PMC,* March:12–13.

Stiller, Brian
   1986   *Understanding Our Times.* Seminar Workbook. Willowdale, Ont.: The Evangelical Fellowship of Canada.
   1991   *Critical Options for Evangelicals.* Markham, Ont.: Faith Today Publications.

Swatos, William H., Jr.
   1991   "Getting the Word Around: A Research Note on Communicating an Evangelistic Crusade." *Review of Religious Research* 33:176–185.
   1992   "Adolescent Satanism: A Research Note on Exploratory Data." *Review of Religious Research* 34:161–169.

Sykes, Charles
   1992   *A Nation of Victims: The Decay of the American Character.* New York: St. Martin's Press.

Tapscott, Don and Art Caston
   1993   *Paradigm Shift: The New Promise of Information Technology.* New York: McGraw-Hill.

Tarter, Donald
   1993   "Treading on the Edge: Practicing Safe Science with SETI." *Skeptical Inquirer* 17:288–296.

Thomas, Joan
   1992   "Leaving a Life That's Fundamentally Flawed." *Globe and Mail,* Facts and Arguments, October 13.

Tillich, Paul
    1966   *On the Boundary.* New York: Scribner's.
Todd, Douglas
    1991   "Faithful Churchgoers Now Get Together via Continent-Wide Computer Network." *Vancouver Sun,* November 19:A3.
    1993   "Bouncing Back from Victimization." *Vancouver Sun,* February 27, 1993:C13.
Toffler, Alvin
    1990   *Powershift.* New York: Bantam Books.
Toneguzzi, Mario
    1992   "Faith on the Field." *Calgary Herald,* November 28:E8.
Troeltsch, Ernst
    1931   *The Social Teaching of the Christian Churches.* 2 vols. Translations by Olive Wyon. New York: Macmillan.
Turner, Gordon
    1987   *Outside Looking In.* Toronto: the United Church of Canada.
Tyler, Tracey
    1993   "Court Discounts Father's Religion in Custody Case." *Toronto Star,* February 22.
Van Ginkel (ed.).
    1992   *Shaping a Christian Vision: Discussion Papers on Canada's Future.* Markham, Ont.: Faith Today Publications.
VanderVennen, Robert E. (ed.)
    1991   *Church and Canadian Culture.* Lanham, Md.: University Press of America.
Van Seters, Arthur
    1992   "The Jazz Factor of Faithful Living." *Presbyterian Record,* January:30–31.
Van Velzen, Andrew
    1989   "Secular Society Gave Couple Their Niche: The Wedding Business." *Globe and Mail,* August 14.
von Gernet, Alexander
    1991   "Culture Contact in the Canadian Wilderness." *Compass,* July-August:19–21.
Wallace, Jim
    1993   "Spirit Stirring in the Cities of Alberta." *Christian Week,* April 13:5.
Wan, Enoch
    1990   "Ethnic Receptivity Factors." In Arnell Motz, ed. *Reclaiming a Nation.* Richmond, B.C.: Outreach Canada Ministries.
Ward, Ken
    1993   "From the Other Side of the Pulpit." *PMC,* March:19–20.
Warner, R. Stephen
    1993   "Work in Progress Toward a New Paradigm for the Sociological Study of Religion in the United States." *American Journal of Sociology* 98:1044–1093.
Weber, Max
    1963   *Sociology of Religion.* Translation by Ephraim Fischoff. Boston: Beacon Press.
Westhues, Kenneth
    1976   "The Adaptation of the Roman Catholic Church in Canadian Society." In Stewart Crysdale and Les Wheatcroft (eds.). *Religion in Canadian Society.* Toronto: Macmillan, pp. 290–306.
Whyte, Mary E.
    1992   "In Solidarity with Women." *Canada Lutheran,* February:16–17.
    1993   "Rooted in Fear." *Canada Lutheran,* April:5.
Williams, Ivor
    1993   "Thanking the Community." *Presbyterian Record,* April:22–23.
Wills, Garry
    1990   *Under God: Religion and American Politics.* New York: Simon and Schuster.

Woodward, Kenneth, et al.
1990 "A Time to Seek: A Generation Returns to Religion." *Newsweek,* December 17:50–56.
Wilson, Bryan
1959 "An Analysis of Sect Development." *American Sociological Review* 24:3–15.
1966 *Religion in Secular Society.* London: C.A. Watts.
1979 "The Return of the Sacred." *Journal for the Scientific Study of Religion* 18:268–280.
1982 *Religion in Sociological Perspective.* London: Oxford University Press.
1985 "Secularization: The Inherited Model." In Phillip E. Hammond (ed.). *The Sacred in the Secular Age.* Berkeley, Calif.: University of California Press. 9–20.
Wilson, David
1993 "Vision TV: Religious Television Comes of Age." *United Church Observer,* June:14–21.
Winter, Terry
1993 "Encouraging Evangelism in Canada." *Christian Week,* May 25:10.
Witvoet, Bert
1993 "Christ the Cloud Rider." *Christian Courier,* May 14:10.
Wolak, R.
1992 "Euthanasia: The Challenge Today." *Our Family,* September:4–7.
Woodbury, Clair
1992 "Estimating Support for a United Church New Church Development Congregation." Research Report. Edmonton: Centre for Research and Training in New Church Development.
Wright, Lawrence
1993a "Remembering Satan — Part I." *New Yorker,* May 17:60–81.
1993b "Remembering Satan — Part II." *New Yorker,* May 24:54–76.
Wuthnow, Robert
1976 "Recent Patterns of Secularization: A Problem of Generations?" *American Sociological Review* 41:850–867.
1988 *The Restructuring of American Religion.* Princeton: Princeton University Press.
Wylie, Betty Jane
1993 "Rethinking What Makes a Family." *United Church Observer,* May:16–20.
Zarzour, Kim
1989 "A Crisis in Faith?" *Toronto Star,* December 23:J1,3.
Zikmund, William and Michael D'Amico
1984 *Marketing.* New York: John Wiley and Sons.
1988 *Marketing.* Rexdale, Ont.: John Wiley and Sons.

INDEX